THE PHILIPPINES PAST AND PRESENT

THE MACMILLAN COMPANY
NEW YORK · BOSTON · CHICAGO · DALLAS
ATLANTA · SAN FRANCISCO

MACMILLAN & CO., LIMITED
LONDON · BOMBAY · CALCUTTA
MELBOURNE

THE MACMILLAN CO. OF CANADA, LTD.
TORONTO

PEACE AND PROSPERITY.

This chance photograph showing General Emilio Aguinaldo as he is to-day, standing with Director of Education Frank L. Crone, beside a field of corn raised by Emilio Aguinaldo, Jr., in a school contest, typifies the peace, prosperity, and enlightenment which have been brought about in the Philippine Islands under American rule.

THE PHILIPPINES
PAST AND PRESENT

BY

DEAN C. WORCESTER

SECRETARY OF THE INTERIOR OF THE PHILIPPINE ISLANDS
1901–1913; MEMBER OF THE PHILIPPINE
COMMISSION, 1900–1913

AUTHOR OF "THE PHILIPPINE ISLANDS
AND THEIR PEOPLE"

IN TWO VOLUMES—WITH 128 PLATES

VOLUME I

New York
THE MACMILLAN COMPANY
1914

All rights reserved

Norwood Press
J. S. Cushing Co. — Berwick & Smith Co.
Norwood, Mass., U.S.A.

CONTENTS

VOL. I

LIST OF ILLUSTRATIONS

VOL. I

THE PHILIPPINES PAST AND PRESENT

THE PHILIPPINES
PAST AND PRESENT

CHAPTER I

View Point and Subject-Matter

It is customary in Latin countries for a would-be author or orator to endeavour, at the beginning of his book or his speech, to establish his status. Possibly I have become partially Latinized as the result of some eighteen years of residence in the Philippines. At all events it is my purpose to state at the outset facts which will tend to make clear my view point and at the same time briefly to outline the subject-matter which I hereinafter discuss.

As a boy I went through several of the successive stages of collector's fever from which the young commonly suffer. First it was postage stamps; then birds' nests, obtained during the winter season when no longer of use to their builders. Later I was allowed to collect eggs, and finally the birds themselves. At one time my great ambition was to become a taxidermist. My family did not actively oppose this desire but suggested that a few preliminary years in school and college might prove useful.

I eventually lost my ambition to be a taxidermist but did not lose my interest in zoölogy and botany. While a student at the University of Michigan I specialized in these subjects. I was fortunate in having as one of my instructors Professor Joseph B. Steere, then at the head of the Department of Zoölogy. Professor Steere, who had been a great traveller, at times entertained his classes with wonderfully interesting tales of adventure on the Amazon and in the Andes, Peru, Formosa, the Philippines and the Dutch Moluccas. My ambition was fired by his stories and when in the spring of 1886 he announced his intention of returning to the Philippines the following year to take up and prosecute anew zoölogical work which he had begun there in 1874, offering to take with him a limited number of his students who were to have the benefit of his knowledge of Spanish and of his wide experience as a traveller and collector, and were in turn to allow him to work up their collections after their return to the United States, I made up my mind to go.

I was then endeavouring to get through the University on an allowance of $375 per year and was in consequence not overburdened with surplus funds. I however managed to get my life insured for $1500 and to borrow $1200 on the policy, and with this rather limited sum upon which to draw purchased an outfit for a year's collecting and sailed with Doctor Steere for Manila. Two other young Americans accompanied him. One of these, Doctor Frank S. Bourns, was like myself afterwards destined to play a part in Philippine affairs which was not then dreamed of by either of us.

We spent approximately a year in the islands. Unfortunately we had neglected to provide ourselves with proper official credentials and as a result we had some embarrassing experiences. We were arrested by suspicious Spanish officials shortly after our arrival and were tried on trumped-up charges. On several subsequent occasions we narrowly escaped arrest and imprisonment.

The unfriendly attitude of certain of our Spanish acquaintances was hardly to be wondered at. They could not believe that sensible, civilized human beings would shoot tiny birds, pay for eggs the size of the tip of one's little finger more than hens' eggs were worth, undergo not a few hardships and run many risks while living in the simplest of native houses on very inadequate food, unless actuated by some hidden purpose. At different times they suspected us of looking for gold deposits, of designing to stir up trouble among the natives, or of being political spies.

When Doctor Bourns came back with the American troops in 1908 and I returned as a member of the first Philippine Commission in 1909, this last supposition became a fixed belief with many of our former Spanish acquaintances who still remained in the islands, and they frankly expressed their regret that they had not shot us while they had the chance.

Over against certain unpleasant experiences with those who could not understand us or our work I must set much kind and invaluable assistance rendered by others who could, and did.

All in all we spent a most interesting year, visiting eighteen of the more important islands.[1]

Throughout this trip we lived in very close contact with the Filipinos, either occupying the *tribunales*, the municipal buildings of their towns, where they felt at liberty to call and observe us at all hours of the day and night, or actually living in their houses, which in some instances were not vacated by the owners during our occupancy.

Incidentally we saw something of several of the wild tribes, including the Tagbanuas of Palawan, the Moros of Joló, Basilan and Mindanao, and the Mangyans of Mindoro.

We experienced many very real hardships, ran not a few serious risks and ended our sojourn with six weeks of fever and starvation in the interior of Mindoro. While we would not have cut short our appointed stay by a day, we were nevertheless delighted when we could turn our faces homeward, and Doctor Bourns and I agreed

[1] Cuyo, Palawan, Balabac, Cagayan de Joló, Joló proper, Basilan, Mindanao, Panay, Guimaras, Negros, Siquijor, Cebu, Bohol, Samar, Leyte, Masbate, Marinduque and Mindoro.

that we had had quite enough of life in the Philippines.

Upon my arrival at my home in Vermont a competent physician told my family that I might not live a week. I however recuperated so rapidly that I was able to return to the University of Michigan that fall and to complete the work of my senior year. I became a member of the teaching staff of the institution before my graduation.

Little as I suspected it at the time, the tropics had fixed their strangely firm grip on me during that fateful first trip to the Far East which was destined to modify my whole subsequent life. I had firmly believed that if fortunate enough to get home I should have sense enough to stay there, but before six months had elapsed I was finding life at Ann Arbor, Michigan, decidedly prosaic, and longing to return to the Philippines and finish a piece of zoölogical work which I knew was as yet only begun.

Doctor Bourns, like myself, was eager to go back, and we set out to raise $10,000 to pay the expenses of a two-years collecting tour, in the course of which we hoped to visit regions not hitherto penetrated by any zoölogist.

Times were then getting hard, and good Doctor Angell, the president of the university, thought it a great joke that two young fellows like ourselves should attempt to raise so considerable a sum to be spent largely for our own benefit. Whenever he met me on the street he used to ask whether we had obtained that $10,000 yet, and then shake with laughter. One of the great satisfactions of my life came when, on a beautiful May morning in 1890, I was able to answer his inquiry in the affirmative.

He fairly staggered with amazement, but promptly recovering himself warmly congratulated me, and with that kindly interest which he has always shown in the affairs of young men, asked how he could help us. Through his kindly offices and the intervention of the State Department we were able to obtain a royal order from the

Spanish government which assured us a very different reception on our return to the Philippines in August from that which had been accorded us on the occasion of our first visit to the islands.

There was now revealed to us a pleasing side of Spanish character which we had largely missed during our first visit. Satisfied as to our identity and as to the motives which actuated us, the Spanish officials, practically without exception, did everything in their power to assist us and to render our sojourn pleasant and profitable. Our mail was delivered to us at points fifty miles distant from provincial capitals. When our remittances failed to reach us on time, as they not infrequently did, money was loaned to us freely without security. Troops were urged upon us for our protection when we desired to penetrate regions considered to be dangerous. Our Spanish friends constantly offered us the hospitality of their homes and with many of them the offer was more than *pro forma*. Indeed, in several instances it was insisted upon so strongly that we accepted it, to our great pleasure and profit.

Officials were quite frank in discussing before us the affairs of their several provinces, and we gained a very clear insight into existing political methods and conditions.

During this trip we lived in even closer contact with the Filipino [1] population than on the occasion of our first visit. Our rapidly growing knowledge of Spanish, and of Visayan, one of the more important native dialects, rendered it increasingly easy for us to communicate with them, gain their confidence and learn to look at things

---

[1] I employ the noun Filipinos to designate collectively the eight civilized, Christianized peoples, called respectively the Cagayans, Ilocanos, Pangasináns, Zambalans, Pampangans, Tagálogs, Bicols and Visayans, or any of them; the adjective Filipino to designate anything pertaining to these peoples, or any of them; the noun Philippines to designate the country, and the adjective Philippine to designate anything pertaining to the country as distinguished from its people.

from their view point. They talked with us most frankly and fully about their political troubles.

During this our second sojourn in the Philippines, which lengthened to two years and six months, we revisited the islands with which we had become more or less familiar on our first trip and added six others to the list.[1] We lived for a time among the wild Bukidnons and Negritos of the Negros mountains.

After my companion had gone to Borneo I had the misfortune to contract typhoid fever when alone in Busuanga, and being ignorant of the nature of the malady from which I was suffering, kept on my feet until I could no longer stand, with the natural result that I came uncommonly near paying for my foolishness with my life, and have ever since suffered from resulting physical disabilities. When able to travel, I left the islands upon the urgent recommendation of my physician, feeling that the task which had led me to return there was almost accomplished and sure that my wanderings in the Far East were over.

Shortly after my return to the United States I was offered a position as a member of the zoölogical staff of the University of Michigan, accepted it, received speedy promotion, and hoped and expected to end my days as a college professor.

In 1898 the prospect of war with Spain awakened old memories. I fancy that the knowledge then possessed by the average American citizen relative to the Philippines was fairly well typified by that of a good old lady at my Vermont birthplace who had spanked me when I was a small boy, and who, after my first return from the Philippine Islands, said to me, "Deanie, are them Philippians you have been a visitin' the people that Paul wrote the Epistle to?"

I endeavoured to do my part toward dispelling this ignorance. My knowledge of Philippine affairs led me

[1] Busuanga, Culion, Tawi Tawi, Tablas, Romblon and Sibuyan.

FORT SAN ANTONIO ABAD, SHOWING THE EFFECT OF THE FIRE FROM DEWEY'S FLEET.

This fort, which marked the southern and western end of the Spanish line of defences around the city of Manila, was bombarded by the United States Fleet as a preliminary to the successful assault of August 13, 1898, on the city. The photograph, although not taken until March, 1899, gives some idea of the havoc wrought by the shells which struck the outer wall. The chief damage was done when they exploded within the fort.

strongly to favour armed intervention in Cuba, where similar political conditions seemed to prevail to a considerable extent, and I fear that I was considered by many of my university colleagues something of a "jingo." Indeed, a member of the University Board of Regents said that I ought to be compelled to enlist. As a matter of fact, compulsion would have been quite unnecessary had it not been for physical disability.

My life-long friend and former travelling companion, Doctor Bourns, was not similarly hampered. He promptly joined the army as a medical officer with the rank of major, and sailed for the islands on the second steamer which carried United States troops there. As a natural result of his familiarity with Spanish and his wide acquaintanceship among the Filipinos, he was ordered from the outset to devote his time more largely to political matters than to the practice of his profession. He did all that he could to prevent misunderstandings between Filipinos and Americans. He assisted as an interpreter at the negotiations for the surrender of Manila on August 13, 1898, after taking part in the attack on the city. Later he was given the rather difficult task of suppressing a bad outbreak of smallpox among the Spanish prisoners of war, which he performed with great success. He was finally made chief health officer of Manila, although he continued to devote himself largely to political matters, got numberless deserving Filipinos out of trouble, and rapidly increased his already wide circle of Filipino friends. Through his letters I was kept quite closely in touch with the situation.

Meanwhile I decided that the Philippines were not for me, asked for and obtained leave for study in Europe, and in December 1898 set out for New York to engage passage for myself and my family. I went by way of Washington in order to communicate to President McKinley certain facts relative to the Philippine situation which it seemed to me ought to be brought to his attention.

I believed that there was serious danger of an outbreak of hostilities between Filipinos and Americans, and that such a catastrophe, resulting from mutual misunderstanding, might be avoided if seasonable action were taken. I have since learned how wrong was this latter belief. My previous experience had been almost exclusively with the Visayans and the wild tribes, and the revolution against the United States was at the outset a strictly Tagálog affair, and hence beyond my ken.

President McKinley very kindly gave me all the time I wanted, displayed a most earnest desire to learn the truth, and showed the deepest and most friendly interest in the Filipinos. Let no man believe that then or later he had the slightest idea of bringing about the exploitation of their country. On the contrary, he evinced a most earnest desire to learn what was best for them and then to do it if it lay within his power.

To my amazement, at the end of our interview he asked me whether I would be willing to go to the islands as his personal representative.

I could not immediately decide to make such a radical change in my plans as this would involve, and asked for a week's time to think the matter over, which was granted. I decided to go.

Meanwhile, the President had evolved the idea of sending out a commission and asked me if I would serve on it. I told him that I would and left for my home to make preparations for an early departure. A few days later he announced the names of the commissioners. They were Jacob Gould Schurman, President of Cornell University; Major-General Elwell S. Otis, then the ranking army officer in the Philippines; Rear-Admiral George Dewey, then in command of the United States fleet in Philippine waters; Colonel Charles Denby, who had for fourteen years served as United States Minister to China, and myself.

Colonel Denby was delayed in Washington by public

business. Mr. Schurman and I reached Yokohama on the morning of February 13, and on arrival there learned, to our deep regret, that hostilities had broken out on the fourth instant. We reached Manila on the evening of March 4, but Colonel Denby was unable to join us until April 2. Meanwhile, as we could not begin our work in his absence, I had an exceptional opportunity to observe conditions in the field, of which I availed myself.

I served with the first Philippine Commission until it had completed its work, and was then appointed to the second Philippine Commission without a day's break in my period of service.

The members of this latter body were William H. Taft of Ohio; Luke E. Wright of Tennessee; Henry C. Ide of Vermont; Bernard Moses of California, and myself. Briefly stated, the task before us was to establish civil government in the Philippine Islands. After a period of ninety days, to be spent in observation, the commission was to become the legislative body, while executive power continued to be vested for a time in the military.

This condition endured until the 4th of July, 1901, on which day Mr. Taft was appointed civil governor. On September 1, 1901, each of the remaining original members of the commission became an executive officer as well. Mr. Wright was appointed secretary of commerce and police; Mr. Ide, secretary of finance and justice; Mr. Moses, secretary of public instruction, and I myself, Secretary of the Interior. On the same day three Filipino members were added to the commission: Dr. T. H. Pardo de Tavera, Sr. Benito Legarda and Sr. José R. de Luzuriaga.

Until the 16th of October, 1907, the Commission continued to serve as the sole legislative body. It is at the present time the upper house of the Philippine Legislature, the Philippine Assembly, composed of eighty-one elective members, constituting the lower house.

I have therefore had a hand in the enactment of all legislation put in force in the Philippine Islands since the American occupation, with the exception of certain laws passed during my few and brief absences.

As secretary of the interior it fell to my lot to organize and direct the operations of a Bureau of Health, a Bureau of Government Laboratories, a Bureau of Forestry, a Bureau of Public Lands, a Bureau of Agriculture, a Bureau of Non-Christian Tribes, a Mining Bureau and a Weather Bureau. Ultimately, the Bureau of Non-Christian Tribes and the Mining Bureau were incorporated with the Bureau of Government Laboratories to form the Bureau of Science, which continued under my executive control. The Bureau of Agriculture was transferred to the Department of Public Instruction in 1909.

I was at the outset given administrative control of all matters pertaining to the non-Christian tribes, which constitute, roughly speaking, an eighth of the population of the Philippines, and until my resignation retained such control throughout the islands, except in the Moro Province, which at an early day was put directly under the governor-general.

I participated in the organization of civil government in the several provinces of the archipelago, and myself drafted the Municipal Code for the government of the towns inhabited by Filipinos, as well as the Special Provincial Government Act and the Township Government Act for that of the provinces and settlements inhabited chiefly by the non-Christian tribes.

At the outset we did not so much as know with certainty the names of the several wild and savage tribes inhabiting the more remote and inaccessible portions of the archipelago. As I was unable to obtain reliable information concerning them on which to base legislation for their control and uplifting, I proceeded to get such information for myself by visiting their territory, much of which was then quite unexplored.

After this territory was organized into five so-called "Special Government Provinces," some of my Filipino friends, I fear not moved solely by anxiety for the public good, favoured and secured a legislative enactment which made it my official duty to visit and inspect these provinces at least once during each fiscal year. I shall always feel indebted to them for giving me this opportunity to become intimately acquainted with some of the most interesting, most progressive, and potentially most important peoples of the Philippines.

When in 1901 I received the news that a central government was soon to be established, I was in the Subprovince of Lepanto on my first trip through the wilder and less-known portions of northern Luzon. During each succeeding year I have spent from two to four months in travel through the archipelago, familiarizing myself at first hand with local conditions.

I have frequently taken with me on these inspection trips representatives of the Bureaus of Forestry, Agriculture, Science and Health to carry on practical investigations, and have made it my business to visit and explore little known and unknown regions. There are very few islands worthy of the name which it has not been my privilege to visit.

The organization of an effective campaign against diseases like bubonic plague, smallpox, Asiatic cholera and leprosy in a country where no similar work had ever previously been undertaken, inhabited by people profoundly ignorant of the benefits to be derived from modern methods of sanitation, and superstitious to a degree, promptly brought me into violent conflict with the beliefs and prejudices of a large portion of the Filipino population.

A similar result followed the inauguration of an active campaign for the suppression of surra, foot and mouth disease, and rinderpest, which were rapidly destroying the horses and cattle.

From the outset I was held responsible for the enforcement of marine and land quarantine regulations, which were at first very obnoxious to the general public.

When the Pure Food and Drugs Act adopted by Congress for the United States was made applicable to the Philippines without any provision for its enforcement, this not altogether pleasant duty was assigned to me.

I did not seek appointment to the Philippine service in the first instance. The political influence at my command has never extended beyond my own vote. During a period of twelve years my removal was loudly and frequently demanded, yet I saw President Schurman, Colonel Denby, General Otis, Admiral Dewey, Commissioner Moses, Governor Taft, Governor Wright, Governor Ide, Governor Smith, Secretary Shuster, Commissioner Tavera, Commissioner Legarda and Governor Forbes, all my colleagues on one or the other of the Philippine commissions, leave the service, before my own voluntary retirement on September 15, 1913.

I had long expected a request for my resignation at any time, and had often wished that it might come. Indeed I once before tendered it voluntarily, only to have President Taft say that he thought I should withdraw it, which I did. I am absolutely without political ambition save an earnest desire to earn the political epitaph, "He did what he could."

During my brief and infrequent visits to the United States I have discovered there widespread and radical misapprehension as to conditions in the Philippines, but have failed to find that lack of interest in them which is commonly said to exist. On the contrary, I have found the American public keenly desirous of getting at the real facts whenever there was an opportunity to do so.

The extraordinary extent to which untrue statements have been accepted at their face value has surprised and deeply disturbed me. I have conversed with three college presidents, each of whom believed that the current expenses of the Philippine government were paid from the United States Treasury.

The preponderance of false and misleading statements about the Philippines is due, it seems to me, primarily to the fact that it is those persons with whom the climate disagrees and who in consequence are invalided home, and those who are separated from the service in the interest of the public good, who return to the United States and get an audience there; while those who successfully adapt themselves to local conditions, display interest in their work and become proficient in it, remain in the islands for long periods during which they are too busy, and too far from home, to make themselves heard.

Incidentally it must be remembered that if such persons do attempt to set forth facts which years of practical experience have taught them, they are promptly accused of endeavouring to save their own bread and butter by seeking to perpetuate conditions which insure them fat jobs.

When I think of the splendid men who have uncomplainingly laid down their lives in the military and in the civil service of their country in these islands, and of the larger number who have given freely of their best years to unselfish, efficient work for others, this charge fills me with indignation.

The only thing that kept me in the Philippine service for so long a time was my interest in the work for the non-Christian tribes and my fear that while my successor was gaining knowledge concerning it which can be had only through experience, matters might temporarily go to the bad. It has been my ambition to bring this work to such a point that it would move on, for a time at least, by its own momentum.

I am now setting forth my views relative to the past and present situation in the islands because I believe that their inhabitants are confronted by a danger graver than any which they have before faced since the time when their fate wavered in the balance, while the question whether the United States should acquire sovereignty over them or should allow Spain to continue to rule them was under consideration.

It is my purpose to tell the plain, hard truth regardless of the effect of such conduct upon my future career. It has been alleged that my views on Philippine problems were coloured by a desire to retain my official position. Nothing could be further from the truth. Indeed, no man who has not served for long and sometimes very weary years as a public official, and has not been a target for numerous more or less irresponsible individuals whose hands were filled with mud and who were actuated by a fixed desire to throw it at something, can appreciate as keenly as I do the manifold blessings which attend the life of a private citizen.

I trust that I have said enough to make clear my view point, and now a word as to subject-matter. It is my intention to correct some of the very numerous misstatements which have been made concerning past and present conditions in the Philippines. I shall quote, from time to time, such statements, both verbal and written, and more especially some of those which have recently appeared in a book entitled "The American Occupation of the Philippines, 1898–1912," by James H. Blount, who signs himself "Officer of the United States Volunteers in the Philippines, 1899–1901 ; United States District Judge in the Philippines, 1901–1905."

Judge Blount has indulged so freely in obvious hyperbole, and has made so very evident the bitter personal animosities which inspire many of his statements, that it has been a genuine surprise to his former associates and acquaintances that his book has been taken seriously.

It should be sufficiently evident to any unprejudiced reader that in writing it he has played the part of the special pleader rather than that of the historian. He has used government records freely, and as is usually the

FELIPE BUENCAMINO.

Perhaps the most prolific writer on political subjects whom the Philippines
have produced. He was at one time a member of Aguinaldo's cabinet and
accompanied Aguinaldo's mother and son when they surrendered in order
to obtain American protection.

case when a special pleader quotes from such records, the nature of the matter which he has omitted is worthy of more than passing attention. I shall hope to be able to fill some of the gaps that he has left in the documentary history of the events which he discusses and by so doing, very materially to change its purport.

As public documents have been so misused, and as a new administration is bestowing on Filipinos political offices, and giving them opportunities, for which they are as yet utterly unprepared, thus endangering the results of years of hard, patient, self-sacrificing work performed by experienced and competent men, it becomes necessary to strike home by revealing unpleasant facts which are of record but have not heretofore been disclosed because of the injury to reputations and the wounding of feelings which would result from their publication. In doing this I feel that I am only discharging a duty to the people of the United States, who are entitled to know the truth if the present possibility of Philippine independence is to be seriously considered, and to the several Filipino peoples who are to-day in danger of rushing headlong to their own utter and final destruction.

At the outset I shall discuss the oft-asserted claim that the Filipino leaders were deceived and betrayed by American officials whom they assisted, and that this unpardonable conduct led to the outbreak of active hostilities which occurred just prior to the arrival at Manila of the first Philippine Commission.

I shall then show that these leaders never established a government which adequately protected life and property, or gave to their people peace, happiness or justice, but on the contrary inaugurated a veritable reign of terror under which murder became a governmental institution, while rape, inhuman torture, burying alive and other ghastly crimes were of common occurrence, and usually went unpunished. The data which I use in establishing these contentions are for the most part taken directly

from the Insurgent records, in referring to which I employ
the war department abbreviation "P. I. R." followed
by a number.

I next take up some of the more important subsequent
historical events, describing the work of the first Philippine Commission, and showing in what manner the
government established by the second Philippine Commission has discharged its stewardship, subsequently discussing certain as yet unsolved problems which confront
the present government, such as that presented by the
existence of slavery and peonage, and that of the non-
Christian tribes.   For the benefit of those who, like Judge
Blount, consider the Philippines "a vast straggly archipelago of jungle-covered islands in the south seas which
have been a nuisance to every government that ever
owned them," I give some facts as to the islands, their
climate, their natural resources and their commercial
possibilities, and close by setting forth my views as to
the present ability of the civilized Cagayans, Ilocanos,
Pampangans, Zambals, Pangasináns, Tagálogs, Bicols
and Visayans, commonly and correctly called *Filipinos*,
to establish, or to maintain when established, a stable
government throughout Filipino territory, to say nothing
of bringing under just and effective control, and of protecting and civilizing, the people of some twenty-seven
non-Christian tribes which constitute an eighth of the
population, and occupy approximately half of the territory, of the Philippine Islands.

I wish here to acknowledge my very great indebtedness
to Major J. R. M. Taylor, who has translated and compiled the Insurgent [1] records, thereby making available a
very large mass of reliable and most valuable information
without which a number of chapters of this book would
have remained unwritten.   Surely no man who bases his

---

[1] I use the word " Insurgents " as a proper noun, to designate the
Filipinos who took up arms against the United States, hence capitalize
it, and the adjective derived from it.

statements concerning Filipino rule on the facts set forth in these records can be accused of deriving his information from hostile or prejudiced sources.

Of them, Major Taylor says : —

"No one reading the Insurgent records can fail to be impressed with the difference between the Spanish and the Tagálog documents. Many of the former are doubtless written with a view to their coming into the hands of the Americans, or with deliberate purpose to have them do so, and are framed accordingly. All Tagálog documents, intended only for Filipinos, say much that is not said in the Spanish documents. The orders of the Dictator [1] to his subjects were conveyed in the latter series of documents."

[1] General Aguinaldo.

CHAPTER II

Was Independence Promised?

It has long been the fashion in certain quarters to allege, or to insinuate, that American consuls and naval officers promised the Insurgent leaders that the independence of the Philippines would be recognized by the United States. It has been claimed by some that the coöperation of the Insurgents in the military operations against Manila was sought for and secured. Others say that they were at least *de facto* allies of the United States, and that they were in the end shamelessly betrayed and wantonly attacked.

These are very serious charges. I shall prove, chiefly by the Insurgent records, that each of them is false. I ask the forbearance of my readers if, in the three chapters which I devote to these matters, I quote documentary evidence at length. When original documents or extracts from them tell a clear and reasonably concise story, I sometimes insert them bodily in the text. In other cases I give my own version of the facts which they set forth, but give the full text in foot-notes. In nearly all instances references are given to sources of documentary information. I greatly regret that Taylor's narrative, with its very numerous supporting documents, is not readily accessible to the student of history. It ought to have been published, but never got beyond the galley-proof stage. In referring to it, I am therefore obliged to use the word Taylor followed by the letters and figures designating the page of this galley proof on which the passage referred to is found. Whenever possible I give the War Department numbers[1] of Insurgent documents, but in a few cases can give only the exhibit numbers assigned by Taylor in printing the documents.

As his exhibits are serially arranged it is easy to find any one of them. Copies of his work may be found in the War Department and in the office of the Chief of the Philippine Constabulary.

Referring to the charge that the Insurgents were deceived, even had deceit been practised as claimed, Aguinaldo would have had no just ground for complaint, for he himself not only frankly advocated its use, but deliberately employed it in his dealings with the Americans, as clearly appears in records hereinafter cited.[2] However, most Americans hold to a standard very different from his. Was it departed from in this instance?

Aguinaldo has specifically and repeatedly charged that Pratt and Dewey promised him the recognition of the independence of the Philippines by the United States.[3]

Judge Blount has referred to the "*de facto* alliance between the Americans and Aguinaldo," and has dwelt at length on "promises, both expressed and implied," which were subsequently repudiated by Consul Pratt, Admiral Dewey and Generals Anderson and Merritt, constantly suggesting, even when he does not specifically charge, bad faith on the part of these officers of the United States.[4]

On analyzing his statements we find that he is discreetly non-committal as to exactly what were the expressed promises, nor does he make it so plain as might be desired what legitimate inferences were deducible from the acts of the Americans in question. He quotes

[1] Beginning with the letters "P. I. R."

[2] See pp. 53, 55, 68.

[3] See pp. 27, 47, 49, 63 of this book for repetitions and variations of this charge of Aguinaldo.

[4] See p. 31 of his book, "The American Occupation of the Philippines," in referring to which I will hereafter use the word Blount, followed by a page number.

an alleged statement of General Anderson to the effect that : —

"Whether Admiral Dewey and Consuls Pratt, Wildman,[1] and Williams [2] did or did not give Aguinaldo assurances that a Philippino government would be recognized, the Phillippinos certainly thought so, judging from their acts rather than from their words. Admiral Dewey gave them arms and ammunition, as I did subsequently at his request."[3]

Before discussing these charges I will briefly review certain historical facts, knowledge of which will be useful in considering them.

In August, 1896, an insurrection against Spain had broken out in the Philippines under the leadership of Emilio Aguinaldo, a resident of Cavite Viejo, who had been a school teacher, and was, at that time, *gobernadorcillo* [4] of his town.

It had been terminated by the so-called "Treaty of Biacnabató," signed in Manila on December 15, 1897.

This document provided for the surrender of "Don Emilio Aguinaldo, Supreme Chief of the Insurgents in arms," and Don Marciano Llanera and Don Baldomero Aguinaldo, his subordinates, together with their soldiers and arms.

"The Excellent Señor General in Chief" of the Spanish forces was to "provide the necessary means for supporting the lives" of those who surrendered before a certain fixed date.

In actual practice what was done was to agree to pay them $800,000[5] in three instalments, the first of $400,000, the second and third of $200,000 each.

Aguinaldo and certain other leaders were to take up

[1] U. S. Consul General Rounseville Wildman of Hongkong.

[2] U. S. Consul O. F. Williams of Manila.

[3] Blount, p. 43.

[4] A term, more or less corresponding to mayor, then applied to the ranking municipal officer of a *pueblo* or town.

[5] Eight hundred thousand Mexican dollars, the actual value of which constantly fluctuated.

THE SAN JUAN BRIDGE.

This bridge is the one near which the first shot was fired when hostilities began between Americans and Filipinos.

their residence outside the islands. Their deportation was duly provided for, and Aguinaldo and twenty-six of his companions were taken to Hongkong, on the Spanish steamer *Uranus;* arriving there on December 31, 1897.

On January 2, 1898, $400,000 were deposited in the Hongkong Bank, to the credit of Aguinaldo and Co.

The Insurgent leaders remaining at Biacnabató had a meeting under the presidency of Isabelo Artacho, an Ilocano [1] who was the ranking officer in the absence of Aguinaldo, and requested that the second instalment, of $200,000, be paid to them. The Spanish governor-general, Primo de Rivera, acceded to their request, and they divided the money, although Aguinaldo denied their right to do so, claiming that it should have been sent to Hongkong.

The third payment of $200,000 was apparently never made. Primo de Rivera, says that he turned over a check for $200,000 to his successor, General Augustin, in April, 1898; giving as his reason for refusing to pay it to the Insurgents that there seemed to him to be no prospect of its being equitably divided among those who were entitled to receive it under the agreement.

Aguinaldo and his associates claimed that certain reforms were promised by the Spanish government at the time the treaty of Biacnabató was negotiated, and as these measures were not put into effect, they organized a junta or revolutionary committee at Hongkong. It included in its membership a number of Filipino political exiles, then residing at that place.

The men who composed this organization soon fell to quarrelling and it became necessary to come to a definite understanding as to its aims. Under the arrangement finally reached, the junta, as a whole, was charged with the work of propaganda outside of the archipelago; with

[1] The Ilocanos are one of the eight civilized peoples who collectively make up the Filipinos. They number 803,942, and inhabit certain provinces in northern Luzon.

all diplomatic negotiations with foreign governments; and with the preparation and shipment of such articles as were needed to carry on the revolution in the Philippines. It was to be allowed voice by Aguinaldo's government in any serious question which might arise abroad, and would aid that government in bringing the civil administration of the Philippines to the level of that of the most advanced nations.

Trouble soon arose among the former Insurgent leaders over the division of the funds deposited at Hongkong.

Taylor gives a trustworthy and concise account of the events of this period, and as it is of historic interest, and makes clear just how Aguinaldo came to go to Singapore, meet Pratt, and enter into negotiations with him, I quote extensive extracts from it.[1]

"From January 4 to April 4, Aguinaldo withdrew from the banks 5786.46 pesos in part interest on the money he had deposited. This was used to pay the expenses of himself and his companions in Hongkong. These expenses were kept at a minimum; the money was drawn and spent by him. If one of the men with him needed a new pair of shoes, Aguinaldo paid for them; if another wanted a new coat, Aguinaldo bought it. Minute accounts were kept, which are on file among his papers, and it is seen from them that his expenses were exceeding his income, which could only be 12,000 pesos a year, while he was living at the rate of 22,000, with constant demands being made upon him by men who came from the Philippines. Life was not easy under these conditions. Aguinaldo's companions were entirely dependent upon him. Their most trivial expenses had to be approved by him, and he held them down with a strong hand. They were men living in a strange land, among a people whose language they did not speak, having nothing to do but quarrel among themselves, exiles waiting for a chance to return to their own country, which they watched with weary eyes while they guarded the embers by which they hoped to light the fires of a new insurrection.

[1] I have not felt at liberty to correct spelling, capitalization, punctuation or grammar in quotations, except in the case of perfectly evident printer's errors. It should be remembered that the results of Taylor's work were left in the form of galley proof.

"The men who had accompanied Aguinaldo to Hongkong were not the only Filipinos domiciled there; a number of men had taken refuge in that British colony after the events of 1872, and some of them at least had prospered. Some of them, like the members of the Cortes family, seem to have had almost no relations with the followers of Aguinaldo; some, like J. M. Basa, knew them and took part in some of the meetings of the governing groups, but were probably not admitted to their full confidence, as Aguinaldo and his immediate following wanted and were working for independence and independence alone, while the Filipinos who had long lived in Hongkong wanted to see the archipelago lost to Spain, but had no confidence in the ability of the country to stand alone or in the fitness of Aguinaldo and ¡his following to direct the councils of a state. The character of the new refugees did not inspire confidence in these older men, who hoped for a protectorate by or annexation to the United States.

"On May 6, 1898, the consul-general of the United States there informed the State Department that D. Cortés, M. Cortés, A. Rosario, Gracio Gonzaga, and José Maria Basa (50), all very wealthy land-owners, bankers, and lawyers of Manila, desired to tender their allegiance and the allegiance of their powerful families in Manila to the United States, and that they had instructed all their connections to render every aid to the United States forces in Manila. On May 14 he forwarded statements of other Filipinos domiciled in Hongkong, not members of the junta, that they desired to submit their allegiance and the allegiance of their families in the Philippine Islands to the United States. One of Aguinaldo's followers, writing somewhat later, spoke with bitterness of the rich old men who went about calling their companions 'beggarly rebels,' but these men were rich, and their names and their apparent adhesion to the cause represented by Aguinaldo would inspire confidence in him among men of property in the Philippines. They were, accordingly, not to be lightly alienated; therefore, at first, at least, no open break took place with them, but their attitude toward the leaders of the insurrection is shown by the fact that after the early summer of 1898 they took no, or very little, part in the insurgent movement, although they were living in Hongkong, the seat of the junta, which conducted the propaganda for the insurgent government of the Philippines.

*   *   *   *   *   *   *

"But, in fact, Aguinaldo had no just conception of the conditions and of the opportunities which were about to open be-

fore the Hongkong junta, for although war between Spain and
the United States was imminent and a United States squadron
was in Hongkong threatening Manila, Aguinaldo was chiefly
concerned in finding how to avoid losing the money which had
been received from the Spanish government as the price of his
surrender.   The importance of his presence near the Philippines
in case of war did not occur to him, or if it did occur to him anything which he could obtain there from the aid of the United
States probably seemed for the moment of little consequence
compared with escaping from his wrangling companions with
enough money to live on in Paris.

" Artacho, who had received 5000 pesos as his share of the
second payment, arrived in Hongkong and on April 5 demanded
200,000 pesos of the insurgent funds, probably under the
agreement that he should establish a company in Hongkong
for the benefit of the former leaders and not merely of those
who had accompanied Aguinaldo. But the leaders in Hongkong had denounced that agreement, and refused to pay.   He
then entered suit before the supreme court of Hongkong, calling
upon Aguinaldo for an accounting of the trust funds deposited
in his hands for the benefit of Artacho and others, and asked
for an injunction restraining Aguinaldo or any member of the
junta from handling or disposing of any part of said funds.   He
filed as evidence copies of the Biacnabató agreement and of
the agreement made by the leaders on December 19.   This
suit was brought not merely in the name of Artacho, but in
that of all the exiles who were described as living in exile in
Hongkong in accordance with an agreement made with the
Spanish Government.   Artacho probably had adherents among
these men, some at least of whom were utterly weary of waiting
in Hongkong and of living upon what was doled out to them.
Some at least saw no chance of any other fate than indefinite
exile spent in dependence upon the inner group for even the
means of existence.

" The suit was in equity, and called for an accounting for the
trust funds which the complainant recognized were legally in
the hands of Aguinaldo.   It could be carried on only with great
difficulty without his presence and without his account books.
Meetings were held, and Artacho was denounced as attempting
to extort blackmail, but he refused to yield, and Aguinaldo,
rather than explain the inner workings of the Hongkong junta
before a British court, prepared for flight.   A summons was
issued for his appearance before the supreme court of Hongkong
on April 13, 1898, but he was by that time beyond its jurisdiction.

" He drew out the 50,000 pesos from the Chartered Bank, which had become due according to the terms of the deposit, and perhaps such other sums as could be drawn upon by check, engaged passage for Europe by way of Singapore for G. H. del Pilar, J. M. Leyba, and himself under assumed names, appointed V. Belarmino to succeed to his functions, and gave him checks signed in blank to draw the interest of the sums on deposit to provide for the support of the exiles. He gave as his reason for departure that he was going to remain under cover until Artacho could be bought off, but he intended to go far afield for this purpose, as he gave his destination as Europe and the United States.

" Aguinaldo and his companions probably sailed from Hong-kong on April 8, 1898, and arrived in Singapore on April 21, after stopping in Saigon. War between the United States and Spain had been rendered inevitable by the resolution of Congress demanding that Spain should withdraw her forces from Cuba, and was declared on April 21. Although Aguinaldo and his followers did not appreciate the influence which conditions on the other side of the world might have upon the future of the Philippines, it happened that in Singapore at that time there was an Englishman named Bray who did. He had been a member of the civil service in India, and had lived for some years in the Philippines, but he had fallen upon evil days and was engaged in writing letters to the Singapore *Free Press* upon the Philippines, and in retailing such information as was in his possession concerning them to the United States consul-general in Singapore, Mr. E. Spencer Pratt, for transmittal to Commodore Dewey. Bray heard of the arrival of Aguinaldo and realized what could be done with him, and that if the matter were well handled it might be to his own advantage. He went at once to see Aguinaldo and informed him that the United States consul-general was anxious to see him. He went to the consul-general and informed him of the importance of Aguinaldo, and that he was in Singapore. Aguinaldo had to be persuaded to agree to a meeting. The consul-general was anxious for it, and it took place, according to Aguinaldo, on the night of April 22 (according to Pratt, on the morning of April 24). The statement made by Aguinaldo is probably correct. According to his account book, he paid $11 on April 23, 1898, for a telegram to the Hong-kong junta concerning the negotiations 'with America.'

" Aguinaldo knew but little English, Pratt knew no Spanish, so in their interview Bray acted as interpreter. An interpreter who is interested in the subject of the discussion may be a dangerous man. It is impossible to say what he told Aguinaldo. Certainly Pratt did not know; but whatever was said during these conversations it is within the limits of possibility that Pratt may have been made to say by the interpreter more than he intended, and that his statements of what would probably be granted by the United States Government and his expression of good wishes for the cause of Filipino independence may have been translated as assurances and as promises. Bray, who, according to his Filipino former friends, was apt to talk too much, may have talked too much on this occasion, and so the myth of the formal agreement between Aguinaldo on behalf of the Filipino insurgents and Pratt on behalf of the United States grew up, a fiction which Bray himself, with a natural desire to add to his own importance, did his best to circulate.

"Bray did not ask for his reward at the time, but probably reckoned upon making himself indispensable as an adviser, so that later he could make his own terms. For a time he wrote letters of advice to Aguinaldo, which may have had some influence upon the line of conduct which he adopted, and later was employed in furnishing from Hongkong news to various newspapers of events and conditions in the Philippines. His cablegrams shortly before the outbreak of hostilities between the United States and the insurgents were more picturesque than veracious, but they were apparently considered effective, as Aguinaldo ordered that he should be given $5000. He wanted more, but the Hongkong junta did not trust him, and he ceased to be in their employment."[1]

As we shall see, Bray did not do all of the interpreting at Singapore, and we shall be able to determine with some accuracy what actually transpired there.

We can now consider understandingly the charges made against Pratt and Dewey.

It has been claimed over and over again, that Pratt promised Aguinaldo recognition of the independence of the Philippines if he and his people would coöperate with the United States forces against Spain.

Aguinaldo himself made the charge in his "Reseña Verídica"[2] in the following words : —

---

[1] Taylor, 42 F Z–43 F Z.
[2] For the history of this document, see p. 51.

"In this interview Consul Pratt told me that because the Spaniards had not complied with the agreement of Biac-na-bató, the Filipinos had a right to renew their interrupted revolution and advised me to take up arms anew against Spain, assuring me that America would give the Filipinos the greatest advantages (mayores ventajas). Then I asked the Consul what advantages the United States would concede to the Philippines, suggesting, when I had the proper opening, the propriety of making an agreement in writing, to which the Consul answered that he would report, by telegraph, on the subject to Mr. Dewey, who was the chief of the expedition against the Philippines, and who had ample powers from President McKinley.

" On the following day, between 10 and 12 in the morning, we again took up the matter, Consul Pratt saying that the admiral had answered my inquiry by saying that the United States would at least recognize the independence of the Philippine government under a naval protectorate, but that there was no necessity to put it in writing, as the words of the admiral and the American consul were sacred and would be fulfilled, not being like those of the Spaniards, and finally, that the Government of North America was a very honourable Government, a very just and very powerful one."[1]

On April 27, 1908, Pratt telegraphed the Secretary of State as follows : —

"General Aguinaldo gone my instance Hongkong arrange with Dewey coöperation insurgents Manila.

"PRATT."

On the 28th he wrote the Secretary, explaining how he had come to meet Aguinaldo, and stating just what he had done. He said : —

"At this interview, after learning from General Aguinaldo the state of an object sought to be obtained by the present insurrectionary movement, which, though absent from the Philippines, he was still directing, I took it upon myself, whilst explaining that I had no authority to speak for the Government, to point out the danger of continuing independent action at this stage ; and, having convinced him of the expediency of coöperating with our fleet, then at Hongkong, and obtained the assurance of his willingness to proceed thither and confer with

[1] P. I. R., 1300. 2.

Commodore Dewey to that end, should the latter so desire, I telegraphed the Commodore the same day as follows, through our consul-general at Hongkong : —

"'Aguinaldo, insurgent leader, here. Will come Hongkong arrange with Commodore for general coöperation insurgents Manila if desired. Telegraph.

"'PRATT.'"

The Commodore's reply read thus : —

"'Tell Aguinaldo come soon as possible.

"'DEWEY.'"

Pratt adds : —

"I received it late at night, and at once communicated to General Aguinaldo, who, with his aide-de-camp and private secretary, all under assumed names, I succeeded in getting off by the British Steamer *Malacca*, which left here on Tuesday the 26th.

"Just previous to his departure, I had a second and last interview with General Aguinaldo, the particulars of which I shall give you by next mail.

"The general impressed me as a man of intelligence, ability, and courage, and worthy the confidence that had been placed in him.

"I think that in arranging for his direct coöperation with the commander of our forces, I have prevented possible conflict of action and facilitated the work of occupying and administering the Philippines.

"If this course of mine meets with the Government's approval, as I trust it may, I shall be fully satisfied ; to Mr. Bray, however, I consider there is due some special recognition for most valuable services rendered.

"How that recognition can best be made I leave to you to decide.

"I have, etc."[1]

It will be noted that Pratt explained to Aguinaldo that he had no authority to speak for the government ; that there was no mention in the cablegrams between Pratt and Dewey of independence or indeed of any conditions on which Aguinaldo was to coöperate, these details being left for

[1] Senate Document 62, part 1, Fifty-fifth Congress, Third Session, P. P. 341 *et seq.*

INSURGENT PRISONERS.

On the day of the Polo fight in province of Bulacan these Insurgent soldiers lay in a trench and fired into a charging company of American troops until the latter came in on top of them. They were taken prisoners, sent to Manila and humanely treated there. This photograph was taken as they were being marched down the railroad track to the Manila train.

future arrangement with Dewey; and that Pratt thought that he had prevented possible conflict of action and facilitated the work of occupying and administering the Philippines.

The particulars as to the second and last interview between Aguinaldo and Pratt were embodied in the following letter: —

"No. 213.   CONSULATE-GENERAL OF THE UNITED STATES.
                    "SINGAPORE, April 30, 1898.
    "SIR: Referring to my dispatch No. 212, of the 28th instant, I have the honor to report that in the second and last interview I had with Gen. Emilio Aguinaldo on the eve of his departure for Hongkong, I enjoined upon him the necessity, under Commodore Dewey's direction, of exerting absolute control over his forces in the Philippines, as no excesses on their part would be tolerated by the American Government, the President having declared that the present hostilities with Spain were to be carried on in strict accord with modern principles of civilized warfare.
    "To this General Aguinaldo fully assented, assuring me that he intended and was perfectly able, once on the field, to hold his followers, the insurgents, in check and lead them as our commander should direct.
    "The general stated that he hoped the United States would assume protection of the Philippines for at least long enough to allow the inhabitants to establish a government of their own, in the organization of which he would desire American advice and assistance.
    "These questions I told him I had no authority to discuss.
    "I have, etc.,
                    "E. SPENCER PRATT,
                        "United States Consul-General."

In a subsequent communication written on July 28, 1898, Pratt made the following statement: —

"I declined even to discuss with General Aguinaldo the question of the future policy of the United States with regard to the Philippines, that I held out no hopes to him of any kind, committed the government in no way whatever, and, in the course of our confidences, never acted upon the assumption that the Government would coöperate with him — General Aguinaldo —

for the furtherance of any plans of his own, nor that, in accepting his said coöperation, it would consider itself pledged to recognize any political claims which he might put forward."[1]

What reason if any is there for denying the truth of this allegation ?

I will give in full Blount's statement as to what occurred at a meeting held at Singapore, to celebrate the early successes of Dewey and Aguinaldo, as it constitutes his nearest approach to a direct claim, that any one at any time promised independence : —

"First there was music by the band.   Then followed the formal reading and presentation of the address by a Dr. Santos, representing the Filipino community of Singapore.   The address pledged the 'eternal gratitude' of the Filipino people to Admiral Dewey and the honored addressee ; alluded to the glories of independence, and to how Aguinaldo had been enabled ; by the arrangement so happily effected with Admiral Dewey by Consul Pratt, to arouse eight millions of Filipinos to take up arms 'in defence of those principles of justice and liberty of which your country is the foremost champion ' and trusted 'that the United States . . . will efficaciously second the programme arranged between you, sir, and General Aguinaldo in this port of Singapore, and secure to us our independence under the protection of the United States.'

" Mr. Pratt arose and 'proceeded, speaking in French,' says the newspaper — it does not say Alabama French, but that is doubtless what it was — 'to state his belief that the Filipinos would prove and were now proving themselves fit for self-government.'   The gentleman from Alabama then went on to review the mighty events and developments of the preceding six weeks, Dewey's victory of May 1st, 'the brilliant achievements of your own distinguished leader, General Emilio Aguinaldo, *coöperating on land with the Americans at sea*,' etc.   ' You have just reason to be proud of what has been and is being accomplished by General Aguinaldo and your fellow-countrymen under his command.   When, six weeks ago, I learned that General Aguinaldo had arrived *incognito* in Singapore, I immediately *sought him out*.   An hour's interview convinced me that he was *the man for the occasion ;* and, having communicated with Admiral Dewey, I accordingly arranged for him to join the latter, which he did at Cavite.   The rest you know.' "[2]

[1] Senate Document 62, part 1, Fifty-fifth Congress, Third Session ; also P. I. R., 496.   [2] Blount, pp. 11–12.

Now, it happens that Dr. Santos himself forwarded his speech, and his version of Pratt's reply thereto, in a letter to Aguinaldo, dated Singapore, June 9, 1898. As he served as interpreter, he, if any one, should know what Pratt said. After describing the change in tone of the Singapore *Free Press*, with which strained relations had formerly existed, and the subsequent friendliness of the editor of this paper and that of the *Straits Times*, he says that on the previous afternoon he went with the other Filipinos to greet Pratt. He continues: —

"This occasion was unusually opportune by reason of ours having been victorious and immediately after the cry of our worthy chief which found an echo in this colony. For this purpose 30 or more Filipinos — 9 of the higher class, 15 musicians and the remainder of the middle class — went to greet Consul A., here, and on the invitation of Mr. Bray we ascended. He received us in his private office, and it was imposing to see that the only decoration was the American flag which covered the desk, and in its centre, a carved wooden frame holding the portrait of our worthy chief. He shook hands with all of us, and I introduced them all. We found there also, and were introduced to, the Editor of the *Straits Times* and the *Free Press* of here, and after being thus assembled, after a musical selection, I read the following speech in French : —

"'His Excellency, the Consul General of the United States of America in Singapore :

"'Your Excellency : The Filipinos of all social classes residing in this port, have come to greet Your Excellency as the genuine representative of the great and powerful American Republic in order to express to you our eternal gratitude for the moral and material support given by Admiral Dewey to our General Aguinaldo in his campaign for the liberty of eight million Filipinos. The latter and we ourselves hope that the United States, your nation, persevering in its humanitarian policy, will without cessation and (with) decided energy continue to support the programme agreed upon in Singapore between Your Excellency and General Aguinaldo, that is to say, the Independence of the Philippine Islands, under an American protectorate. Accept our cordial acknowledgments and congratulations on being the first one in accepting and supporting this idea which time and events have well developed to the great satisfaction of our nation. Finally, we request you, Most Excellent Sir, to express to your worthy President and the American Republic, our sincere acknowledgments and our fervent wishes for their prosperity. I have concluded.'

"The Consul replied hereto in French, in more or less the following terms: —

"'You have nothing to thank me for, because I have only faithfully followed the instructions received from my Government; the fact of the sudden departure of your General will permit you to infer that I have done so. I shall in any case inform my Government of your good wishes and I thank you in its name. You know that your wishes are mine also, and for this reason at the last interview I had with Mr. Aguinaldo, I repeated to him that he should observe the greatest humanity possible in the war, in order that our army, our soldiers, our nation and all the other nations may see that you are humane and not savages, as has erroneously been believed.'

"After this there was enthusiastic applause for the Consul; he offered us all cigars, glasses of very fine sherry, and lemonade for the musicians and the majority. The toasts were offered with the sherry by your humble servant, Sres. Cannon, Enríquez, Celio, Reyes, the Consul, the editors of the *Free Press*, *Straits Times* and Mr. Bray. We drank to America and her humanitarian work of redemption; to the Philippines with America; we gave thanks to the Consul, to Mr. Bray as an important defender; we drank to the *Free Press* for taking such an interest in our affairs, and to the *Straits Times* (sarcastically); but I was very careful not to propose a toast to our general, which was done at the proper time by 'Flaco'[1] when we gave three cheers; for the sake of courtesy we cheered for England, which had been so hospitable to us, and when everybody had become quiet, the Editor of the *Straits Times* took his glass in his hand and cried in a loud voice, 'The Philippine Republic,' to which we all responded. 'Flaco' disappeared a moment, and when he returned he brought with him the American flag, and formally presented it to us in French, which I interpreted to all in Spanish, as follows: 'Gentlemen: The American Consul, with his deep affection for us, presents us this flag as the greatest and most expressive remembrance which he can give us. The red stripes stand for the generous blood of her sons, shed to obtain her liberty; the white stripes stand for her virginity and purity as our country; the blue background indicates the

[1] Pratt.

sky and each star represents a free and independent State; this is America, and the Consul is desirous that we also should have so glorious a history as hers and that it may be as brilliant as could be wished, securing peace with respect, and may God be our help and guide in securing liberty. Viva and with it our most sincere thanks for so signal a courtesy.' Hereupon, to the surprise of everybody as no one expected it, the Consul requested that some Filipino airs be played which seemed to please him very much. Finally, about 6.15, we left, very well satisfied with the reception accorded us and the kindness of the Consul. Mr. Bray asked me for the text of my speech, which I insert above and I secured from the Consul his French text, which I enclose in my letter to Naning. Without anything further for the present, awaiting your reply and your opinion as to the above, as also orders and instructions for the future, I am,

" Yours, etc.

(Signed)   " ISIDORO DE LOS SANTOS."

To this letter Major Taylor has appended the following note : —

"(*Note by Compiler.* — In a letter written in Tagálog to Aguinaldo on June 6 by Santos he describes the American consul general as having cried out 'Hurrah for General Aguinaldo, hurrah for the Republic of the Philippines' and then, having apparently taken several drinks, he passed up and down the room waving the American flag before giving it to the assembled Filipinos (P. I. R., 406. 7).)"[1]

This final statement does not present the representative of the United States government at Singapore in a very favourable light, but I take the facts as I find them. If now we compare the speech actually made by Dr. Santos with Blount's version of it, we shall find that with the exception of the words "eternal gratitude" the passages which he encloses in quotation marks are not in the original at all. The glories of independence are not alluded to, nor is there so much as a suggestion that Aguinaldo had been enabled to arouse eight millions of Filipinos to take up arms, which he certainly had not done.

[1] P. I. R., 516. 4.

Dr. Santos in his speech did resort to a stereotyped Filipino procedure so very commonly employed that those of us who have dealt much with his people have learned to meet it almost automatically. It consists in referring to one's having said just exactly what one did not say, and then if one fails to note the trap and avoid it, in claiming that because one did not deny the allegation one has admitted its truth.

Aguinaldo himself later repeatedly resorted to this procedure in his dealings with Dewey and others.

In the present instance Santos employed it rather cleverly when he expressed the hope that the United States would "continue to support the programme agreed upon in Singapore, between your Excellency and General Aguinaldo, that is to say, the independence of the Philippine Islands under an American protectorate."

Now if this was agreed to, Aguinaldo later constantly violated his part of the agreement, for we shall see that he stated over and over again, in correspondence with members of the junta and others, that a protectorate would be considered only if absolute independence finally proved unattainable, but there is no reason to believe that any such agreement was made.

Dr. Santos read his speech to Mr. Pratt in French. Blount implies, whether rightly or wrongly I do not know, that Pratt's knowledge of French was poor.   At all events Pratt in his reply made not the slightest reference to the hope expressed by Santos that the United States would continue to support the programme which Santos said had been agreed upon between Pratt and Aguinaldo, and claim of a promise of independence based on these speeches must obviously be abandoned.   There is no doubt that Pratt personally sympathized with the ambitions of the Filipino leaders, and openly expressed his sympathy on this and other occasions, but to do this was one thing and to have attempted to compromise his government would have been another and very different one.   The shrewd

Filipinos with whom he was dealing understood this difference perfectly well.

It is a regrettable fact that there exists some reason to believe that his sympathy was not purely disinterested. Aguinaldo claims that Pratt wished to be appointed "representative of the Philippines in the United States to promptly secure the official recognition of our independence" and that he promised him "a high post in the customs service."[1]

It will be noted that several sentences and phrases in Blount's statement are enclosed in quotation marks. From what were they quoted? The next paragraph in his book tells us: —

"Says the newspaper clipping which has preserved the Pratt oration: At the conclusion of Mr. Pratt's speech, refreshments were served, and as the Filipinos, *being Christians, drink alcohol*, there was no difficulty in arranging as to refreshments."[2]

The use of this clipping from the Singapore *Free Press* illustrates admirably Blount's methods. The *Free Press* had at first displayed a marked coldness toward the insurgent cause, but its editor, Mr. St. Clair, was opportunely "seen" by Bray, who reported that as a result of his visit, both the editor and the paper would thereafter be friendly, and they were. In other words, the *Free*

---

[1] "The Consul — after telling me that, before arriving in Hongkong harbor, a launch would be sent by the Admiral to secretly take us to the North American squadron, a secrecy which pleased me also, as it would avoid giving publicity to my acts — then advised me that I should appoint him the representative of the Philippines in the United States to promptly secure the official recognition of our independence. I answered that whenever the Philippine government should be formed, I would nominate him for the office he desired, although I considered that but small recompense for his aid, and that in case of our having the good fortune to secure our independence I would bestow upon him a high post in the customs service besides granting the commercial advantages and the participation in the expenses of the war which the Consul asked for his Government in Washington, since the Filipinos agreed in advance to what is here stated, considering it a proper testimonial of gratitude." — P. I. R., 1300. 2.

[2] Blount, p. 12.

Press became the Singapore organ of the insurrection, and its editor, according to Bray,"a true and loyal friend" of Aguinaldo.

Blount claims to have made "an exhaustive examination of the records of that period." [1]   Why then did he use as evidence a newspaper clipping from an Insurgent organ, instead of Santos's letter?

Blount endeavours to make capital out of the fact that Pratt forwarded to the State Department a proclamation which he says was gotten up by the Insurgent leaders at Hongkong and sent to the Philippines in advance of Aguinaldo's coming.   He says that it was headed "America's Allies" and quotes from it as follows: —

"COMPATRIOTS: Divine Providence is about to place independence within our reach. . . .   The Americans, not from mercenary motives, but for the sake of humanity and the lamentations of so many persecuted people, have considered it opportune, etc. [Here follows a reference to Cuba.] At the present moment an American squadron is preparing to sail for the Philippines. . . .   The Americans will attack by sea and prevent any reënforcements coming from Spain ; . . . we insurgents must attack by land. Probably you will have more than sufficient arms, because the Americans have arms and will find means to assist us. *There where you see the American flag flying, assemble in numbers; they are our redeemers!*" [2]

The translation that he used is that given in Senate Document No. 62, L. 60, and is none too accurate.   He allows it to be inferred that this proclamation was actually issued.   It was not.   Its history is as follows: —

On May 16, 1898, J. M. Basa, a Filipino, who had lived in Hongkong since 1872, on account of his connection with the troubles of that year, wrote letters [3] to a number

[1] Blount, pp. 8–9.   [2] *Ibid.*, p. 9.
[3] The following is one of them : —

"H. KONG, May 16, 1898.
"SEÑOR DON JOSÉ ENRIQUE BASA:
"MY DEAR ENRIQUE : As an aid to the American policy in the Philippines, — America being the most liberal and humanitarian nation in

TYPICAL INSURGENT TRENCHES.

The Insurgents built long lines of well-constructed trenches from which they could escape without exposing themselves to the fire of the American troops.

of friends recommending the widest possible circulation of a proclamation enclosed therewith, as an aid to the American policy in the Philippines "in the war against the tyrannical friars and the Spaniards."

With these letters there were sent two different proclamations, each beginning with the words "Fellow Countrymen." The first, which is the one referred to by Blount, continues : —

"Divine Providence places us in a position to secure our independence, and this under the freest form to which all individuals, all people, all countries, may aspire.

"The Americans, more for humanity than for self-interest, attentive to the complaints of so many persecuted Filipinos, find it opportune to extend to our Philippines their protective mantle, now that they find themselves obliged to break their friendship with the Spanish people, because of the tyranny they have exercised in Cuba, causing all Americans, with whom they have great commercial relations, enormous damages.

"At this moment an American fleet is prepared to go to the Philippines.

"We, your fellow-countrymen, fear that you will make use of your arms to fire upon the Americans. No, brothers; do not make such a mistake; rather (shoot) kill yourselves than treat our liberators as enemies.

"Do not pay attention to the decree of Primo de Rivera, calling on you to enlist for the war, for that will cost you your lives: rather die than act as ingrates toward our redeemers, the Americans.

*   *   *   *   *   *   *

"Note well that the Americans have to attack by sea, at the same time avoiding reënforcements which may come from Spain; therefore the insurrection must attack by land. Per-

the world, — I earnestly recommend the widest possible circulation of the proclamation which I send herewith in order that the Americans may be supported in the war against the tyrannical friars and the Spaniards who have connived with them, and that public order, so necessary under the present conditions, be preserved.

"Thy relative, twenty-six years an emigrant.

(Signed) "J. M. BASA."

—P. I. R., 1204–10.

haps you will have more than sufficient arms, as the Americans have arms, and will find the means to aid you.

"Whenever you see the American flag, bear in mind that they are our redeemers." [1]

On the margin is written: "Viva, for America with the Philippines!"

Apparently what Basa here means by independence is independence from Spain, for it is known that he was in favour of annexation to the United States, and in the second proclamation we find the following: —

"This is the best opportunity which we have ever had for contriving that our country (all the Philippine Archipelago) may be counted as another Star in the Great Republic of the United States, great because of its wisdom, its wealth, and its constitutional laws.

"Now is the time to offer ourselves to that great nation. With America we shall have development in the broadest sense (of advancement) in civilization.

"With America we shall be rich, civilized and happy.

"Fellow patriots, add your signatures to those which have already been given. Explain to all our fellow countrymen the benefits of this change, which will be blessed by Heaven, by men and by our children.

"Viva America with the Philippines! ! !" [2]

The letters were undoubtedly given to Aguinaldo for delivery on his arrival. They were never delivered, and it is reasonable to suppose, especially as Basa, who was a man of importance and means, was a member of the group who desired annexation to the United States, that Aguinaldo took the letters along in order to avoid a rupture with him and then quietly suppressed them. Obviously, however, he sent or gave a copy of the first one to Pratt, presumably without the written words: "Viva, for America with the Philippines!"

And now comes a bit of evidence as to what occurred at Singapore which I consider incontrovertible.

Aguinaldo returned promptly to Hongkong and on

---

[1] P. I. R., 1204–10.   [2] *Ibid.*, 1204–10.

May 4, 1898, a meeting of the junta was held. The minutes of this meeting,[1] signed by each of the several Filipinos present, form a part of the Insurgent records which have come into the possession of the United States Government. They state among other things that: —

"The temporary Secretary read the minutes of the preceding meeting, which were approved. The temporary President reported that D. Emilio Aguinaldo had just arrived from Singapore and it became necessary for him to take possession of the office to which he has been elected."

After the transaction of some further business Aguinaldo was summoned, appeared at the meeting, and was duly installed as President. Then: —

"The President described the negotiations which took place during his absence in Singapore with the American Consul of that English colony. Both agreed that the President should confer with the Admiral commanding the American squadron in Mirs Bay, and if the latter should accept his propositions, advantageous, in his judgment, to the Philippines, he would go to said country in one of the cruisers which form the fleet for the purpose of taking part in the present events. And as he did not find the Admiral, he thought it well to have an interview with the American Consul of this colony on the day of his arrival, but was not satisfied with such interview.

"Considering the critical conditions in the Philippines at present, he begged the committee to discuss the advisability of his going to said islands with all the leaders of prominence in the last rebellion residing in this colony, in case the Admiral gave them an opportunity to do so."

Note that there is here absolutely not one word of any promise of independence made to Aguinaldo by Pratt or any one else. Is it conceivable that Aguinaldo in describing "the negotiations which took place during his absence in Singapore with the American Consul of the English Colony" would, by any chance, have failed to inform his associates in Hongkong of such an extraordinary and fortunate occurrence as the promising by

[1] P. I. R., 53-2.

Mr. Pratt and Admiral Dewey that the United States would recognize Philippine independence?

Sandico [1] thought that Aguinaldo ought to go, for —

"From conferences which he had with the Admiral of the American fleet and with the American Consul in this colony, he believed that under present conditions it was absolutely necessary for the President to go to the Philippines, since, according to the American Consul, Manila had been taken by said fleet, and a provisional government was now being formed in that capital. The intervention of the President in the formation of that government is undoubtedly essential, since his prestige, which everybody recognizes, would evidently prevent dissensions among the sons of the country, and it would be possible thereby to obtain a perfect organization both for the military and civil evolution of that country.

"Srs. Garchitorenā [2] and Apacible [3] expressed themselves in similar terms. Notwithstanding the previous remarks, the President insisted that he considered it reckless for him to go to the Philippines without first making a written agreement with the Admiral, as it might happen, if he placed himself at his orders, that he might make him subscribe to or sign a document containing proposals highly prejudicial to the interests of the country, from which might arise the following two very grave contingencies:

"1st. If he should accept them, he would undoubtedly commit an unpatriotic act, and his name would justly be eternally cursed by the Filipinos.

"2d. If he should refuse, then the break between the two would be evident.

"And to avoid this sad dilemma, he proposed to the committee that the four parties (?) of the insurgents now here, under charge of the competent chiefs authorized in writing by him, should go to the Philippines to intervene, after a conference with the Admiral, in these important questions; such means, in his opinion, should be first employed to ascertain in

[1] Teodoro Sandico, an influential Tagálog leader, who spoke English well and afterward served as a spy while employed by the Americans as an interpreter.

[2] Señor Garchitorena was a wealthy Tagálog of Manila, and, at this time, a prominent member of the Hongkong junta.

[3] Dr. Galicano Apacible, a very intelligent and rather conservative Tagálog physician. After Aguinaldo left Hongkong, he was the leading member of the junta.

an authentic manner what the intentions of the United States in regard to that country are; and if his intervention is absolutely necessary, he would not object to go at once to the Philippines, endeavouring by all the means in his power to remedy the critical condition of the country, to which he had offered, and always would willingly offer, to sacrifice his life."

Why adopt means to learn from the admiral what the intentions of the United States were in regard to the Philippines if both he and Pratt had already promised recognition of independence?

"Srs. Sandico, Garchitorena, Gonzaga [1] and Apacible replied that they were fully convinced the Admiral of the American squadron would furnish the President all the arms which he might desire, since the former was convinced that the fleet could do nothing in the Philippines unless it were used in conjunction with the insurgents in the development of their plans of war against the Spanish government. . . , The authority to treat which the President desired to give to the other chiefs, without reflecting at all upon their personal qualifications, they did not believe would be as efficacious as his personal intervention which is necessary in grave affairs, such as those the subject of discussion; there would be no better occasion than that afforded them to insure the landing of the expeditionary forces on those islands and to arm themselves at the expense of the Americans and to assure the situation of the Philippines in regard to our legitimate aspirations against those very people. The Filipino people, unprovided with arms, would be the victims of the demands and exactions of the United States; but, provided with arms, would be able to oppose themselves to them, struggling for independence, in which consists the true happiness of the Philippines. And they finished by saying that it made no difference if the Spanish government did demand the return of the ₱400,000, and if the demand were allowed in an action, since the object of the sum would be obtained by the Admiral furnishing the Filipinos the arms which they required for the struggle for their legitimate aspirations."

Here, then, was a definite plan to obtain arms from the Americans to be used if necessary "against those very people" later.

[1] Sr. Graco Gonzaga, a prominent Filipino lawyer of the province of Cagayan.

"The President, with his prestige in the Philippines, would be able to arouse those masses to combat the demands of the United States, if they colonized that country, and would drive them, if circumstances rendered it necessary, to a Titanic struggle for their independence, even if they should succumb in shaking off the yoke of a new oppressor. If Washington proposed to carry out the fundamental principles of its constitution, there was no doubt that it would not attempt to colonize the Philippines, or even to annex them. It was probable then that it would give them independence and guarantee it; in such case the presence of the President was necessary, as he would prevent dissensions among the sons of the country who sought office, who might cause the intervention of European powers, an intervention which there was no reason to doubt would be highly prejudicial to the interests of the country. . . . What injury could come to the Philippines, even if we admitted that the Admiral would not give arms to the President on account of his refusal to sign a document prejudicial to the country, after he had taken all means to provide for her defence? None. Such an act of the President could not be censured, but, on the other hand, would be most meritorious, because it would be one proof more of his undoubted patriotism."

Not one word of any promise of independence do we find in this remarkable document. On the contrary it furnishes conclusive proof that no such promise had been made and that the future relations between Filipinos and Americans were still completely uncertain.

And now comes some direct evidence. Bray and St. Clair, the latter the editor of the Insurgent organ in Singapore, were present on the occasion when independence was said to have been promised by Pratt. Bray subsequently declared in the most positive terms that it was promised. St. Clair wrote him a letter taking him roundly to task for this claim, in the following very interesting terms : —

"I felt it to be my duty to let Pratt know that you still hold that you and Santos have evidence that will controvert his, (and) he was, of course, extremely disappointed, because he (is) quite aware of what took place in Spanish, and as to turning of his conversation into a pretense of agreement he knows nothing.

Inside View of Insurgent Trenches at the Bagbag River.

He says very truly: 'My own party, the Democrats, will say if they read this book — If this man takes it upon himself to be a Plenipotentiary without authority, we had better not employ him any more — I frankly cannot understand your action, as to its unwisdom I have no doubt at all.

"Admiral Dewey goes home, it is believed, to advise the President on Naval and Colonial Affairs, he knows exactly what did take place and what did not, and I should know if he had any ground to think that the slightest promise was made by Pratt to Aguinaldo he would declare it unauthorized and decline to sanction it. I am certain Pratt reported what he supposed took place accurately; he had no surety on what you might have said, naturally.

"And, curiously, you never mentioned to me anything of the agreement as having taken place then, nor in the paper you communicated to me was there any mention of one, nor did Pratt know of any. It is only more recently that the fiction took shape. 'The wish father to the thought,' or the statement repeated till it has become believed by the —,[1] this is common.

"Now I would like to urge you, from the practical point of view, to drop any such foolishness. The vital thing, and nothing else counts, is what Dewey said and did when he at last met Aguinaldo. That, that, that, is the thing, all else is empty wind.

"Supposing that Pratt and Wildman had covered inches of paper with 'Clauses' and put on a ton of sealing wax as consular seals, what, pray, to any common sense mind would all that have been worth? Nothing!! Nothing!! And yet, where is the agreement, where is the seal? Where are there any signatures? And if you had them — waste paper — believe me, that all this potter about Pratt and Wildman is energy misdirected. The sole thing to have impressed upon the public in America would be the chaining of Dewey and Aguinaldo together as participants in common action; you surely comprehend this means! Think and think again; it means success as far as it is possible. The other work is not only lost, but does not gain much sympathy, especially this criticism of the conduct of American troops; things may be true that are not expedient to say. Sink everything into Dewey-Aguinaldo coöperation, that was on both sides honest even if it did not imply any actual arrangement, which, of course, Dewey himself could not make. That here you have the facts, — undenied — incontrovertible." [2]

---

[1] There is an illegible word in the original.   [2] P. I. R., 406–5.

The following letter of Bray to Aguinaldo, dated January 12, 1899, seems to me to throw much light on the question of how these claims relative to the promised recognition of Filipino independence sometimes originated and were bolstered up : —

"With regard to your proclamation, there is still a trump card to be played. Did you not say that the basis of any negotiation in Singapore was the Independence of the Philippines under an American protectorate? This is what Consul Pratt telegraphed and to which Dewey and Washington agreed; as I figured up the 'price' of the telegram, I know very well what occurred, and I am ready to state it and to swear to it when the proper time comes. There are five of us against one in the event of Consul Pratt receiving instructions to deny it. Furthermore, Mr. St. Clair knows what happened and I am certain that he also would testify. St. Clair still has the rough draft as an historical relic, and St. Clair is a true and loyal friend of yours, as is your humble servant." [1]

The utter unscrupulousness of Bray is shown by his claim that St. Clair would confirm his false statements, made as it was after receiving St. Clair's letter above quoted.

But Bray did not wait for Aguinaldo to play this trump card. He tried to play it himself by cabling Senator Hoar, on the same day, that as the man who introduced General Aguinaldo to the American government through the consul at Singapore he was prepared to swear that the conditions under which Aguinaldo promised to coöperate with Dewey were independence under a protectorate.[2]

[1] P. I. R., 398. 9.

[2] "HONGKONG, 12 Jan. 1899, — 2 P.M.
"SENATOR HOAR, Washington.
"As the man who introduced General Aguinaldo to the American government through the consul at Singapore, I frankly state that the conditions under which Aguinaldo promised to coöperate with Dewey were independence under a protectorate. I am prepared to swear to this. The military party suborned correspondents are deceiving the American nation by means of malevolent lying statements. If your powerful influence does not change this insensate policy there will be a hopeless conflict with the inevitable results disastrous for the Americans.   "BRAY."
                                                —P. I. R., 853–4.

Let us now trace Aguinaldo's subsequent movements, and see what promises, if any, were made to him by Wildman and Dewey. He had returned to Hongkong with two companions, all travelling under assumed names. Only his most trusted friends among the members of the junta were at first allowed to know where he was living.

His situation was a difficult one. It was necessary for him to come to some sort of a temporary arrangement with Artacho, if he was to avoid legal difficulties, and to reëstablish himself with some of his companions, who had accused him of deserting with the intention of going to Europe to live on money which belonged to them. When harmony had been temporarily restored through the good offices of Sandico, Aguinaldo had an interview with Consul General Wildman. He has since claimed that Wildman, too, promised him independence, but the truth seems to be that he himself said he was anxious to become an American citizen. This being impossible, he wanted to return to the Philippines and place himself under Dewey's orders. He wanted to help throw off the yoke of Spain, and this done, would abide by the decision of the United States as to the fate of the Philippines.[1]

[1] "Then Aguinaldo had an interview with the United States consul in Hongkong, in which he told him that he was anxious to become an American citizen, but this being impossible, he desired to .be allowed to return to the Philippines and place himself under the orders of Commodore Dewey. According to the brother of that Consul, who certainly must have had opportunities for knowing the facts in the case, he made no demands for independence, but said that he hoped that the Americans would not leave the Filipinos to their fate, but would annex the Philippines and protect them against the Spaniards. He promised the Consul that he would fight with the Americans and not attempt to foment a revolution against the United States. His highest expressed aim was to throw off the Spanish yoke, and, that once accomplished, he would abide by the decision of the United States as to the ultimate disposition of the Philippines. If Aguinaldo had expressed his real intentions of obtaining arms and using them only for his own purposes, and, if he found it expedient, against the United States, it is not to be thought that he would have been returned to the Philippines on a United States vessel."*

* Taylor, 44 F Z.

Any claim that Aguinaldo had been promised independence by Wildman, or, indeed, that the latter had been allowed to know that the Filipinos desired it, seems to me to be negatived, not only by Wildman's own statements, but by a letter from Agoncillo to Aguinaldo written on August 5, 1908, in which he says : —

"The American consul left my house to-day at 3 o'clock, as I had requested an interview with him before his departure, and I was unable to go to the Consulate on account of the swelling of my feet. From our conversation I infer that independence will be given to us. I did not, however, disclose to him our true desires. . . . Said consul approved my telegram to McKinley, which has been sent to-day through him, a copy of which is herewith enclosed. If they accept our representative in the commission, we may arrive at a friendly understanding, and it will enable us to prepare for the fight in case they refuse to listen to our request. On the other hand, if at the very beginning they refuse to admit our representative, we will at once be in a position to know what should be done, *i.e.* to prepare for war."[1]

On May 4, 1898, the Hongkong junta voted that Aguinaldo ought to go to the Philippines, and go he did. It would seem that he at first gave up the idea of joining Dewey, for on May 11 he wrote a cipher letter, giving minute directions for the preparation of signals to assist his ship in making land, by day or by night, at Dingalan Bay on the east coast of Luzon ; directing the capture of the town of San Antonio, just back of Capones Islands, in Zambales, and ending with the words : "We will surely arrive at one of the two places above mentioned, so you must be prepared."

Something led him again to change his mind, and he finally sailed on the *McCulloch.*

In his "Reseña Verídica" written later for political purposes, Aguinaldo has definitely claimed that Dewey promised him that the United States would recognize the independence of the Filipino people. I will let

[1] P. I. R., 471. 7.

him tell his own story, confronting his statements with those of the admiral.

> "May 19, 1898.
>
> "The *McCulloch* started at eleven o'clock on the morning of the 17th of May for the Philippines; we anchored, between twelve and one o'clock on the afternoon of the 19th, in the waters of Cavite, and immediately the launch of the Admiral — with his aid and private secretary — came to convey me to the *Olympia*, where I was received, with my aid, Sr. Leyva, with the honors of a general, by a section of marine guards." [1]

Relative to this matter, Admiral Dewey has testified : [2]

> "*The Chairman.* You, of course, never saluted the flag?
> "*Admiral Dewey.* Certainly not; and I do not think I ever called Aguinaldo anything but Don Emilio; I don't think I ever called him 'General.'
> "*The Chairman.* And when he came on board ship was he received with any special honors at the side?
> "*Admiral Dewey.* Never."

The "Reseña Verídica" continues : —

> "The Admiral received me in a salon, and after greetings of courtesy I asked him 'if all the telegrams relative to myself which he had addressed to the Consul at Singapore, Mr. Pratt, were true.' He replied in the affirmative, and added, 'that the United States had come to the Philippines to protect its natives and free them from the yoke of Spain.'
> "He said, moreover, that 'America was rich in territory and money, and needed no colonies,' concluding by assuring me, 'to have no doubt whatever about the recognition of Philippine independence by the United States.' Thereupon he asked me if I could get the people to arise against the Spaniards and carry on a rapid campaign." [3]

As we have seen, Dewey sent only one telegram to Pratt about Aguinaldo. It merely directed that the latter be sent.

---

[1] P. I. R., 1300. 2.

[2] Admiral Dewey's testimony, from which I quote extracts, will be found in Senate Documents, Vol. 25, 57 Congress, 1st session, pp. 2928, 2941.

[3] P. I. R., 1300. 2.

"I then expressed to him my profound acknowledgement for the generous help which the United States was giving the Filipino people, as well as my admiration for the magnificence and goodness of the American people.   I also stated to him that 'before leaving Hongkong, the Filipino Colony had held a meeting, at which was discussed and considered the possibility that — after defeating the Spaniards—the Filipinos might have a war with the Americans, if they should refuse to recognize our independence, who were sure to defeat us because they should find us tired out, poor in ammunitions and worn out in the war against the Spaniards,' requesting that he pardon my frankness.

"The Admiral replied that he 'was delighted at my sincerity, and believed that both Filipinos and Americans should treat each other as allies and friends, clearly explaining all doubts for the better understanding between both parties,' and added that, 'so he had been informed, the United States would recognize the independence of the Filipino people, guaranteed by the word of honor of the Americans, — more binding than documents which may remain unfulfilled when it is desired to fail in them as happened with the compacts signed by the Spaniards, advising me to form at once a Filipino national flag, offering in virtue thereof to recognize and protect it before the other nations, which were represented by the various squadrons then in the Bay; although he said we should conquer the power from the Spaniards before floating said flag, so that the act should be more honourable in the sight of the whole world, and, above all, before the United States, in order that when the Filipino ships with their national flag would pass before the foreign squadrons they should inspire respect and esteem.'

"Again I thanked the Admiral for his good advice and generous offers, informing him that if the sacrifice of my life was necessary to honor the Admiral before the United States, I was then ready to sacrifice it.

"I added that under such conditions I could assure him that all the Filipino people would unite in the revolution to shake off the yoke of Spain; that it was not strange that some few were not yet on his side on account of lack of arms or because of personal expediency.

"Thus ended this first conference with Admiral Dewey, to whom I announced that I would take up my residence at the Naval Headquarters in the Cavite Arsenal." [1]

[1] P. I. R., 1300. 2.

Further on, in the same document, Aguinaldo advances the claim that on the occasion of the visit of General Anderson and Admiral Dewey the latter again promised him independence.

He says : —

"In the same month of July, the Admiral, accompanied by General Anderson, presented himself, and after greetings of courtesy said to me: 'You have seen confirmed all of what I promised and said to you. How pretty your flag is. It has a triangle, and it looks like Cuba's. Will you give me one as a reminder when I return to America?'

"I replied to him that I was convinced of his word of honour and that there was no necessity whatever to draw up in documentary form his agreements, and as for the flag, that he could count on it, even at that very moment.

"Dewey continued: 'Documents are not complied with when there is no honour, as has happened with your agreement with the Spaniards, who have failed in what was written and signed. Trust in my word for I hold myself responsible that the United States will recognize the independence of the country. But I recommend to you [plural. — Tr.] to keep everything which we have talked about and agreed upon with a great deal of secrecy for the present. And, moreover, I entreat you [plural. — Tr.] to be patient if our soldiers should insult some Filipino, because, as volunteers, they are yet lacking in discipline.'" [1]

Admiral Dewey has testified as follows, concerning the recognition of Philippine independence by him : —

"*The Chairman.* You remember the question of your recognizing his republic was a good deal discussed and you wrote me a letter, which I read in the senate. Of course, I am only asking now about what you said in the letter. There was no recognition of the republic?

"*Admiral Dewey.* Never. I did not think I had any authority to do it and it never occurred to me to do it. There was a sort of a reign of terror; there was no government. These people had got power for the first time in their lives and they were riding roughshod over the community. The acts of cruelty which were brought to my notice were hardly credible.

[1] Taylor, 4 MG., E.

I sent word to Aguinaldo that he must treat his prisoners kindly, and he said he would."

He has further testified that he never as much as heard of independence until the appearance of Aguinaldo's proclamation of June 15, 1898 : —

"*Admiral Dewey*. . . . Then when I heard that our troops were coming I asked him to withdraw his troops from Cavite and make room for our men. He demurred at this, but finally withdrew and established headquarters across the bay at a place called Bacoor, from which place on the 15th of June he sent me a proclamation declaring the independence of the Philippines.

"*The Chairman*. Was that the first?

"*Admiral Dewey*. That was the first intimation; the first I had ever heard of independence of the Philippines.

"*The Chairman*. He had said something to you —

"*Admiral Dewey*. Not a word. He had done what I told him. He was most obedient; whatever I told him to do he did. I attached so little importance to this proclamation that I did not even cable its contents to Washington, but forwarded it through the mails. I never dreamed that they wanted independence."

Remembering that Admiral Dewey was not being interrogated as to the statements of the "Reseña Verídica," it will be seen that he has, nevertheless, covered them fully.

It was my good fortune to be long and intimately associated with Admiral Dewey while serving on the first Philippine commission. He always grew indignant when the subject of any promises relative to independence said to have been made by him was so much as mentioned, and gave to the commission in writing the following : —

" The statement of Emilio Aguinaldo, under date of Sept. 23, published in the *Springfield Republican,* so far as it relates to reported conversations with me, or actions of mine, is a tissue of falsehood. I never, directly or indirectly, promised the Filipinos independence. I never received Aguinaldo with military honors, or recognized or saluted the so-called Filipino flag. I never considered him as an ally, although I did make

GENERAL HENRY W. LAWTON.

This photograph was taken by the author at General Lawton's Manila residence, two months before his death.

use of him and the natives to assist me in my operations against the Spaniards." [1]

As Dewey's allegations flatly contradict those of Aguinaldo, we must choose between the two. While I have no doubt as to where the choice will fall, I will now submit some additional matter of interest. Let us first consider the history of the "Reseña Verídica" in which Aguinaldo makes the charges above quoted. On September 12, 1899, Buencamino wrote of it to Apacible in Hongkong, saying : —

"This work is entitled 'Reseña Verídica de la Revolución Filipina' in which Don Emilio relates in detail his acts with Admiral Dewey. It has been distributed to the Consuls and you are ordered to reprint it there translated into English and send some copies to the United States, even though only a thousand, if you deem it advisable. Send copies also to Europe, Señor Agoncillo taking charge of the publication. If the Agent you may have selected for the United States should still be there, it would be advisable for him to take a copy of the pamphlet with him for its publication.

"This is an order of the Government which I take pleasure in transmitting to you for due execution." [2]

But there was a change of heart about giving the pamphlet to the consuls, for under date of September 30 Buencamino wrote : —

"We have not distributed them here in order that Otis may not counteract the effects that we desire to produce with this publication, through his usual machinations. Nor do we believe it advisable to make this pamphlet public in those colonies before your arrival in the United States." [3]

To this letter he added in cipher the following postscript to Pablo Ocampo, in charge of Aguinaldo's correspondence in Manila : —

"At last moment — Nota bene:
"Don't deliver any copy of the 'Reseña Verídica' to the

[1] Report of the Philippine commission to the President. January 31, 1900. Vol. I, p. 121.
[2] P. I. R., 396. 3.　　　　　[3] Ibid., 396. 3.

Consuls, even though it was so directed in the beginning of the letter. All except one, which is for you, will be sent to Hong-kong, Don Pedro de la Viña being bearer of the same, as also of the other documents. The copy intended for you is neither to be divulged nor published, for strict reserve is required until those which are being sent arrive at their destination." [1]

The reason for preserving such secrecy relative to this document until it could reach its destination and work its harm is of course obvious. Its statements were so outrageously false that they would have been instantly and authoritatively contradicted had it been issued seasonably at Manila.

The truth is that Aguinaldo's claim that he had been promised independence was a gradual growth. Let us trace it.

On May 21, he wrote a circular letter to "My dear brother," inviting the recipients and their companions to meet him at once, and arrange the best way to entrap all the enemy in their homes.

In this he says that he has promised the American admiral that they will "carry on modern war" and adds: "Even if a Spaniard surrenders, he must be pardoned and treated well, and then you will see that our reputation will be very good in all Europe, which will declare for our independence; but if we do not conduct ourselves thus, the Americans will decide to sell us or else divide up our territory. As they will hold us incapable of governing our land, we shall not secure our liberty, rather the contrary; our own soil will be delivered over to other hands." [2]

---

[1] P. I. R., 461. 4.

[2] "My Dear Brother: I inform you that we arrived here in Cavite at eleven o'clock and disembarked at four o'clock in the afternoon after our conference with the American Admiral. Everything appears to be favourable for obtaining our independence. I cannot say more on that subject as it would take too long.

"I have no other object in writing this except to ask you and your companions to meet at once and arrange the best way to entrap all the enemy in your town, employing deceit, for instance, make a

In this letter, written on the very day of the interview at which he subsequently claimed that Admiral Dewey had promised independence, does he make any claim that this had occurred? No, he very distinctly implies the contrary. Is it believable that if he could truly have said "The United States, through its representatives Dewey and Pratt, has promised to recognize our independence" he would have failed to do so when this would instantly have secured him the vigorous support which he was then uncertain of obtaining? I think not.

In this letter Aguinaldo specifically directs that deceit be employed and that Spanish officers be treacherously attacked. The practising of deceit was a carefully considered part of the insurgent policy. In a letter from Hongkong dated July 21, 1898, Agoncillo writes as follows to Mabini:[1] —

*   *   *   *   *   *   *

"the time will come when disguises must be set aside and we will see who is deceiving whom. The statements made by some

present of whatever you think best to the chiefs successively and then at once enter the houses and attack them, or if not this, do what you think best. Show valor and resolution, brothers, the hour has arrived for the Philippines to belong to her sons and not to them, only one step and we shall reach Independence; be constant, brothers, and be united in feelings, do not imitate those who show two faces, whatever such people do sooner or later they will be slaves. Respect foreigners and their property, also enemies who surrender.

" I want you to know that in respect to our conduct I have promised the American Admiral and other nations, that we shall carry on modern war. Even if a Spaniard surrenders, he must be pardoned and treated well and then you will see that our reputation will be very good in all Europe which will declare for our Independence; but if we do not conduct ourselves thus the Americans will decide to sell us or else divide up our territory as they will hold us incapable of governing our land, we shall not secure our liberty; rather the contrary; our own soil will be delivered over to other hands.

" Therefore, my brethren, I urge that we strive to unite our efforts, and let us fire our hearts with the idea of vindicating our country. Many nations are on our side." — P. I. R., 12. 1.

[1] Mabini was a Tagálog paralytic of exceptional ability. In my opinion he was the strongest man whom the revolution produced.

of the commanders of the fleet here to Don Emilio and myself were to the effect that the exclusive purpose of the Government at Washington with regard to the Filipinos, is to grant this country independence, without any conditions, although I said to myself that such a purpose was too philanthropical. Don Emilio knew what I thought then, and I still think the same; that is to say that we are the ones who must secure the independence of our country by means of unheard of sacrifices and thus work out its happiness."[1]

Aguinaldo himself frankly advocated the use of deceit. He practised what he preached. Simeon Villa, one of his companions on his subsequent flight through Northern Luzon, before he finally took refuge at Palanan, kept a diary, which constitutes an official record of this long journey. In it he has inserted some bits of history of other days, of which none is more interesting than his account of the beginning of hostilities against the Spaniards, in August, 1896. From it we learn that Aguinaldo, who was known to the friar of his town to be both a mason and a chief of the Katipúnan, was in danger during August, and on the night of the 29th of that month called a meeting of all the compromised persons of the place, who agreed that on the following day he should "make representations to the governor of the province." Villa says that he was greatly beloved by the governor and his wife. Early on the following morning, he "presented himself to the governor, and in the name of the people of Cavite Viejo, offered him their respects and their loyalty to Spain," at the same time asking a garrison of a hundred men for his town, which the governor promised to send at once if the captain-general approved.

That afternoon he reported the results of his efforts to his fellow-conspirators, "and told them that then was the opportune moment for rising against the Spaniards." He initiated the uprising himself the next morning.[2]

[1] P. I. R., 451. 1.
[2] Extract from the Journal of Simeon Villa.
"The memorable month of August, 1896, arrived. Aguinaldo was

Could deceit be more deliberately practised or treachery more frankly employed?

'master' of the Cavite Lodge. Moreover, he was a member of the 'Katipúnan' Society and the chief of the many members who were in the pueblo of Cavite Viejo. What was to be done? Aguinaldo, not knowing what to do, and mindful of the fact that the curate there knew positively that he was not only a mason, but also the chief of the Katipúnans of his pueblo, considered it expedient on the night of August 29 to at once call a meeting of all the compromised persons in his town. Aguinaldo made clear to them their grave situation.

"They all agreed that on the following day Aguinaldo, their chief, should make representations to the Governor of Cavite; so he went away very early the following morning, presented himself to the governor, and in the name of the people of Cavite Viejo offered him their respects and their loyalty to Spain, at the same time requesting him to condescend to send to his town a garrison of 100 men for its security. The governor replied that he would first consult the captain-general, and if the proposition was approved he would send the garrison at once.

"As Aguinaldo was greatly beloved by the governor and his wife, they offered him wine and sweetmeats. As soon as this was over he took his leave and returned happy to his town. On arrival in the town he assembled all the compromised persons and informed them of the brilliant result of his efforts. Continuing, he told them that then was the opportune moment for rising in arms against the Spaniards. To this they unanimously replied by saying it was terrible, because no arms were available, and that for this reason it would certainly prove to be a disaster for them.

"But Aguinaldo, in company with his godfather, the lamented Candido Tirona, insisted on convincing them with their strong arguments. They made them understand that Spanish cruelty would annihilate them without fail, and for no other reason than that they were members of the Katipúnan.

"As it happened, at that very time there were two 'Guardia Civil' soldiers in the court-house. So at about 2 o'clock in the morning, Aguinaldo and Tirona went directly to the court-house. Arriving there, these two determined insurgent chiefs intimated to the guards that they should surrender their equipments. These replied that it was impossible, and said they would die first. Instantly a struggle ensued between the four men, which lasted nearly an hour. But it resulted in favor of the insurgent chiefs who succeeded in taking the guns and cartridges. Once in possession of these armaments, the two chiefs, accompanied by a number of the town people, directed themselves to the convent in order to capture the curate. Very unfortunately for them, the curate was no longer there when they arrived; he had made his escape. While the struggle was going on with the

I have indulged in this digression to show that Aguinaldo could hardly have complained had the methods which he used against others been employed against him. He was never deceived by the Americans, but his claims relative to independence grew rapidly, and he was soon deceiving his own people.

On May 24th, he issued no less than four proclamations. One of these, doubtless intended to be seen by Americans, made no mention of Independence, but said : [1] —

guards in the court-house, he received the news and fled at once by embarking in a native boat.

" The insurgent chiefs then returned to the court-house and immediately prepared a communication to all the municipal captains in the provinces of Cavite, Batangas and Laguna, inviting them to at once rise against Spain, and stating that their own town of Cavite Viejo was already freed from slavery.

" Each one of these communications was sent out by a mounted courier, so that before the expiration of many hours all the towns in Cavite Province were informed of what had taken place in Cavite Viejo.

" On the following day some of the towns took up arms. At the same time Aguinaldo, in company with many people from his town, marched on Imus in order to attack the Spanish troops who were there. When he arrived in Imus the people of this town at once joined him and they all went to the convent, in which were the friars and the soldiers of the 'Guardia Civil.' Just as he arrived at the atrium of the Church his companions did not wish to follow him, for fear that the soldiers were occupying the church tower. So Aguinaldo advanced alone until he reached the door of the convent. Once here, he called his companions to aid him. But these were not so determined as he was, and only about five responded. When these got to where Aguinaldo was, he commenced breaking in the door which was soon open. They went upstairs, but they found nobody, since the friars and soldiers had crossed over to the treasury building.

" Aguinaldo's companions were now numerous, because the others followed him when they saw that nothing happened to those who went up into the convent ; and all of these went immediately to the treasury building, in which were the friars and soldiers whom they were hunting. When they reached it they found the doors closed, so they could not pass. Aguinaldo ordered the house burned. Those in hiding inside the house were without any other remedy and had to surrender ; but meanwhile some of them had been burned to death, among these a lieutenant of the 'Guardia Civil.' By this victory Aguinaldo succeeded in taking 17 rifles and two 2½ pounder guns." — P. I. R., 869.

[1] "My Beloved Countrymen: I accepted the agreement of peace

"The great powerful North American nation has offered its disinterested protection to secure the liberty of this country."

In another proclamation, doubtless intended for a different use, he made the statement that the great North American nation had come to give decisive and disinterested protection, "considering us as sufficiently civilized and capable of governing ourselves." [1]

proposed by Don Pedro A. Paterno after his consultation with the Captain-General of the islands (Philippines), agreeing in consequence thereof to surrender our arms and disband the troops under my immediate command under certain conditions, as I believed it more advantageous for the country than to continue the insurrection, for which I had but limited resources, but as some of the said conditions were not complied with, some of the bands are discontented and have not surrendered their arms. Five months have elapsed without the inauguration of any of the reforms which I asked in order to place our country on a level with civilized people — for instance, our neighbor, Japan, which in the short space of twenty years has reached a point where she has no reason to envy any one, her strength and ascendency being shown in the last war with China. I see the impotence of the Spanish Government to contend with certain elements which oppose constant obstacles to the progress of the country itself and whose destructive influence has been one of the causes of the uprising of the masses, and as the great and powerful North American nation has offered its disinterested protection to secure the liberty of this country, I again assume command of all the troops in the struggle for the attainment of our lofty aspirations, inaugurating a dictatorial government to be administered by decrees promulgated under my sole responsibility and with the advice of distinguished persons until the time when these islands, being under our complete control, may form a constitutional republican assembly and appoint a president and cabinet, into whose hands I shall then resign the command of the islands.

"EMILIO AGUINALDO.
"Given at Cavite, May 24, 1898." —P. I. R. 206. 6.

[1] "The great North American nation, the cradle of genuine liberty and therefore the friend of our people oppressed and enslaved by the tyranny and despotism of its ruler, has come to us manifesting a protection as decisive as it is undoubtedly disinterested toward our inhabitants, considering us as sufficiently civilized and capable of governing ourselves and our unfortunate country. In order to maintain this high estimate granted us by the generous North American nation we should abominate all those deeds which tend to lower this opinion, which are pillage, theft, and all sorts of crimes relating to persons or

On June 5, having practically gained control of Cavite Province, he felt strong enough to announce that independence would be proclaimed on June 12, and on that date he did proclaim it in a decree.

The Admiral of the American Squadron, with the commanders and officers of his command, was invited to the ceremonies, but none of them went. As it was important for Aguinaldo to have some one there to pose as a representative of the United States, he utilized for this purpose a certain "Colonel" Johnson, an ex-hotel keeper of Shanghai, who was running a cinematograph show. He appeared as Aguinaldo's chief of artillery and the representative of the North American nation.[1]

Even as late as October 3, 1898, Agoncillo in a memorandum addressed to President McKinley did not claim that independence had been promised, but said : —

"As soon as the Spanish-American war began, the American representatives and officials in Singapore, Hongkong and Manila, invited the natives of the Philippines to assist the American arms, which they did gladly and loyally, as allies, with the conviction that their personality would be recognized, as well as their political, autonomous and sovereign rights." [2]

property, with the purpose of avoiding international conflict during the period of our campaign." — P. I. R., 43. 3.

[1] Of this extraordinary occurrence Taylor says : —

"Invitations to the ceremony of the declaration of independence were sent to Admiral Dewey; but neither he nor any of his officers were present. It was, however, important to Aguinaldo that some American should be there whom the assembled people would consider a representative of the United States. 'Colonel' Johnson, ex-hotel keeper of Shanghai, who was in the Philippines exhibiting a cinematograph, kindly consented to appear on this occasion as Aguinaldo's Chief of Artillery and the representative of the North American nation. His name does not appear subsequently among the papers of Aguinaldo. It is possible that his position as colonel and chief of artillery was a merely temporary one which enabled him to appear in a uniform which would befit the character of the representative of a great people upon so solemn an occasion !" *

[2] P. I. R., 451. 4.

* Taylor, 26 A J.

FEEDING FILIPINO REFUGEES.

Before the Insurgent troops retired from Parañaque near Manila, they plundered their own people and left them without food. Our army fed them. This photograph shows a typical scene when food distribution was about to begin.

In it he does, however, claim that the organization of a government independent of America and Spain was accomplished with the tacit consent of the admiral commanding the fleet and with that of the general and military and political commanders of the United States of North America in the Philippines.

"Who, knowing these facts, not only did not object but accepted them as a consummated legal act, and maintained official relations with the new organization, making use thereof in its subsequent actions and for the subsequent development of the campaign, which was consequently brought to such a happy end." [1]

This is a second illustration of the stereotyped insurgent procedure of announcing a policy and then claiming that failure to attack it meant acquiescence in it. Admiral Dewey says that he did not even read this proclamation. There was no reason why he should have done so, as it did not deal with matters which he was authorized to settle. He had no instructions relative to the recognition of new governments, and he sent this document to Washington without comment, as he should have done. [2]

Apropos of this claim that American officers tacitly recognized the Insurgent government, certain passages from an unsigned document in the handwriting of Mabini, prepared about July 15, 1898, are of interest. Mabini, speaking of the attitude of the Americans, says, "Notwithstanding all this and in spite of their protestations of friendship, they have always refused to recognize that government." Also, "If they persist in refusing to recognize our government, we shall see ourselves compelled to come to an agreement with any other government that will consent to recognize us on friendly terms." [3]

[1] P. I. R., 451. 4.   [2] See p. 50.

[3] "They are aware that a Government has been established here from the beginning: first the Dictatorial, and afterwards, when several provinces had been freed from Spanish domination, there was implanted in the same a proper organization, and thus a new Government was established in the form best adapted to the principles of liberty; but

This statement is certainly sufficiently specific as to whether Americans had recognized the Insurgent government on or before the date when it was written.

Let us now consider the relations between Aguinaldo and General Anderson.

Blount attempts to make much of a cablegram, sent by the latter, in which, after describing the Filipinos, he adds, "The people expect independence." Blount says : —

"That cablegram of July 22nd, above quoted, in which the commanding general of our forces in the Philippines advises the Washington Government, 'The people expect independence' is the hardest thing in the public archives of our government covering that momentous period for those who love the memory of Mr. McKinley to get around. After the war with the Filipinos broke out, McKinley said repeatedly in public speeches, 'I never dreamed they would turn against us.' "[1]

If there is nothing harder than this to get around the memory of President McKinley will not suffer, as the

notwithstanding all this and in spite of their protestations of friendship, they have always refused to recognize that government.

" The things they request involve the recognition of a right which we cannot and ought not to grant, unless they recognize our Government and unless the limits of the powers of both sides be defined. If they wish us to recognize them in Cavite, let them recognize our rights in Parañaque.

" The United States are our creditors more than any other nation; not only are they due the gratitude of the Filipino people, but also they should be allowed to profit by the advantages this people can grant them without loss of our legitimate right to a free and independent life. Therefore we are disposed to make a treaty or convention with them. They will be no longer able to allege the lack of national character, for in the near future there is to be assembled the Revolutionary Congress composed of the Representatives of the provinces.

" They should understand that they have come to make war on the Spaniards; that the Filipinos have risen in arms against the same enemy to achieve their liberty and independence; and that in consequence they cannot exercise dominion over us without violation of international law. If they persist in refusing to recognize our Government, we shall see ourselves obliged to come to an agreement with any other government that will consent to recognize us on friendly terms."
— P. I. R., 58.

[1] Blount, p. 24.

important thing is not what Aguinaldo had led his people to expect, but what the American officials had promised him. The President was certainly not bound to believe that the Filipinos would turn against us even if they did then expect independence. Blount has seen fit to leave unmentioned certain other facts which are very pertinent in this connection.

Apparently sometime during September, 1898, Sandico made the following statement in a letter to Aguinaldo: —

"I also have to inform you that Señores Basa, Cortés and Co. have congratulated the Government of the United States upon the capture of Manila, stating at the same time that now that Filipino soil had been soaked with American blood, the Islands must remain American. I believe that a telegram should be sent immediately, to counteract that sent by them." [1]

Probably Sandico did not know that on August 15, 1898, Agoncillo had transmitted another telegram to President McKinley through Consul-General Wildman, reading as follows: —

"Agoncillo, my Commissioner and Ambassador-Extraordinary, representing the provisional government of the Philippine Islands, in its name and the name of its President, Emilio Aguinaldo, congratulates you on the successful termination of the war, and commends the occupancy of Manila. I assure the United States of the allegiance and unquestioning support of our people, and petition that we be granted one or more representatives on the commission that is to decide the future of our Islands." [2]

It would appear, therefore, that the President had more information on this subject than was transmitted by General Anderson !

Not only did the latter passively refrain from recognizing Aguinaldo's pretensions, but on July 22, 1898, he wrote to him as follows: —

"I observe that your Excellency has announced yourself Dictator and proclaimed martial law. As I am here simply

[1] P. I. R., 416. 1.   [2] *Ibid.*, 102. 5.

in a military capacity, I have no authority to recognize such an assumption. ` I have no orders from my government on the subject." [1]

The effort to keep Americans in ignorance of the true state of affairs was kept up until further deception was useless. Consul Williams, for instance, wrote on June 16, 1898 : —

"For future advantage, I am maintaining cordial relations with General Aguinaldo, having stipulated submissiveness to our forces when treating for their return here. Last Sunday, 12th, they held a council to form provisional government. I was urged to attend, but thought best to decline. A form of government was adopted, but General Aguinaldo told me to-day that his friends all hoped that the Philippines would be held as a colony of the United States of America." [2]

Yet on Sunday, June 12, Aguinaldo had in reality proclaimed the independence of the Philippines. Few Americans at this time knew any Spanish and none understood Tagálog, so that it was comparatively easy to deceive them. What Consul Williams reported was what Aguinaldo considered it expedient to have him believe.

The following undated letter from Aguinaldo to Mabini, supposed to have been sent at this time, is of especial interest in this connection : —

"MY DEAR BROTHER : I do not want to go there [where the addressee is] until after the visit of the American Consul, because I do not wish the negotiations to end in an ultimatum, and in order that you may tell him all that is favourable for the cause of our Nation. I charge you with the task of giving him a reply, and if he should ask about me tell him that since the time of his last visit there I have not recovered from my illness. If anything important should happen we can communicate with each other by telegraph, using a code in matters that require secrecy." [3]

In a letter supposed to have been written during November, 1898, prepared for Aguinaldo's signature and

[1] Senate Document 208, 1900, p. 9.
[2] Taylor, 26 A J.   [3] P. I. R., 5. 10.

addressed to Señor McKinley, President of the Republic of the United States of North America, but apparently never sent, Aguinaldo renews the charge [1] previously made in his " Reseña Verídica," that Pratt and Dewey promised independence. It need not be further discussed.

The climax was finally reached in an official protest against the Paris Treaty written by Agoncillo in Paris on the 12th of December, 1898, in which occurs the following : —

"The United States of America, on their part, cannot allege a better right to constitute themselves as arbitrators as to the future of the Philippines.

"On the contrary, the demands of honour and good faith impose on them the explicit recognition of the political status of the people, who, loyal to their conventions, were a devoted ally of their forces in the moments of danger and strife. The noble general Emilio Aguinaldo and the other Filipino chiefs were solicited to place themselves at the head of the suffering and heroic sons of that country, to fight against Spain and to second the action of the brave and skilful Admiral Dewey.

" At the time of employing their armed coöperation, both the Commander of the *Petrel* and Captain Wood in Hongkong, before the declaration of war, the American Consuls-General Mr. Pratt in Singapore, Mr. Wildman, in Hongkong, and Mr. Williams in Cavite, acting as international agents of the great American nation, at a moment of great anxiety offered to

[1] " Going to Singapore, I had several interviews with the Consul of the United States, Mr. Spencer Pratt, who informed me that the war was directed against Spain only and that in addition your action in the Philippines had as an object the independence of my beloved country.

" The Commander of the *MacCulloch* telegraphed me also from Hongkong, offering in the name of Commodore Dewey, to take me to Cavite, in order to raise the Filipinos against Spain.

"Without any written treaty, counting only upon the sacred word of American citizens, I went to Hongkong, embarked on the *MacCulloch* and a few days later had the honor to make the acquaintance of the victorious Commodore Dewey, who likewise informed me that he had come to make war against Spain, that he had annihilated the fleet of Admiral Montojo and that the United States desired to give the Philippines their independence." — P. I. R., 441. 2.

recognize the independence of the Filipino nation, as soon as triumph was obtained.

"Under the faith of such promises, an American man-of-war, the *McCulloch* was placed at the disposal of the said leaders and which took them to their native shores; and Admiral Dewey himself, by sending the man-of-war; by not denying to General Aguinaldo and his companions the exacting of his promises, when they were presented to him on board his flag-ship in the Bay of Manila; by receiving the said General Aguinaldo before and after his victories and notable deeds of arms, with the honours due the Commander-in-Chief of an allied army, and chief of an independent state; by accepting the efficacious coöperation of that Army and of those Generals; by recognizing the Filipino flag, and permitting it to be hoisted on sea and land, consenting that their ships should sail with the said flag within the places which were blockaded; by receiving a solemn notification of the formal proclamation of the Philippine nation, without protesting against it, nor opposing in any way its existence; by entering into relations with those Generals and with the national Filipino authorities recently established, recognized without question the corporated body and autonomous sovereignty of the people who had just succeeded in breaking their fetters and freeing themselves by the impulse of their own force." [1]

It will be noted that the claim constantly grows. The commander of the *Petrel* Captain Wood, Consul Wildman and Consul Williams are now included among those alleged to have promised independence, and it is claimed that Aguinaldo was received with the honours due the chief of an independent state when he visited Admiral Dewey, whereas his own original claim was that he was received with the honours due a general, which is quite a different matter.

As a matter of fact, American officers usually addressed and treated Aguinaldo as a general. The extent to which they were able to use his organization to further the ends of their government will be set forth later.

In a letter to Wildman, dated August 7, 1898, Aguinaldo admits that there is no agreement, but says that he cannot

[1] P. I. R., 102. 1.

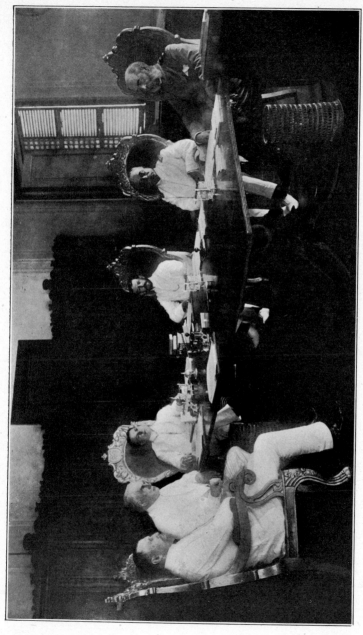

THE FIRST PHILIPPINE COMMISSION.

This photograph taken in the room where the commission held its hearings is the only one ever obtained which shows all the members. From left to right : the author, Colonel Charles Denby, President Jacob Gould Schurman, Mr. John R. MacArthur, Secretary to the Commission, Admiral George Dewey and General E. S. Otis.

tell the peoples that it does not exist, "fearing that I may not be able to restrain the popular excitement." [1] He begs Wildman to use his influence on his government so that it will realize the inadvisability of deciding the fate of the people "without considering their will duly represented by my government." Is it conceivable that, if there had been any ground for claiming a promise of independence, Aguinaldo would have failed to mention it at this time?

We may summarize the well-established facts as follows: —

Consul-General Pratt was, or professed to be, in hearty sympathy with the ambition of the Filipino leaders to obtain independence, and would personally have profited from such a result, but he refrained from compromising his government and made no promises in its behalf.

Admiral Dewey never even discussed with Aguinaldo the possibility of independence.

There is no reason to believe that any subordinate of the Admiral ever discussed independence with any Filipino, much less made any promise concerning it.

Neither Consul Wildman nor Consul Williams promised it, and both were kept in ignorance of the fact that it was desired up to the last possible moment.

It is not claimed that either General Anderson or General Merritt made any promise concerning it.

The conclusion that no such promise was ever made by any of these men is fully justified by well-established facts.

Aguinaldo himself carefully refrained at the outset from saying, in any document which Americans could read, that independence had been promised, and advanced this claim only when the growing strength of his land force had given him confidence. He repeated it, with increasing emphasis, as his army increased in size, ultimately openly threatening war if his pretensions were not recognized. In doing this, he was merely carrying

[1] P. I. R., Books C-1.

out a carefully prearranged plan, agreed upon by the Hongkong junta.

And now let us examine the claim that the insurgents were our "faithful allies" and "coöperated" with us in the taking of Manila. We shall find that this subject richly repays investigation.

CHAPTER III

INSURGENT "COÖPERATION"

I HAVE previously [1] called attention to the minutes of a session of the Hongkong junta held on May 4, 1898, from which it indirectly appears that the Filipino leaders at that time hoped to secure arms at the expense of the Americans and purposed to attack them later if it seemed advisable.

The treacherous policy then outlined was never departed from by Aguinaldo and his associates, who sailed for Manila with their eyes wide open, knowing full well that they had been promised nothing; prepared to match their wits against those of Admiral Dewey, and intent on deceiving him and on securing from him arms to be used first against the Spaniards and later against the Americans, after they had been employed to help bring about the downfall of Spain.

There exists a significant circular signed "J.M.B." [2] believed to have been an outright forgery, both from its tenor and from the fact that the signature "J.M.B." is not in the handwriting of Basa's letter hereinbefore quoted.

It contains the following statements: —

"The true patriots have organized a committee to which I belong, naming Aguinaldo as President and Agoncillo as Vice-President. The latter and three others have commenced diplomatic negotiations with the Admiral and American Consul, and we infer that they are trying to make colonies of us, although they said they would give us independence. The Committee deemed it advisable to simulate belief, at the same time equipping ourselves with arms.

[1] P. 39. [2] For J. M. Basa.

67

"We have accepted arms offered by the Admiral which will be disembarked in the Philippines by the squadron.

"A part of our forces will aid the Americans by fighting with them in order to conceal our real intentions, and part will be held in reserve. If America triumphs and proposes a colony, we shall reject such offer and rise in arms.

"A separate expedition will disembark at whatever point may be considered suitable.

"José Alejandrino embarked with the American squadron in order to give secret instructions to the Chiefs.

"Be very cautious about this exceedingly delicate point; you will communicate with prudent and intelligent chiefs who will recognize the gravity of the subject." [1]

Here, then, in a faked-up letter on which Basa's initials were forged in order to gain the prestige of his name for this treacherous plan, we have definitely set forth the purpose of the Filipinos to deceive the Americans by allowing a part of the Insurgent force to fight with them, and then to attack them.

Reference has already been made to Agoncillo's advice to Aguinaldo, given under date of August 26, 1898, to the effect that friendly relations should be maintained with the Americans until the diplomatic negotiations at Paris should end; that an effort should be made to find out the future status of the islands "by deceitful means," and that confidence should never be put in the Americans.

Aguinaldo put the whole matter in a nutshell in a postscript to this letter, saying : —

"You should issue an order commanding that all our chiefs should employ a policy of friendship toward the Americans until our status is defined; but said order should be confidentially given. Try to mislead them." [2]

Bray also very strongly advised awaiting the results of the Paris conference.[3]

[1] P. I. R., 507–7.   [2] P. I. R., 477. 1.

[3] "Until the Philippine question is finally decided, you would do well in not having any controversy with the Americans. After having secured the extinction of Spanish control for good, you may then liquidate accounts with the United States in the event that they wish

Blount claims that the Filipinos hoped that the Treaty of Paris would leave their country to them as it left Cuba to the Cubans,[1] and adds that having helped us take the city of Manila, they "felt that they had been 'given the double cross,'" "believed that the Americans had been guilty of a duplicity rankly Machiavellian, and that was the cause of the war." [2]

The quotations already given from Insurgent records show plainly that the principal thing for which the Filipinos were waiting was the ousting of Spain from the Philippines by the United States; those which follow show that war was by no means inevitable as a result of a a decision at Paris adverse to Filipino hopes, for the question of whether a United States protectorate, or even annexation to the United States, might be considered, was left open to a very late date.[3]

It has been claimed not only that the Insurgents whipped the Spaniards without our assistance, but whipped them so thoroughly that Spanish sovereignty had practically disappeared from the islands at the time Manila surrendered. It has further been alleged that "decrepit" Spain "could not possibly have sent any reënforcements to the Philippines. Besides, the Filipinos would have 'eaten them up.'" [4]

to control in the interior; but in the meantime, let what will occur, do not allow yourself to have any controversy with them. Matters are in a very delicate state at the present time." — P. I. R., 398. 3.

In a postscript to the same letter Bray says: —

"America is a great nation and does not wish that conditions be dictated to her. I am more than ever convinced that you must be patient and await what they propose, without opposing their wishes and insanities, before the questions before the Paris Congress are definitely settled and the islands ceded by Spain; then there would still be time to show your teeth if they try to govern the country. I would not object at present to them taking up their residence there and acting in the capacity of guard for good government, placing our trust for the future in Providence which will never abandon the Philippines." — P. I. R., 398. 3.

[1] Blount, p. 283.   [2] *Ibid.*, p. 283.   [3] See p. 74.

[4] "Both Spanish fleets had been destroyed and Spain had but one left to protect her own coast cities. The death knell of her once proud

But the Filipinos had fought Spain before and were by no means sanguine. Their more intelligent and reasonable men clearly foresaw that they could not win unaided. Señor Antonio Regidor was at the time residing in London. He was a Filipino of unusual intelligence and exceptionally good education. He took a keen interest in the situation, and on July 28, 1898, telegraphed Agoncillo as follows : —

"In the name of the Filipinos, you should immediately send a telegraphic message to MacKinley, requesting him not to abandon the islands, after having fought as brothers for a common cause. Pledge him our unconditional adhesion, especially of well-to-do people. To return to Spain, in whatever form, would mean annihilation, perpetual anarchy. Filipinos en masse should visit the consuls at Hongkong, Singapore. London commerce support it. Influence Aguinaldo to accept American flag, flying it everywhere, thus obliging them to remain." [1]

This leaves no room for doubt as to Regidor's views, but Agoncillo did not share them. He replied on July 29 : —

"Provisional government's aspiration is independence. Make this campaign." [2]

Regidor was not to be persuaded. On July 30 he replied as follows, addressing his communication to Basa :

"America vacillating as to remaining fears conflicts later with natives international question other difficulties necessary to encourage her all of you submit united unconditionally raising American flag great demonstrations necessary to influence outside opinion show islands resolved united America high circles advise in view present circumstances only feasible programme is protectorate." [3]

colonial empire had sounded. Decrepit as she was, she could not possibly have sent any reënforcements to the Philippines. Besides, the Filipinos would have 'eaten them up.'" — BLOUNT, p. 127.

[1] P. I. R., 471. 4.   [2] *Ibid.*, 471. 4.   [3] *Ibid.*, 450. 2.

Obviously, Agoncillo was somewhat impressed by this cablegram, for on August 1 in a letter to Aguinaldo he made the following statements and inquiries : —

"If the American troops leave us alone there, the questions which will arise are these : Have we sufficient arms to maintain the war against Spain in order to secure our independence? If the other nations are opposed to our independence and wish that we should continue under the Spanish sovereignty, have we sufficient strength to wage a war and obtain victory over Spain and over them in the future? If you think that we have not sufficient strength to fight against them, should we accept independence under the American protectorate? And if so, what conditions or advantages should we give to the United States? You should carefully consider the preceding questions, and I suggest that you should, in a confidential manner, consult them with your cabinet-in-banc, as well as with your private secretary and military chiefs of rank; and your decision be notified to our representatives abroad in order that they may know what they must do in their negotiations. You will see from the telegram addressed to me by Regidor that he suggests to me to send a message to MacKinley requesting him not to abandon us, and to submit to them [the U. S.] unconditionally. As I do not agree with him and as I cannot take any action which is against the instructions of the government, I replied to him that the only desire of our government is independence. This may be seen from the enclosed telegram. On account of this reply, he was, I think, somewhat offended, as he afterwards sent a telegram to Joviales [Basa] instead of to me. The latter, upon receiving the telegram, convened all the boastful patriots, and they adopted a resolution to send a message to MacKinley requesting annexation. Fortunately, in the meeting there was present Dr. Justo Lucban, who protested against such measure. In view of this protest, they again agreed that I should be present in the meeting, since I am the representative of our government. At the meeting where I was present, I pointed out the inadvisability of their resolution, stating, as one of the reasons, that we should await your instructions in regard to the matter before sending any message of that character. So the message was not sent; but I was later informed that Basa had, after all, sent it yesterday, because he believed that it would not injure our cause. Upon learning this, I was carried away by passion and went so far as to say to Basa the following: 'Many of us, especially myself, think ourselves to be wise, without being so;

politicians for what we hear from others; we claim to be patriots, but we are only so in words; we wish to be chiefs, but none of us act in a way worthy of a chief.' To this he did not reply. Perhaps his conscience accused him of an act of treachery, since we agreed in the meeting to await your letter. What union can you expect from this people?"[1]

Note that the Basa here referred to is the man whose initials were forged on the letter quoted on page 67.

In the course of the above-mentioned letter Agoncillo came back once more to the question of independence under a protectorate and made it very clear that at this late day he did not know whether this was or was not what the Filipinos desired.[2]

On August 21, Apacible obviously did not think that it would be an easy matter to escape from Spanish domination, much less that the islands were already rid of it, for he wrote to Mabini that the United States were likely again to deliver the Filipinos into the hands of Spain. He said that "if events will be what their telegrams indicate, we have a dark and bloody future before us. To be again in the hands of Spain will mean a long and bloody war, and it is doubtful whether the end will be favourable to us. . . . Spain free from Cuba and her other colonies will employ her energy to crush us and will send here the 150,000 men she has in Cuba."[3]   Apacible

[1] P. I. R., 471. 4.

[2] "You should not forget what I have stated at the beginning of this letter; because I am of the opinion that those questions should be well considered by all of you. If our people desire independence under the American protectorate, it is necessary that our representatives to the United States be given instructions as to the conditions which we should grant to the United States. The peace negotiations are in full blast, and it is probable that we will be rather late in sending our representatives. Therefore, if you agree to independence under a protectorate, you should recommend it at once. I leave it, however, to your care, as you are better qualified than myself concerning the conditions of our country." — P. I. R., 471. 4.

[3] "My Dear Friend: . . . The last telegrams from Europe which Felipe will send you by this mail are alarming for our future. The preliminaries of peace are announced. The demand of America is, annexation of Porto Rico and the Ladrone Islands, independence of

THE SECOND PHILIPPINE COMMISSION.

From left to right: General Luke E. Wright, Professor Dean C. Worcester, Professor Bernard Moses, Judge William H. Taft, and Judge Henry C. Ide.

thought that the best thing was independence under an American protectorate.

On August 7, 1898, Aguinaldo warned Agoncillo that in the United States he should "not accept any contracts or give any promises respecting protection or annexation, because we will see first if we can obtain independence." [1]

Even annexation to the United States was not excluded by Aguinaldo from the possible accepted solutions, for in outlining the policy of the Philippine government to Sandico on August 10, 1898, he wrote: —

Cuba under an American protectorate and an American coaling station in the Philippines. That is, they will again deliver us into the hands of Spain. On the other hand, all the powers will unite to prevent the annexation of the Philippines, according to the telegrams of Regidor; the American cabinet hesitates about including us in the negotiations for peace from fear of a conflict with us and the Filipinos in Europe advise us to send a message to America giving our unconditional adhesion. If events will be what these telegrams indicate, we have a dark and bloody future before us. To be again in the hands of Spain will mean a long and bloody war, and it is doubtful whether the end will be favourable to us. The treaty of peace sanctioned by the other powers will assure the dominion of Spain. Spain free from Cuba and her other colonies will employ all her energy to crush us and will send here the 150,000 men she has in Cuba. I do not think that the Filipinos will again submit to their tyrants and there will be a long and bloody war. And on account of the treaty the other powers will aid Spain to completely dominate us and place all possible obstacles in our way to prevent shipment of arms and all kinds of revolutionary labours. In view of all this and bearing in mind the present urgency of the matter, it is necessary for that government to establish and publish its policy. We believe that the best for us and the only feasible one, if we want to establish negotiations with America, is independence under an American protectorate." — P. I. R., 453. 3.

[1] "The policy which you will pursue in the United States is the following one: —

"Make them understand that whatever may be their intention towards us, it is not possible for them to overrule the sentiments of the people represented by the government, and they must first recognize it if we are to come to an agreement. Still do not accept any contracts or give any promises respecting protection or annexation, because we will see first if we can obtain independence. This is what we shall endeavour to secure; meanwhile, if it should be possible to do so, still give them to understand in a way that you are unable to bind yourself but that once we are independent, we will be able to make arrangements with them." — P. I. R., Books C-1.

"The policy of the government is as follows: 1st. To struggle for the independence of 'the Philippines' as far as our strength and our means will permit. Protection or annexation will be acceptable only when it can be clearly seen that the recognition of our Independence, either by force of arms or diplomacy, is impossible." [1]

On August 26, 1898, Aguinaldo was still ready to consider annexation if necessary.[2] He was apparently not sanguine at this time as to the result of a continued struggle with Spain. At all events, he wanted the help of the Americans if such a struggle was to come, and desired to know on what terms it could be had.[3]

Meanwhile the Filipinos in Hongkong who favoured annexation made themselves heard.

On July 18, 1898, Consul-General Wildman wrote from that place: —

"I believe I know the sentiments of the political leaders and of the moneyed men among the insurgents, and, in spite of all statements to the contrary, I know that they are fighting for annexation to the United States first, and for independence secondly, if the United States decides to decline the sovereignty of the Islands. In fact, I have had the most prominent leaders

[1] P. I. R., 5. 7.

[2] In a letter written on that date to Agoncillo he says: —

"Notwithstanding, I enclose you the credentials as requested; thereby you will see that in addition to your representing us at Washington, you may assist the commission they have formed for the purpose of determining the future condition of the Philippines.

"But you must act in such manner that they may not be able to say that we have accepted the said commission, because it is my wish to protect [protest? D. C. W.] at all times against their being charged with determining our destiny. You must bear in mind that the policy of the government is to obtain absolute independence, and if perchance we should know by the course of events that such cannot be the case, we will then think of protection or annexation." — P. I. R., Books C–1.

[3] On August 30, 1898, Aguinaldo wrote Agoncillo: —

"It is said that General Merritt is going away to take part in the work of the Commission. On this account it is important that you proceed as quickly as possible to America, in order to know what takes place. If perchance we should go back to Spanish control, ask them to help us as the French helped them during their own revolution and ask also the terms." — P. I. R., Books C–1.

call on me and say they would not raise one finger unless I could assure them that the United States intended to give them United States citizenship if they wished it." [1]

We have already noted the action of Basa and the Cortez family who insisted that the Islands must remain American,[2] and that of Agoncillo, who cabled President McKinley in Aguinaldo's name and his own, congratulating him on the outcome of the war, commending the occupation of Manila, and assuring the people of the United States of the allegiance and unquestioning support of the Filipinos,[3] but it is to be feared that the sending of this cablegram was only one more move in the Insurgent game of deceit.

There were annexationists in Manila as well as in Hongkong.[4] Indeed we know that some of the strongest and best of the Filipinos there were in favour of it.

Felipe Buencamino, writing in 1901, said : —

"In June of 1898, Don Cayetano Arellano[5] addressed to Don Felipe Buencamino and Don Ambrosio Rianzares Bautista a letter written from the town of Pagsanján, province of Laguna, in reply to one addressed to him by those two gentlemen. In this letter Don Cayetano outlined the idea of union with the United States and said : 'Avoid all doing and undoing, and when America has established a stable order of affairs, then it will be time enough to make laws.' Mabini, whose influence at that time was in the ascendant in Aguinaldo's government, paid no heed to this wise advice. In October of 1898, while the Philippine government was established in Malolos, and before congress

---

[1] Taylor, 18 AJ. [2] See p. 61. [3] *Ibid.*

[4] Some time during August, 1898, Sandico wrote a letter to Aguinaldo of which the postscript reads as follows : —

"P.S. — If you think of appointing me as Delegate to Manila, please send me my credentials. There are also annexationists here [*i.e.*, in Manila. — D. C. W.]." — P. I. R., 416. 3.

[5] Now Chief Justice of the Supreme Court of the Philippine Islands. He is a man of excellent character, high attainments and great ability. He held important legal positions under the Spanish government. In October, 1898, he was appointed Secretary of Foreign Relations of the "Philippine Republic," but never served as such officer. He was given the degree of Doctor of Law by Yale University in 1904.

had promulgated a Philippine constitution, Messrs. Arellano and Pardo[1] still more earnestly advocated union with America, the first as secretary of foreign affairs and the latter as chief diplomat.   Their plan consisted in asking the United States to acknowledge the independence of the country under a protectorate through the mediation of General Otis, and this plan was accepted at a cabinet meeting by Don Emilio Aguinaldo.   But on the following day Sandico came and told Aguinaldo that he had had a conference with the Japanese consul and had been told by him : 'that if Aguinaldo would support absolute independence the Japanese Government would help.'   Aguinaldo believed Sandico's story (which turned out to be absolutely false) and did not carry out the resolution adopted by the cabinet.   Messrs. Arellano and Pardo, after this affront, separated themselves from the Malolos government.   Aguinaldo told me afterwards that he had received a letter from Agoncillo, dated Washington, assuring him that a majority of the American people were inclined to acknowledge the independence of the Philippines and of Cuba." [2]

But annexationists were not confined, in the Philippines, to the vicinity of Manila.

As late as September 6 Consul Williams reported that a delegation from four thousand Visayan soldiers, a delegation which also represented southern business interests, had come to him and pledged loyalty to annexation.[3]

Clearly, then, the situation early in September was as follows : All were agreed that the assistance of the United States was necessary in getting rid of Spanish sovereignty.

Under the plan of Aguinaldo and his followers friendly relations were to be maintained with the United States, if possible, until Spain was ousted from her Philippine territory, and then they were to "show their teeth," and see "who was deceiving whom," resorting to "force of arms" if necessary.   Protection or annexation would be accepted only when it could be clearly seen that the

[1] Dr. T. H. Pardo de Tavera, one of the most brilliant living Filipinos.   He had spent many years in Paris, was a talented physician, and under American rule served for more than seven years as a member of the Philippine Commission.   [2] Taylor, 55 AJ.   [3] Taylor, 26 AJ.

recognition of independence, won either by force of arms or by diplomacy, was impossible.

Other influential and patriotic Filipinos favored annexation to the United States or a United States protectorate, but their views were in the end ignored by Aguinaldo and his following, and as the latter had the guns their ideas prevailed.

The Treaty of Paris, which terminated Spanish sovereignty in the Philippines, was signed on December 10, 1898. It is important to bear this date in mind later, when considering the Insurgent records relative to the preparations which were so carefully made for attacking the American troops.

And now let us consider the actual facts as to the coöperation alleged to have been asked by Americans and given by Filipinos. The following points are not in dispute : —

Pratt asked Aguinaldo to coöperate with Dewey.

Aguinaldo was taken to Manila with the understanding that he would do so.

Dewey assisted Aguinaldo by destroying the main Spanish fleet; by bringing him and his associates back to the Philippines; by furnishing them arms and ammunition; by blockading Manila and by keeping at a safe distance the Spanish mosquito fleet, which would have made dangerous, or impossible, the landing of the arms subsequently imported by the Insurgents.

Aguinaldo successfully attacked the Spanish garrisons in the provinces and used the arms and ammunition captured, or brought in by deserters, to equip a force which surrounded and attacked Manila, drove large numbers of people into the walled city, thus rendering the position of the Spanish garrison very difficult in the face of a possible bombardment, and prevented this garrison from betaking itself to the provinces, as it might otherwise have done, leaving Manila to shift for itself.

Aguinaldo was powerless to take the place by assault.

It lay at the mercy of Dewey's guns, and it would have been possible for the Admiral to take it at any time, but he could not at first have garrisoned it with United States forces, and never thought of attempting to use Insurgent forces for this purpose.

Did Dewey really want or need Aguinaldo's help? Let us consider his testimony on the subject : —

"*Senator Carmack.* You did want a man there who could organize and rouse the people?

"*Admiral Dewey.* I didn't want anybody. I would like to say now that Aguinaldo and his people were forced on me by Consul Pratt and Consul Wildman ; I didn't do anything —

"*Senator Carmack.* Did they have any power to force him upon you?

"*Admiral Dewey.* Yes ; they had in a way. They had not the official power, but one will yield after a while to constant pressure. I did not expect anything of them ; I did not think they would do anything. I would not have taken them ; I did not want them ; I did not believe in them ; because, when I left Hongkong, I was led to suppose that the country was in a state of insurrection, and that at my first gun, as Mr. Williams put it, there would be a general uprising, and I thought these half dozen or dozen refugees at Hongkong would play a very small part in it."[1]

The picture of the poor admiral, busy getting his fleet ready for battle, pestered by officious consuls on the one hand and by irresponsible Filipinos on the other, is pathetic ; but it had its humorous features, which were not lost on the Admiral himself. I quote the following : —

"*Senator Patterson.* Was there any communication between you and Pratt in which the matter of a written pledge or agreement with Aguinaldo was discussed with reference to the Philippine Islands?

"*Admiral Dewey.* No.

"*Senator Patterson.* What became of the correspondence, Admiral, if you know?

"*Admiral Dewey.* It is all in the Navy Department. When I turned over my command my official correspondence was all sent to the Navy Department.

[1] Senate Documents, Vol. 25, Fifty-seventh Congress, First Session, p. 2969.

"*Senator Patterson.* You retained all of your letters from any United States officials?

"*Admiral Dewey.* No; they went to the Department.

"*Senator Patterson.* I mean you did not destroy them.

"*Admiral Dewey.* No; I did not destroy them.

"*Senator Patterson.* And you turned them over to the Navy Department?

"*Admiral Dewey.* Yes; our regulations require that. I may say that for my own information I kept copies of certain telegrams and cablegrams. I don't think I kept copies of Mr. Pratt's letters, as I did not consider them of much value. He seemed to be a sort of busybody there and interfering in other people's business and I don't think his letters impressed me.

"*Senator Patterson.* He was the consul-general?

"*Admiral Dewey.* Yes; but he had nothing to do with the attack on Manila, you know.

"*Senator Patterson.* I understand that.

"*Admiral Dewey.* I received lots of advice, you understand, from many irresponsible people.

"*Senator Patterson.* But Pratt was the consul-general of the Government there?

"*Admiral Dewey.* Yes; he was consul-general.

"*Senator Patterson.* And he communicated with you, giving you such information as he thought you might be interested in, and among other information he gave you was this concerning Aguinaldo?

"*Admiral Dewey.* I don't remember; no, I really don't remember his telling me anything about Aguinaldo more than that cablegram there, and I said he might come. And you see how much importance I attached to him; I did not wait for him.

"*Senator Patterson.* What you said was: 'Tell Aguinaldo to come as soon as possible.'

"*Admiral Dewey.* Yes; but I did not wait a moment for him.

"*Senator Patterson.* Yes; but there was a reason for that.

"*Admiral Dewey.* I think more to get rid of him than anything else.

"*Senator Carmack.* Rid of whom?

"*Admiral Dewey.* Of Aguinaldo and the Filipinos. They were bothering me. I was very busy getting my squadron ready for battle, and these little men were coming on board my ship at Hongkong and taking a good deal of my time, and I did not attach the slightest importance to anything they could do, and they did nothing; that is, none of them went with me when I went to Mirs Bay. There had been a good deal of talk, but when the time came they did not go. One of them didn't go because he didn't have any toothbrush.

"*Senator Burrows.* Did he give that as a reason?

"*Admiral Dewey.* Yes; he said, 'I have no toothbrush.'" [1]

However, Dewey ultimately yielded to the pressure exercised on him by Pratt and Wildman, and allowed Aguinaldo and some of his associates to be brought to Manila. Having them there he proposed to get assistance from them, not as allies, but as a friendly force attacking a common enemy, in its own way.

Let us continue with his testimony as to coöperation between Aguinaldo and the naval forces of the United States:—

"*Senator Patterson.* Then, Admiral, until you knew that they were going to send land forces to your assistance you thought there was a necessity to organize the Filipinos into land forces, did you?

"*Admiral Dewey.* No; not a necessity.

"*Senator Patterson.* You thought it might prove of value to you?

"*Admiral Dewey.* I testified here, I think, in a way that answers that. I said to Aguinaldo, 'There is our enemy; now, you go your way and I will go mine; we had better act independently.' That was the wisest thing I ever said.

"*Senator Patterson.* But you stated that you were using these people and they were permitted to organize, that you might use them.

"*Admiral Dewey.* They were assisting us.

"*Senator Patterson.* Very well, they were to assist you. Did you not either permit them or encourage them — I do not care which term you use — to organize into an army, such as it was, that they might render you such assistance as you needed?

"*Admiral Dewey.* They were assisting us, but incidentally they were fighting their enemy; they were fighting an enemy which had been their enemy for three hundred years.

[1] Senate Documents, Vol. 25, pp. 2931–2932.

THE RETURN OF MR. TAFT.

This photograph, taken on the occasion of the return of Mr. Taft to the Philippines after his appointment as secretary of war, shows him in a stand on the Luneta reviewing the procession organized in his honor, in which thousands of Filipinos participated.

"*Senator Patterson.* I understand that, Admiral.

"*Admiral Dewey.* While assisting us they were fighting their own battles, too.

"*The Chairman.* You were encouraging insurrection against a common enemy with which you were at war?

"*Admiral Dewey.* I think so. I had in my mind an illustration furnished by the civil war. I was in the South in the civil war, and the only friends we had in the South were the negroes, and we made use of them; they assisted us on many occasions. I had that in mind; I said these people were our friends, and 'we have come here and they will help us just exactly as the negroes helped us in the civil war.'

"*Senator Patterson.* The negroes were expecting their freedom —

"*Admiral Dewey.* The Filipinos were slaves, too.

"*Senator Patterson.* What were the Filipinos expecting?

"*Admiral Dewey.* They wanted to get rid of the Spaniards; I do not think they looked much beyond that. I cannot recall but I have in mind that the one thing they had in their minds was to get rid of the Spaniards and then to accept us, and that would have occurred — I have thought that many times — if we had had troops to occupy Manila on the 1st day of May before the insurrection got started; these people would have accepted us as their friends, and they would have been our loyal friends — I don't know for how long, but they would have been our friends then.

"*Senator Patterson.* You learned from Pratt, or Wildman, or Williams, very early, did you not, that the Filipinos wanted their own country and to rule their own country; that that is what they were expecting?

"*Admiral Dewey.* I heard from Williams that there was an insurrection there against the Spaniards. The Spaniards were very cruel to them, and I think they did not look much beyond getting rid of them. There was one, Dr. Rizal, who had the idea of independence, but I don't think that Aguinaldo had much idea of it.

"*Senator Carmack.* Then what useful purpose did the Filipino army serve; why did you want the Filipino army at all?

"*Admiral Dewey.* I did not want them.

"*Senator Carmack.* Did you not want the Filipino forces?

"*Admiral Dewey.* No, not really. It was their own idea coming over there. We could have taken the city at any moment we had the troops to occupy it."

Admiral Dewey has made the following statements relative to the importance of Aguinaldo's military operations : —

"Then he began operations toward Manila, and he did wonderfully well.   He whipped the Spaniards battle after battle, and finally put one of those old smoothbore guns on a barge, and he wanted to take this up — wanted me to tow it up so he could attack the city with it.   I said, 'Oh, no, no ; we can do nothing until our troops come.'   I knew he could not take the city without the assistance of the navy, without my assistance, and I knew that what he was doing — driving the Spaniards in — was saving our own troops, because our own men perhaps would have had to do that same thing.   He and I were always on the most friendly terms ; we had never had any differences. He considered me as his liberator, as his friend.   I think he had the highest admiration for us because we had whipped the Spaniards who had been riding them down for three hundred years.

*   *   *   *   *   *   *

"*Senator Patterson* (continuing).   You sent this short dispatch to the Secretary of the Navy : —

"'Aguinaldo, the revolutionary leader, visited the *Olympia* yesterday.   He expects to make general attack on May 31. Doubt his ability to succeed.   Situation remains unchanged.'

"Do you recall that visit ?

"*Admiral Dewey.*   Yes.

"*Senator Patterson.*   He came to tell you, did he, that he was going to make a general attack, and you —

"*Admiral Dewey.*   Yes.

"*Senator Patterson.*   And you doubted his ability to succeed ?

"*Admiral Dewey.*   And he wanted me to assist him.   He wanted me to tow one of his guns up into position.   I knew he could not take the city ; of course he could not.

"*Senator Patterson.*   Did you urge that he should not make the attack ?

"*Admiral Dewey.*   I do not remember that ; very likely I did.

"*Senator Patterson.*   And was he not persuaded or restrained by you from doing so ?

"*Admiral Dewey.*   I do not remember ; but it is very likely.   I did not want to see a lot of them killed unnecessarily, because I knew they could not take that walled city.   They had no artillery, and they could not take it, I knew very well, and I wanted the situation to remain as it was until our troops came to occupy it.

"*Senator Patterson.* But you found that whenever you expressed a strong objection to anything being done at that time that Aguinaldo yielded to your request?

"*Admiral Dewey.* Up to the time the army came he did everything I requested. I had not much to do with him after the army came." [1]

But Dewey's influence over Aguinaldo was not sufficient to prevent his looting, as the following extracts from his testimony show: —

"*Senator Patterson.* Is that what you mean when you say he looted — that he made reprisals for his army, took provisions and whatever was necessary? That is what you meant?

"*Admiral Dewey.* That is one part of it.

"*Senator Carmack.* This was taking provisions for the use of the army?

"*Admiral Dewey.* That is one thing he did.

"*Senator Carmack.* You said you did not object to that at the time?

"*Admiral Dewey.* No. It would have been useless; he got beyond me very soon — he got out of my hands very soon.[2]

"*Senator Carmack.* You said yesterday you suspected that Aguinaldo took the lion's share of the provisions that were gathered for the army. What was the ground upon which you made that accusation?

"*Admiral Dewey.* Because he was living in Malolos like a prince, like a king, in a way that could only have come about by his taking the lion's share. Then, in regard to his looting, I repeat what I said yesterday. He began within forty-eight hours after he landed in Cavite to capture and take everything he wanted. I know these things of my own knowledge, because I saw the loot brought in; and I know that every dollar that was taken from the workingmen at the navy-yard was taken at the threat of death.[3]

* * * * * * *

"*Senator Patterson.* Do you believe in this proclamation he was uttering falsehoods to the Filipino people?

[1] Senate Documents, Vol. 25, p. 2956.   [2] *Ibid.*, p. 2966.
[3] *Ibid.*, p. 2965.

"*Admiral Dewey.* Yes; I do absolutely. I think he was there for gain — for money — that independence had never up to that time entered his head. He was there for loot and money. That is what I believe, since you ask me my belief; I believe that implicitly.[1]

*   *   *   *   *   *   *

"*Senator Patterson.* And you found nothing to cause any doubt as to his loyalty up to the time until after Manila surrendered?

"*Admiral Dewey.* His loyalty to whom?

"*Senator Patterson.* To you and to the cause for which he was fighting?

"*Admiral Dewey.* I began to suspect he was not loyal to us about the time our troops arrived, when he demurred at moving out of Cavite to make room for our troops.

"*Senator Patterson.* Do you mean by that that you feared that he was commencing to think more of independence than the success of the American cause?

"*Admiral Dewey.* Yes." [2]

We have seen to what extent Aguinaldo coöperated with the marine forces of the United States. Now let us examine the claim that he coöperated with the land forces after their arrival.

One of the things which the Insurgents are said to have accomplished was the maintenance of an effective land blockade which prevented the entrance of provisions, and produced a very serious food shortage. Both Otis and Dewey have stated that they did this, but we learn from the Insurgent records how erroneous was this conclusion.[3]

[1] Senate Documents, Vol. 25, p. 2955.

[2] *Ibid.*, p. 2952.

[3] The following passage is an extract from an unsigned order dated July 22, 1898: —

"For the preservation of peace and good order in the community and to put an end to the acts of those who within and without the city of Manila and in the neighboring provinces not under the control of the Spanish Government, are evading the orders issued by these Headquarters, and in view of the large number of those who are storing and monopolizing food and other most necessary articles, under the pretence of desiring to sell them to the Americans, but whose real intention is to ship them secretly to Manila where they receive higher

The landing of the American troops for the attack on Manila was not actively opposed by the Filipinos, but it was narrowly and distrustfully watched.

Necessary transportation requested by General Anderson was ultimately furnished by Aguinaldo, but only grudgingly after a three weeks' delay, and as a result of threats that it would be seized if not voluntarily supplied.

The necessary positions in the trenches around Manila from which to make the attack on that city were, in part at least, yielded to the Americans by the Filipinos upon the request of the former.

The Insurgents twice informed the Spaniards in advance of projected American attacks.

They carried out their own attack on the city without regard to the plans, or the requests, of the Americans. They secretly treated with the Spaniards in the endeavour to secure the surrender of the city to themselves.

prices for their merchandise, without regard for the injury they are doing the cause of our independence, I have seen fit to decree the following: . . ." P. I. R., 45. 5 and 125. 3.

Relative to this matter, Taylor says : —

"The defection of Buencamino and Pilar had opened the road to Aguinaldo, but at first the blockade was not effective. There were too many natives there with friends and relations in Aguinaldo's camp to make him desire to subject the city to the hardships of an effective siege. And, furthermore, he did not have the force, nor did his men have the necessary discipline, to prevent the ingress of supplies. It was not until the first part of July that the price of provisions increased. It was at no time found necessary by the authorities to take over all the stores of provisions in the city. Indeed, there seems to have been a fairly steady traffic in supplies between Manila and the country to the north. It was a traffic in which it has been charged that certain Spanish officers of rank made large sums. Aguinaldo permitted it, and on July 26, 1898, signed an order directing that food should be sent into Manila from the north to prevent starvation in the city, and ordered the heads of the towns in the vicinity not to interfere with this traffic (P. I. R., 1087–4). The entrance of food supplies was confined to the northern line, for then it would not be known to the Americans who, after July 30, occupied the entrenchments in front of San Antonio Abad. It was not expedient for them to see too much of Aguinaldo's methods." *

* Taylor, 14 AJ.

After the capitulation to the Americans had been agreed upon, and on the very morning of the day of the surrender, they endeavoured to push home an attack. Disregarding the request that they keep out of the final assault, they crowded into the city with, and after, the American troops. They fired on Spanish soldiers on the city wall while a flag of truce was flying, provoking a return fire which killed and wounded American soldiers.

They demanded for themselves Malacañan palace and. other buildings and a share in "the war booty." They promptly looted the parts of the city which they occupied, and ultimately retired from their positions within the city limits on the evening of their last day of grace after being warned by General Otis that if they did not do so they would be driven out.

I will now quote from the records in support of these statements.

The following is the programme of "coöperation" out-lined to Aguinaldo by Bray in a letter dated June 30, 1898 : —

"I am very anxious to receive the news of the capitulation of Manila and I hope that General Augustín will be obliged to turn over his sword to you in person and not to the Americans. You are by right entitled to it and I should like to see it so from a political standpoint, as I am of the opinion that you should declare the independence of the Philippines before the arrival of General Merritt, appointed by the President to be Governor with full powers to establish a provisional government.

*   *   *   *   *   *   *

Any attempt on the part of the Americans to garrison the interior towns with their troops or any other act which might be construed as a conquest, should meet with resistance.

*   *   *   *   *   *   *

"After having written these lines, I had another conference with Mr. St. Clair of the *Free Press*, who sent for me regard-ing the question of independence. He has had a consultation with the Supreme Judge of this place, and he is of opinion that you should proclaim independence at once, notwithstanding what Admiral Dewey and Consul Williams say against it, and this should be done before General Merritt can arrive. A Government having been thus constituted in due form, the Americans would have no right to invade the Philippines without committing a violation of international law. They are no longer fighting against the Spaniards against whom they declared war. The advice of Consul Williams to delay this, is a diplomatic play to gain time until the arrival of General Merritt, because he is well aware of the false position said General would find himself in. The key to the situation is now in your hands; do not permit any one to take it away from you. The Americans have done nothing but bombard and destroy the Spanish fleet on the high seas; they have not conquered any land, but in the meantime the control of the Philippines has passed by conquest from the hands of the Spaniards and the Americans have no right to enter further. Under certain conditions and guarantees, permit the landing of American troops; but be very careful, they must not be permitted to land until they execute an agreement with the duly constituted government of the Philippines, respecting all its institutions, and they must under no pretext whatever be permitted to garrison any place except the municipal limits of Manila, Cebú, and Iloílo, and even therein care should be observed. . . . You must not permit a single soldier to land without having these guarantees." [1]

When General Anderson, with the first United States troops of occupation, arrived at Manila Bay, Aguinaldo did not call on him, as an " ally " might have been expected to do. Later, however, Admiral Dewey and General Anderson went to see Aguinaldo, but without any of the ceremony of an official military call, the Admiral saying to General Anderson : —

"Do not take your sword or put on your uniform, but just put on your blouse. Do not go with any ceremony." [2]

And they went in that way.

On July 4, 1898, General Anderson wrote Aguinaldo definitely requesting his coöperation in the following words : —

"For these reasons I desire to have the most amicable relations with you, and to have you and your force coöperate with us in the military operations against the Spanish forces." [3]

[1] P. I. R., 398. 2.   [2] Senate Document 331, p. 2976, 1902.
[3] P. I. R., 102-10.

On July 5 Aguinaldo replied, thanking General Anderson for the

"amicable sentiments which the natives of these islands inspire in the Great North American nation,"[1]

and also for his desire to have friendly relations with the Filipinos and treat them with justice, courtesy and kindness. There is, however, not a word relative to coöperation in his reply, and Anderson apparently never renewed his request for coöperation in military operations.

On July 6 he wrote to Aguinaldo again, saying: —

"I am encouraged by the friendly sentiment expressed by Your Excellency in your welcome letter received on the 5th instant, to endeavour to come to a definite understanding, which I hope will be advantageous to both. Very soon we expect large additional land forces, and it must be apparent to you as a military officer that we will require much more room to camp our soldiers and also store room for our supplies. For this I would like to have Your Excellency's advice and coöperation, as you are best acquainted with the resources of the country."[2]

To this letter there was no reply. However, in a letter dated July 9, 1898, to the Adjutant-General of the United States Army, General Anderson says of Aguinaldo: —

"When we first landed he seemed very suspicious, and not at all friendly, but I have now come to a better understanding with him and he is much more friendly and seems willing to coöperate. But he has declared himself Dictator and President, and is trying to take Manila without our assistance. This is not probable, but if he can effect his purpose he will, I apprehend, antagonize any attempt on our part to establish a provisional government."[3]

Evidently, however, coöperation, even in the matter of getting necessary transportation, did not materialize, for on July 17 S. R. Jones, Chief Quartermaster, wrote Aguinaldo as follows: —

"We will want horses, buffaloes, carts, etc., for transportation, bamboo for shelter, wood to cook with, etc. For all this

[1] P. I. R., Books C–1.   [2] P. I. R., 102–10.   [3] *Ibid.*

GOVERNOR-GENERAL JAMES F. SMITH WITH A BONTOC IGOROT ESCORT.

Up to the time of Governor-general Smith, no governor-general had ever penetrated the land of the Luzon head-hunters. He crossed Bontoc and Ifugao, in company with the author, in 1907. This photograph shows him on the crest of the Polis range, at the boundary line between these two sub-provinces, sixty-four hundred feet above the sea.

we are willing to pay a fair price, but no more. We find so far that the native population are not willing to give us this assistance as promptly as required. But we must have it, and if it becomes necessary we will be compelled to send out parties to seize what we may need. We would regret very much to do this, as we are here to befriend the Filipinos. Our nation has spent millions in money to send forces here to expel the Spaniards and to give good government to the whole people, and the return we are asking is comparatively slight.

"General Anderson wishes you to inform your people that we are here for their good, and that they must supply us with labor and material at the current market prices. We are prepared to purchase five hundred horses at a fair price, but cannot undertake to bargain for horses with each individual owner."

Aguinaldo sent this letter by a staff officer to General Anderson inquiring whether it was sent by authority of the latter, who then indorsed on it in a statement that it was. Nevertheless, Major Jones reported on July 20 that it was impossible to secure transportation except upon Aguinaldo's order and that the natives had removed their cart wheels and hidden them, from which it is to be inferred that the transportation requested had not been furnished.

Obviously General Anderson was informed that Aguinaldo had given orders against furnishing the transportation desired, for on July 21 he wrote the Adjutant-General of the Army as follows: —

"Since I wrote last, Aguinaldo has put in operation an elaborate system of military government, under his assumed authority as Dictator, and has prohibited any supplies being given us, except by his order. As to this last, I have written to him that our requisitions on the country for horses, ox carts, fuel, and bamboo (to make scaling ladders) must be filled, and that he must aid in having them filled."

On July 23 General Anderson wrote Aguinaldo as follows: —

"GENERAL: When I came here three weeks ago I requested Your Excellency to give what assistance you could to procure means of transportation for the American Army, as it was to fight the cause of your people. So far we have received no response.

"As you represent your people, I now have the honor to make requisition on you for five hundred horses and fifty oxen and ox carts. If you cannot secure these I will have to pass you and make requisition directly on the people.

"I beg leave to request an answer at your earliest convenience.

"I remain with great respect, etc."[1]

To this letter, Aguinaldo replied as follows: —

"Replying to your letter of yesterday, I have the honor to manifest to Your Excellency that I am surprised beyond measure at that which you say to me in it, lamenting the non-receipt of any response relative to the assistance that you have asked of me in the way of horses, carabaos, and carts, because I did reply through the bearer that I was disposed to issue proper orders whenever you advised me of the number of these, giving me notice in advance.

"I have sent orders to the nearest provinces in order that within the shortest time possible horses be brought for sale, but I cannot assure Your Excellency that we will have the number of 500 that you need, because there are not many horses in this vicinity, owing to deaths from epizoötic diseases in January, February, and March last.

"Whenever we have them collected, I shall have the pleasure to advise Your Excellency.

"I have also ordered to be placed at my disposal 50 carts that I shall place at your disposition when you need them, provided you give me previous notice four days in advance."[2]

General Anderson replied : —

"Your favour of the 26th ultimo in relation to requisitions for cattle, horses, etc., is satisfactory I regret that there should have been any misunderstanding about it. The people to whom we applied even for the hiring of carromatas, etc., told our people that they had orders to supply nothing except by your orders. I am pleased to think that this was a misapprehension on their part."[3]

From this series of communications it appears that it took three weeks, and a very direct threat to seize trans-

[1] P. I. R., 102. 10.   [2] *Ibid.*, Books C–1.   [3] *Ibid.*, 102–10.

portation, to bring about Aguinaldo's promise of assistance in securing it. What help had he given, meanwhile, in other matters?

On July 14, 1899, General Anderson wrote asking him to assist American officers in making reconnaissance of the approaches to Manila, and to favor them with his advice.[1]

On July 19, 1899, he again wrote Aguinaldo asking him to allow Major J. F. Bell,[2] who was gathering information for General Merritt, to see maps, and further requesting him to place at Bell's disposal any available information about the force of the enemy and the topography of the country.[3]

On July 21 he wrote again asking for passes for a Lieutenant E. I. Bryan and party, who were making a reconnaissance.[4]

Such records as I have been able to find do not show what response, if any, Aguinaldo made to these several requests, but General Anderson's original views as to the willingness of the Insurgents to coöperate with him underwent an early change, for on July 18, 1898, in a letter to the Adjutant-General of the United States Army he makes the following statement: —

"The Insurgent chief, Aguinaldo, has declared himself Dictator and self-appointed President. He has declared martial law and promulgated a minute method of rule and administration under it.

"We have observed all official military courtesies, and he and his followers express great admiration and gratitude to the great American republic of the north, yet in many ways they obstruct our purposes and are using every effort to take Manila without us.

"I suspect also that Aguinaldo is secretly negotiating with the Spanish authorities, as his confidential aide is in Manila."[5]

This suspicion was entirely justified, as we shall see later.

On July 24 Aguinaldo wrote a letter to General Anderson in effect warning him not to disembark American

---

[1] P. I. R., 102–10.   [2] Now a major-general.
[3] P. I. R., 102–10.   [4] *Ibid.*   [5] *Ibid.*

troops in places conquered by the Filipinos from the Spaniards without first communicating in writing the places to be occupied and the object of the occupation.[1]

Aguinaldo's assumption of civil authority on July 15, 1899, did not pass unnoticed. On July 21 General Anderson wrote the Adjutant-General of the army concerning it : —

"His assumption of civil authority I have ignored, and let him know verbally that I could, and would, not recognize it, while I did not recognize him as a military leader. It may seem strange that I have made no formal protest against his proclamation as Dictator, his declaration of martial law, and publication and execution of a despotic form of government. I wrote such a protest, but did not publish it, at Admiral Dewey's request, and also for fear of wounding the susceptibilities of Major-General Merritt, but I have let it be known in every other way that we do not recognize the Dictatorship. These people only respect force and firmness. I submit, with all deference, that we have heretofore underrated the natives. They are not ignorant, savage tribes, but have a civilization of their own; and although insignificant in appearance, are fierce fighters, and for a tropical people they are industrious. A small detail of natives will do more work in a given time than a regiment of volunteers."

[1] "Debtor to the generosity of the North Americans, and to the favors we have received through Admiral Dewey and (being) more desirous than any other person of preventing any conflict which would have as a result foreign intervention, which must be extremely prejudicial, not alone to my nation, but also to that of Your Excellency, I consider it my duty to advise you of the undesirability of disembarking North American troops in the places conquered by the Filipinos from the Spanish, without previous notice to this government, because as no formal agreement yet exists between the two nations the Philippine people might consider the occupation of its territories by North American troops as a violation of its rights.

"I comprehend that without the destruction of the Spanish squadron the Philippine revolution would not have advanced so rapidly. Because of this I take the liberty of indicating to Your Excellency the necessity that before disembarking, you should communicate in writing to this government the places that are to be occupied and also the object of the occupation, that the people may be advised in due form and (thus) prevent the commission of any transgression against friendship." — P. I. R., Books C–1.

Because he was invited as general rather than as president, Aguinaldo refused to attend a parade and review on the 4th of July. This fact is, in itself, an answer to his claim that the Americans were tacitly recognizing his pretensions.

After referring to this incident, Blount says : —

"On subsequent anniversaries of the day in the Philippines it was deemed wise simply to prohibit the reading of our declaration before gatherings of the Filipino people. It saved discussion." [1]

This statement is incorrect. I myself was present the following year when the declaration was read on the Luneta to a considerable gathering of Filipinos among whom were many school children, and it has often been read since.

The landing of American troops at Parañaque and their going into camp near that town on July 15 caused much excitement, and a lively interchange of telegrams between Insurgent officers followed.[2]

They were suspicious of the intentions of the Americans,[3] and trouble soon began.

On July 16 General Noriel telegraphed Aguinaldo as follows : —

[1] Blount, p. 59.

[2] On July 15 General Noriel telegraphed Aguinaldo as follows : —
"Urgent. Received a telegram from the captain adjutant, who is in Parañaque, of the following tenor : 'I inform your excellency that two cascos of armed Americans have arrived at this point. I await orders from Your Excellency.' Which I hasten to communicate to Your Excellency for the proper action." — P. I. R., 849.

Later on the same day Arevalo telegraphed Aguinaldo as follows : —
"Lieutenant-Colonel Duboce with three hundred men waiting for more troops from Cavite, and also orders, but not to attack." — P. I. R., 849.

[3] Captain Torres telegraphed Aguinaldo on July 15 as follows : —
"I have read all your telegrams and carried out the same, and I incidentally questioned them about their purposes, [they] replying that they will aid ; let time demonstrate it. They also intend to encamp over here at Parañaque. I will report to you any occurrence." — P. I. R., 69. 6.

"An American has come here who says that he is a Colonel of the Army whom we should obey; and that it is your desire. We did not listen to him, awaiting your order."

On the back of the telegram is written the following: —

"Reply. — You should not obey. What this American Colonel says is a lie. Be cautious so as not to be deceived. You should require from him proof. Be always vigilant, but upright, also all of the officers and soldiers must be strict and not timid." [1]

Obviously there was no real coöperation between American and Filipino troops at this time. General Anderson ignored General Aguinaldo's request for information as to places where American troops were to land in Filipino territory and the objects of disembarking them.

The Americans proceeded with their plans for the attack upon Manila, and it became desirable to occupy some of the Insurgent trenches. On July 29 Arévalo telegraphed Aguinaldo as follows: —

"In conference with General Greene I asked for an official letter, a copy of which I send you: 'Headquarters 2nd Brigade, U. S. Expeditionary Forces, Camp Dewey, near Manila, July 29th, 1898. EL SEÑOR NORIEL, GENERAL DE BRIGADE. Sir: In pursuance of our conversation of yesterday and the message which Captain Arévalo brought to me during the night, I beg to inform you that my troops will occupy the intrenchments between the Camino Real and the beach, leaving camp for that purpose at 8.00 o'clock this morning. I will be obliged if you will give the necessary orders for the withdrawal of your men. Thanking you for your courtesy, I remain, very respectfully, your obedient servant, F. V. GREENE, BRIGADIER GENERAL, commanding.'" [2]

This clear direct declaration of intention by General Greene is the actual transaction referred to by Blount as "Jockeying the Insurgents out of their trenches." He bases his statements concerning the matter on a newspaper report.

[1] P. I. R., 69. 5.   [2] Ibid., 849.

The attitude of the army officers in the matter of obtaining permission to occupy the trenches needed in preparing for the assault on the city could not have been more correct.

On August 10 General Merritt gave the following emphatic instructions relative to the matter : —

"No rupture with Insurgents. This is imperative. Can ask Insurgent generals or Aguinaldo for permission to occupy their trenches, but if refused not to use force."

On the same day General Anderson wrote to Aguinaldo, asking permission to occupy a trench facing blockhouse No. 14, in order to place artillery to destroy it. The permission was granted on the following day.

During the early part of August, Aguinaldo seems to have avoided conferences with American officers. On the second of the month Mabini wrote him how he had put off Admiral Dewey's aid with a false statement that he did not know Aguinaldo's whereabouts.[1]

The landing of American troops at Parañaque for the assault on Manila led to the concentration of Insurgent troops at the neighbouring town of Bacoor.[2]

On August 8 Fernando Acevedo [3] wrote to General Pío

---

[1] "Admiral Dewey's Aide was here to-day. I told him I was ignorant of your whereabouts and, if he had no objection, he might talk with me as I am your representative; but he said that he could not do so, as he had orders to speak with you personally, about something very important. He then departed." — P. I. R., 1179. 5.

[2] The following telegram was addressed to the President or the Secretary of War by Sulpicio at Bacoor, on August 8, 1898 : —

"Last night I received a telegram from General Noriel, asking for 100 cavanes of rice which he needs immediately, since he has ordered to send him all the troops here on account of the landing of Americans in Parañaque. General Mascardo will send him the troops which are here. There are 56 bundles [of rice. — Tr.] deposited in this storehouse." — P. I. R., 1179. 5.

[3] This man's record is not known to me. Apparently he was an officer in the Spanish army, for he is later reported as surrendering to the Insurgents at Santa Ana on August 13, 1898. See footnote 4, p. 104.

del Pilar that the Americans were going to attack the next day and that, —

"It is requisite and necessary before their attack takes place to-morrow, that you to-morrow or to-night annihilate them, sparing none, for the way they have deceived us, and will again without fail, in the contract signed by Sr. Emilio; and convince yourself, my friend, that it is necessary to do this; and when it is done the whole world will wonder and say that we have done well, and will not be able to give out that the people here are fools spending the time sucking their fingers." [1]

Worse yet, information was sent to the Spaniards of the proposed American attack on the 13th instant, as is shown by the following letter : —

"(Battalion of Cazadores, No. 2. Expeditionary. Office of the Lieutenant-Colonel. Private.)

"SEÑOR DON ARTEMIO RICARTE : [2]

"MY DEAR SIR : I have received to-day your kind letter giving warning of the attack on Manila, and I thank you for your personal interest in me, which, on my part, I reciprocate. I assure you that I am yours, most truly and sincerely,

"LUIS MARTINEZ ALCOBENDAS.
"SINGALON, August 10, 1898." [3]

According to Taylor, this was not the first occurrence of this sort. He says : —

"The officers of the United States Army who believed that the insurgents were informing the Spaniards of the American movements were right. Sastrón has printed a letter from Pío del Pilar, dated July 30, to the Spanish officer commanding at Santa Ana, in which Pilar said that Aguinaldo had told him that the Americans would attack the Spanish lines on August 2 and advised that the Spaniards should not give way, but hold their positions. Pilar added, however, that if the Spaniards should fall back on the walled city and surrender Santa Ana to himself, he would hold it with his own men. Aguinaldo's information was correct, and on August 2 eight American soldiers were killed or wounded by the Spanish fire." [4]

[1] Taylor, 33 AJ.   [2] Artemio Ricarte was one of the ranking Insurgent generals directing operations against Manila.
[3] P. I. R., 1087. 5.   [4] Taylor, 30 AJ.

GOVERNOR-GENERAL FORBES IN THE WILD MAN'S COUNTRY.

Mr. Forbes has made frequent trips through the wild man's country in Northern Luzon, and knows it from end to end. Its people know and like him. This photograph shows a crowd of Ifugaos welcoming him on his arrival at Banaue in May, 1913. They are clapping their hands over their heads in true Ifugao fashion.

Taylor continues : —

"And yet Aguinaldo claimed to be an ally of the Americans. It is not probable that these were the only two such letters written. Aguinaldo had by this time found out that although he could defeat the scattered Spanish detachments, he could not defeat the Spanish force holding the lines of Manila. He did not want the Americans in the Philippines. They were in his way, and he had already made up his mind that if they did not give him what he wanted, he would drive them out by force. He saw very early that it was extremely improbable that he should obtain from them what he wanted; accordingly all losses both among Spaniards and Americans would, from Aguinaldo's point of view, inure to his benefit. The best possible thing for him would be to hold his own force intact while they wore each other out. The Spanish losses, small as they were, occurred in front of the American lines, not in front of the Filipinos. There is no reason, accordingly, for believing that the Filipinos suffered heavily. To arrange that the Spaniards should inflict losses upon the Americans, while he saved his own men, showed ingenuity on the part of Aguinaldo; but it was decidedly not the conduct of an ally." [1]

The feeling toward the American troops at this time is further shown by a telegram from General Pío del Pilar, sent from San Pedro Macati on August 10, 1898 : —

"Commandant Acebedo writes that the Spaniards are about to surrender because they want to turn over the place; the Americans want them to leave only the batteries and say that they will station themselves in said batteries. It appears that they want to deceive us; they do not want to give us arms, and if they do not give us arms, we shall attack them and drive them out. I await your reply." [2]

This is perhaps not quite the kind of coöperation that Admiral Dewey and Generals Anderson and Merritt had expected.

The truth is that the Insurgents were determined to capture Manila for themselves, not only because of the "war booty," for which they were hungry, but because of the status which they felt that the taking of the capital

---

[1] Taylor, 30 AJ.   [2] P. I. R., 849.

of the Philippines would assure them. The great importance which they attached to this plan is shown in communications written by Agoncillo, Aguinaldo and others.[1]

Of conditions at this time, Taylor says : —

"On July 7, Aguinaldo appointed Artemio Ricarte and Pantaleón García to negotiate the surrender of Manila by the Spaniards to him (Exhibit 155). On July 5 Pantaleón García was planning to enter Manila by way of Tondo or of Santa Cruz (P. I. R., 243. 7). On the 9th Aguinaldo ordered that rice should be gathered from the towns of Manila Province for the use of his troops in the decisive attack upon Manila which he intended making in a few days (P. I. R., 1087. 5).

"Aguinaldo, finding that his chance of obtaining Manila for himself was growing steadily less, now determined to force himself into the city with the Americans and demand a consideration for the assistance he had rendered them during the siege. It is true he had assisted them, but his assistance had not been intentional. It was the result of the operations he was carrying on for his own ends. The operations of the Filipinos and the Americans were against Spain as a common enemy of both; but the operations were not joint operations, and although their purpose was a common purpose, it was not a mutual one. On August 8 Aguinaldo appointed General

[1] On August 2, 1899, Agoncillo wrote Mabini : —
"I send Don Emilio the information I have been able to obtain here, in order that in view thereof you [plural] may consider the best solution of our present political problem, which is an exceptional case in history. In my opinion, the most critical moment, which I call agonizing, whether correctly or not I know not, is the capture of Manila, where General Merritt will constitute a provisional government, in compliance with the instructions from his Government. It is unnecessary to recommend that you observe great tact, great prudence, when this event occurs. Ascertain the real wishes of the people in this conflict and the war resources at our disposal and those which you may count on during the struggle until its termination."
— P. I. R., 451. 3.

In his document entitled "Means for Attaining Filipino Independence" Aguinaldo had written : —
"VIII. Exterior attack. Above everything the Revolutionists must occupy all Manila including the Walled City with the object and purpose that the nation possessing the Philippines according to the decision of the Powers will be forced to come to an understanding with the Filipinos to avoid the shedding of blood." — P. I. R., 457. 5.

Ricarte commander in the operations about Manila, ordered him to respect the property of all foreigners, and told him that in case his troops succeeded in entering Manila they were to carry their flag and plant it there (P. I. R., 703. 2). Judging from an unsigned draft of a letter, he must have warned the foreign consuls in Manila about the same time to gather under the protection of their flags all of their fellow-citizens who had not taken refuge on the vessels in the bay, so that when his troops entered the city no foreign lives would be taken, and no foreign property would be injured. The earnestness with which he urged that all foreigners not Spaniards should take steps to identify themselves and their property shows that he considered the persons and property of Spanish civilians as fair booty of war." [1]

There was certainly no need of Insurgent assistance in the assault on Manila.

The reports which reached Aguinaldo that the surrender of Manila had been agreed upon in advance were correct, as is shown by the following testimony of Admiral Dewey:

"*Senator Patterson.* When did you reach an understanding with the Spanish commander upon the subject,[2] — how long before the 12th or 13th of August?

"*Admiral Dewey.* Several days before.

"*Senator Patterson.* To whom did you communicate the arrangement that you had?

"*Admiral Dewey.* General Merritt and, of course, all of my own captains — General Merritt, and I think a council of officers on board of one of the steamers. I think there were several army officers present when I told the General that; and I may say here that I do not think General Merritt took much stock in it.

"*Senator Patterson.* What statement did you make to them, Admiral, in substance?

"*Admiral Dewey.* That the Spaniards were ready to surrender, but before doing so I must engage one of the outlying forts. I selected one at Malate, away from the city.[3] They said I must engage that and fire for a while, and then I was to make a signal by the international code, 'Do you surrender?' Then they were to hoist a white flag at a certain bastion; and

[1] Taylor, 29 AJ.   [2] That is, the surrender of Manila.
[3] Fort San Antonio A'bad.

I may say now that I was the first one to discover the white flag. We had 50 people looking for that white flag, but I happened to be the first one who saw it. I fired for a while, and then made the signal according to the programme. We could not see the white flag — it was rather a thick day — but finally I discovered it on the south bastion; I don't know how long it had been flying there when I first saw it." [1]

On August 12, the day before Manila surrendered, Buencamino telegraphed Aguinaldo, urging him in the strongest terms to attack that night so that Americans might be obliged to ask him to stop, with the result that the Insurgents would be included in the official negotiations. He further advised Aguinaldo that he must not suspend his attack because the Americans suspended theirs.[2]

General Anderson tells us that, on the evening of August 12, he received an order from General Merritt to notify Aguinaldo to forbid the Insurgents under his command from entering Manila. This notification was delivered to Aguinaldo that night, and was received by him with anger.[3]

On the following morning the Insurgents actually made an independent attack of their own, as planned.[4] It

[1] Senate Documents, Vol. 25, p. 2943.

[2] "I must tell you that I feel as you should feel in regard to our government not having officially participated in the capitulation of Manila. Accordingly the war must be continued with Spain, because, if we attack to-night, the Americans, acting upon the request of the Spaniards and foreigners in addition to those who took part in the capitulation, will have to ask us to suspend operations; hence we shall be included in the negotiations and this will work to our advantage.

"To-night at 2 A.M. you will attack without fail in order that we may be included in the capitulation which the Americans made to-day. You must not stop the attacks because they do, and this is also the opinion of our partisans among the foreigners."
— P. I. R., 1179. 5 & 427. 5.

[3] "Our Rule in the Philippines," The North American Review, 1900, No. 170.

[4] General Ricarte to Aguinaldo, August 12, 1898, 11.15 P.M.:
"Have received the telegram from your honourable person regarding attack at four o'clock in the morning, although we will make the

promptly led to trouble with the Americans, and at 8 A.M. Aguinaldo received a telegram from General Anderson sternly warning him not to let his troops enter Manila without the consent of the American commander on the south side of the Pasig River.[1]

Aguinaldo apparently took no action in response to this request, except to direct General Riego de Dios, who was at Cavite, to go with Buencamino without losing a moment and ask for an explanation, in writing if possible.[2]

At 10.50 A.M. he telegraphed General Anderson saying that his troops were being forced, by threats of violence, to retire from positions which they had taken, and asking Anderson to order his troops to avoid difficulty with the Insurgent forces. Aguinaldo said that he had directed his men to aid the American forces if the latter are attacked by a common enemy, but was discreetly silent on the subject of their entering Manila.[3]

attack anyway. I have directed Gen. Pío Del Pilar begin firing cannon at the hour set. At the present time we are making preparations and will also give orders to the chiefs of the columns."
— P. I. R., 849.

[1] "August 13, 1898. "Dated. Camp Dewey 13. To General Aguinaldo. Commanding Philippine Forces, Bacoor: Do not let your troops enter Manila without the permission of the American commander on this side of Pasig river. You will be under our fire.
"ANDERSON, Brig. General."
— P. I. R., 102–10.

[2] "Copy: Gen. Riego, Cavite: Have just received a note from Gen. Anderson saying to me he does not permit my troops to enter Manila without permission from the American commander on this side of the Pasig River. They will be under his fire. Go with Señor Buencamino and ask for an explanation, in writing if possible, as to the motive for said note, without losing a moment. August 13, '98. E. A."
— P. I. R., 849.

[3] "I received a telegram. My interpreter is in Cavite. In consequence of this I have not answered until now. My troops are forced by yours, by means of threats of violence, to retire from positions taken. It is necessary to avoid conflict, which I should lament, that you order your troops that they avoid difficulty with mine, as until now they have conducted themselves as brothers to take Manila. I have given

Fifteen minutes later, at 11.05, he received a reply to his telegram to General Riego de Dios, in which that officer communicated the views of Araneta [1] and Buencamino, who had been unable to find General Anderson. This important communication follows : —

"Most urgent. Araneta and Buencamino having been consulted in regard to your telegram of to-day, they confirm capitulation, and in regard to the telegraphic note of General Anderson they are of the opinion, first that we should continue hostilities while we ask for an explanation; second, that explanation should be in the following terms: Inquire reason for note and ask why our troops are not to enter Manila without permission of the American commander; third, in case the (terms of ?) capitulation is given as the reason, to answer that we do not suspend our attempt to enter Manila. Its capitulation is not favourable to our independence. General Anderson is not here. General Merritt is probably in Manila. Only Admiral Dewey is in the Bay. We ask authorization to express our explanation in the proposed terms and to have a conference with Admiral Dewey in order to have our claims reach General Merritt." [2]

An indorsement written by Mabini and signed by Aguinaldo on the above paper reads : —

"I authorize every assertion of right, but state that we believe that we have the right to enter Manila without permission as we have a part in the surrender of the Spaniards. They would not have surrendered if our troops had not cut off their retreat to the interior. Besides but for us the landing of troops would have cost them much blood. Obtain an answer as soon as possible in order to lay a protest before the consuls in case it is necessary." [3]

strict orders to my chiefs that they preserve strict respect to American forces and to aid them in case they are attacked by a common enemy."

[1] Gregorio Araneta, later a member of the Philippine Commission and Secretary of Finance and Justice. He was Secretary of Justice under the Malolos government, and was also secretary of the Insurgent Congress. He was at this time a bright young lawyer of good ability and character.

[2] P. I. R., 849.   [3] *Ibid.*

Naturally, trouble followed. At 1.30 P.M. General Ricarte telegraphed to Aguinaldo : —

"Americans wish to put us out. Give directions." [1]

Apparently about the same hour he wired more at length, as follows : —

"Most urgent. American troops rearguard our trenches. Mabolo and San José warn us that they will fire on us when the time comes. Impossible to remain there without disagreeing with them. Since 5 o'clock this morning we have been furiously attacking. Americans firing incessantly, Spaniards silent. No losses yet." [2]

At 3.52 he wired again : —

"General Pío del Pilar informs me of the following : 'Come here, if possible, as our soldiers at the barrio of Concepción are not allowed to go out and we are prohibited to move on any farther. We it was who succeeded in capturing that place. Come here or there will be trouble, since they are driving me away, and refusing to listen to what I say.' I am at this very moment going to aforesaid place." [3]

At 5 P.M. another was sent by Ricarte to Aguinaldo as follows : —

"Colonel San Miguel arrived here from Ermita. Regional Exposition, Agricultural College and other buildings are ours. Our flag flies already at Ermita. Colonel Agapito Donzón with his troops is in the Pérez building, Paco. Colonels Julian Ocampo and Isidoro Tolentino are in the convent of Ermita. All houses without flag are guarded by our soldiers." [4]

At 6.15 P.M. he telegraphed as follows : —

"I inform you that the chiefs of our troops have reported to me that our flag at Singalong church (visita) was removed by the Americans and they hoisted theirs instead, not allowing us to approach thereto. General Pío del Pilar is at present at the barrio of Concepción. Americans prohibited him to move on any farther. How can he enter Manila?" [5]

[1] P. I. R., 849.   [2] Ibid., 849.   [3] Ibid., 1179. 5.
[4] Ibid.   [5] Ibid.

No attention was paid to General Anderson's request that the Insurgent troops should not enter Manila without permission. They crowded forward with and after the American forces. Coming out on Bagumbayan drive, they found American and Spanish troops confronting each other but not firing, the former on the drive, the latter on the neighbouring city wall. A flag of truce was waving from the south bastion, nevertheless the Insurgents fired on the Spanish forces, provoking a return fire which killed and wounded American soldiers. Of this incident General Greene has said : —

"At this point the California regiment a short time before had met some insurgents who had fired at the Spaniards on the walls, and the latter, in returning the fire, had caused a loss in the California regiment of 1 killed and 2 wounded." [1]

Some of these matters must have come to the attention of General Anderson, for he sent Aguinaldo a telegram, received by the latter at 6.35 P.M., as follows : —

"Dated Ermita Headquarters 2nd Division 13 to Gen. Aguinaldo. Commanding Filipino Forces.—Manila, taken. Serious trouble threatened between our forces. Try and prevent it. Your troops should not force themselves in the city until we have received the full surrender then we will negotiate with you.
"ANDERSON, commanding." [2]

It appears that the Insurgent troops took the suburb of Santa Ana, and captured Spanish and Filipino officers and men.[3]

[1] Report of War Dept., 1898, Vol. I, part 2, p. 69.
[2] Taylor, Exhibit 739.
[3] The following two telegrams were sent by General Pío del Pilar to Aguinaldo at 9.30 P.M. : —
"I inform you that the Bayambang troops who have presented themselves before me when we entered Santa Ana this afternoon, are : 4 lieutenants, 171 soldiers with their respective rifles and ammunitions, Major Fernando Acevedo, Captain Licerio Geronimo, 1 Spanish lieutenant, and 1 prisoner by the name of Enrique Flores. All of them I put under your orders." — P. I. R., 1179. 5.

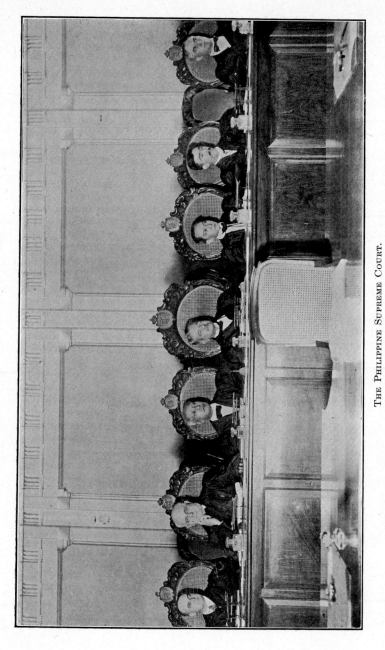

THE PHILIPPINE SUPREME COURT.

From left to right, Justice Moreland, Justice Johnson, Justice Torres, Chief-Justice Arlleano, Justice Mapa, Justice Carson, and Justice Trent.

In view of the known facts, how absurd becomes the following contention of Aguinaldo, advanced in his "Reseña Verídica" : —

"Our own forces could see the American forces land on the beach of the Luneta and of the Paseo de Santa Lucía. The Spanish soldiers, who were on the walls of the city, drew the attention of every one because they did not fire on the former, a mystery which was explained at nightfall of that day, by the news of the capitulation of the place by General Señor Jáudenes [1] to the American General, Mr. Merritt, a capitulation which the American Generals claimed for themselves, an infraction of what had been agreed upon with Admiral Dewey, in regard to the formation of plans for the attack and taking of Manila by the two armies, American and Filipino, together and in combination.

"This inexplicable line of conduct on the part of the American officers was made clearer by the telegrams, which General Anderson addressed to me, from Maytubig on the said 13th day, requesting that I should order our troops not to enter Manila, which request was refused, inasmuch as it was contrary to what was agreed upon, and to the high ends of the Revolutionary Government, which, on taking upon itself the immense work of besieging Manila, during the two months and a half, sacrificing thousands of lives and millions in material interests, could not surely have done so with any object other than that of capturing Manila and the Spanish garrison which with firmness and tenacity defended that place." [2]

On August 14 Aguinaldo telegraphed General Anderson as follows : —

"My troops, who have been for so long besieging Manila, have always been promised that they could appear in it, as you know and cannot deny, and for this reason, and on account of the many sacrifices made of money, and lives, I do not consider it prudent to issue orders to the contrary, as they might be disobeyed against my authority. Besides, I hope that you will allow the troops to enter because we have given proofs many

"Very urgent. I inform you of the capture made by my soldiers: 2 lieutenants of the Marine Corps, 2 lieutenants of the Spanish Infantry, 52 soldiers. Rifles about 400. I put them under your orders and await your instructions." — P. I. R., 1179. 5.

[1] The Spanish Governor-General.   [2] P. I. R., 1300. 2.

times of our friendship, ceding our positions at Parañaque, Pasay, Singálon and Maytubig. Nevertheless, if it seems best to you, and in order to enter into a frank and friendly understanding and avoid any disagreeable conflict before the eyes of the Spaniards, I will commission Don Felipe Buencamino and others, who will to-day go out from our lines and hold a conference with you, and that they will be safe during the conference."[1]

Aguinaldo and his associates pressed the demand for joint occupation. On August 13 Admiral Dewey and General Merritt informed the government that since the occupation of Manila and its suburbs the Insurgents outside had been insisting on this, and asked how far they might proceed in enforcing obedience in the matter.

They were informed by a telegram dated August 17 that the President of the United States had directed : —

"That there must be no joint occupation with the Insurgents. The United States in the possession of Manila city, Manila bay and harbor must preserve the peace and protect persons and property within the territory occupied by their military and naval forces. The insurgents and all others must recognize the military occupation and authority of the United States and the cessation of hostilities proclaimed by the President. Use whatever means in your judgment are necessary to this end."[2]

This left the military and naval commanders no option in the premises, and in any event dual occupation was out of the question because of the lawlessness of the Insurgent troops.

At this very time they were looting the portions of the city which they occupied, and as is abundantly shown by their own records were not confining their attacks to Spaniards, but were assaulting their own people and raiding the property of foreigners as well.[3] The continuation of such a condition of affairs was manifestly impossible.

The Insurgents promptly demanded their share in the

[1] Taylor, 58 HJ.   [2] *Ibid.*, 59.   [3] See footnote 2, p. 108.

"war booty," and asked certain other extraordinary concessions as follows : —

"(4) Our sacrifices in coöperating in the siege and taking of Manila being well known, it is just that we should share in the war booty.

"(5) We demand for our use the palace of Malacañang and the Convents of Malate, Ermita and Paco or San Fernando de Dilao.

"(6) We demand that the civil offices of Manila be filled by North Americans and never by Spaniards ; but if General Merritt should require some Filipinos we should be pleased if he will grant our President, Don Emilio Aguinaldo, the favour of recommending select and skilled Filipinos. The jurisdiction of the authorities of Manila shall not be recognized beyond the municipal radius.

"(7) The American forces shall not approach nor penetrate our military positions without permission of the respective commanders thereof and shall evacuate all the positions which they occupy at the present time beyond the municipal radius ; Spaniards who pass our lines without permission of the commander will be considered as spies.

*　　*　　*　　*　　*　　*　　*

"(10) Lastly we state clearly that our concessions and petitions do not signify on our part that we recognize the sovereignty of North America in these islands, as they are made necessary by the present war." [1]

Under the instructions of the President these demands could not be acceded to. Nor could they have been acceded to had there been no such instructions. In this connection the following extract from General Jáudenes's cablegram for June 8th to his home government is highly significant : —

"Population of suburbs have taken refuge in walled city from fear of outrages of insurgents, preferring to run risks of bombardment, which has not yet begun." [2]

It would seem that the population of the suburbs did not have a high idea of Insurgent discipline.

[1] P. I. R., Books C–1.　　[2] Taylor, 15 AJ.

That their apprehensions were not groundless is shown by a passage in a letter sent the following day to Governor-General Augustin by Buencamino : —

"Manila being surrounded by land and by sea, without hope of assistance from anywhere, and Señor Aguinaldo being disposed to make use of the fleet in order to bombard, if Your Excellency should prolong the struggle with tenacity, I do not know, frankly, what else to do other than to succumb dying, but Your Excellency knows that the entrance of 100,000 Indians,[1] inflamed with battle, drunk with triumph and with blood, will produce the hecatomb from which there will not be allowed to escape either women, children, or Peninsular friars, — especially the friars ; and, I believe that the rights of humanity, imperilled in such a serious way, should be well considered by Your Excellency, for however dear glory and military duty may be, although worth as much or more than existence itself there is no right by which they should be won at the cost of the rights of humanity, and the latter outweigh every consideration and all duty." [2]

Don Felipe knew his own people. He also knew, none better, what they had in mind at this time.

As it was the Insurgent forces made the most of such opportunity as they had, and their own records show it.

In the suburbs of Manila they sacked and committed outrages, threatening people with their arms, and this was still going on a week after the fall of Manila.[3]

General Pío del Pilar was believed to be responsible for much of this misconduct, and Mabini proposed that as it was necessary for him to leave the vicinity of Manila, and they could not remove him by force, he be promoted.[4]

[1] The word Indios, here translated "Indians," means Malayan Filipinos of pure blood as distinguished from *mestizos* or people of mixed blood. [2] P. I. R., 918. 2.

[3] The following telegram was sent by Colonel José to Aguinaldo : —
"Urgent. August 20, 1898 : Colonel López reports that our troops are still sacking and committing outrages in Malate, Paco and Ermita, even menacing people with their arms. Urge you to take proper measures to stop these abuses." — P. I. R., 1167. 3.

[4] Extract from a letter of August 20, 1899, from Mabini to Aguinaldo :
"Señor López, your adjutant, arrived and told me of many complaints regarding the behaviour of the soldiers. He says that our offi-

Some time during this month Sandico wrote Aguinaldo as follows : —

"The Americans have already heard of the frequent cases of kidnapping (*dukut*) occurring in Tondo, San Sebastián and San Miguel. Last night some of ours were surprised in the act of kidnapping a person. I have also heard that many persons are asking for contributions of war. I tell them [1] that you know nothing of all this and that if some persons are kidnapped it is due to the hate of the natives for the Spanish spies and secret police, which is great." [2]

Evidently Sandico continued to interest himself in the matter of preventing disorder, for on September 24, 1898, he wrote Aguinaldo from Manila as follows : —

"By authority of General Don Pío del Pilar and accompanied by the War Auditor, Señor Urbano, we entered a prison where the individuals Mariano de la Cruz and Mariano Crisóstomo were kept. They were almost prostrated. They had lately been released from Bilibid where they had been confined for political crimes. On being asked the reason for their imprisonment they began by showing us their bodies from which blood still issued as the result of the barbarous treatment received from Major Carmona who, by the way, is the same person of whom I spoke to you in one of my previous letters; I declared to you then that he had assaulted, revolver in hand, a man in the middle of one of the most frequented streets of the suburb of Paco on pure suspicion.

"The prisoners in question stated that if they admitted the accusations made against them it was for fear of greater punishments promised by said Major. The officer of the guard took

cers carry off many horses, some of them belonging to foreigners. If the foreigners should enter a protest against such doings, I do not know what will be thought of our government.

" It is also absolutely necessary that a stop should be put to the passes, and that the tax on merchandise entering Manila, should no longer be exacted. It is absolutely necessary, if you think well of it, for us to promote General Pío, and make him your second in command. It is necessary for him to leave the vicinity of Manila, as we cannot remove him by force; and do not reprimand him.

" If you approve, I will write a Decree, but I reflect that nothing will succeed, if our commanders are not obliged to comply."

— P. I. R., 472. 13.

[1] *I.e.* the Americans.　　　　　[2] P. I. R., 458. 8.

the liberty of striking with his fist the one who dared to express himself so.

"Before such a spectacle Major Bell found himself forced to tell them that brutal acts are not precisely a recommendation for a country that wished to be free and that they, the Americans, do not arrest any one without just cause.[1]

"I take the liberty of calling your attention to the matter in question and other abuses in order that the measures you may think fit be adopted to remedy this evil. In fact, we are making a target of ourselves in the sight of all nations, especially so in that of the Americans who note any act of ours and judge us secretly now in order to do so later in public. To make light of this is to plant a seed of future injury to us, because many will desire to place themselves under the protection of the American flag, seeing that ours refuses to defend the citizens' individual rights.

"I, for my part, ask that Major Carmona be arrested together with his accomplices in the matter so that it may serve as a lesson not only for him but also for those who think like him." [2]

Obviously Sandico's protest of September 24 did not produce the desired result, for on September 28 he wrote Aguinaldo a long letter complaining that in Manila personal security did not exist, people were being tortured and murdered, kidnapping and theft were very frequent, and these abuses were being committed by Filipino officers and men. Some of the things which had come to his knowledge were of such a nature that he preferred to speak to Aguinaldo privately about them.[3]

[1] Major J. F. Bell accompanied Sandico on this trip.

[2] P. I. R., 1166. 12.

[3] "I regret very much to have to inform you that as long as personal property is not respected here in Manila especially, by some of our men, as long as personal security does not exist and as long as prisoners are tortured, we cannot hope to deserve the confidence of the other governments. Murders, thefts of carriages and horses, are very frequent here, as is kidnapping, . . .

"Sergeant Barcena, of the Fifth Company of the Second Zone, that is the zone of General Pío del Pilar, informed me that the cruel officers of that Zone, were Major Carmona and a lieutenant who was formerly a barber.

"I know that the Government has ordered that private persons and property be respected and has withdrawn from the military the

Murder, pillaging, torture of prisoners, kidnapping, theft — these are not pleasant things, but they continued to occur, and Aguinaldo, who apparently desired to prevent them, was powerless to do so. He did not dare discipline General Pío del Pilar, nor remove him from the vicinity of Manila, and the soldiers of that officer continued to work their will on their own unfortunate and helpless people.

Aguinaldo at first flatly refused to direct the disorderly Insurgent forces to leave Manila. The American commander showed great forbearance and negotiations continued.

On August 16, 1898, the Diplomatic Commission (Buencamino and Gregorio Araneta) telegraphed Agui-

power of trying civilians; but in view of the fact that notwithstanding this restriction some of them continue to discharge powers of which they have been divested, I find it necessary to call your attention thereto, in order that more energetic measures may be adopted so that other nations may not be led to believe that our government is very weak.

"In the jurisdiction of the Americans, I have surprised small groups of officers, who devote themselves to summoning persons before them and arresting them. These groups can be found in Binondo, Tondo and Trozo. I have used all friendly measures to secure their dissolution, but if they continue their conduct, I shall be obliged to turn them over to the American authorities, although I inform you that I shall not make use of such measures, until diplomatic means are exhausted.

"I understand very well that in endeavouring to stop the abuses committed by our officers and by the Filipinos who claim to belong to us, in Manila, I expose myself to becoming a victim of their vengeance; nevertheless, this does not terrify me, because my duty to the country requires it.

"I beg of you that if you take any steps against Major Carmona and the barber lieutenant, to be very careful and call General Pío del Pilar and come to an understanding with him as to the mode of punishment of these officers. . . .

"I have discovered grave cases which are occurring in the Presidio of Manila, which I propose to relate to you when I shall have the honor to see you personally. The Americans are already aware of these cases, and are working in their own interest untiringly.

"I could tell you a good many other things, but I do not do so on account of lack of time, and because I wish to reserve them until I can speak to you privately. In the meantime, order me as you will, etc."
— P. I. R., 416. 7.

naldo that a clause in a proposed agreement requiring prior permission of Insurgent officers before American troops could pass or approach their lines had greatly displeased General Anderson who declined to treat until after the withdrawal of Noriel's troops from Manila.[1]

Aguinaldo's reply, sent on August 17, 1898, shows that he had already made up his mind to fight the Americans, for it contains the following significant words: "The conflict is coming sooner or later and we shall gain nothing by asking as favours of them what are really our rights." [2]

While negotiations were pending General Merritt sent Major J. F. Bell to Aguinaldo with a letter and also with a memorandum in which were the words: —

"In case you find Aguinaldo inclined to be generous in his arrangements with us, you may communicate to him as follows: . . ."

There follow six paragraphs, of which the third is of special importance. It reads as follows: —

"(3) That I have every disposition to represent liberally the Government at Washington, which I know is inclined to

[1] "General Anderson received us very well, but in the proposed agreement the clauses requiring the prior permission of our commanders before American troops could pass or approach our lines displeased him very much. Gen. Anderson refuses to treat until after the withdrawal of Noriel's troops. I think it prudent to yield. This telegram is in amplification of another which, at the request of Gen. Anderson, we sent through his telegraph station to your excellency." — P. I. R., 849.

[2] "It is impossible to order General Noriel to fall back because if we order it they will ask the same thing from General Pío and we shall get nothing ourselves. And the worst is that after we have evacuated Manila and its environs they will follow us up to our new positions to take them too without our being able to obtain from them any formal statement of the concession signed in due form. The conflict is coming sooner or later and we shall gain nothing by asking as favours of them what are really our rights. We shall maintain them as long as we are able, confiding in Providence and in Justice. I confirm my last telegram. Tell General Anderson that we shall hold a meeting of the council of Government in order to decide. Please return here soon with your companions. I inclose the map which I hope you will return." — P. I. R., 427. 1.

AN UNSANITARY WELL.

This is a typical old-style well, with the family washing going on beside it.
Under such circumstances infection of the well water invariably resulted.

A FLOWING ARTESIAN WELL.

There is no way in which the water from such a well can become infected.
More than eight hundred fifty have been sunk, and the death rate in some
towns fortunate enough to possess them has fallen off fifty per cent, as a
result.

deal fairly with him and his people; but not knowing what the policy of that Government will be, I am not prepared to make any promises, except that in the event of the United States withdrawing from these islands care will be taken to leave him *in as good condition as he was found by the forces of the Government.*" [1]

Relative to the italicized portion of this statement Major Bell says: —

"I was pressed to explain further just what meaning General M. meant to convey by the underscored portion of this remark, but I replied that I had repeated the language General M. had used to me, and I preferred they should seek any further explanation from him, lest I might unwittingly fall into error if I undertook to explain his meaning myself. Their lack of definiteness and my unwillingness to comment upon the language seemed to arouse their apprehensions and suspicions. They have been trying ever since to obtain in writing some definite promise on this subject." [2]

Aguinaldo ordered that the machinery of the water works be started up at once, a thing which was very necessary as Manila was suffering from lack of water. I should be glad if I could leave this matter here, but I cannot, for Major Bell elsewhere makes the further statement: —

"Attention is invited to General Merritt's promise made known to Aguinaldo by me verbally, namely, that in the event of the United States withdrawing from these islands, care would be taken to leave Aguinaldo in as good condition as he was found by the forces of the Government. From a remark the General made to me I inferred he intended to interpret the expression 'forces of the Government' to mean the naval forces, should future contingencies necessitate such an interpretation." [3]

Let us hope that Major Bell misunderstood General Merritt's intention. If this is not the case, I must say in all frankness that in my opinion it was General Merritt's intention to indulge in sharp practice.

[1] Senate Document No. 208, p. 22.　[2] *Ibid.*, p. 23.　[3] *Ibid.*, p. 26.

Obviously, the American naval forces did not find Aguinaldo in any "condition," in the sense in which General Merritt uses the term. On the contrary, they brought him from Hongkong and assisted him in starting a revolution. The negotiations in question were relative to the positions held by the Insurgents at the time the negotiations took place, and General Merritt's promise could not legitimately be interpreted to refer to anything else.

Had Aguinaldo accepted his offer, a most embarrassing situation would have resulted. General Merritt was obviously not authorized to make such a proposition in the first instance, and the only honourable course left open to him would have been to advise Washington of his improper action and beg the Government to support him in it and thus save the honour of the country.

Fortunately, Aguinaldo did not act upon the promise nor accept the offer. On the contrary, he promptly and indignantly denied that he was committed to anything, and sought to impose new conditions which were not acceded to.

Meanwhile some one doubtless got hold of General Merritt and called his attention to the fact that in making this offer he had grossly exceeded his authority, for in his reply to Aguinaldo's protest General Merritt says : —

"So far as any promises as to what should be done in the event of a conclusion of a treaty between the United States and Spain are concerned, it is utterly impossible for me as the military representative only of the United States to make any promises such as you request. As you have already been informed, you may depend upon the good will of the Americans out here and the Government, of which you already know the beneficence, to determine these matters in the future." [1]

Coming, as this statement did, after the offer made in the memorandum hereinbefore referred to, it must have aroused the suspicions of Aguinaldo and his associates,

[1] Senate Document No. 208, p. 24.

and in my opinion Merritt's conduct in making such a proposal in the first instance was inexcusable.

Before he could terminate the negotiations which followed he was called away, and turned this matter, together with other unfinished business, over to his successor, General E. S. Otis.

On August 31, 1898, the latter official wrote to Aguinaldo as follows: —

"GENERAL AGUINALDO, BACOOR:

"Referring to promise made by General Merritt to reply to your letter of August 27 within four days, I desire to state that he was unexpectedly ordered away and had not opportunity to reply. Being unacquainted with the situation, I must take time to inform myself before answering, which I will do at the earliest opportunity.   "OTIS."

On September 8 General Otis wrote Aguinaldo a long letter fully discussing the whole situation in the light of the complete information which he had meanwhile obtained. Since so much has been made of this incident by Blount and others, I invite attention to the following extracts from General Otis's letter, which embody a fair and judicial statement of the conditions which existed: —

"You designate certain lines within the suburbs of the city of Manila, to which you promise to retire your troops, and name as conditions precedent: First, protection to your shipping by the United States Navy, and the free navigation of your vessels within the waters in United States occupation; second, restitution to your forces of all positions which are now occupied by your troops, in the event that treaty stipulations between the United States and Spain surrender to the last-named government the territory occupied by the former; and thirdly, that United States troops now occupying positions beyond the lines you name shall retire within the same.

"A discussion of your proposition to hold, jointly, with the United States Government, the city of Manila, involves consideration of some of the other concessions you desire to be made, and to that I will at once refer. I wish to present the matter, in the first instance, in its legal aspect, although, from remarks contained in former correspondence, I am of the opinion that you are fully aware how untenable the proposition is.   The United States and Spain were and are belligerent parties to a war, and were so recognized by the civilized world. In the course of events the entire city of Manila, then in full possession of Spanish forces, was surrendered to the first-named belligerent power.   The articles of agreement and capitulation gave the United States Government full occupancy of the city and defences of Manila, and that Government obligated itself to insure the safety of the lives and property of the inhabitants of the city to the best of its ability.   By all the laws of war and all international precedents the United States authority over Manila and its defences is full and supreme, and it cannot escape the obligations which it has assumed.

*   *   *   *   *   *   *

"But conceding, as you do, the strictly legal right of my Government to hold and administer the affairs of the city of Manila and its suburbs (I thus conclude from expressions contained in former correspondence and from my appreciation of your intellectual attainments), you base your proposition — a joint occupation — upon supposed equitable grounds, referring to the sacrifices your troops have made and the assistance they have rendered the American forces in the capture of Manila. It is well known they have made personal sacrifices, endured great hardships, and have rendered aid.   But is it forgotten that my Government has swept the Spanish navy from the seas of both hemispheres; sent back to Spain the Spanish army and navy forces, recently embarked for your destruction, and the secure holding of the Philippine possessions; that since May 1 last its navy has held the city of Manila at its mercy, but out of consideration of humanity refused to bombard it, preferring to send troops to demand surrender, and thereby preserve the lives and property of the inhabitants?   Is it forgotten that the destruction of the Spanish navy and the retention of Spanish armed men in its European possessions has opened up to you the ports of the Island of Luzon and held Spain helpless to meet its refractory subjects?

*   *   *   *   *   *   *

"Apart from all legal and equitable considerations, and those having their origin in personally conceived ideas of justice, I wish respectfully to call your attention to the impracticability of maintaining a joint occupation of Manila and its suburbs, and in this I know that I shall have the approval of your excellent judgment.   It would be extremely difficult to prevent friction between our respective forces, which might result in unfortunate consequences, labor as we may for continued harmonious relations. Located in close proximity, irresponsible members of our organizations, by careless or impertinent action, might be the means of inciting grave disturbances; and in this connection I call to your attention the recent shooting affair at Cavite, which still requires investigation. There might also arise conflict of authority between our subordinate officers. Even now, within precincts in entire actual possession of our troops, I find that permits are given to citizens, who are styled local presidents, to make arrests, to carry arms, etc., in violation of our instructions and authority, and that several cases of kidnapping have taken place. In pursuance of our obligations to maintain, in so far as we can, domestic tranquillity, our officers have arrested suspected parties, and they have asserted (with what element of truth I know not) that the insurgent forces are the offenders. I have declined to accept their statements, as I prefer to believe the contrary, although it would appear that officers connected with those forces have issued the permits to which I allude. Such interference with our administration of civil affairs must eventually result in conflict.

". . . And here permit me to remark upon a view of the subject you have advocated in support of the plea for dual occupation of the city's suburbs. Your forces, you say in substance, should have a share in the booty resulting from the conquest of the city, on account of hardships endured and assistance rendered. The facts on which you base your conclusion granted, your conclusion, under the rules of war which are binding on my Government, does not follow, for it has never recognized the existence of spoils of war, denominated 'booty,' as have many European governments. No enemy's property of any kind, public or private, can be seized, claimed by, or awarded to, any of its officers or men, and should they attempt to appropriate any of it for their individual benefit, they would be very severely punished through military tribunals, on which have been conferred by law very sweeping jurisdiction. The enemy's money and property (all that is not necessary to be expended in administering local affairs in the enemy's territory) must be preserved for final arbitrament or settlement by and between the supreme authorities of the nations concerned. My troops cannot acquire booty nor any individual benefit by reason of the capture of an enemy's territory. I make this comment, believing that you hold erroneous opinions in respect to individual advantages which occupation bestows.

"I request your indulgence while I briefly consider the concessions you ask us to make as conditions precedent to the retirement of your forces to the lines indicated by your note of the 27th ultimo.

"The first is: Protection to your shipping and free navigation to your vessels. Neither the extent of protection nor the limit of free navigation you request is understood. Certainly you could not mean protection on the high seas, or in the ports not in the rightful possession of the United States. That, as you are fully aware, could only be effected by treaty, or guarantee, following international recognition of the belligerent rights of the Philippine revolutionary government. While the existing armistice continues, the United States are in rightful possession, in so far as the navigable waters of the Philippine Islands are concerned, only of the bay of Manila and its navigable tributaries. Within the same all vessels of trade and commerce and the war vessels of recognized national powers sail freely as long as the sovereignty of my Government is not assailed nor the peace of the locality threatened. In this respect, whatever concessions are extended by way of relaxation of trade restrictions, incident to war, to the citizens of these islands will be extended to all alike, and discrimination in this regard is neither intended nor permitted. Admiral Dewey exercises supervision over all naval matters, and they are in no way related to the duties conferred upon me by law. Nor would it avail should I seek his consent for greater latitude of action, for even if disposed to grant special concessions he could not do so, and I doubt if the supreme authority of my Government could now, under the prevailing truce with Spain, invest him with the requisite powers to do so and at the same time preserve its international obligations.

"The second concession named by you is restitution of positions in the city of Manila to your forces, in case the treaty of peace remands to Spain the territory surrendered under the late capitulatory articles; and the third and last is a promise to retire our troops within the lines indicated by you, as the lines on which you desire your troops to remain permanently. These propositions, having a kindred nature, may be considered together, and, indeed, have already been impliedly answered. From previous statements of facts and logical conclusions made and stated in this communication, concerning the nature of the obligations resting on the United States with regard to the territory to which they have the legal right of possession under contracting articles with Spain, it is evident that neither in law or morals can the concessions be made. I would be powerless to grant them in any aspect of the case, being nothing more than an agent to carry out the instructions of the executive head of my Government and not being vested with discretionary power to determine matters of such moment. In the present instance I am not only powerless to accede to your request, but have been strictly enjoined by my Government, mindful of its international promises and national honour, which it has never broken nor sacrificed, not to accede joint occupation of the city and suburbs of Manila and am directed specially to preserve the peace and protect persons and property within the territory surrendered under the terms of the Spanish capitulation. These mandates must be obeyed.

"Thus have I endeavoured with all candor and sincerity, holding nothing in reserve, to place before you the situation as understood by me, and I doubt not by the Republic which I represent. I have not been instructed as to what policy the United States intends to pursue in regard to its legitimate holdings here, and hence I am unable to give you any information on the subject. That it will have a care and labor conscientiously for the welfare of your people I sincerely believe. It remains for you, beneficiaries of its sacrifices, to adopt a course of action which will manifest your good intentions and show to the world the principles which actuate your proceedings.

* * * * * * *

"It only remains for me to respectfully notify you that I am compelled by my instructions to direct that your armed forces evacuate the entire city of Manila, including its suburbs and defences, and that I shall be obliged to take action with that end in view within a very short space of time should you decline to comply with my Government's demands; and I hereby serve notice on you that unless your troops are withdrawn beyond the line of the city's defences before Thursday, the 15th instant, I shall be obliged to resort to forcible action, and that my Government will hold you responsible for any unfortunate consequences which may ensue.

* * * * * * *

"In conclusion, I beg to inform you that I have conferred freely with Admiral Dewey upon the contents of this communication and am delegated by him to state that he fully approves of the same in all respects; that the commands of our Government compel us to act as herein indicated, and that between our respective forces there will be unanimity and complete concert of action."

This calm and temperate discussion of the situation, coupled with the firm statement of intention with which it closed, produced a decided effect on Aguinaldo. Concerning the events to which it led, General Otis has made this statement: —

"On September 13, a commission sent by Aguinaldo and consisting of three members, one of whom was the treasurer and another the attorney-general of the insurgent government, called for the purpose of discussing the subject of my letter of the 8th. They asked me to withdraw it and simply request in writing that the insurgent troops retire to the line designated by General Merritt, which I refused to do, stating that unless they withdrew as directed we would be obliged to resort to force. They then asked that I withdraw the letter and issue a request unaccompanied by any threat to use force, as Aguinaldo was fearful that he would be unable to remove his troops upon a demand. To which I replied that the letter of the 8th instant would stand. They then said that as the demands of that letter must remain unchanged, the insurgents would withdraw as directed therein, but that if I would express in writing a simple request to Aguinaldo to withdraw to the lines which I designated — something which he could show to the troops and induce them to think that he was simply acting upon a request from these headquarters — he would probably be able to retire his men without much difficulty; that, of course, they themselves understood the direction to withdraw, which would be obeyed, and thereupon repeated their desire to obtain a note of request, whereupon I furnished them with the following: —

"'OFFICE U. S. MILITARY GOVERNOR IN THE
"'PHILIPPINE ISLANDS,
"'MANILA, P. I., September 13, 1898.

"'THE COMMANDING GENERAL OF THE PHILIPPINE FORCES:

"'SIR: Referring to my communication of September 8, I have the honour to inform you that I have had a most agreeable conversation with certain gentlemen who are in the interests of your revolutionary government upon the matters therein contained. We have discussed at length the complications now existing, which will exist, and will doubtless increase, while our troops continue to occupy jointly certain districts of the city of Manila. I have urged upon them the necessity of the withdrawal of your troops in order that the friendly relations

AN UNIMPROVED STREET IN THE FILIPINO QUARTER OF MANILA.

The condition of the streets formerly made it impossible to remove night-soil and garbage from this district, and cholera was rampant there when this photograph was taken.

which have always been maintained by and between them and the forces of the United States Government may be perpetuated. I am sure that the gentlemen fully appreciate my sentiments and will clearly report them to you. May I ask you to patiently listen to their report of our conversation?

" ' It is my desire that our friendly intercourse and mutual amicable relations be continued; that they be not jeopardized if we can by consistent action avoid it, and such, I am certain, is the desire of yourself and associates.

" ' May I ask, therefore, that you withdraw your troops from Manila?

" ' Permit me to add in conclusion that I have that confidence in your ability and patriotism which will lead you to accede to this request.

" ' I am, with great respect, your most obedient servant,
(Signed) " ' E. S. OTIS,
" ' Major-General, U. S. V.,
" ' United States Military Governor in the Philippines.'

" In reply to which, on the 16th, the following was received : —

" ' MALOLOS, BULACAN, September 16, 1898.

" ' THE COMMANDING GENERAL OF THE AMERICAN FORCES :

" ' MY DEAR SIR : Referring to your esteemed communication, dated the 13th instant, I have the honour to inform you that I have given appropriate orders that my troops should abandon their most advanced positions within some of the suburbs, and that they should retire to points where contact with yours would be more difficult, in order to avoid all occasion for conflict.

" ' I hope that by these presents you will be fully convinced of my constant desire to preserve amicable relations with the American forces, even at the risk of sacrificing a part of the confidence placed in my government by the Philippine people.

" ' A consideration of my many occupations will serve to excuse me for not having answered with the promptness desired.

" ' Your very respectful servant,
(Signed) " ' EMILIO AGUINALDO.'

" On the evening of the 15th the armed insurgent organizations withdrew from the city and all of its suburbs, as acknowledged by their leaders, excepting from one small outlying district. This certain agents of Aguinaldo asked on the previous day to be permitted to retain for a short time, on the plea that the general officer in command[1] would not obey instructions, and they proposed to remove his men gradually by organizations and thereafter to punish him for his disobedience. The withdrawal was effected adroitly, as the insurgents marched out in excellent spirits, cheering the American troops."[2]

I have given the facts thus fully for the reason that this is the one instance I have found in which a promise was made, fortunately in the form of an offer which was not accepted, and then withdrawn. It has seemed to me that the reasons why General Merritt should never have made it, and why General Otis could not possibly have renewed it, should be fully set forth.

On September 7, 1898, General Otis had cabled to Washington that Admiral Dewey and he considered conditions critical, and that the number of armed Insurgents in the city was large and rapidly increasing. He stated that on the 8th he would send a notification to Aguinaldo that unless the latter's troops were withdrawn beyond the line of the suburbs of the city before September 15 he would be obliged to resort to forcible action and that the United States would hold Aguinaldo responsible for any unfortunate consequences which might ensue.

Aguinaldo still hoped to obtain recognition of his government by the United States, but did not consider such recognition probable, and pushed preparations to attack if a favorable opportunity should offer.

Before occupying ourselves with these preparations, let us briefly review the results of our investigations as to Insurgent coöperation with the American forces up to this time.

Taylor has made the following excellent summary of the case : —

"Up to this time Aguinaldo had continued a desultory warfare with the Spanish troops in Manila. That none of his

---

[1] Pío del Pilar.
[2] Report of the War Department, 1899, Vol. I, part IV, pp. 5–10.

attacks were very serious is shown from the Spanish reports of casualties; but although he had failed to secure the surrender of the city to himself, he had kept its garrison occupied and within their works. The American force on land was now strong enough to begin offensive operations. So far the relations between the Americans and Aguinaldo had not been really friendly. They were in his way, and yet he could not break with them, for he hoped to use them for the attainment of the designs which he had by this time frankly declared. The Americans had listened to these declarations, and had not answered them, nor was it possible to answer them. The American forces were there under the instructions of the President to make war on Spain and to establish a military government in the Philippines. Aguinaldo had declared himself a dictator and the Philippines independent. To have recognized him in his civil capacity, to have dealt with him in his civil capacity, would have meant a recognition of his government by the military commander in the field — a thing impossible and unlawful. Officers of the United States forces are not empowered to recognize governments; that function is reserved to the President of the United States; and in this case he, in his orders to the Secretary of War, dated May 19, copies of which were forwarded to General Merritt for his guidance, informed him that the army of occupation was sent to the Philippines 'for the twofold purpose of completing the reduction of the Spanish power in that quarter and of giving order and security to the islands while in the possession of the United States.' These instructions contemplated the establishment of a military government in the archipelago by military officials of the United States.

*   *   *   *   *   *   *

"It is true that in spite of the date of these instructions General Merritt in San Francisco had received no copy of them on August 28, three days after the departure of General Anderson, and what that officer knew of them could only have been what General Merritt remembered of the contents of an unsigned copy of them shown him at the White House, but they were in accordance with the practice of the United States Government in occupying conquered territory, that practice General Anderson well knew, and his relations with Aguinaldo were guided by it.

*   *   *   *   *   *   *

"It has been claimed that Aguinaldo and his followers received the impression at this time from their conversation with American officers that the United States would undoubtedly recognize the independence of the Philippines, and that the coöperation of the insurgents was due to this impression. There was no coöperation. That he attempted in vain to secure the surrender of Manila to himself was not coöperation. That he refrained from attacking the Americans and occasionally permitted them to be furnished supplies, for which they paid, was not coöperation. The fact that for a time their plans and his plans were parallel does not mean coöperation. Aguinaldo was forced by the exigencies of the situation, by the necessity of strengthening his hold upon the people, by the necessities of his operations against the Spaniards, to make Spaniards and natives alike believe that all that he did was with the aid of the Americans by whom he would be supported in all his acts. He needed their support, and if he could not obtain that he needed the appearance of their support for the attainment of his ends; and this he was forced to purchase by compliance, or apparent compliance, with their demands. But his compliance with them, as all American officers serving there well knew, was never willing, was never complete, and was never given except under pressure. It is true that writers upon the subject, speaking with the confidence which is born of insufficient and incomplete information, assure their readers that any government but that of the United States, any colonial administrators but Americans, would have been able to obtain the hearty coöperation of Aguinaldo and his followers by judicious concessions to them at this time. The only concession which would have obtained that hearty coöperation would have been the recognition of the independence of the Philippines under a United States protectorate, of Aguinaldo clothed with the plenitude of the powers of the Katipúnan as dictator, and a promise to promptly withdraw from the islands. This promise the Government of the United States could not make. Until the ratification of a treaty of peace with Spain the insurgents of the Philippine Islands were rebellious subjects of Spain, and with them, except as fighting men, no relations could be had.

*   *   *   *   *   *   *

"No report of operations or returns of strength were rendered by Aguinaldo at this or any other time to any American commander, and no American commander ever rendered such returns to him. At the time of General Merritt's arrival, and until Manila was occupied by the Americans, the insurgents and United States troops were united solely by the fact that they had Manila as a common objective. Conditions were such that the Americans, in order to obtain its surrender, had to avoid doing anything which might cause the insurgents to attack them and perhaps make terms with Spain; while Aguinaldo and his followers, in order to accomplish the surrender of Manila to themselves, had to maintain such relations with the Americans as would induce the Spaniards to believe that their fleet was at his disposal,[1] and also such apparent harmony and coöperation with them in the execution of their plans that the recalcitrant among the Filipinos would be forced to believe that the Americans would in all ways use their forces to support Aguinaldo in the attainment of his desires.

"General Merritt saw this and the necessity for immediately taking such steps as would lead to his occupation of Manila. With the arrival of the third expedition he was able to pass through the insurgent lines between Camp Dewey and Manila, for he had sufficient force to accept no refusal from Aguinaldo.

"In his report he said that the insurgents had obtained positions of investment opposite the Spanish lines along their full extent, and that on the bay front their lines ran within 800 yards of San Antonio Abad. The approaches to the beach and village of Pasay were in their possession.

"'This anomalous state of affairs, namely, having a line of quasi-hostile native troops between our forces and the Spanish position, was, of course, very objectionable, but it was difficult to deal with owing to the peculiar conditions of our relations with the insurgents. . . . As General Aguinaldo did not visit me on my arrival nor offer his services as a subordinate military leader, and as my instructions from the President fully contemplated the occupation of the islands by the American land forces, and stated that "the powers of the military occupant are absolute and supreme and immediately operate upon the political condition of the inhabitants," I did not consider it wise to hold any direct communication with the insurgent leader until I should be in possession of the city of Manila, especially as I would not until then be in a position to issue a proclamation and enforce my authority in the event that his pretensions should clash with my designs. For these reasons the preparations for the attack on the city were pressed and the military operations conducted without reference to the situation of the insurgent forces. The wisdom of this course was subsequently fully established by the fact that when the troops at my command carried the Spanish entrenchments, extending from the sea to the Pasay road on the extreme Spanish right, we were

---

[1] See Buencamino's letter to Jáudines, p. 108.

under no obligation, by prearranged plans of the mutual attack, to turn to the right and clear the front still held by the insurgents, but were able to move forward at once and occupy the city and the suburbs.'" [1]

All that the Insurgents and the Americans ever had in common was an enemy. They each fought that enemy in their own way. There was no coöperation. On the part of the Insurgents there was treachery. I will submit further evidence of this fact.

[1] Taylor 36 AJ. *et seq.*

CHAPTER IV

The Premeditated Insurgent Attack

It will be remembered that the minutes of the session of the Hong Kong junta at which Aguinaldo reported the result of his negotiations with Pratt and received his instructions relative to the trip to Manila, recorded the fact that there would be no better occasion for the expeditionary forces "to arm themselves at the expense of the Americans," and that provided with arms the Filipino people would be able to oppose themselves to the United States and combat their demands if they attempted to colonize the country.[1]

The possible, if not the probable, desirability of attacking the United States troops was, it is evident, clearly foreseen from the beginning. Active preparations for doing this now soon began.

Although Insurgent officers in full uniform freely visited Manila at all times, Aguinaldo wrote on October 1 to his commander in Laguna Province that he must not permit Americans there without passes. He was to get rid of them civilly, but he was to keep them out and inform all authorities there of his instructions.

On August 24 an American soldier was killed and others were wounded in Cavite by Insurgent troops who fired from behind. An Insurgent officer in Cavite at the time reported on his record of services that he —

"took part in the movement against the Americans on the afternoon of the 24th of August, under the orders of the commander of the troops and the adjutant of the post."

[1] See p. 41.

127

This shows that the movement was ordered, but the Insurgents promptly realized that it was ill advised.

On August 28 General Llanera was reported to be preparing for operations against the Americans. He was ordered to suspend his preparations. The same day General P. Mercado Rizal, commanding in Laguna Province, wrote Mabini asking whether they were to consider the Americans as their allies or their enemies. He wanted to know whether the war was to stop or continue becoming more furious. This not because he desired to ask questions about the secrets of the government, but because he wished to prepare the minds of the people for the future. Mabini's answer has not been found.

We have already noted that on August 8 Fernando Acevedo wrote General Pío del Pilar recommending that he attack and annihilate the American troops; that on August 10 Pilar wrote Aguinaldo suggesting that the Americans be attacked, and that on August 17 Aguinaldo stated: "The conflict is coming sooner or later."[1]

At this time Sandico entered the service of the Americans as an interpreter and acted as a spy, endeavouring to keep his people fully informed relative to the plans and acts of his employers. Incidentally he endeavoured to convince the latter that the barbarities really committed by Insurgent officers and troops in Manila were perpetrated by enemies of the Insurgent cause who wished to discredit it.

In a letter dated September 21, 1898, Apacible says that the conflict will come sooner or later and asks Aguinaldo if it would not be better for them to provoke it before the Americans concentrate their troops.[2]

[1] P. I. R., 427. 1.
[2] "The insolent commentary of the American Consul here, if it is true, clearly shows the intention of America to impose her will upon us by force. In this case, the conflict will come sooner or later. Would it not be better for us to provoke the conflict while the Americans

AN IMPROVED STREET IN THE FILIPINO QUARTER OF MANILA.

The construction of such streets and drains makes it possible successfully to combat disease.

On September 10 General Garcia reported to Aguinaldo that on the previous night the Americans had attempted to push back his line at San Lazaro, and that morning had concentrated and penetrated the Insurgent territory, making a reconnaissance through the fields about Sampaloc. Aguinaldo put an indorsement on this communication saying that he had long since ordered that the Insurgent line should not be passed. He instructed Garcia to throw troops in front of the Americans at Sampaloc, and order them to leave, and to warn the bolo men. Obviously, little more was needed to provoke an Insurgent attack.[1]

An unsigned draft of an order in Aguinaldo's handwriting dated Malolos, September 13 (?), 1898,[2] shows how tense was the situation while the question of withdrawal of the Insurgent forces from the city of Manila was under consideration. It contains instructions for General Pío del Pilar, General P. Garcia and General Noriel or Colonel Cailles. Their purpose is hardly open to doubt.

General Pío del Pilar was directed : —

"To have a detachment posted in the interval from the branch of the river of Paco in a northerly direction to the bridge and so on up to the Pasig river in the direction of Pandacan, the river serving as a line until the suburb of Panque is reached which will be under our jurisdiction. Proceed to exe-

have not as yet concentrated their troops there? Or would it be better to wait for the results of the Congress of Paris? This question should be answered immediately by the committee on foreign relations of the Congress of representatives and the decision should be sent at once to us so that we can proceed according to your instructions."
— P. I. R., 453. 11.

[1] "I gave an order long ago not to permit our line to be passed, and to say frankly that it was by my order. To be prepared to defend our rights you are ordered to place troops in front of American position at Sampaloc and to tell them plainly to leave, to warn the Sandatahan [bolo men. — D. C. W.] and get everything ready; you must warn the commanders of the zones about Manila. Do not forget, whenever in doubt." — P. I. R., 849.

[2] P. I. R., 88. 9.

cute this order on its receipt, posting detachments where they are necessary and trenches will be made without loss of time working day and night.   Do not rest for by doing so we may lose the opportunity ; beg of the troops to assist in the formation of intrenchments.   Matters have a bad aspect, we especially expect something Wednesday and Thursday, the 15th and 16th of this month.   The danger is imminent on the mentioned days, also in the time that follows.

" Keep strict vigilance at all hours.   In case you receive orders to leave that place, do not do so on any account without my orders, happen what may. . . .

" Concentrate all your forces in Santa Ana before the day arrives.

" Warn your soldiers against firing at random as the Spaniards did, if possible have them calculate the number of their antagonists and how much ammunition there is in comparison with the number of the attacking force, in fact, there are occasions when each shot fired kills as many as four men.

" I hope you will see to the execution of these instructions and that you will maintain the honour of the Philippines by your courage and in no way permit your rights to be trampled underfoot." [1]

General Garcia was instructed as follows : —

"On Wednesday, the 14th of this month, you will post detachments in the points indicated by lines on the enclosed plan. On receipt of this and as soon as you learn its contents, proceed secretly to determine the most suitable places to post detachments and immediately post our troops and have intrenchments made employing day and night in this work.   Beg this of our soldiers." [2]

The instructions to Noriel or Cailles read as follows : —

"At eight o'clock in the morning of Wednesday, the 14th, withdraw your command from the town of Malate as indicated on the enclosed plan, from the bridge in Singalong and in a straight line from there to the branch of the river in Paco will be the line of our jurisdiction even though we may not be of one mind in the matter.   On receipt of this proceed to determine the most suitable places to post our troops even if they are not supplied with batteries ; on posting the detachments give instructions to have intrenchments made immediately without

[1] P. I. R., 88. 9.   [2] *Ibid.*

resting, especially on the days of the 15th and 16th. Since affairs have a serious aspect, do not lose vigilance and be on the alert at all times. . . .

"Concentrate all the forces and have a call to arms in Cavite so that all the troops may be in Pasay on Wednesday night.

"In case the Americans attempt to order you out do not leave your posts, happen what may, but exercise prudence and be prepared leaving them to give the provocation. Answer them that you have no instructions given you with regard to what they ask." [1]

Obviously the maintenance of peace at this time hung by a very slender thread. On September 14 the governor of Cavite telegraphed Aguinaldo as follows : —

"Most urgent. I desire to know from you the result of the ultimatum. Advise me if we must prepare our troops for action to-morrow. I await a reply." [2]

But war was not to begin at this time. On September 23 Bray wrote to Aguinaldo advising him to maintain a defensive attitude until the result of the negotiations at Paris should become known, giving way to the Americans and not showing his teeth. He could take the offensive later if advisable and should have little difficulty in settling accounts with the American soldiers. [3]

Bray suggested the possibility of an alliance between the American and the Spanish soldiers if a conflict should arise before the departure of the latter. [4]

[1] P. I. R., 88. 9.   [2] *Ibid.*, 849.

[3] "Until the decision of the Paris Congress is known, all of us here are of the opinion that you should maintain a defensive attitude regarding the Americans, giving way to them with regard to Manila and its suburbs or in anything they may wish, although apparently only, and not show them your teeth. After the decision of the Congress is known, you may take the offensive if advisable, and according to the information we may have of the American soldiers it should not be difficult for you and your army to settle accounts with them."

                        —P. I. R., 398. 6.

[4] "If you and the Americans should happen to come in conflict before the departure of the Spanish soldiers, it might happen that the Yankees would enter into an alliance with them to combat the Filipinos. Think well over this." — P. I. R., 398. 6.

Meanwhile preparations for the attack progressed. During September, Sandico wrote Aguinaldo suggesting the urgent necessity of reorganizing the "masons" and the Katipúnan,[1] and that all be furnished with knives, to be kept hidden so that they might be "ready for any event."

In spite of efforts to keep the Insurgent soldiers in hand, feeling among them ran high, and they wanted to fight.[2] On November 30, 1898, General Mascardo telegraphed from San Fernando to Aguinaldo asking if he might begin firing in order to prevent the American troops from disembarking, and Aguinaldo promptly answered in the affirmative.[3]

On December 5 Malvar telegraphed from Lipa that according to a despatch from Batangas, American divers were working unceasingly and that a subordinate had ordered that they be fired on if they attempted to land. Aguinaldo replied that he did not mind their working at sea, but that they must not be allowed to land under any circumstances.[4]

---

[1] "It is also of urgent necessity, Señor President, to reëstablish committees in all the suburbs and that the masons and the Katipúnan be reorganized, and it is advisable that all be provided with knives ready for any event, but it is proper that these arms be hidden." — P. I. R., 466. 9.

[2] "Our soldiers are always desirous of fighting in order to bring affairs to an end, as they are very resentful with regard to the evacuation of the suburbs mentioned." — P. I. R., Books C–1.

[3] "Most urgent. Have received telegraphic order from War Dept., which says: 'Prevent American troops from disembarking.' In case they insist what am I to do? May I begin firing?"

This telegram was indorsed by Aguinaldo: —

"Answered affirmatively December 1, 1898." — P. I. R., 849.

[4] "Most urgent. According to despatch from Captain detached at Batangas, American divers are working unceasingly. He says that he ordered them to be fired on in case they try to land. Await your reply."

Aguinaldo's reply ran as follows: —

"I do not mind their working at sea, but you must under no conditions allow them to land troops; be brave for the sake of your Tagálog heart. Approve your action." — P. I. R., 1179. 2.

On December 6 Sandico telegraphed Aguinaldo as follows: —

"The difficulty of last night at the San Juan picket with the American troops has been adjusted without prejudice. Our preparations ought to continue. Awaiting orders." [1]

San Juan was where the firing commenced on February 4, 1899.

On December 9 Cailles wired Aguinaldo as follows: —

"Report to you that there are 3000 Americans in front of our position at Singalong. I do not know what they wish; if they enter Pineda I open fire." [2]

By this time the Insurgents had made up their minds that the Americans, who had been bearing their insults in silence, were cowards. Aguinaldo's indorsement on this telegram reads: —

"Answered: Nevertheless the 3000 American soldiers are few against my Colonel and his 300 soldiers, and I believe you have more than that number. E. A., Dec. 12, 1898." [3]

Relative to the insults which were at this time showered upon Americans, Taylor has made the following statement: [4] —

"Fortune had been good to Aguinaldo and his associates in the eight months during which the United States had prevented Spain from relieving her beleaguered garrisons in the Philippines, and she might still be kind. The men about Aguinaldo who had risen farthest and fastest could not endure the thought of having to accept subordinate positions in a government not directed by themselves. The halberdiers at the door of the palace of the president saluted them as the halberdiers at the doorway of his lordship the governor-general in Manila had struck the marble steps with their halberds at the coming of the Spanish generals. They swaggered down the streets of Malolos, clashing their swords behind them, and they knew that if they won, the Philippines would be divided into fiefs which they, as dukes and marquises, would hold in feudal tenure from a Malay potentate. They were confident. They

---

[1] P. I. R., 849.   [2] *Ibid.*   [3] *Ibid.*   [4] 56 AJ.

held Luzón. They held the people. They had no intention
of returning to office stools or to the life of outlaws and hunted
men. The United States force in Manila was small and
America was far. It was true that they might have to fight for
the prize which they had seized, but the military leaders about
Aguinaldo were confident of winning in case they fought. They
believed the Americans were afraid of them and would be easily
beaten. American soldiers had been seized and had been insulted by the followers of Aguinaldo and no resort had been
made to force. The Americans had been ordered to avoid
bringing on an engagement and had obeyed. It is also probable
that many of the insults to which they had been subjected were
not appreciated by them. A tall soldier from western America
paid no attention to the insults hurled at him in a language
which he did not understand. And yet the small excited Filipinos might retire feeling that the American had tamely submitted to insult worse than a blow."

By the middle of December, Aguinaldo had placed in
position in the vicinity of Manila all of the field guns in
his possession.

The Treaty of Paris was signed on December 10. It
provided for the termination of Spanish sovereignty in
the Philippines. This was what the Insurgents had been
waiting for, and thereafter things moved rapidly. It is
obvious that an attack was definitely planned for at this
time, for on December 21, Commandant F. E. Rey telegraphed Aguinaldo that the second chief of the second
zone of Manila had directed him to assist by entering
that city as soon as they opened fire against the American
troops.[1]

On the following day Cailles reported that he had
occupied blockhouse No. 12, which was within the
American lines, and added the following significant
statement : —

---

[1] "We are constantly alarmed here by American troops who wish
to come within the military line. To-day received word from second
chief, second zone, Manila, that as soon as they opened fire against
the American troops I assist by entering Manila. I have no orders
in this matter; I await your directions." — P. I. R., 849.

"The order of yesterday was, on hearing the first shots from Santa Ana, for my whole force to hurl themselves on the American line of trenches, and to follow the living to Manila. The dead can lie with the dead. Yesterday we were content waiting for the arming of the San Quintin." [1]

San Quintin's Day was the anniversary of the Sicilian vespers, the massacre of the French in Sicily in 1268. Obviously the Insurgents were planning something similar for Manila.

For some reason the attack was not made as planned, but there was no intention of abandoning it. Within fifteen days of January 1 some 40,000 Filipinos left Manila. Why? On January 7, Aguinaldo wrote to Señor Benito Legarda at Manila, saying: —

"I beg you to leave Manila with your family and come here to Malolos, but not because I wish to frighten you — I merely wish to warn you for your satisfaction, although it is not yet the day or the week." [2]

Many details of the plan of attack have come into our possession. Doctor Manuel Xeres Burgos wrote Aguinaldo during January relative to a plan for an uprising of the prisoners in Bilibid Prison, saying that it should by all means come "before the movement is begun anywhere else," and calling attention to the necessity of stationing men to prevent the American soldiers near by in the Zorilla theatre from coming to the rescue. On the back of this letter there is a sketch plan showing where bolo men were to be stationed, ready to attack these soldiers. [3]

[1] P. I. R., 849.

[2] Taylor, 70 AJ.

[3] "It is absolutely necessary that an order be received here permitting the uprising of those in prison before the movement is begun anywhere else; in the prison the word shall be given at the moment the bugle sounds retreat; it is indispensable that some of our party be prepared in the vicinity of the Iris bridge, San Pedro street and Dulumbrayan bridge, in order to prevent the Americans quartered in the Pennsylvania barracks (Zorilla theatre) from aiding those in the prison." — P. I. R., 73. 3.

In his message to Congress dated January 1, 1899, Aguinaldo said : —

"I consider arguments unnecessary in support of the proposed amendments, every one knows that our newborn Republic now has to fight for its existence against giants in ambition and in power." [1]

An unsigned letter addressed to Apacible on January 4, 1899, contains the following statement : —

"It appears that conflict with the Americans is imminent and inevitable. Several of their vessels with thousands of soldiers commanded by General Miller were sent to Iloilo on December 20th last to take that port together with the whole of Visayas and Mindanao." [2]

On January 4 the following significant telegram was sent out : —

"Circular Telegram from the Secretary of the Interior to Provincial Presidents, wherever there may be Telegraphic Service, to be communicated to the Local Chiefs of each Town.

"MALOLOS, January 4, 1899, 9.35 A.M.
"To the Provincial President of the Province of Pangasinán :
"Hasten the preparation of all the towns in order to oppose the American invasion. See that all the inhabitants prepare their bolos and daggers; also that in each street and barrio national militia is organized, each six of whom should be commanded by a corporal, each thirteen by a sergeant, each twenty-six by a second lieutenant, each fifty-two by a first lieutenant, and each one hundred and four by a captain, directing that the soldiers of the national militia elect their own officers, informing all that upon our attitude depends our salvation.

"LINGAYEN, January 4, 1899."

There is a note thereon which reads : —

"Communicate this to all of the local chiefs, and to the commanding general."

(Signed by initials which are illegible, but evidently those of the Provincial President.) [3]

[1] P. I. R., 40. 8.   [2] *Ibid.*, Books C–1.   [3] *Ibid.*, 1141. 3.

DISINFECTING BY THE ACRE.

During the last cholera epidemic chemical fire engines were used to disinfect whole native sections of Manila.

On January 5, 1899, Aguinaldo issued a proclamation which contains the following statement : —

"The said generals accepted my concessions in favor of peace and friendship as indications of weakness. Thus it is, that with rising ambition, they ordered forces to Iloilo on December 26, with the purpose of acquiring for themselves the title of conquerors of that portion of the Philippine Islands occupied by my govermnent.

* * * * * * *

"My government cannot remain indifferent in view of such a violent and aggressive seizure of a portion of its territory by a nation which has arrogated to itself the title, 'champion of oppressed nations.' Thus it is that my government is ready to open hostilities if the American troops attempt to take forcible possession of the Visayan Islands. I announce these rights before the world, in order that the conscience of mankind may pronounce its infallible verdict as to who are the true oppressors of nations and the tormentors of human kind.

"Upon their heads be all the blood which may be shed." [1]

Three days later this proclamation, which was rather dangerously like a declaration of war, was reissued with a significant change in the last one of the passages quoted, the words "attempt to take forcible possession of any part of the territory submitted to its jurisdiction" being substituted for the words "attempt to take forcible possession of the Visayan Islands."

On January 8, 1899, at 9.40 P.M., Sandico telegraphed Aguinaldo as follows : —

"NOTE. — In consequence of the orders of General Rios to his officers, as soon as the Filipino attack begins the Americans should be driven into the Intramuros district and the Walled city should be set on fire." [2]

Preparations for the attack, which was to begin inside the city of Manila, were now rapidly pushed to conclusion. I quote Taylor's excellent summary of them : —

"After Aguinaldo's proclamation of January 5 the number of organizations charged with an attack within the city in-

[1] P. I. R., 1186. 10.   [2] *Ibid.*, 849.

creased rapidly and it is possible that those which had been formed during Spanish rule had never been disbanded.   Sandico's clubs for athletic exercises and mutual improvement formed a nucleus for these bodies and the directing boards of the popular committees took up the work of recruiting, while some of the members became officers of the militia or sandatahan.   On January 6 the commander of militia in Trozo, Manila, reported that 1130 soldiers had been enrolled by the popular committee.   On January 7 Bonifacio Arévalo forwarded to the head of the central committee a list of the officers of the battalion which had just been organized in Sampaloc for the defence of their liberties.   Apparently about the same time J. Limjap submitted to Sandico a project for arming the prisoners in Bilibid Prison with the arms of the American soldiers quartered in the Zorrilla Theatre across the street.   He said : —

"'Jacinto Limjap having been proclaimed commander of the volunteers of the penitentiary, I ask you to authorize the creation of a disciplinary battalion and the provisional appointments of officers for 600 sandatahan, or militia, ready to provide themselves by force with the American rifles in the Zorrilla Theatre.'

"He followed by a statement of the officers desired.   It was not difficult for him to obtain volunteers there to rob, to burn, to rape and to murder.   These were the crimes for which they were serving sentences.   The political prisoners had been released. . . .

"On January 18 Sandico approved of the officers for the first battalion organized by the committees of Sampaloc ; on January 27 he approved those of the second battalion.   By January 22 two battalions had been organized in Quiapo.   At least one regiment of eight companies was raised in Binondo, for on January 23 its commander forwarded a roll of the officers to Aguinaldo for his approval. . . .   On January 25 T. Sandico, at Malolos, submitted for approval the names of a number of officers of the territorial militia in the city of Manila.   On January 30, 1899, a roll of four companies just organized in Malate was forwarded approved by T. Sandico, and on the same day the committee of Trozo, Manila, applied to T. Sandico for permission to recruit a body for the defence of the country.   The regiment of 'Armas Blancas' had already been raised in Tondo and Binondo.   It was in existence there in December, 1898, and may have been originally organized to act against Spain.   On February 2 all officers of the territorial militia in Manila reported

at Caloocan, in accordance with orders of Sandico, for the purpose of receiving their commissions and taking the oath to the
flag.   A man who took part in this ceremony wrote that a multi-
tude of men were present in uniform, and that the oath was administered by Gen. Pantaleón García.   There is no reason for
believing that this is a complete statement of sandatahan organized in Manila by the end of January, and yet this statement
gives a force of at least 6330 men.   General Otis said that this
force had been reported to him as being 10,000 men.   It is probably true that only a small number of them had rifles ; but
armed with long knives and daggers they could have inflicted
much damage in a sudden night attack in the narrow and
badly lighted streets of Manila.   On January 9, 1899, Aguinaldo wrote his instructions for the sandatahan of Manila.
Members of this body were to enter the houses of the American
officers on the pretext of bringing them presents.   Once in they
were to kill.   The sentinels at the gates of the barracks were to
be approached by men dressed as women and killed.   The gates
of the barracks held and as many officers as possible treacherously murdered, the sandatahan were to rise throughout the
city, and by attacking in the rear the United States troops on
the outer line were to aid in opening a way for Aguinaldo's
force.   To further increase the confusion and perhaps to punish
the natives who had not joined them, the sandatahan were to
fire the city.

*   *   *   *   *   *   *

" It is a fair deduction from Luna's orders for an uprising in
Manila, from Aguinaldo's instructions for the sandatahan,
from other documents among the papers of the insurgents and
from what was done in Manila on February 22 that Aguinaldo
and his advisers about the middle of January, 1899, drew up a
plan of attack upon Manila which would, if carried out, have
inflicted a severe blow upon the Americans.   It was not carried
out, but that was not the fault of Aguinaldo or of Luna.

"It is true that the instructions were general ; but that particular instructions were given by Aguinaldo himself for the
murder of General Otis is shown by his note on the back of a
document presented to him.[1]

". . . And then there was nothing abhorrent to Aguinaldo
and the men about him in beginning a war by the murder of
the commanding general on the other side.

*   *   *   *   *   *   *

[1] See p. 733.

". . . Aguinaldo and all his followers have declared that on February 4 the Americans attacked the unsuspecting Filipinos who were using their utmost efforts to avoid a war.   And yet here in Aguinaldo's own handwriting is the record of the fact that on January 10, 1899, he ordered the murder of the American commander.

"The attack which Aguinaldo was preparing to deliver upon and in Manila was not to be a mere raid such as the bandits of Cavite were in the habit of making upon the defenceless towns.   The plan was a piece of calculated savagery in which murder and outrage were considered means to accomplish a purpose.   The servants were to kill their employers; organized bands, dressed in the dress of civilians, living in the city of Manila under the government of the Americans, in many cases employed by the Americans, were to suddenly fall upon the barracks of the American soldiers and massacre the inmates; all Americans in the streets were to be killed, the city was to be fired and its loot was to be the reward of loyalty to Aguinaldo. If this plan had been carried out no white man and no white woman would have escaped.   The reënforcements from the United States would have arrived to find only the smoking ruins of Manila.   Buencamino had warned General Augustín what the fate of Manila would be if taken by a horde of Indians drunk with victory.   That fate was now deliberately planned for the city.   Aguinaldo planned to occupy the capital not as it had been occupied by the Americans.   He planned to take it as Count Tilly took Magdeburg.

"The authors of this plan were not savages.   Mabini, Sandico, and Luna, Asiatics educated in European schools, were men of trained and subtle minds.   With them cruelty and assassination was not a matter of savage impulse but of deliberate calculation; with them assassination was employed as an effective addition to political propaganda, and murder as an ultimate resource in political manœuvres." [1]

Some portions of Aguinaldo's instructions to the *sandatahan* are particularly worthy of perpetuation, as they illustrate his ideas as to the conduct which should be observed by cultured, patriotic, honourable and very humane men, who were not cruel : —

"ART. 3.   The chief of those who go to attack the barracks should send in first four men with a good present for the Ameri-

[1] Taylor, 68–69 AJ.

can commander.   Immediately after will follow four others who will make a pretence of looking for the same officer for some reason and a larger group shall be concealed in the corners or houses in order to aid the other groups at the first signal.   This wherever it is possible at the moment of attack.

"ART. 4.   They should not, prior to the attack, look at the Americans in a threatening manner.   To the contrary, the attack on the barracks by the sandatahan should be a complete surprise and with decision and courage.   One should go alone in advance in order to kill the sentinel.   In order to deceive the sentinel one of them should dress as a woman and must take great care that the sentinel is not able to discharge his piece, thus calling the attention of those in the barracks.   This will enable his companions who are approaching to assist in the general attack.

"ART. 5.   At the moment of the attack the sandatahan should not attempt to secure rifles from their dead enemies, but shall pursue, slashing right and left with bolos until the Americans surrender, and after there remains no enemy who can injure them, they may take the rifles in one hand and the ammunition in the other.

"ART. 6.   The officers shall take care that on the tops of the houses along the streets where the American forces shall pass there will be placed four to six men, who shall be prepared with stones, timbers, red-hot iron, heavy furniture, as well as boiling water, oil and molasses, rags soaked in coal oil ready to be lighted and thrown down, and any other hard and heavy objects that they can throw on the passing American troops. At the same time in the lower parts of the houses will be concealed the sandatahan, who will attack immediately.   Great care should be taken not to throw glass in the streets, as the greater part of our soldiers go barefooted.   On these houses there will, if possible, be arranged, in addition to the objects to be thrown down, a number of the sandatahan, in order to cover a retreat or to follow up a rout of the enemy's column, so that we may be sure of the destruction of all the opposing forces.

"ART. 7.   All Filipinos, real defenders of their country, should live on the alert to assist simultaneously the inside attack at the very moment that they note the first movement in whatever barrio or suburb, having assurance that all the troops that surround Manila will proceed without delay to force the enemy's line and unite themselves with their brothers in the city.   With such a general movement, so firm and decided against the Americans, the combat is sure to be a short one, and

I charge and order that the persons and goods of all foreigners shall be respected and that the American prisoners shall be treated well.

*　　*　　*　　*　　*　　*　　*

"ART. 9.   In addition to the instructions given in paragraph 6, there shall be in the houses vessels filled with boiling water, tallow, molasses and other liquids, which shall be thrown as bombs on the Americans who pass in front of their houses, or they can make use of syringes or tubes of bamboo.   In these houses shall be the sandatahan who shall hurl the liquids that shall be passed to them by the women and children.

"ART. 10.   In place of bolos or daggers, if they do not possess the same, the sandatahan can provide themselves with lances and arrows with long sharp heads, and these should be shot with great force in order that they may penetrate well into the bodies of the enemy, and these should be so made that in withdrawal from the body the head will remain in the flesh.

*　　*　　*　　*　　*　　*　　*

"ART. 12. . . . . Neither will you forget your sacred oath and immaculate banner; nor will you forget the promises made by me to the civilized nations, whom I have assured that we Filipinos are not savages, nor thieves, nor assassins, nor are we cruel, but on the contrary, that we are men of culture and patriotism, honourable and very humane." [1]

Aguinaldo enjoined order on his subordinates.[2]

The Filipinos were now ready to assume the offensive, but desired, if possible, to provoke the Americans into firing the first shot.   They made no secret of their desire for conflict, but increased their hostile demonstrations and pushed their lines forward into forbidden territory. Their attitude is well illustrated by the following extract from a telegram sent by Colonel Cailles to Aguinaldo on January 10, 1899 : —

"Most urgent.   An American interpreter has come to tell me to withdraw our forces in Maytubig fifty paces.   I shall

[1] P. I. R., 206–207.

[2] "Above all I expect that you will respect the persons and goods of private persons of all nationalities, including the Chinese; that you will treat well the prisoners and grant life to those of the enemy who surrender.   And that you be on the sharp lookout for those traitors and enemies who, by robbery, will seek to mar our victory."

not draw back a step, and in place of withdrawing, I shall advance a little farther. He brings a letter from his general, in which he speaks to me as a friend. I said that from the day I knew that Maquinley (McKinley) opposed our independence I did not want any dealings with any American. War, war, is what we want. The Americans after this speech went off pale." [1]

Aguinaldo approved the hostile attitude of Cailles, for there is a reply in his handwriting which reads : —

"I approve and applaud what you have done with the Americans, and zeal and valour always, also my beloved officers and soldiers there. I believe that they are playing us until the arrival of their reënforcements, but I shall send an ultimatum and remain always on the alert. — E. A. Jan. 10, 1899." [2]

On this same day Aguinaldo commissioned Feliciano Cruz and Severino Quitiongco to assassinate General Otis. [3]

On January 13 Noriel and Cailles telegraphed Aguinaldo as follows : —

"We desire to know results of ultimatum which you mention in your telegram, and we also wish to know what reward our Government is arranging for the forces that will be able first to enter Manila."

This telegram is indorsed in Aguinaldo's handwriting :

"As to the contents of your telegram, those who will be the heroes will have as their rewards a large quantity of money, extraordinary rewards, promotions, crosses of Biak-na-bató, Marquis of Malate, Ermita, Count of Manila, etc., besides the congratulations of our idolizing country on account of their being patriotic, and more, if they capture the regiments with their generals, and, if possible, the chief of them all who represents our future enemies in Manila, which (lot ?) falls to you, or, better said, to General Noriel and Colonel Cailles.

"The ultimatum has not been sent, but it will be within a few days.

(Signed) "E. A.
"MALOLOS, Jan. 14, 1899." [4]

[1] P. I. R., 849.   [2] Ibid.
[3] For the document on which this statement is based see p. 733.
[4] P. I. R., 849.

On January 14, 1899, the people at Aparri shouted: "Death to the Americans," and held a review to celebrate the rupture of friendly relations with the United States.[1]

At this time Aguinaldo had a dream about a victorious attack upon Manila and telegraphed it to some of his officers. General García replied from Caloocan on January 17 that the dream would come true as soon as the conflict with the Americans began.[2]

In January 21, 1899, Aguinaldo was still not quite ready, and ordered that the Filipino soldiers in the walled city keep on good terms with the Americans, in order to deceive them, "since the hoped-for moment has not yet arrived."[3]

The Insurgents grew surer and surer that the Americans were cowards,[4] and openly boasted that when the attack began they would drive them into the sea.

[1] Taylor, 81 AJ.

[2] "In reply to your telegram concerning your dream of entering Manila after four hours of combat. I have the honour to inform you for myself and the officers and soldiers under my command that your dream will come true as soon as the conflict with the Americans begins, since we shall advance at any cost." — P. I. R., 849.

[3] On January 21, 1899, the commander of the fourth zone, Caloocan, wired Aguinaldo that:

"Julian Santo, commander of the territorial militia of Trozo, informs me that 400 native soldiers of the Spanish army to-day incorporated in his militia. He lives in the walled city, and he wants to know your opinion upon the present situation, since the Americans want to hold them as prisoners or confine them in Bilibid prison."

(Indorsed, handwriting of Aguinaldo:) "Tell the Filipino soldiers in the walled city affiliated to our cause that they must keep on good terms with the Americans, in order to deceive them, and prevent their confining them, since the hoped-for moment has not yet arrived."
— P. I. R., 849.

[4] On January 20, 1899, a correspondent wrote to one of the Insurgents abroad:

"In some places (in Manila) there have been fights with bolos between Filipinos and Americans who wanted to tear down the proclamation of our president while the people defended it with their bolos. They say that it amuses them to see the Americans run when they draw their knives. It is said that some 10,000 servants have gone on strike. Some Americans have already disappeared by the method of 'dukut' but it will not be proper to publish this in my opinion."
— P. I. R., 980. 82.

AN OLD-STYLE PROVINCIAL JAIL.

Lieutenant Gilmore, of the United States Navy, and his fellow prisoners were detained in this building for a time.

On January 21 General Otis wrote to Admiral Dewey that : —

"The insurgents will not now permit us to cross their lines and have been very insulting to our officers, calling to them that very shortly they will give us battle. My best information is that they have fully determined to attack both outside and within the city before our additional troops arrive, and the least spark may start a conflagration." [1]

As the date of the proposed attack drew near, the work of strengthening the Insurgent positions around Manila was pushed with all possible speed.[2]

About the middle of January General Otis stationed the First Nebraska Regiment upon the high ground at Santa Mesa for sanitary reasons. Of conditions at this time, and of the circumstances leading to the actual outbreak of hostilities Taylor says : —

"During the latter part of January General Otis was informed on good insurgent authority that the insurgents meditated an attack upon those troops, and he was advised to remove them, as in their exposed position they would kill them all. General MacArthur, under whose command the regiment was,

[1] Taylor, AJ. 73.
[2] (Telegram received by E. Aguinaldo :)
"To the President of the Republic, Malolos, from the Provincial Governor of Manila, San Juan del Monte, Jan. 29, 1899, 10.25 A.M. : I yesterday visited the military road in process of construction, Santa Ana to Pineda. To-morrow it will be sufficiently completed to permit passage, and in two days after it will be finished. Considering opening another military road direct from Caloocan to San Juan. Desire authority.
(Indorsed, handwriting of Aguinaldo :) "Telegram received. I am very much satisfied, and in the name of the government I congratulate you and the presidents of Santa Ana and Pineda with their inhabitants for their efforts for the public good. You are authorized to open another military road from Caloocan to San Juan del Monte, and I want you to endeavor to finish it this week, as I am certain you will." — P. I. R., 849.
(Telegram received by E. Aguinaldo :)
"To the Secretary of the Interior, Malolos, from San Juan del Monte — Received Feb. 3, 1899 from the Provincial Governor Manila : Road marked out ; work began Wednesday. I shall put forth every effort to finish by middle of the coming week." — P. I. R., 849.

placed two guns in position there, as it was fully expected that the insurgents would direct their attack upon that point, as in fact they did. On February 4, 1899, the tents of the regiment covered the ridge, and its outposts extended along the San Juan River, a small stream which formed part of the line of delimitation between the Americans and the insurgents.

"For some days before the outbreak of hostilities the pressure of the insurgents was constant along this position, so constant indeed that in the light of subsequent events it indicated a premeditated purpose on the part of some one in the insurgent army to force a collision at that point. On February 2 General MacArthur, commanding the Second Division of the Eighth Army Corps, wrote to the commanding general of the Filipino troops in the third zone in front of him that —

"'An armed party from your command now occupies the village in front of blockhouse No. 7, at a point considerably more than a hundred yards on my side of the line, and is very active in exhibiting hostile intentions. This party must be withdrawn to your side of the line at once. From this date if the line is crossed by your men with arms in their hands they must be regarded as subject to such action as I may deem necessary.'

"Colonel San Miguel, who commanded at San Juan del Monte, replied upon the receipt of this communication that the action of his troops was foreign to his wishes and that he would give immediate orders for them to retire. At about half past 8 on the night of February 4 a small insurgent patrol entered the territory within the American lines at blockhouse No. 7 and advanced to the little village of Santol in front of an outpost of the Nebraska regiment. This was the same point from which the insurgents had been compelled to retire on February 2. An American outpost challenged, and then as the insurgent patrol continued to advance the sentinel fired, whereupon the insurgent patrol retired to blockhouse No. 7, from which fire was immediately opened upon the Americans. This fire spread rapidly down the American and insurgent lines and both forces at once sprang to arms." [1]

General Otis's account of the opening of active hostilities follows : —

"On the night of February 2 they sent in a strong detachment to draw the fire of our outposts, which took up a position

[1] Taylor, 73 AJ.

immediately in front and within a few yards of the same. The outpost was strengthened by a few of our men, who silently bore their taunts and abuse the entire night. This was reported to me by General MacArthur, whom I directed to communicate with the officer in command of the insurgent troops concerned. His prepared letter was shown me and approved, and the reply received was all that could be desired. However, the agreement was ignored by the insurgents and on the evening of February 4 another demonstration was made on one of our small outposts, which occupied a retired position at least 150 yards within the line which had been mutually agreed upon, an insurgent approaching the picket and refusing to halt or answer when challenged. The result was that our picket discharged his piece, when the insurgent troops near Santa Mesa opened a spirited fire on our troops there stationed.

"The insurgents had thus succeeded in drawing the fire of a small outpost, which they had evidently labored with all their ingenuity to accomplish, in order to justify in some way their premeditated attack. It is not believed that the chief insurgent leaders wished to open hostilities at this time, as they were not completely prepared to assume the initiative. They desired two or three days more to perfect their arrangements, but the zeal of their army brought on the crisis which anticipated their premeditated action. They could not have delayed long, however, for it was their object to force an issue before American troops, then en route, could arrive in Manila." [1]

Thus began the Insurgent attack, so long and so carefully planned for. We learn from the Insurgent records that the shot of the American sentry missed its mark. There was no reason why it should have provoked a hot return fire, but it did.

The result of the ensuing combat was not at all what the Insurgents had anticipated. The Americans did not drive very well. It was but a short time before they themselves were routed and driven from their positions.

Aguinaldo of course promptly advanced the claim that his troops had been wantonly attacked. The plain fact is that the Insurgent patrol in question deliberately drew the fire of the American sentry, and this was just as much

[1] Taylor, 73 AJ.

an act of war as was the firing of the shot.   Whether
the patrol was acting under proper orders from higher
authority is not definitely known.

In this connection the following telegram sent by Captain
Zialcita from Santa Ana on February 4, 1899, at 9.55 P.M.,
to Major Gray, San Juan del Monte, is highly interesting :

"I received the telegram forwarded from Malolos.   General
Ricarte is not here.   I believe (that if the) Americans open fire
we shall attack.   Will ask instructions (of) Malolos." [1]

This looks as if Zialcita at least knew that something
was to be done to draw the American fire.

Aguinaldo's first statement relative to the opening of
hostilities is embodied in a general order dated Malolos,
February 4, 1899, and reads in part as follows : —

"Nine o'clock P.M., this date, I received from Caloocan station a message communicated to me that the American forces,
without prior notification or any just motive, attacked our
camp at San Juan del Monte and our forces garrisoning the
blockhouses around the outskirts of Manila, causing losses
among our soldiers, who in view of this unexpected aggression and
of the decided attack of the aggressors, were obliged to defend
themselves until the firing became general all along the line.

"No one can deplore more than I this rupture of hostilities.
I have a clear conscience that I have endeavoured to avoid it
at all costs, using all my efforts to preserve friendship with the
army of occupation, even at the cost of not a few humiliations
and many sacrificed rights.

    *   *   *   *   *   *   *

". . . I order and command : —
"1. Peace and friendly relations between the Philippine
forces and the American forces of occupation are broken, and
the latter will be treated as enemies, with the limits prescribed
by the laws of war.

"2. American soldiers who may be captured by the Philippine forces will be treated as prisoners of war.

"3. This proclamation shall be communicated to the accred-
ited consuls of Manila, and to congress, in order that it may
accord the suspension of the constitutional guarantees and the
resulting declaration of war." [2]

[1] P. I. R., 2018.   [2] Ibid., 1090. 5.

Aguinaldo's protestations relative to his efforts to avoid hostilities are absurd, in view of his own instructions concerning the attack to be made simultaneously within and without the city of Manila.

There is other correspondence which throws light on the situation which existed immediately prior to the outbreak of hostilities. On January 25, 1899, Agoncillo cabled from Washington to Apacible in Hongkong: "Recommend you await beginning American aggression, justifying our conduct nations." [1]

Apacible apparently did not take this view of the matter, for on January 31 he wrote to Aguinaldo that the Senate in Washington would take final vote upon the treaty of peace between the United States and Spain on February 6, and said : —

"It is urgently necessary for America to answer us immediately before the ratification of the treaty. A conflict after the ratification of the treaty would be unfavorable to us in public opinion." [2]

Obviously this letter might be interpreted as a recommendation that hostilities begin before February 6 if America did not answer meanwhile. It was evidently well understood in Hongkong that Aguinaldo's receipt of Apacible's letter might cause war to begin, for on February 3, 1899, Bray, anticipating the outbreak of hostilities of the following day, cabled Senator Hoar at Washington as follows : —

"Receive caution news hostilities Manila discredited here denied Filipino circles supposed political move influence vote Senate to-day any case insignificant skirmish due intentional provocation.

"BRAY." [3]

The extracts from the Insurgent records above quoted leave no escape from the conclusion that the outbreak of hostilities which occurred on February 4, 1899, had been

[1] P. I. R., 453. 4.   [2] P. I. R., 453. 2.   [3] P. I. R., 493. 12.

carefully prepared for and was deliberately precipitated by the Filipinos themselves.

Blount says : —

"It would be simply wooden-headed to affirm that they ever expected to succeed in a war with us." [1]

It may have been wooden-headed for the Filipinos to expect this, but expect it they certainly did. We have seen how they held their soldiers in check until after Spain had been ousted from the Philippines by the Treaty of Paris as they had originally planned to do. It now only remained to carry out the balance of their original plan to get rid of the Americans in one way or another.

General Otis states that "when Aguinaldo had completed his preparations for attack he prepared the outlines of his declaration of war, the full text of which was published at Malolos on the evening, and very shortly after, hostilities began. This declaration was circulated in Manila on the morning of February 5." [2]

The Insurgents brought down upon themselves the punishment which they received on February 4 and 5.

Blount has stated [3] that if the resolutions of Senator Bacon introduced on January 11, 1899, had passed, we never should have had any war with the Filipinos. The resolutions in question concluded thus : —

"That the United States hereby disclaim any disposition or intention to exercise sovereignty, jurisdiction, or control over said islands except for the pacification thereof, and assert their determination when an independent government shall have been duly erected therein entitled to recognition as such, to transfer to said government, upon terms which shall be reasonable and just, all rights secured under the cession by Spain, and to thereupon leave the government and control of the islands to their people."

I must take issue with Blount as to the effect which these resolutions might have had if passed. The Insur-

[1] Blount, p. 190.   [2] Taylor, 86 AJ.   [3] Blount, p. 175.

gents felt themselves to be fully competent to bring about such pacification of the islands as they deemed necessary. At the time the resolutions were presented in the Senate their soldiers were straining at the leash, ready to attack their American opponents upon the most slender excuse. Aguinaldo himself could not have held them much longer, and it is not impossible that they got away from him as it was. They would have interpreted the passage of the Bacon resolutions as a further evidence of weakness, and hastened their attack. As we have seen, "war, war, war" was what they wanted.

Blount has endeavoured to shift the responsibility for the outbreak of hostilities to the United States by claiming that certain words italicized by him in what he calls the "Benevolent Assimilation Proclamation" were necessarily, to the Insurgents, "fighting words." The expressions referred to have to do with the establishment of United States sovereignty and the exercise of governmental control in the Philippine Islands.

These words were not "fighting words," the Insurgent policy being, as I have shown by the records, to consider the acceptance of a protectorate or of annexation in the event that it did not prove possible to negotiate absolute independence, or probable that the American troops could be driven from the islands.

The growing confidence of the Insurgents in their ability to whip the cowardly Americans, rather than any fixed determination on their part to push a struggle for independence to the bitter end, led to their attack.

CHAPTER V

INSURGENT RULE AND THE WILCOX-SARGENT REPORT

THE Good Book says, "By their fruits ye shall know them, whether they be good or evil," and it seems proper to apply this test to the Insurgents and their government.

The extraordinary claim has been advanced that the United States destroyed a republic in the Philippines and erected an oligarchy on its ruins. Various writers and speakers who have not gone so far as this have yet maintained that Aguinaldo and his associates established a real, effective government throughout the archipelago during the interim between his return and the outbreak of hostilities with the United States.

In summarizing conditions on September 15, 1898, Judge Blount says : [1] —

"Absolute master of all Luzon outside Manila at this time, with complete machinery of government in each province for all matters of justice, taxes, and police, an army of some 30,000 men at his beck, and his whole people a unit at his back, Aguinaldo formally inaugurated his permanent government — permanent as opposed to the previous provisional government — with a Constitution, Congress, and Cabinet, patterned after our own,[2] just as the South American republics had done before him when they were freed from Spain, at Malolos, the new capital."

He refers to our utter failure to understand "what a wonderfully complete 'going concern' Aguinaldo's government had become throughout the Philippine Archipelago before the Treaty of Paris was signed." [3]

[1] Blount, p. 98.
[2] The constitution used was most certainly not patterned after our own. See p. 265.
[3] Blount, p. 111.

152

He bases his claim as to the excellent state of public order in the Insurgent territory at this time on a report of Paymaster W. E. Wilcox and Naval Cadet L. R. Sargent of the United States Navy, who between October 8 and November 20, 1898, made a long, rapid trip through northern Luzon, traversing the provinces of Bulacan, Pampanga, Tarlac, Pangasinán, Nueva Ecija, Nueva Vizcaya, Isabela, Cagayan, South Ilocos and Union, in the order named, thence proceeding to Dagupan and down the railroad through Pangasinán, Tarlac, Pampanga and Bulacan to Manila.

He says that these gentlemen found the authority of Aguinaldo's government universally acknowledged, the country in a state of perfect tranquillity and public order,[1] with profound peace and freedom from brigandage and the like.[2]

Now if it be true that Aguinaldo established complete machinery of government throughout all of Luzon outside of Manila for all matters of justice, taxes and police, so that life and property were safe and peace, tranquillity and justice assured, we may well dispense with quibbling as to whether the proper name was applied to such government. But did he?

Let us examine with some care the history of the Wilcox–Sargent trip, and see if we can gain further light from other sources relative to the condition of public order in the territory which they traversed.

I propose, for the most part, to let the captured Insurgent records speak for themselves, as it is fair to assume that Insurgent officers were at no pains to repre-

[1] "The light Messrs. Sargent and Wilcox throw on the then universal acknowledgment of the authority of the Aguinaldo government and the perfect tranquillity and public order maintained under it, in the Cagayan valley." — Blount, pp. 114–115.

[2] "The country in fact, as Aguinaldo always claimed in his proclamations of that period seeking recognition of his government by the Powers, in a state of profound peace and tranquillity — free from brigandage and the like." — Blount, p. 115.

sent conditions as worse than they really were. In view of the fragmentary character of these records, we may also assume that the complete story would be still more interesting and instructive than the one which I have been able to reconstruct.

Messrs. Sargent and Wilcox were almost everywhere hospitably received, and were entertained with dinners and dances after the inimitable fashion of the hospitable Filipino everywhere. They gained a very favourable impression of the state of public order in the provinces through which they passed for the reason that from the very start their trip was strictly personally conducted. They saw exactly what it was intended that they should see and very little more. Their progress was several times interrupted for longer or shorter periods without adequate explanation. We now know that on these occasions the scenery so carefully prepared in advance for them had become a little disarranged and needed to be straightened up. Facts which I will cite show that most shocking and horrible events, of which they learned nothing, were occurring in the territory through which they passed.

For a considerable time before their departure American visitors had been carefully excluded from the Insurgent territory, but the Filipino leaders decided to let these two men go through it to the end that they might make as favourable a report as possible. How carefully the way was prepared for American visitors is shown by the following telegram : —

"SAN PEDRO, MACATI,
"July 30, 1898.

"To the Local Presidente of Pasig :

"You are hereby informed that the Americans are going to your town and they will ask your opinion [of what the people desire. — Tr.] You should answer them that we want a republican government. The same answer must be given throughout your jurisdiction.

(Signed)   "Pío DEL PILAR,
"General of the Second Zone."[1]

[1] P. I. R., 958. 11

RETREAT AT BILIBID PRISON, MANILA.

Now General Pilar had an uncomfortable way of killing people who did not obey his orders, and under the rules of the Insurgent government he was abundantly justified in so doing. His suggestions as to what visiting Americans should be told or shown would be likely to be acceded to. Certainly this seems to have been the case in the present instance, for on the same day General Noriel reported as follows : [1] —

"President R. G., Bacoor, from Gen. Noriel, Pineda, July 30, 12.10 P.M. : I inform your excellency that some commissioners of the American admiral are making investigations in the region around Pasay as to the wishes and opinion of the people as to the government. To-day I received a statement from some, giving the answer : 'Free government under American protectorate [copy mutilated, two or three words missing here] the President.'"

Blount quotes with approval Admiral Dewey's statement made shortly after the return of Wilcox and Sargent that in his opinion their report "contains the most complete and reliable information obtainable in regard to the present state of the northern part of Luzon Island." [2] This was true.

The admiral might have gone further and said that it contained practically the only information then obtainable in regard to conditions in the territory in question, but as I shall conclusively show it was neither complete nor reliable.

Judge Blount in describing the experiences of Messrs. Wilcox and Sargent naïvely makes the statement that :

"The tourists were provided at Rosales by order of Aguinaldo with a military escort, 'which was continued by relays all the way to Aparri.'" [3]

It certainly was !

Very little Spanish was then spoken in Nueva Vizcaya, Isabela or Cagayan. What opportunity had these two

[1] P. I. R., 849.   [2] Blount, p. 108.   [3] *Ibid.*, p. 109.

men, ignorant as they were of the native dialects, to learn the sinister facts as to what had been and was occurring in the territory which they visited?

No one can fail to be delighted with Filipino hospitality, which was lavishly bestowed upon them everywhere, and it is only natural that they should have reported favourably upon what they saw. It was about this time that an order was issued [1] that fronts of buildings should be whitewashed, streets cleaned and fences repaired with a view to showing every one, and especially travellers through the territory of the Insurgents, that they were "not opposed to a good such as a refined and civilized people should have." Doubtless the report of the two men from Dewey's fleet was made in the best of faith. I will now endeavour to show what were some of the actual conditions in the territory through which they passed.

Bulacan

They first visited Bulacan. They do not mention hearing of the activities of a Chinaman named Ignacio Paua, who had been given the rank of colonel by Aguinaldo and assigned the task of extorting contributions for the revolution from his countrymen. In a letter to Aguinaldo written on July 6, 1898, Paua states that he has collected more than $1,000 from the Chinese of these small towns, but asks for an order "prohibiting the outrages that are being committed against such merchants as are not our enemies." He further says, "When the contributions from the Chinamen of all the pueblos shall have been completed I wish to publish a proclamation forbidding any injury to the Chinamen and any interference with their small business enterprises," and adds that "the

---

[1] "With a view to showing every one and especially foreigners travelling through the territory of the Republic, that we are not opposed to a good such as a refined and civilized people should have, the fronts of buildings should be whitewashed, streets should be cleaned and fences repaired." — P. I. R., 292. 3.

natives hereabouts themselves are the people who are committing said abuses." [1]

Apparently Paua had no objection to the committing of outrages against merchants that were the enemies of the cause, nor does he seem to have objected to injury to Chinamen before contributions were completed. His own methods were none too mild. On August 27, 1898, General Pío del Pilar telegraphed Aguinaldo that five Insurgent soldiers, under a leader supposed to be Paua, had entered the store of a Chinaman, and tried to kidnap his wife, but had left on the payment of $10 and a promise to pay $50 later, saying that they would return and hang their fellow countryman if the latter amount was not forthcoming. [2]

Paua was later made a general in consideration of his valuable services !

[1] "It would be a great satisfaction to me to aid you with all my strength ; and the only thing that I see to object to is that the Commanders and Generals in this province are getting pretty abusive toward our brethren and allow themselves to be bribed by the Tagálog merchants so as to allow them to enter Manila with their goods, which is of great assistance to our enemies.

"Concerning the contributions which I have collected from the Chinamen, it amounts to more than ₱2,000 here in Tambobong, Meycauayan and Polo alone ; and those from the other pueblos have not yet come to see me. Furthermore, I would like an order from you prohibiting the outrages that are being committed against such merchants as are not our enemies ; and when the contributions from the Chinamen of all the pueblos shall have been completed, I wish to publish a proclamation forbidding any injury to the Chinamen and any interference with their small business enterprises ; since this is a disgrace to our government and to your name ; for the natives of hereabouts themselves are the people who are committing said abuses, and in hopes of putting a stop to them, I await your decision at the earliest possible moment concerning the proclamation referred to." — P. I. R., 355. 11.

[2] "Last night in the place known as Santo Cristo (Manila ?) the store of J. Ricafort, a Chinaman, was entered by five soldiers of our army under an unknown commander supposed to be Colonel Paua. They tried to kidnap the wife of Ricafort. At the request of P. García they desisted upon payment of 20 pesos and the agreement that 100 pesos would be paid later. If this was not done they would return and hang them. To quiet these people I gave them a pass to assure their personal safety, and exacted at the same time a promise that they should not report the matter to the Americans. Paulino García is now at Pedro Macati." — P. I. R., 1187. 4.

Pampanga

Our travellers next visited Pampanga. Here they apparently overlooked the fact that Aguinaldo did not have "his whole people a unit at his back." The citizens of Macabebe seem not to have approved of the Aguinaldo régime, for the Insurgent records show that : —

"Representatives of the towns of Pampanga assembled in San Fernando on June 26, 1898, and under the presidency of General Maximino, Hizon agreed to yield him complete 'obedience as military governor of the province and representative of the illustrious dictator of these Philippine Islands.' The town of Macabebe refused to send any delegates to this gathering." [1]

It may be incidentally mentioned that Blount has passed somewhat lightly over the fact that he himself during his army days commanded an aggregation of sturdy citizens from this town, known as Macabebe scouts, who diligently shot the Insurgents full of holes whenever they got a chance. He incorrectly refers to them as a "tribe or clan." [2] It is absurd to call them a tribe. They are merely the inhabitants of a town which has long been at odds with the neighbouring towns of the province.

Things had come to a bad pass in Pampanga when its head wrote that the punishment of beating people in the plaza and tying them up so that they would be exposed to the full rays of the sun should be stopped. He argued that such methods would not lead the people of other

[1] P. I. R., 223.

[2] "Early in the war we had availed ourselves of a certain tribe, or clan, known as the Maccabebes, who look nowise different from all other Filipinos, but who had, under the Spanish government, by reason of long-standing feuds with their more rebellious neighbours, come to be absolutely loyal to the Spanish authorities. When we came they had transferred that loyalty to us, and had now become a recognized and valuable part of our military force." — Blount, pp. 333-334.

nations to believe that the reign of liberty, equality and fraternity had begun in the Philippines.[1]

When it is remembered that persons tied up and exposed to the full rays of the sun in the Philippine lowlands soon die, in a most uncomfortable manner, we shall agree with the head of this province that this custom has its objectionable features !

Tarlac

While the failure of Messrs. Wilcox and Sargent to learn of the relations between the Tagálogs of Macabebe and their neighbours, or of the fact that people were being publicly tortured in Pampanga, is perhaps not to be wondered at under the circumstances, it is hard to see how they could have failed to hear something of the seriously disturbed conditions in Tarlac if they so much as got off the train there.

On August 24 the commissioner in charge of elections in that province asked for troops to protect him, in holding them in the town of Urdaneta, against a party of two thousand men of the place, who were going to prevent them.

On September 22 the secretary of the interior ordered that the requirements of the decree of June 18, establishing municipal governments, should be strictly complied with, as in many of the towns "the inhabitants continue to follow the ancient methods by which the friars exploited us at their pleasure and which showed their great contempt for the law." [2]

[1] "On July 28, 1898, the head of the province of Pampanga wrote that the punishment of beating people in the plaza and tying them up so that they would be exposed to the full rays of the sun should be stopped. He complained that these methods had been carried so far that even people of good social position had been so punished. It was especially undesirable to employ such punishments, as the people of other nations seeing them would not believe that the reign of liberty, equality, and fraternity had begun in the Philippines."
— P. I. R., 196. 3.

[2] Taylor, 47 AJ.

The following letter to Aguinaldo, from Juan Nepomuceno, Representative from Tarlac, speaks for itself as to conditions in that province on December 27, 1898, shortly after the American travellers passed through it on their return : —

"I regret exceedingly being compelled to report to you that since Sunday the 25th instant scandalous acts have been going on in the Province of Tarlac, which I represent. On the night of the Sunday mentioned the entire family of the Local Chief of Bamban was murdered, and his house and warehouse were burned. Also the Tax Commissioner and the Secretary, Fabian Ignacio, have been murdered. Last night Señor Jacinto Vega was kidnapped at the town of Gerona ; and seven travellers were murdered at O'Donnel, which town was pillaged, as well as the barrio of Matayumtayum of the town of La Paz. On that day various suspicious parties were seen in the town of Panique and in the same barrio, according to reliable reports which I have just received.

"All this general demoralization of the province, according to the information which I have obtained, is due to the fact that the province is dissatisfied with the Provincial Chief, Señor Alfonso Ramos, and with Major Manuel de León ; for this is substantiated by the fact that all the events described occurred since last Sunday, when Señor Alfonso Ramos returned, to take charge of the Office of Provincial President, after having been detained for several days in this town. Wherefore, I believe that in order to restore tranquillity in the province, consideration be given to various documents that have been presented to the Government and to the standing Committee of Justice ; and that there be removed from office Señor Alfonso Ramos, as well as said Señor Manuel de León, who has no prestige whatever in this province. Moreover on the day when fifty-four soldiers of the command deserted, he himself left for San Fernando, Pampanga." [1]

On November 30, 1898, General Macabulos sent Aguinaldo a telegram [2] from which it evidently appears

[1] P. I. R., 944.

[2] "I have the honour to inform you that I have been in this town since yesterday afternoon issuing, in a proclamation, conciliatory orders to the populace that the people comprised in the uprising must present themselves and express aversion and repudiation of it, promising them consideration and pardon as long as they lay aside arms. In

BILIBID PRISON HOSPITAL.

The Philippine Government has been charged with the neglect of prisoners. The truth is that it has made the prisons of the Philippines the most sanitary structures of their kind in the tropics, and gives its sick prisoners the best of care.

that there was an armed uprising in Tarlac which he was endeavouring to quell and that he hoped for early success. Apparently, however, his efforts to secure tranquillity were not entirely successful, for on December 18 he telegraphed Aguinaldo as follows : —

"In a telegram dated to-day Lieut. Paraso, commanding a detachment at Camilin, informs me that last night his detachment was attacked by Tulisanes (robbers). The fire lasted four hours without any casualties among our men. This afternoon received another from the captain commanding said detachment, informing me of the same, and that nothing new has occurred. The people of the town await with anxiety the result of the charges they have made, especially against the local president and the justice of the peace, the original of which I sent to your high authority." [1]

Obviously the police machinery was not working quite smoothly when a detachment of Insurgent troops could be kept under fire for four hours by a robber band, and perhaps the attacking party were not all "robbers." Soldiers do not ordinarily carry much to steal.

We obtain some further information from the following telegram of December 27, 1898, sent by the secretary of the interior to the President of the Revolutionary Government : —

"Most urgent. According to reports no excitement except in Bangbang, Tarlac, which at 12 A.M., 25th, was attacked by Tulisanes [bandits or robbers, — D. C. W.]. The local presidente with his patrols arrested six of them. On continuing the pursuit he met in Talacon a party too large to attack. At 7 A.M. of the 26th the town was again attacked by criminals, who killed the tax collector, and others who burnt some houses, among them that of the local presidente, and his stables, in which he lost two horses. I report this for your information." [2]

compliance with and following the earlier published proclamation, they presented two guns and innumerable bolos. I hope soon for tranquillity among the people there through these efforts. I ask dispense with assembly of the Junta. CAMILIN, November 30, 1898." — P. I. R., 849.

[1] P. I. R., 849.   [2] *Ibid.*

Evidently tax collectors were not popular in Tarlac.

Still further light is shed on the situation by a telegram from the secretary of the interior to Aguinaldo, dated December 28, 1898 : —

"According to my information the excitement in Tarlac increases. I do not think that the people of the province would have committed such barbarities by themselves. For this reason the silence of General Macabulos is suspicious; to speak frankly, it encourages the rebels. Some seven hundred of them, with one hundred and fifty rifles, entered Pañique, seized the arms of the police, the town funds, and attacked the houses of the people. I report this for your information. All necessary measures will be taken." [1]

Note also the following from the secretary of the interior, under date of December 27, 1898, to Aguinaldo : —

"I have just learned that not only in Bangbang, but also in Gerona, Onell, and other places in Tarlac, men have been assaulted by numerous Tulisanes, armed with rifles and bolos, who are killing and capturing the inhabitants and attacking travellers, robbing them of everything they have. The President should declare at once that that province is in state of siege, applying martial law to the criminals. That — (remainder missing)." [2]

The secretary of agriculture took a more cheerful view of the situation. Under date of December 28 he telegraphed Aguinaldo as follows : —

"The events in Bangbang, Tarlac Province, according to a witness here worthy of credit, have arisen from an attempt to procure vengeance on the local presidente, and robbery of Chinese shops. Hence they are without political importance. The tax collector killed, and a countryman servant of the local presidente wounded. They burnt two houses of the local presidente, a stable, and a warehouse for sugar-cane." [3]

Obviously the robbery of Chinese shops and the killing of a few individuals was at first considered by the secretary of agriculture to be without political importance. Evi-

[1] P. I. R., 849.   [2] *Ibid.*   [3] *Ibid.*

dently he changed his mind, however, for on the same day, December 28, 1898, he telegraphed Aguinaldo as follows :—

"I think it necessary to send Aglipay [1] to quiet Tarlac. Send for him. If you desire, I will go to Tarlac to investigate the causes of the disorders, in order to find a remedy for them." [2]

At this stage of events Aguinaldo was summoned to Malolos by a telegram from Mabini under date of December 29, which reads as follows : —

"Most urgent. You must come here immediately. Trías is sick. We can come to no decision in regard to the Tarlac matter. Cannot constitute a government without you." [3]

The measures which were actually taken are set forth in another telegram of the same date from the secretaries of war and interior to Aguinaldo, which reads as follows : —

"We have sent civil and military commissioners to Tarlac; among them the Director of War and persons of much moral influence, in order to stifle the disturbances. The necessary instructions have been given them and full powers for the purpose, and as far as possible to satisfy the people. Have also sent there six companies of soldiers with explicit instructions to their commander to guard only the towns, and make the people return to a peaceful life, using a policy of attraction for the purpose." [4]

Let us hope that the commander was able to attract the people with his six companies of soldiers, and make them return to a peaceful life.

Still further light is thrown on the situation in Tarlac by the following extract from "Episodios de la Revolucion Filipina" by Padre Joaquin D. Duran, an Augustinian priest, Manila, 1901, page 71 :—

"At that period the Filipinos, loving order, having been deceived of the emancipation promise, changed by the Katipúnan into crimes and attacks on the municipality of the pueblos, dis-

---

[1] Gregorio Aglipay, an Ilocano Catholic priest who became an active Insurgent leader. Later he abandoned the Catholic faith and set up a new church which gained many adherents in the Philippines.

[2] P. I. R., 849.   [3] *Ibid.*   [4] *Ibid.*

content broke out in all parts, and, although latent in some provinces, in that of Tarlac was materialized in an ex-sergeant of the late Spanish civil guard. A valorous and determined man, he lifted up his flag against that of Aguinaldo. One hundred rifles were sufficient to terrorize the inhabitants of said province, crushing the enthusiastic members of the revolutionary party. . . . Having taken possession of four towns, Pecheche would have been everywhere successful if ambition and pride had not directed his footsteps. In January, 1899, the Aguinaldista commander of Tarlac province, afraid that his whole province would espouse the cause of the sergeant, attempted by every means in his power to interrupt his career, not hesitating to avail himself of crime to destroy the influence of Pecheche with the many people who had been incensed by the Katipúnan and had in turn become firm partisans of the Guards of Honour.

"The Ilocano Tranquilino Pagarigan, local presidente at that time of Camiling, served as an admirable instrument for this purpose. . . . Pecheche was invited to a solemn festivity organized by Tranquilino, who pretended to recognize him as his chief, and rendering himself a vassal by taking an oath to his flag. He accepted the invitation, and after the mass which was celebrated went to a meal at the convent, where, after the meal was over, the members of the K. K. K. surrounded Pecheche and 10 of his officers and killed them with bolos or tied them and threw them out of the windows and down the staircase. Some priests were held captive in the building where this took place and were informed of what had taken place immediately afterwards."

This extract shows how easy it then was for any man of determination to acquire a following, especially if he could dispose of a few rifles. It also gives an excellent idea of the methods employed by the Insurgents in dealing with those who opposed their rule.

General Fred D. Grant once told me, with much amusement, of an interesting experience during a fight on Mt. Arayat in Pampanga. His men took a trench and captured some of its occupants. Several of these were impressed as guides and required to show the attacking forces the locations of other trenches. At first they served unwillingly, but presently became enthusiastic and rushed the works of their quondam fellow-soldiers in the van of the American attack. Finally they begged for guns. Grant added that he could start from Bacolor for San Fernando any morning with a supply of rifles and pick up volunteers enough to capture the place, and that on the return trip he could get enough more to attack Bacolor!

Pangasinán

And now we come to Pangasinán, the most populous province of Luzon, and the third in the Philippines in number of inhabitants.

"In July, 1898, the officer in Dagupan wrote to the commanding general of Tarlac Province that he would like to know whom he was required to obey, as there were so many officials of all ranks who gave him orders that it was impossible for him to know where he stood." [1]

In a letter dated August 17, 1898, to Aguinaldo, Benito Legarda complained that a bad impression had been produced by the news from Dagupan that when the Insurgents entered there, after many outrages committed upon the inmates of a girls' school, every officer had carried off those who suited him. [2]

What should we say if United States troops entered the town of Wellesley and raped numerous students at the college, the officers subsequently taking away with them the young ladies who happened to suit them? Yet things of this sort hardly caused a ripple in the country then under the insurgent flag, and I learned of this particular incident by accident, although I have known Legarda for years.

I quote the following general description of conditions in Pangasinán from a letter addressed by Cecilio Apóstol to General Aguinaldo on July 6, 1898 : —

"You probably know that in the Province of Pangasinán, of one of the towns in which your humble servant is a resident,

[1] P. I. R., 1231. 2.   [2] Taylor, 62 AJ.

the Spanish flag through our good fortune has not flown here for the past few months, since the few Spaniards who lived here have concentrated in Dagupan, a place not difficult of attack, as is said.

"But this is what is going on in this Province: There exist here two Departmental Governments, one calling itself that of Northern Luzón and of which Don Vicente del Prado is the President, and the other which calls itself that of Northern and Central Luzón, presided over by Don Juliano Paraiso. Besides these two gentlemen, there are two governors in the province (!) one Civil Political Military, living in Lingayen, named Don Felipe J. Bartolomé, and another living in Real Guerrero, a town of Tayug, named Don Vicente Estrella. And in addition there are a large number of Administrators, Inspectors, Military Judges, Generals, . . . they cannot be counted. It is a pandemonium of which even Christ, who permits it, cannot make anything. Indeed, the situation is insupportable. It reminds me of the schism in the middle ages when there were two Popes, both legitimate, neither true. Things are as clear as thick chocolate, as the Spaniards say. In my poor opinion, good administration is the mother-in-law of disorder, since disorder is chaos and chaos produces nothing but confusion, that is to say, death.

"I have had an opportunity, through the kindness of a friend, to read the decree of that Government, dated June 18th, of the present year, and the accompanying 'Instructions for the government of towns and provinces.' Article 9 of the said decree says that the Superior Government will name a commissioner for each province with the special duty of establishing there the organization set forth in the decree. Very well so far: which of the so-called Presidents of Northern or of Northern and Central Luzón is the commissioner appointed by that government to establish the new organization in that province? Are military commanders named by you for Pangasinán? I would be very much surprised if either of them could show his credentials. Aside from these, the fact remains that in those instructions no mention is made of Presidents of Departments, there is a manifest contradiction in their jurisdictions, since while one calls himself president of a Departmental Government, of Northern Luzón, the other governs the Northern and Central portion of the Island, according to the seals which they use.

"And, nevertheless, a person calling himself the General Administrator of the Treasury and the said Governor of the

Province, both of whom live in Tayug, came to this town when the Spaniards voluntarily abandoned it and gathered all the people of means, and drew up an act of election, a copy of which is attached. From it you will see how this organization violates the provisions of the decree of the 18th of June.

"Another item: They got up a contract with the people of means of this town, and did the same thing in the other towns, in which contract they exact from us $1250 which they call contributions of war (see document No. 2 attached). Among the doubtful powers of these gentlemen is the one to exact these sums included? Have they express orders from that Government?

"Perhaps these blessed gentlemen — they are high flyers there is no doubt about that, — have struck the clever idea of calling themselves generals, governors, etc., in order to enjoy a certain prestige and to give a certain color of legality to their acts — this, although they don't know an iota of what they are doing. But what I am sure of, and many other men also, is that there is no order, that here there is not a single person in authority whom to obey. This superfluity of rulers will finally lead to strained relations between them and the towns of this province will end by paying the piper.

"But we poor ignorant creatures in so far as the republican form of government is concerned, in order to avoid worse evils took them at their word, obeyed them like automatons, hypnotized by the title of 'Insurgents' which they applied to themselves. But when I had an opportunity to read the said decree, doubts were forced upon me, I began to suspect — may God and they pardon me — that they were trying to impose upon us nicely, that, shielded by the motto, 'have faith in and submit to the will of the country' they came to these towns 'for business.'

"In order to dissipate this doubt, in order to do away with abuses, if there are abuses, I made up my mind to send you this account of the condition of things here. I flatter myself that when you learn of the lamentable situation of this province, you will soon deign to take steps to establish order, because thereon depends the tranquillity of Pangasinán and in the end a strict compliance with your superior orders.

"There will be no limit to the thanks of the people of this province if their petitions secure favourable consideration and an immediate response from the high patriotism and honourable standpoint of the Supreme Dictator of the Philippines." [1]

[1] P. I. R., 77.

It will be noted that the picture thus drawn by Señor Apóstol differs in certain important particulars from that painted in such engaging colours by Judge Blount.

In September, 1898, the civil governor of Pangasinán had to have an escort of troops in passing through his province.[1]

On November 20, 1898, the head of the town of San Manuel wrote the provincial governor that his people could no longer support the troops quartered on them, as the adherents of the Katipúan had burned or stolen all of their property.[2]

The sum total of Blount's description of affairs in this, the most populous province of Luzón, is derived from the narrative of Messrs. Wilcox and Sargent and reads as follows : —

"In Pangasinan 'the people were all very respectful and polite and offered the hospitality of their homes.'"[3]

Doubtless true, but as a summary of conditions perhaps a trifle sketchy.

Nueva Ecija

Nueva Ecija was the next province visited by Wilcox and Sargent.   They have failed to inform us that : —

"In December, 1899, certain men charged with being members of this society [Guards of Honour] were interrogated in Nueva Ecija as to their purposes.   One of those questioned said : —

"'That their purpose was one day, the date being unknown to the deponent, when the Ilocanos of Batac came, to rise up in arms and kill the Tagálos, both private individuals and public employees, excepting those who agreed to the former, for the reason that honours were granted only to the Tagálos, and but few to the Ilocanos.'"[4]

Blount has assured us that the Filipinos were a unit at Aguinaldo's back and were and are an united people, and

[1] P. I. R., 47. 7.   [2] *Ibid.*, 951. 3.
[3] Blount, p. 109.   [4] P. I. R., 1006.

Modern Contagious Disease Ward, San Lazaro Hospital.

here are the Ilocanos of Nueva Ecija spoiling his theory by remembering that they are Ilocanos and proposing to kill whom? Not certain individual Filipinos, who might have offended them, but the Tagálogs!

That there were other troubles in Nueva Ecija is shown by the following statement: —

"On January 7, 1899, the commissioner of Aguinaldo's treasury sent to collect contributions of war in Nueva Ecija Province reported that the company stationed in San Isidro had become guerillas under command of its officers and opposed his collections, stating that they were acting in compliance with orders from higher authority." [1]

And now, in following the route taken by our tourist friends, we reach Nueva Vizcaya and the Cagayan valley.

[1] P. I. R., 870. 4.

CHAPTER VI

INSURGENT RULE IN THE CAGAYAN VALLEY

NUEVA VIZCAYA is drained by the Magát River, a branch of the Cagayan. While the provinces of Isabela and Cagayan constitute the Cagayan valley proper, Blount includes Nueva Vizcaya in the territory covered by this designation, and for the purpose of this discussion I will follow his example.

Especial interest attaches to the history of Insurgent rule, in the Cagayan valley, as above defined, for the reason that Blount himself served there as a judge of the court of first instance. He says:[1] —

"The writer is perhaps as familiar with the history of that Cagayan valley as almost any other American."

He was. For his action in concealing the horrible conditions which arose there under Insurgent rule, with which he was perfectly familiar, and in foisting on the public the account of Messrs. Wilcox and Sargent, as portraying the conditions which actually existed there, I propose to arraign him before the bar of public opinion. In so doing I shall consider these conditions at some length. We have much documentary evidence concerning them in addition to that furnished by the Insurgent records, although the latter quite sufficiently demonstrate many of the more essential facts.

In describing the adventures of Messrs. Wilcox and Sargent in this region, Judge Blount says:[2] —

"There[3] they were met by Simeon Villa, military commander of Isabela province, the man who was chief of staff to Aguinaldo

[1] Blount, p. 113.   [2] *Ibid.*, p. 111.   [3] At Carig, Isabela.

170

afterwards, and was captured by General Funston along with Aguinaldo in the spring of 1901."

The facts as to Villa's career in the Cagayan valley are especially worthy of note as they seem to have entitled him, in the opinion of his superiors, to the promotion which was afterward accorded him. He was an intimate friend of Aguinaldo and later accompanied him on his long flight through northern Luzon.

On August 10, 1898, Colonel Daniel Tirona, a native of Cavite Province and one of the intimates of Aguinaldo, was ordered to proceed to Aparri in the Insurgent steamer *Filipinas* and establish the revolutionary government in northern Luzon. In doing this he was to hold elections for office-holders under Aguinaldo's government and was authorized to approve or disapprove the results, his action being subject to subsequent revision by Aguinaldo. His forces were composed of four companies armed with rifles.

Tirona reached Aparri on August 25 and promptly secured the surrender of the Spaniards there.

He was accompanied by Simeon Villa, the man under discussion, and by Colonel Leyba, who was also very close to Aguinaldo.

Abuse of the Spanish prisoners began at once. It is claimed that the governor of North Ilocos, who was among those captured, was grossly mistreated.

Taylor briefly summarizes subsequent events as follows:[1] —

"Whatever the treatment of the Spanish governor of Ilocos may really have been, there is testimony to show that some of the other prisoners, especially the priests, were abused and outraged under the direction of S. Villa and Colonel Leyba, both of whom were very close to Aguinaldo. Some of the Spanish civil officials were put in stocks and beaten, and one of the officers who had surrendered at Aparri was tortured to death. This was done with the purpose of extorting money from them,

[1] Taylor, 42 AJ.

for it was believed that they had hidden funds in place of turning them over. All the Spaniards were immediately stripped of everything they had. The priests were subjected to a systematic series of insults and abuse under the direction of Villa in order to destroy their influence over the people by degrading them in their eyes. It was for this that they were beaten and exposed naked in the sun; and other torture, such as pouring the wax of burning candles into their eyes, was used to make them disclose where they had hidden church vessels and church funds. The testimony of a friar who suffered these outrages is that the great mass of the people saw such treatment of their parish priests with horror, and were present at it only through fear of the organized force of the Katipúnan."

Taylor's statement is mildness itself in view of the well-established facts.

The question of killing the Spanish prisoners, including the friars, had previously been seriously considered,[1] but it was deemed wiser to keep most of the friars alive, extort money from them by torture, and offer to liberate them in return for a large cash indemnity, or for political concessions. Day after day and week after week Villa presided at, or himself conducted, the torture of ill-fated priests and other Spaniards who fell into his hands. Even Filipinos whom he suspected of knowing the whereabouts of hidden friar money did not escape.

The following information relative to the conduct of the Insurgents in the Cagayan valley is chiefly taken from a manuscript copy of *"Historia de la Conquista de Cagayan por los Tagalos Revolucionarios,"* in which the narratives of certain captured friars are transcribed and compiled by Father Julian Malumbres of the Dominican Order.

The formal surrender of Aparri occurred on August 26. Tirona, his officers and his soldiers, promptly pillaged the *convento*.[2] The officers left the Bishop of Vigan ten pesos, but the soldiers subsequently took them away from him. Wardrobes and trunks were broken

---

[1] See p. 731.   [2] The parsonage, or residence of the priest.

open; clocks, shoes, money, everything was carried off. Even personal papers and prayer-books were taken from some of the priests, many of whom were left with absolutely nothing save the few remaining clothes in which they stood.

On the same day Villa, accompanied by Victa and Rafael Perea,[1] went to the *convento* and told the priests who were imprisoned there that their last hour had come. He shut all of them except the bishop and five priests in a room near the church, then separated the Augustinians, Juan Zallo, Gabino Olaso, Fidel Franco, Mariano Rodriguez, and Clemente Hidalgo, from the others and took them into the lower part of the *convento* where he told them that he intended to kill them if they did not give him more money. The priests told him that they had given all they had, whereupon he had their arms tied behind their backs, kicked them, struck them and whipped them with rattans.

Father Zallo was thrown on his face and savagely beaten. Meanwhile two shots were fired over the heads of the others and a soldier called out "One has fallen," badly frightening the priests who had remained shut in the room. Villa then returned with soldiers to this room, ordered his men to load, and directed that one priest step forward to be shot. Father Mariano Ortiz complied with this request, asking that he be the first victim. Villa, however, contented himself with threatening him with a revolver and kicking and striking him until he fell to the floor. He was then beaten with the butts of guns.

Father José Vazquez, an old man of sixty years, who had thrown some money into a privy to keep it from falling into the hands of the Insurgents, was stripped and compelled to recover it with his bare hands, after which he was kicked, and beaten with rattans.

Father Aquilino García was unmercifully kicked and beaten to make him give up money, and this sort of

[1] Insurgent officers.

thing continued until Villa, tired out with the physical exertion involved in assaulting these defenceless men, departed, leaving his uncompleted task to others, who continued it for some time.

The net result to the Insurgents of the sacking of the *convento* and of the tortures thus inflicted was approximately $20,000 gold in addition to the silver, bank notes, letters of credit, jewels, etc., which they obtained.

On September 5 Villa had Fathers Juan Recio and Buenaventura Macia given fifty blows each, although Father Juan was ill.

Villa then went to Lalloc, where other priests were imprisoned. On September 6 he demanded money of them, causing them to be kicked and beaten. Father Angel was beaten in an especially cruel manner for the apparent purpose of killing him, after which he was thrust into a privy. Father Isidro Fernandez was also fearfully abused. Stripped of his habit, and stretched face down on the floor, he was horribly beaten, and was then kicked, and struck with the butt of a revolver on the forehead.

A little later the priests were offered their liberty for a million dollars, which they were of course unable to furnish. Meanwhile the torture continued from time to time.

On August 30 Tuguegarao was taken by the Insurgents without resistance. Colonel Leyba promptly proceeded to the *convento* and demanded the money of the friars as spoil of war. He found only eight hundred pesos in the safe. Father Corujedo was threatened with death if he did not give more. Other priests were threatened but not tortured at this time. The prisoners in the jail were liberated, but many of them had promptly to be put back again because of the disorder which resulted, and that same evening Leyba was obliged to publish a notice threatening robbers with death.

At midnight on September 3 Father Corujedo was taken from the *convento* by Captain Diego and was again asked for money.   Replying that he had no more to give, he was beaten with the hilt of a sabre and stripped of his habit, preparatory to being executed.   A mock sentence of death was pronounced on him and he was placed facing to the west to be shot in the back.   Diego ordered his soldiers to load, adding, "When I count three all fire," but the fatal count was not completed.   Three priests from Alcala were given similar treatment.

The troubles of the priests imprisoned at Tuguegarao were sufficiently great, but they were augmented a thousand fold when Villa arrived on September 11. He came to the building where they were imprisoned, bearing a revolver, a sabre and a great quantity of rattans. He ordered the priests into the corner of the room in which they were confined, and beat those who did not move quickly enough to suit him.   He threatened them with a very rigorous examination, at the same time assuring them that at Aparri he had hung up the bishop until blood flowed from his mouth and his ears, and that he would do the same with them if they did not tell him where they had their money hidden.   There followed the usual rain of kicks and blows, a number of the priests being obliged to take off their habits in order that they might be punished more effectively.

Fathers Calixto Prieto and Daniel Gonzales, professors in educational institutions, he ordered beaten because they were friars.

Fathers Corujedo and Caddedila were beaten, kicked and insulted.   Both were gray-haired old men and the latter was at the time very weak, and suffering from a severe attack of asthma.   Father Pedro Vincente was also brutally beaten.

The following is the description given by an eye-witness of conditions at Tuguegarao : —

"Even the Indios of Cagayan complained and were the victims of looting and robbery on the part of the soldiery.   So lacking in discipline and so demoralized was that army that according to the confession of a prominent Filipino it was of imperative necessity to disarm them.[1] On the other hand we saw with real astonishment that instead of warlike soldiers accustomed to battle they were nearly all raw recruits and apprentices. From an army lacking in discipline, and lawless, only outrages, looting and all sorts of savagery and injustice were to be expected. Witnesses to their demoralization are, aside from the natives themselves who were the first to acknowledge it, the Chinese merchants whose losses were incalculable; not a single store or commercial establishment remained that was not looted repeatedly. As to the Spaniards it goes without saying because it is publicly known, that between soldiers and officers they despoiled them to their heart's content, without any right except that of brute force, of everything that struck their fancy, and it was of no avail to complain to the officers and ask for justice, as they turned a deaf ear to such complaints. At Tuguegarao they looted in a manner never seen before, like Vandals, and it was not without reason that a prominent Filipino said, in speaking to a priest: 'Vandalism has taken possession of the place.' These acts of robbery were generally accompanied by the most savage insults; it was anarchy, as we heard an eye-witness affirm, who also stated that no law was recognized except that of danger, and the vanquished were granted nothing but the inevitable duty of bowing with resignation to the iniquitous demands of that soulless rabble, skilled in crime."

Villa now set forth for Isabela. Meanwhile the jailer of the priests proceeded to steal their clothes, including shirts, shoes and even handkerchiefs. Isabela was taken without resistance on September 12. Dimas Guzman[2] swore to the priests on his life that he would work without rest to the end that all friars and all Spaniards might be respected, but he perjured himself.

On September 12 Villa and others entered the town of Cabagan Viejo, where Villa promptly assaulted Father Segundo Rodriguez, threatening him with a revolver, beating him unmercifully, insulting him in every possible way and robbing him of his last cent. After the bloody

[1] Their own commander so reported. See p. 202.
[2] Shortly afterward "elected" governor.

FILIPINA TRAINED NURSES.
This photograph shows the members of the first class to graduate from the government training school.

scene was over he sacked the *convento*, even taking away the priests' clothes.

Villa also cruelly beat a Filipino, Quintin Agansi, who was taking care of money for masses which the priests wished to save from the Insurgents.

After Father Segundo had suffered torture and abuse for two hours he was obliged to start at once on a journey to Auitan. The suffering priest, after being compelled to march through the street shouting "Vivas!" for the Republic and Aguinaldo, spent the night without a mouthful of food or a drink of water.

Father Deogracias García, a priest of Cabagan Nuevo, was subjected to torture because he had sent to Hongkong during May a letter of credit for $5000 which belonged to the Church. Villa and Leyba entered his *convento* and after beating him ordered his hands and feet to be tied together, then passed a pole between them and had him lifted from the ground, after which two great jars of water were poured down his nose and throat without interruption.[1] In order to make the water flow through his nose better, they thrust a piece of wood into the nasal passages until it came out in his throat. From time to time the torture was suspended while they asked him whether he would tell the truth as to where he had concealed his money. This unfortunate priest was so sure he was going to die that while the torture was in progress he received absolution from a fellow priest. After the torture with water there followed a long and cruel beating, and the unhappy victim was finally thrust into a filthy privy.

Meanwhile Father Calzada was assaulted by a group of soldiers and badly beaten, after which he was let down into the filth of a privy, first by the feet and afterwards by the head.

On the 14th a lieutenant with soldiers entered the

---

[1] This form of torture is commonly referred to in the Philippines as the "water cure."

convento of Tumauini and as usual demanded money of the occupants, who gave him $80, all they had at the time. This quantity not being satisfactory, a rope was sent for and the hands of the two priests were tied while they were whipped, kicked and beaten. They were, however, released when Father Bonet promised to get additional money. They had a short respite until the arrival of Villa, who still demanded more money of Father Blanco, and failing to get it for the reason that the father had no more, leaped upon him and gave him a dreadful beating, his companions joining in with whips, rattans and the butts of guns. They at last left their victim stretched on the ground almost dead. This priest showed the marks of his ill treatment six months afterward. Not satisfied with this, Villa gave him the so-called "water cure."

Meanwhile his followers had also beaten Father Bonet. Villa started to do likewise but was too tired, having exhausted his energies on Father Blanco. While the tortures were going on, the *convento* was completely sacked. Father Blanco's library was thrown out of the window.

Villa entered Ilagan on the 15th of September at 8 o'clock at night. Hastening to the *convento*, with a company of well-armed soldiers, he had his men surround the three priests who awaited him there, then summoned the local priest to a separate room and demanded money. The priest gave him all he had. Not satisfied, Villa leaped upon him, kicking him, beating him and pounding him with the butt of a gun. Many of his associates joined in the disgraceful attack. The unfortunate victim was then stripped of his habit, obliged to lie down and received more than a hundred lashes. When he was nearly senseless he was subjected to torture by water, being repeatedly lifted up when filled with water, and allowed to fall on the floor. While some were pouring water down his nose and throat, others spilled hot wax on his face and head. The torment repeatedly rendered the priest senseless, but he was allowed to recover from time to time so that he might suffer when it was renewed.

The torturing of this unhappy man lasted for three hours, and the horrible scene was immediately succeeded by another quite as bad. Villa called Father Domingo Campo and, after taking from him the little money that he had, ordered him stripped. He was then given numberless kicks and blows from the butts of rifles and 150 lashes, after which he was unable to rise. There followed the torture with water, on the pretext that he had money hidden away.

Meanwhile the houses of Spaniards and the shops of the Chinese were completely sacked, and the men who objected were knocked down or cut down with bolos. Numerous girls and women were raped.

On September 15 Leyba received notice of the surrender of Nueva Vizcaya. I quote the following from the narrative above referred to : —

"Delfin's soldiers[1] were the most depraved ever seen : their thieving instincts had no bounds; so they had hardly entered Nueva Vizcaya when they started to give themselves up furiously to robbery, looking upon all things as loot; in the very shadow of these soldiers the province was invaded by a mob of adventurous and ragged persons from Nueva Ecija; between the two they picked Nueva Vizcaya clean. When they had grown tired of completely shearing the unfortunate Vizcayan people, leaving them poverty-stricken, they flew in small bands to the pueblos of Isabela, going as far as Angadanan, giving themselves up to unbridled pillage of the most unjust and disorderly kind. Some of these highwaymen demanded money and arms from the priest of Angadanan, but Father Marciano informed them 'that it could not be, as Leyba already knew what he had and would be angry.'

"To this very day the people of Nueva Vizcaya have been unable to recover from the stupendous losses suffered by them

[1] Major Delfin commanded the expedition which took Nueva Vizcaya.

as regards their wealth and industries. How many curses did they pour forth and still continue to level against the Katipúnan that brought them naught but tribulations!"

Confirmation of these statements is found in the following brief but significant passage from the Insurgent records: —

"At the end of December, 1898, when the military commander of Nueva Vizcaya called upon the Governor of that province to order the police of the towns to report to him as volunteers to be incorporated in the army which was being prepared for the defence of the country, the Governor protested against it and informed the government that his attempt to obtain volunteers was in fact only a means of disarming the towns and leaving them without protection against the soldiers who did what they wanted and took what they wished and committed every outrage without being punished for it by their officers." [1]

The effect of the surrender of Nueva Vizcaya on Leyba and Villa is thus described by Father Malumbres: —

"Mad with joy and swollen with pride Leyba and company were like men who travelled flower-strewn paths, crowned with laurels, and were acclaimed as victors in all the towns on their road, their intoxication of joy taking a sudden rise when they came to believe themselves kings of the valley. It was then that their delirium reached its brimful measure and their treatment of those whom they had vanquished began to be daily more cruel and inhuman. In Cagayan their fear of the forces in Nueva Vizcaya kept them from showing such unqualifiable excesses of cruelty and nameless barbarities, but the triumph of the Katipúnan arms in Nueva Vizcaya completely broke down the wall of restraint which somewhat repressed those sanguinary executioners thirsting to fatten untrammelled on the innocent blood of unarmed and defenceless men. From that melancholy time there began an era of unheard of outrages and barbarous scenes, unbelievable were they not proved by evidence of every description. The savage acts committed in Isabela by the inhuman Leyba and Villa cannot possibly be painted true to life and in all their tragic details. The blackest hues, the most heartrending accents, the most vigorous language and the most fulminating anathemas would be

[1] P. I. R., 246. 3.

a pale image of the truth, and our pen cannot express with true ardour the terrifying scenes and cruel torments brought about by such fierce chieftains on such indefensive religious. It seems impossible that a fleshly heart could hold so much wickedness, for these petty chiefs were veritable monsters of cruelty who surpassed a Nero; men who were entire strangers to noble and humane sentiments and who in appearance having the figure of a man were in reality tigers roaring in desperation, or mad dogs who gnashed their teeth in fury."

On September 18 Leyba continued his march, while Villa remained behind at Ilagan to torture the prisoners who might be brought in from Isabela.

On arrival at Gamut, Leyba at once entered the *convento* and as usual immediately demanded money from the priests. Father Venancio gave him all he had. He was nevertheless given a frightful whipping, six persons holding him while others rained blows upon him. A determined effort was made to force the priest to recant, and when this failed Leyba leaped upon him, kicking and beating him. He then ordered him thrown down face uppermost, and asked for a knife with the apparent intention of mutilating him. He did not use the knife, however, but instead, assisted by his followers, gave the unhappy priest another terrific beating, even standing upon him and leaping up and down. The priest was left unable to speak, and did not recover for months.

Later Leyba had torture by water applied to Father Gregorio Cabrero and lay brother Venancio Aguinaco, while Father Sabanda was savagely beaten.

On the 19th of September Father Miguel Garcia of Reina Mercedes was horribly beaten in his *convento* by a captain sent there to get what money he had.

In Cauayan, on September 20, Fathers Perez and Aguirrezabal were beaten and compelled to give up money by five emissaries of Leyba, and the latter priest was cut in the face with a sabre. The *convento* was sacked. On the 25th Leyba arrived and after kicking and beating Father Garcia compelled him to give up

$1700. He then informed the priests that if it were not for Aguinaldo's orders he would kill all the Spaniards.

On the afternoon of the 24th three priests and a Spaniard named Soto arrived at Ilagan. The following is the statement of an eye-witness as to what happened: —

"They led the priests to the headquarters of the commanding officer where the tyrant Villa, always eager to inflict suffering on humanity, awaited them. The scene witnessed by the priests obeisant to the cruel judge was horrifying in the extreme. Four lions whose thirst for vengeance was extreme in all, threw themselves, blind with fury, without a word and with the look of a basilisk, upon poor Señor Soto giving him such innumerable and furious blows on head and face that weary as he was from his past journey, the ill-treatment received at Angadanan and weighted down by years, he was soon thrown down by his executioners under the lintel of the door getting a terrible blow on the head as he fell; even this did not satisfy nor tame down those fierce-hearted men, who on the contrary continued with their infamous work more furious than before, and their cruelty did not flag on seeing their victim at their feet. They could have done no worse had they been Silípan savages dancing in triumph around the palpitating head cut from the body of some enemy.

"The priests who witnessed this blood-curdling scene trembled like the weak reed before the gale, waiting their turn to be tortured, but God willed that cruel Villa should be content with the butchery perpetrated upon unhappy Sr. Soto. Villa dismissed the priests after despoiling them of their bags and clothes telling them, to torment them: 'Go to the *convento* until the missing ones turn up so that I may shoot you all together.'"

Leyba entered Echague on September 22, promptly going to the *convento* as usual and demanding money of the priest, Father Mata. When the latter had given him all he had, he received three terrific beatings at the hands of some twelve men armed with whips and sticks, after which Leyba himself struck him with his fist and his sabre. He was finally knocked down by a blow with the sabre and left disabled. It took six months for him to recover.

Shortly after Leyba's arrival in Nueva Vizcaya on the afternoon of the 25th, five priests were summoned to Solano and there abused in the usual fashion in an effort to extort money from them. Only one escaped ill treatment and one was nearly killed.

Leyba now went to Bayombong to carry out the established programme with the priests. There he found Governor Perez of Isabela, who had taken with him certain government moneys and employed them to pay salaries of soldiers and other employees. He insisted on the return of the total amount and threatened to shoot Perez if it was not forthcoming. The Spaniards of the vicinity subscribed $700 which they themselves badly needed and saved him from being shot. The priests of the place were then summoned to Leyba's quarters and were beaten and tortured. One of them was thrown on the floor and beaten nearly to death, Leyba standing meanwhile with his foot on the unfortunate man's neck. Another was given six hundred lashes and countless blows and kicks. Leyba stood on this man's neck also. When the victim's back ceased to have any feeling, his legs were beaten. Leyba terminated this period of diversion by kicking Father Diez in the solar plexus and then mocking him as he lay gasping on the floor. That afternoon one of the priests, so badly injured that he could not rise unaided, was put on a horse and compelled to ride in the hot sun to Solano.

Villa and Leyba had their able imitators, as is shown by the following description of the torturing of Father Ceferino by Major Delfin at Solano, Nueva Vizcaya, on September 27 : —

"They wished to give brave evidence of their hate for the friar before Leyba left, and show him that they were as brave as he when it came to oppressing and torturing the friar. This tragedy began by Jimenez again asking Father Ceferino for the money. The priest answered as he had done before. Then Jimenez started to talk in Tagalog to the commanding officer and surely it was nothing good that he told him, for suddenly Delfin left the bench and darting fire from his eyes, fell in blind fury upon the defenceless priest; what harsh words he uttered in Tagalog while he vented his fury on his victim, striking him with his clenched fist, slapping him and kicking him, I do not know, but the religious man fell at the feet of his furious executioner who, being now the prey of the most stupendous rage, could scarcely get his tongue to stutter and continued to kick the priest, without seeing where he kicked him.   Getting deeper and deeper in the abyss and perhaps not knowing what he was about, this petty chief made straight for a sabre lying on a table to continue his bloody work.   In the meantime the priest had risen to his feet and awaited with resignation new torments which certainly were even worse than the first, for he gave him so many and such hard blows with the sabre that the blade was broken close to the hilt.   This accident so infuriated Delfin that he again threw himself upon the priest, kicking him furiously and striking him repeatedly until he again threw him to the ground; and not yet satisfied, his vengefulness led him to throw himself upon his victim with the fury of a tiger after his prey, beating him on the head with the hilt of the saber until the blood ran in streams and formed pools upon the pavement.   The priest, more dead than alive, shuddered from head to foot, and appeared to be struggling in a tremendous fight between life and death; he had hardly enough strength to get his tongue to ask for God's mercy.   At this most critical juncture, and when it seemed as if death were inevitable, the martyr received absolution from Father Diez, who witnessed the blood-curdling picture with his heart pierced with grief at the sight of the sufferings of his innocent brother, feeling as must the condemned man preparing for death who sees the hours fly by with vertiginous rapidity.   The blood flowing from the wounds on the priest's head appeared to infuriate and blind the heart of Delfin who, rising from his victim's body, sped away to the armory in the court house, seized a rifle, and came back furious to brain him with the butt and finish killing the priest; but God willed to free his servant from death at the hands of those cannibals, so that generous Lieutenant Navarro interfered, took the rifle away from him and caught Delfin by the arm, threatening him with some words spoken in Tagalog.   Then Navarro, to appease Delfin's anger, turned the priest over with his face to the ground and gave him a few strokes with the bamboo, and feigning anger and indignation, ordered him away.

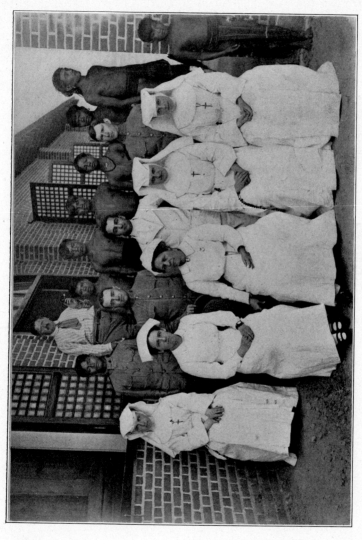

STAFF OF THE BONTOC HOSPITAL.

This photograph shows the doctors, nurses, and some of the servants. The man in the doorway is Dr. Rembe of the Philippine General Hospital, who accompanied the author on his northern inspection trip in 1912, in order to study eye troubles among the wild men.

"Those who witnessed the horrible tragedy, the brutality of the tyrant and the prostration of the friar were persuaded that the latter would never survive his martyrdom. The religious man himself holds it as a veritable portent that he outlived such a terrible trial; but even this did not satisfy them as subsequently the Secretary again called Father Ceferino to subject him to a further scrutiny, as ridiculous as it was malicious, though it did not go beyond words or insults."

Señor Perez, the governor of Isabela, and Father Diez were compelled to go to Ilagan. After they had arrived there on October 2d, Villa proceeded to torture them. At the outset ten soldiers, undoubtedly instructed beforehand, beat the governor down to the earth, with the butts of their guns. Villa himself struck him three times in the chest with the butt of a gun and Father Diez gave him absolution, thinking he was dying. Father Diez was then knocked down repeatedly with the butts of guns, being made to stand up promptly each time in order that he might be knocked down again. Not satisfied with this, Villa compelled the suffering priest to kneel before him and kicked him in the nose, repeating the operation until he left him stretched on the floor half-senseless with his nose broken. He next had both victims put in stocks with their weight supported by their feet alone. While in this position soldiers beat them and jumped onto them and one set the governor's beard on fire with matches. Father Diez was kept in the stocks four days. He was then sent to Tuguegarao in order that personal enemies there might take vengeance on him, Villa bidding him good-by with the following words: "Go now to Tuguegarao and see if they will finish killing you there." Señor Perez was kept in the stocks eight days and it is a wonder that he did not die.

Upon the 25th of September Villa went to the *convento* in Ilagan prepared to torture the priests, but he succeeded in compelling a number of them to sign indorsements in his favour on various letters of credit payable by the Tabacalera Company and departed again in fairly good humour, having done nothing worse than strike one of them.

Later, however, on the pretext that Fathers Aguado and Labanda had money hidden away, he determined to torture them with water. The first to be tortured was Father Labanda. Villa had him taken to the prison where the priest found his two faithful Filipino servants who had been beaten cruelly and were then hanging from a beam, this having been done in order to make them tell where his money was.

He was tied after the usual fashion and water poured down his nose and throat. During the brief respites necessary in order to prevent his dying outright he was cruelly beaten. They finally dragged him out of the prison by the feet, his head leaving a bloody trail on the stones. After he had been taken back to his companions, one of the men who had tortured him came to beg his pardon, saying that he had been compelled to do it by Villa.

Father Aguado was next tortured in one of the rooms of the *convento*. Villa finished the day's work by announcing to the band of priests that he would have them all shot the next day on the plaza, and ordering them to get ready.

On the 29th the barbarities practised by this inhuman fiend reached their climax in the torturing to death of Lieutenant Piera. The following description gives some faint idea of one of the most diabolical crimes ever committed in the Philippines : —

"Villa's cruelty and sanguinary jeering grew without let or hindrance from day to day; it seemed that this hyena continually cudgelled his brains to invent new kinds of torture and to jeer at the friars. On the night of the 29th of September the diabolical idea occurred to him of giving the *coup de grace* to the prestige of the friars by making them pass through the streets of Ilagan conducting and playing a band of music. He carried out his nonsensical purpose by calling upon Father Diogracias to play the big drum, and when this priest had started playing Villa learned that Father Primo was a musician and could therefore play the drum and lead the band with all skill, so he called upon Father Primo to come forward, and with one thing and another this ridiculous function was carried on until the late hours of the night.

*   *   *   *   *   *   *

"While these two priests were serenading Villa and his gang, the most dreadful shrieks were heard from the jail, accompanied by pitiful cries that would melt the coldest heart. The priests hearing these echoes of sorrow and pain, and who did not know for what purpose Fathers Deogracias and Primo had been separated from them, seemed to recognize the voices of these two priests among the groans, believing them to be cruelly tortured; for this reason they began to say the rosary in order that the Most Holy Virgin might imbue them with patience and fortitude in their martyrdom. Great was their surprise when these priests returned saying that they had contented themselves with merely making fun of them by obliging them to play the big drum and lead the band.

"Although this somewhat tempered their sorrow, a thorn remained in their hearts, fearing that the moving lamentations and the mortal groans came from the lips of some hapless Spaniard. This fatidical presentiment turned out unfortunately to be a fact. The victim sacrificed that melancholy night, still remembered with a shudder by the priests, was Lieutenant Salvador Piera. This brave soldier, who had made up his mind to die in the breach rather than surrender the town of Aparri, was persuaded to capitulate only by the prayers and tears of certain Spanish ladies who had been instructed to do so by a man who should have been the first one to shoulder a rifle. After having been harassed in Aparri he was taken to Tuguegarao at the request of Esteban Quinta or Isidoro Maquigat, two artful filibusters thirsting to revenge themselves on the Lieutenant, who during the time of the Spanish government had justly laid his heavy hand upon them. In the latter part of September they conducted him on foot and without any consideration whatever to the capital of Isabela. In this town he was at once placed in solitary confinement in one of the rooms of the *convento* and allowed no intercourse with any one. The sin for which they recriminated Piera was his having charged Dimas [1] with being a filibuster, and their revengefulness reached an incredible limit. The heartrend-

[1] Dimas Guzman.

ing moans of this martyr to his duty still resound in that *convento* converted into the scene of an orgy of blood. The unfortunate man was heard to shout: 'For God's sake, for God's sake, have pity,' and trustworthy persons tell that under the strain of torture he would challenge them to fight in a fair field by saying: 'I will fight alone against twenty of you;' but the cowardly torturers, a reproach to the Filipino race, looked upon it as an amusement to glut their spite on a defenceless man whose hands were tied. They had him strung up all night with but insignificant refreshment and rest, sometimes being suspended by his arms which finally became disjointed and useless, and at others he was hung up by his feet, the blood rushing to his head and placing him in imminent danger of sudden death. It was the intention of these brutes to torture him as much as possible before killing him, just as a member of the feline race plays with, tosses in the air and pirouettes around the victim which falls into his claws. If to the torture of the rope are added the blows with cudgels and the butts of rifles which were frequently rained upon the victim it will be no surprise that early on the morning of the 30th he was in the throes of death in the midst of which the sufferer had just enough strength to say that he was hungry and thirsty; then those cannibals (the heart is filled with fury in setting forth such cruelty) cut a piece of flesh from the calf of the dying man's leg and conveyed it to his mouth and instead of water they gave him to drink some of his own urine. What savagery!

"The blood from the wound finished the killing of the fainting Piera. The blood shed served to infuriate more the barbarous executioners who in order to give the finishing stroke to the martyr, as an unrivalled expression of their savage ferocity, thrust a red-hot iron into his mouth and eyes. That same night these treacherous and ferocious tyrants whose sin made them hate the light, buried the body in the darkness of the night in a patch of cogon grass adjoining the *convento*."

Piera's torture was by no means confined to this last night of his life, as the following account of it shows: —

"In the first days of this accursed month, while the padres were bemoaning their fate in jail, a dark drama was being enacted in the *convento*, whose hair-raising scenes would have inspired terror to Montepiu himself.

"Lieutenant Salvador Piera of the Guardia Civil, commanding officer at Aparri, who, realizing that all resistance was useless, gave way to the persistent solicitations of Spaniards and natives and surrendered that town on honourable terms, which the Katipúnan forces did not respect after the capitulation had been signed, was sent for by Villa, the military authority of Isabela.   Something terrible was going to happen as Piera himself felt confident, for it is said that before leaving Aparri he went to confession where he settled the important business of his conscience in a Christian manner with a representative of God.

"And so it turned out, for as soon as he arrived in Ilagan he was taken to the *convento* and placed incomunicado in one of its apartments.   Soon after, three or four vile fiends, — for they do not deserve the name of men, — bound him with strong cords and hanged him to a beam.   Then they began to charge him with having prosecuted a certain Mason, and inflicted upon him the most frightful tortures.   The pen refuses to set forth so many atrocities.   For three days they had him in that position while his vile assassins made a martyr of him. Our hair stands on end to think of such crimes.   The heart-rending cries of this unfortunate man while prey to such barbarous torments could be heard in every part of the town and carried panic to the homes of all the inhabitants.

"The late hours of the night were always chosen by those treacherous fiends to give Piera the *trato de cuerda* (this form of torture consists in tying the hands of the victim behind his back and hanging him by them by a rope passed through a pulley attached to a beam; his body is lifted as high as it will go and then allowed to fall by its own weight without reaching the ground); but this torture was administered to him in a form so terrible that all the pictures of this kind of torment found in the dreadful narratives of the calumniators of the Holy Office, pale into insignificance in comparison with the atrocious details of the tortures here recited; at each violent jerk the unhappy victim feeling that his limbs were being torn asunder would cry out 'My God! My God!'   This terrifying cry reverberating through the jail would freeze the very blood of the poor priests therein incarcerated.

"On the third day, when those infuriated hyenas appeared to have spent their diabolical rage; after they had thrust a red-hot iron into his eyes and left him with sightless sockets; the poor martyr, the prey of delirium, cried out that he was hungry, and one of those *sicarii* cut a piece of flesh from Piera's thigh and was infamous enough to carry it to his mouth.   On the night of the seventh of the month very late a number of wretches buried in the *convento* garden a body still dripping warm blood from the lips of which there escaped the feeble plaints of anguish of a dying man."

The feeling of the Spaniards relative to this matter is well shown by the following statement of Father Malumbres : —

"This horrible crime cannot be pardoned by God or man, and is still uninvestigated, crying to Heaven for vengeance with greater reason than the blood of the innocent Abel. So long as the criminals remain unpunished it will be a black and indelible stigma and an ugly stain on the race harbouring in its midst the perpetrators of this unheard-of sin. Words of reprobation are not enough, justice demands exemplary and complete reparation, and if the powers of earth do not take justice into their own hands, God will send fire from Heaven and will cause to disappear from the face of the earth the criminals and even their descendants. A murder so cruel and premeditated can be punished in no other way.

"If the courts here should wish to punish the guilty persons it would not be a difficult task; the public points its finger at those who dyed their hands in the blood of the heroic soldier, and we shall set them forth here echoing the voice of the people. The soulless instigator was Dimas Guzman. The executioners were a certain José Guzman (alias Pepin, a nephew of Dimas) and Cayetano Pérez."

The matter was duly taken up in the courts, and Judge Blount himself tried the cases.

The judge takes a very mild and liberal view of the occurrence. He says of it :[1] —

"Villa was accompanied by his aide, Lieutenant Ventura Guzman. The latter is an old acquaintance of the author of the present volume, who tried him afterwards, in 1901, for playing a minor part in the murder of an officer of the Spanish army committed under Villa's orders just prior to, or about the time of, the Wilcox-Sargent visit. He was found guilty, and sentenced, but later liberated under President Roosevelt's amnesty of 1902. He was guilty, but the deceased, so the people in the Cagayan Valley used to say, in being tortured to death,

[1] Blount, p. 112.

got only the same sort of medicine he had often administered thereabouts. At any rate, that was the broad theory of the amnesty in wiping out all these old cases."

He adds : —

"I sentenced both Dimas and Ventura to life imprisonment for being accessory to the murder of the Spanish officer above named, Lieutenant Piera. Villa officiated as arch-fiend on the grewsome occasion. I am quite sure I would have hung Villa without any compunction at that time, if I could have gotten hold of him. I tried to get hold of him, but Governor Taft's attorney-general, Mr. Wilfley, wrote me that Villa was somewhere over on the mainland of Asia on British territory, and extradition would involve application to the London Foreign Office. The intimation was that we had trouble enough of our own without borrowing any from feuds that had existed under our predecessors in sovereignty. I have understood that Villa is now practising medicine in Manila. More than one officer of the American army that I know afterwards did things to the Filipinos almost as cruel as Villa did to that unhappy Spanish officer, Lieutenant Piera. On the whole, I think President Roosevelt acted wisely and humanely in wiping the slate. We had new problems to deal with, and were not bound to handicap ourselves with the old ones left over from the Spanish régime." [1]

But it happens that this was the Filipino régime. Piera's torture occurred at the very time when, according to Blount, Aguinaldo had "a wonderfully complete 'going concern' throughout the Philippine archipelago."

Furthermore, it occurred in the Cagayan valley where Blount says "perfect tranquillity and public order" were then being maintained by "the authority of the Aguinaldo government" in a country which Messrs. Wilcox and Sargent, who arrived on the scene of this barbarous murder by torture four weeks later, found so " quiet and orderly."

Not only was Blount perfectly familiar with every detail of this damnable crime, but he must of necessity

[1] Blount, p. 114.

have known of the torturing of friars to extort money, which preceded and followed it.

The following statement seems to sum up his view of the whole matter : —

"It is true there were cruelties practised by the Filipinos on the Spaniards. But they were ebullitions of revenge for three centuries of tyranny. They do not prove unfitness for self-government. I, for one, prefer to follow the example set by the Roosevelt amnesty of 1902, and draw the veil over all those matters." [1]

The judge drew the veil not only over this, but, as we have seen, over numerous other pertinent matters which occurred in this land of "profound peace and tranquillity" just at the time Wilcox and Sargent were making their trip. My apologies to him for withdrawing the veil and for maintaining that such occurrences as those in question demonstrate complete and utter unfitness for self-government on the part of those who brought them about!

If it be true that Blount knew more than one officer of the American army who did things to the Filipinos almost as cruel as Villa did to Lieutenant Piera, why did he not report them and have the criminals brought to justice?

Such an attack on the army, in the course of which there is not given a name or a fact which could serve as a basis for an investigation, is cowardly and despicable.

I do not for a moment believe that Blount speaks the truth, but if he does, then his failure to attempt to bring to justice the human fiends concerned brands him!

It has been the fashion in certain quarters to make vile allegations of this sort against officers of the United States army, couching them in discreetly general terms. This is a contemptible procedure, for it frees those who make reckless charges from danger of the criminal proceedings which would otherwise doubtless be brought against them.

[1] Blount, p. 113.

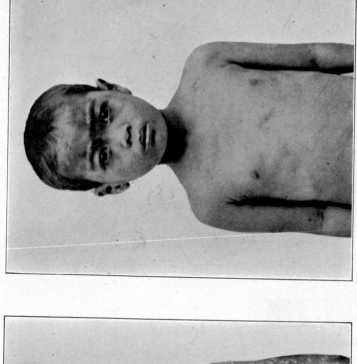

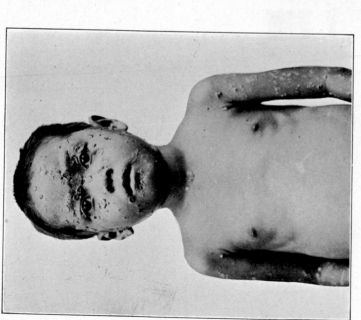

A Victim of Yaws before and after Treatment with Salvarsan.

The discovery that salvarsan was a specific for the disfiguring disease known as yaws was made by Dr. R. P. Strong of the Bureau of Science. The effect of this drug is almost miraculous. A single injection usually cures completely.

On arrival at Ilagan, the town where Piera was tortured to death, Blount says [1] that Messrs. Wilcox and Sargent were

"given a grand *baile* [ball] and *fiesta* [feast], a kind of dinner-dance, we would call it. . . . From Ilagan they proceeded to Aparri, cordially received everywhere, and finding the country in fact, as Aguinaldo always claimed in his proclamations of that period, seeking recognition of his government by the Powers, in a state of profound peace and tranquillity — free from brigandage and the like."

Within sight of the banquet hall, within hearing of the music, lay a lighter on which were huddled eighty-four priests of the Catholic Church, many of them gray-haired old men, innocent of any evil conduct, who for weeks had suffered, mentally and physically, the tortures of the damned.

Of the events of this evening and the following day Father Malumbres says : —

"From the river the *convento* could be seen profusely illuminated and the strains of music could be heard, an evident sign that they were engaged in revelry. This gave us a bad start, as we came to fear that Villa had returned from the expedition undertaken to come up with two Americans who had crossed the Caraballo range and were thinking of coming down as far as Aparri. It was late to announce to Villa our arrival at Ilagan, so that we were obliged to pass the night on the lighter. In the morning our boat was anchored in front of the pueblo of Ilagan, where we were credibly informed that Villa had returned. This accursed news made us begin to fear some disagreeable incident.

"Our Matias went ashore and delivered the official communication regarding our transfer to Villa, while we waited impatiently for his decision. Sergeant Matias at length returned with orders for our disembarkation ; we put on the best clothes we had and the rowers placed a broad plank between the lighter and the arsenal and we left our floating prison two abreast. Matias called the roll and the order to march, we were eighty-four friars in a long column climbing the steep ascent to Ilagan.

[1] Blount, p. 114.

"When we had arrived in front of the building used for head-quarters, we faced about in front thereof, and the first thing we saw in one of the windows were the sinister features of Falaris, who with a thundering brow and black look was delighting himself in the contemplation of so many priests surrounded by bayonets and filled with misery. Any other person but Villa would have melted on seeing such a spectacle, which could but incite compassion. The two American tourists were also looking on at this horrible scene as if stupefied, but they soon withdrew in order, perhaps, not to look upon such a painful picture. It was, indeed, heartrending to contemplate therein old gray-haired men who had passed their lives in apostolic work side by side with young men who had just arrived in this ungrateful land, and many sick who rather than men seemed to be marble statues, who had no recourse but to stand in line, without one word of consolation; therein figured some who wore religious garb, others in secular dress limited to a pair of rumpled trousers and a cast-off coat, the lack of this luxurious garment being replaced in some instances by a native shirt.

"For two long hours we were detained in the middle of the street under the rays of a burning sun and to the scandal of the immense crowd which had been gathered together to witness the denouement of the tragedy. The priests had hardly come into the presence of Villa when Fathers Isidro and Florentino were called out for the purpose of having heaped upon them a flood of insults and affronts. Father Isidro was ordered by Villa to interview Sr. Sabas Orros, who, Villa supposed, would wreak his revenge blindly upon him, but he was greatly mis-taken, as said gentleman treated the priest with great respect; the tyrant remained talking to Father Florentino in the recep-tion room of the headquarters building, and when it appeared that such talk would come to blows, the elder of the Americans left one of the rooms toward the reception room, and the scene suddenly changing, Villa arose and addressing the priest said: 'I am pleased to introduce to you an American Brigadier-General, Mr. N.' The latter returned a cordial greeting in Spanish to the priest who made a courteous acknowledgment; after this exchange of courtesies, Villa resumed his defamatory work, pouring out a string of absurdities and infamous insults upon the friars, going so far as to say in so many words: 'from the bishop down you are all thieves and depraved' he added another word which it would be shameful to write down, and so he went on from one abyss to another without regard to reputations or the respect due to venerated persons.

"The American let his disgust be seen while Villa was talking, and the latter understood these protests and ordered the priest to withdraw, the comedy coming to an end by the American shaking hands with the priest and offering him assistance. Villa would not shake hands with him, as was natural, but the priest was able to see that he was confused when he saw the distinction and courtesy with which an American general had treated a helpless friar. What a narrow idea did the Americans form of the government of Aguinaldo, represented by men as savage and inhuman as Villa !

"The natives averred that the Americans referred to were spies who had come to explore those provinces and were making maps of the strategic points and principal roads, so that a very careful watch was kept upon them and Villa took measures to have them go down the river without landing at any place between Echague and Ilagan. At Ilagan they were given an entertainment and dance, Villa being a skilled hand in this sort of thing, and a few days later he accompanied them to Aparri[1] without allowing them to set foot on land. The government of Aguinaldo no longer had everything its own way, and secret orders had been given to have every step of the explorers followed. The commanding and other leading officers of the Valley, supporting the orders of the government, circulated an order throughout the towns which read as follows : —

"'To all Local Officers:

"'You will not permit any maps to be made or notes to be taken of strategic points by Americans or foreigners; nor will you allow them to become acquainted with the points of defence; you will endeavour to report immediately to this Government any suspicious persons; you will make your investigations secretly, accompanying suspected persons and feigning that their investigations are approved, and finally when it shall seem to you that such suspected persons have finished their work, you will advise without loss of time, in order that their notes may be seized.'

"Despite this order the Americans were able to inform themselves very thoroughly of the forces in the Valley and its state of defence, and Filipinos were not lacking who for a few pesos would put them abreast of all information regarding the plans and projects of Aguinaldo's government."

Relative to this Wilcox-Sargent trip Taylor says : —

[1] A distance of 120 miles.

"In October and November, 1898, Paymaster W. B. Wilcox, U.S.N., and Naval Cadet L. R. Sargent, U.S.N., travelled through Northern Luzon from which they returned with a favourable impression of the government which had been set up by Aguinaldo's agents.

"It was realized by the subtle men whom they met that it was highly expedient that they should make a favourable report and accordingly they were well received, and although constant obstacles were thrown in the way of their seeing what it was not considered well for them to see yet the real reasons for the delays in their journey were carefully kept from them. At least some of their letters to the fleet were taken, translated, and sent to Aguinaldo, who kept them, and constant reports upon them and their movements were made."

Blount refers to the fact that Mr. Sargent tells a characteristic story of Villa,[1] whose vengeful feeling toward the Spaniards showed on all occasions.

It would doubtless have interested the travellers to know that the "robbery" consisted in taking the funds out of the province to save them from falling into Villa's hands, and in paying them to soldiers in Nueva Vizcaya to whom money was due. It would further have interested them to know that this unfortunate Spaniard had been twice tortured within an inch of his life by Villa.

But let us continue our interrupted narrative : —

"The presence of the Americans in Ilagan soon freed us from certain forms of savagery and barbarous intentions on the part of Villa. There can be no doubt that the tyrant was constantly cudgelling his brains to invent new methods of showing his contempt for the friars; at the unlucky time we write of he conceived the infamous plan of ordering a circular enclosure of cane to be made, put a pig into it — we trust the reader will pardon the details — with a bell hung to his neck, blindfolded the priests and compelled them to enter the enclosure with sticks in their hands, and in this ridiculous attitude,

[1] "The former Spanish Governor of the Province was of course a prisoner in Villa's custody. Villa had the ex-Governor brought in, for the travellers to see him, and remarked, in his presence to them, 'This is the man who robbed this province of twenty-five thousand dollars during the last year of his office.'" — Blount, p. 115.

obliged them to strike about when the sound of the bell appraised them of the animal's proximity; it is obvious that the principal purpose of the fiendish Villa was to have the priests lay about them in such a way as to deal each other the blows instead of the pig. The tyrant also had the idea of making us and the other priests in Ilagan parade the streets of that town dancing and playing the band. The wish to consummate his plan was not lacking but he was deterred by the presence of the Americans and the arguments of Sr. Sabas Orros to whom we also owed the signal favour that Villa did not take us to our prisons at Tumauini and Gamut on foot and with our clothing in a bundle at our backs."

On October 2 a banquet was given in Villa's honour at Ilagan and the pleasant idea occurred to him to have four of the friars dance at it for his amusement. The people of the town put their handkerchiefs before their faces to shut out the sight, and some wept. Father Campo, one of the priests who was obliged to dance, had great ulcers on his legs from the wounds caused by the cords with which he had been bound when he was tortured with water, and was at first unable to raise his feet from the floor; but Villa threatened him with a rattan until he finally did so. This caused the sores on his legs to burst open so that the bones showed.

On the 3d of October a number of the friars were compelled to get up a band and go out and meet Leyba with music on his arrival. The people of the towns closed their windows in disgust at the sight. A great crowd had gathered to receive Leyba, and the priests were compelled to dance in the middle of the street, but this again only caused disgust. A couple of priests were then beaten in the usual fashion in a private house. This caused murmuring even among those of the soldiers who were natives of the Cagayan valley. At the same time two other priests were horribly whipped in the prison.

This has been a long story, but the half has not been told. Those who escaped torture had their feelings

harrowed by the sight of the sufferings of their fellows.
They were constantly and grossly insulted; were often
confined in the most unsanitary quarters; given poor
and insufficient food and bad water, or none at all;
robbed of their clothing; compelled to march long dis-
tances under a tropical sun when sick, wounded and
suffering; obliged to do servants' work publicly; forced
to make a ridiculous spectacle of themselves in the public
streets; ordered to recant, and heaven knows what
not!

The torments practised on them had two principal
objects: to compel them to give up money, and to discredit them with the common people. They failed to
accomplish this latter result. There is abundant evidence
that the natives of the Cagayan valley clothed and fed
them when they could, and wept over the painful humiliations and the dreadful sufferings which they were
powerless to prevent or relieve.

The tormentors were men from distant provinces, with
no possible personal grievances against the priests whom
they martyrized. Their action was the result, not of an
"ebullition of revenge for three centuries of tyranny"
as stated by Blount, but of insensate greed of gold and
damnable viciousness. I believe the American people
will hold that such cruelities brand those who practise
them as unfit to govern their fellows, or themselves.

Lest I be accused of basing my conclusions on *ex parte*
statements I will now return to the Insurgent record of
events in the Cagayan valley.

At the outset the Spanish officers of the Tabacalera
Company [1] fared comparatively well. In a letter dated
September 27, 1898, and addressed to the secretary of
war of the revolutionary government, Leyba says of
the taking of Tuguegarao that the only terms of the surrender were to respect life. He therefore felt at liberty

---

[1] *La Compañia General de Tabacos de Filipinas*, a very strong commercial organization.

to seize all the money that the friars had hidden, "which was accomplished by applying the stick." He adds that they did nothing to the agents of the great Tabacalera Company, then the most powerful commercial organization in the Islands, for the significant reason that they had found that its stock was largely held by Frenchmen and feared trouble.[1]

On December 4, 1898, Leyba, concerning whose ideas as to public order we are already informed, wrote a most illuminating letter setting forth the conditions which had existed there. He does not claim that there had been Octavian peace!

It should be borne in mind that this letter covers the very time during which Messrs. Wilcox and Sargent passed through the Cagayan valley. It paints a vivid picture of conditions, and as the painter was the ranking Insurgent officer in the valley during this entire period, he cannot be accused of hostile prejudice. I therefore give the letter in full : —

"APARRI, December 4, 1898.
"DON BALDOMERO AGUINALDO,
    "THE SECRETARY OF WAR :

"DEAR SIR AND OF MY GREATEST ESTEEM : I take the liberty of addressing this to you in order to state that owing to the lack of discipline in the soldiers whom we have brought, since they are all volunteers and whom I am not able to reduce

---

[1] "I call your attention to the fact that the only terms to the surrender were to respect life, and it was for this reason that I seized all the money they [*i.e.* the friars, — D. C. W.] had hidden away, which was accomplished by applying the stick. In this capital I found thirty-four thousand dollars in silver and a draft on the Compañia General de Tabacos for twenty thousand dollars which can be collected here. . . .

"The bearer can give you more details concerning the abuses committed in this province of Vizcaya by the forces of Major Delfin Esquizel. Also, I wish to inform you that we have done nothing to the Compañia General de Tabacos, for we have learned from their records that much of their stock is held by Frenchmen, and consequently we fear a conflict. For this reason we await your orders on this matter. We took all the arms we found in their possession, however." — P. I. R., 271. 2.

to rigorous subordination, for the revolution would find itself without soldiers with whom to win triumph, they committed many abuses and misdeed which, for the lack of evidence, I was not able to punish, although I knew of these abuses but had no proof, and as a lover of my country and of the prestige of the Revolutionary Army, I took care not to disclose the secret to any one, in this way avoiding the formation of an atmosphere against the cause of our Independence to the grave injury of us all.   But it happened that, in spite of the good advice which I have given them and the punishments which I have given to some of the 3d Company of Cauit, they did not improve their conduct but have gone to the extreme of committing a scandalous robbery of 20,800 pesos which sum the German, Otto Weber, was taking to the capital, which deed has caused me to work without ceasing, without sleeping entire nights, for I understood what a serious matter it was to take money from a foreigner. After making many inquiries, it was discovered that a very large part of the money which reached the sum of $10,000, a little more or less, was buried under the quarters which the said company occupied, this with the sanction of all the officers, it appears to me, because it is impossible that such a sum could be brought into a house where so many soldiers are living without the knowledge of the officers.

"Indignant at such shameful behaviour, I reprimanded the officers and preferred charges against the ones I deemed to blame in the matter.

"Afterwards I found out that they had attempted to murder me for trying to find out the originators of the crime.   On account of this, and in order to prevent a civil war which would have broken out against the said soldiers if precautions had not been taken, I decided to disarm them, to the great displeasure of the Colonel who was not aware of my motives.

"This bad conduct has been copied by the soldiers of the 4th Company stationed in Ilagan, and I believe the Colonel, guided by my warning, will take the same measures in regard to them.

"As the officers are the first ones to commit abuses and misdeeds, it is easily seen that the soldiers under their orders, guided by them, will commit worse ones than the chiefs, and as these seem to lack the moral strength to control and reprimand them, I propose to you, if it meets your approval, that all these soldiers and some of the officers be returned to their homes by the steamer *Luzon*, if there should be sufficient coal, or in another if you order it, since they tell me themselves that

THE CULION LEPER COLONY.

Here all known Philippine lepers have been isolated and humanely cared for. As a result, leprosy is rapidly disappearing from the Islands.

because they are far away from their homes they do not wish to continue in the service in this province. This is easily arranged as there are now men stationed in this province for instructing the native volunteers, many of whom have been students, and will therefore make good officers and non-commissioned officers, and in this way a battalion could be formed, well disciplined from the beginning and disgraceful things would be avoided not only towards the natives of this province but also towards foreigners, which is the most important. Having stated my case, I place myself always at your disposal, requesting you will attend to this affair.

"With reference to the 4th Company stationed in the Province of Isabela, whose captain is Don Antonio Monzon of Panamitan, there are many complaints of thefts and assaults committed by the soldiers, and in answer to my questions, Don Simeón Adriano y Villa, Major and Sanitary Inspector and doctor of this battalion, whom I have stationed there for lack of a competent person, tells me that he has always punished and offered advice to officers and soldiers in order to prevent the recurrence of thefts and assaults, but he has never been able to suppress them completely, because the soldiers are abandoned by their officers, and because of lack of example on the part of the latter; they do not understand that it is a great blot when they commit these abuses, since when they discover the goods or house of a Spaniard they believe they have a right to appropriate everything which they encounter.

"I have learned lately, that some foreigners, residents in that province, among them some employees of the Tobacco Factory, 'El Oriente' and of the firm of Baer Senior & Co., who have Spanish employees in various pueblos of that province, have some very serious complaints to make of assaults committed against them prejudicial to their interests; however, I hope that now with the arrival of General Tirona he will regulate matters, although I believe that this gentleman is not sufficiently energetic in proceeding against the officers and soldiers, as I have seen when I reprimanded and punished them for faults committed he has pardoned them, and it appears that he censures energetic acts which we must use in order to subject them to rigorous discipline. The same thing happened when Major Sr. Victa wished to discipline them; it appears that the Colonel reprimanded him when he punished some soldiers for gambling in their quarters, since, as you know, that gentleman believes that he who is right is the one who comes to him first, and who is best able to flatter him.

"The Colonel has agreed with me that his first act on arrival at the province of Isabela should be to disarm and take all the money he finds among the soldiers of the 4th Company (Panamitan) in order to serve as indemnity for the property of the foreigners in case they should make any claim.

"I request that you send some leader or officer in order to superintend our actions, and to lift the doubt which hangs over the person who has worked faithfully and honourably in the sacred cause of our Independence.

"I am filling the position of First Chief in the Port of Aparri temporarily on account of the absence of the Colonel who has conferred on me all his duties and power. After the military operations which were carried on as far as the last town in Isabela, being tired and somewhat sick, I was put in charge of these military headquarters, which I found to be very much mixed up, the town, moreover, being desperate on account of the assaults committed by my predecessor, Rafael Perca, who was appointed by the Colonel, and who was formerly 2d Captain of the steamer *Filipinas*. After arriving and taking charge, having received numerous complaints against him, I had him arrested and I found that he had been guilty of robbery, unlawful use of insignia, illegal marriage, rape and attempted rape. I hold him in custody only awaiting the arrival of the Colonel in order to convene a court-martial for his trial, in which the Colonel will act as President and I as Judge Advocate.

"With nothing more to communicate, I hope you will attend to my just claim and send a special delegate to investigate our acts and see the truth, for perhaps if a statement comes direct from me you will not believe it.

"I am your affectionate and faithful subordinate, who kisses your hand,

(Signed)   "J. N. LEYBA." [1]

Blount states that conditions existed "just like this, all over Luzon and the Visayan Islands." [2]   Unfortunately this was only too true !

The troops complained of by Leyba were made up of Aguinaldo's fellow townsmen. They never obeyed any

[1] P. I. R. 192. 4.

[2] "I was in that town, for a similar purpose, with Governor Taft in 1901, after a bloody war which almost certainly would not have occurred had the Paris Peace Commission known the conditions then existing, just like this, all over Luzon and the Visayan Islands." — Blount, p. 116.

one else, and left a trail of murder and rapine behind them. Aguinaldo never punished them, and from the time when one of them tried to murder their commander until a guard composed of them murdered General Antonio Luna in June, 1899, they are mentioned only with fear and execration.

Blount describes with enthusiasm the establishment of civil government in Cagayan.

Perhaps Americans will be interested in knowing who was its head and how it worked. The "elections" were held on December 9, 1898, and Dimas Guzman was chosen head of the province. He was the man subsequently sentenced to life-imprisonment by Blount, for complicity in the murder of Lieutenant Piera. In describing his method of conducting his government he says that the people doubted the legality of attempts to collect taxes; that the abuses of heads of towns caused rioting in the towns, in which only Ilocanos took part; and that he not only did not report these things but contrived to conceal them from foreigners in the province.[1]

His failure to report these troubles and disorders to his government is of interest, as Blount alleges [2] that dif-

---

[1] "On account of this the vulgar people doubted the legality of our actions in the collection of taxes, and accordingly it became difficult; and this, coupled with the inveterate abuses of the heads of the towns, which the head of the province was not able to perceive in time to check, caused a tumult in Echague, which, owing to wise councils and efforts at pacification, was appeased without it being followed by serious consequences; but I have no doubt that this tumult was due only to the suggestions of ungovernable and passionate persons animated by the spirit of faction, since those who took part in it were all Ilocanos, no native of Echague having any hand in it. The same thing occurred in Naguilian, where the disorders were also quieted. Not only did I make no report of all this to the government of the republic on account of the abnormality of the present conditions, but I also succeeded in concealing them from the foreigners here so that they should not succeed in discovering the truth, which would be to the prejudice of our cause." — Taylor, 42 AJ.

[2] "I may add that as judge of that district in 1901–2 there came before me a number of cases in the trial of which the fact would be brought out of this or that difference among the local authorities hav-

ferences between the local authorities were in a number of cases referred to the Malolos government for settlement.

Blount says [1] that General Otis's reports were full of inexcusable blunders about the Tagálogs taking possession of provinces and making the people do things, and cites the relations between Villa and Dimas Guzman to illustrate the error of these allegations.

He has elsewhere [2] referred to Villa as the "arch-fiend" in the matter of torturing the unhappy Spaniards as well as the Filipinos who incurred his ill-will. We have seen that Guzman proved an apt pupil and did credit to his instructor in connection with the torturing of Lieutenant Piera, but it nevertheless appears from Guzman's own statements that his relations with the Insurgent officers and their subordinates involved some rather grave difficulties. Of Major Canoy, for instance, he says:—

"I must add that the said Major Canoy is such a remarkable character that he saw fit to give my cook a beating for not taking off his hat when he met him. He insulted the delegate of rents of Cabagan Viejo for the same reason. He struck the head man of the town of Bagabag in the face. He put some of the members of the town council of Echague in the stocks, and he had others whipped." [3]

It was really incautious for Governor Guzman to complain of these conditions because Major Canoy and his party won, and the Governor had to resign.

But the day of reckoning came. It was in consequence

ing been referred to the Malolos Government for settlement. And they always waited until they heard from it." — Blount, p. 115.

[1] "General Otis's reports are full of the most inexcusable blunders about how 'the Tagals' took possession of the various provinces and made the people do this or that. Villa's relations with Guzman were just about those of a New Yorker or a Bostonian sent up to Vermont in the days of the American Revolution to help organize the resistance there, in conjunction with one of the local leaders of the patriot cause in the Green Mountain State." — Blount, p. 112.

[2] Blount, p. 114.

[3] Taylor, 42 AJ.

of the atrocities committed by the Tagálog soldiers in the Cagayan valley that Captain Batchelder was able a little later to march practically unopposed through the provinces of Nueva Vizcaya, Isabela and Cagayan with one battalion of American negro troops, for whom he had neither food nor extra ammunition, and that Tirona surrendered the Insurgent forces in the valley without attempting resistance !

CHAPTER VII

INSURGENT RULE IN THE VISAYAS AND ELSEWHERE

REFERRING to the conditions alleged to have been found by Sargent and Wilcox in the Cagayan valley, Blount says : —

"Had another Sargent and another Wilcox made a similar trip through the provinces of southern Luzón about this same time, under similar friendly auspices, before we turned friendship to hate and fear and misery, in the name of Benevolent Assimilation, they would, we now know, have found similar conditions." [1]

So far as concerns the provinces of Mindoro and Palawan, and the great island of Mindanao, he dodges the issue, alleging the unimportance of Mindoro and Palawan, and claiming that "Mohammedan Mindanao" presents a problem by itself. Under such generalities he hides the truth as to what happened in these regions.

I agree with him that there was essential identity between actual conditions in the Cagayan valley and those which prevailed under Insurgent rule elsewhere in Luzón and in the Visayas. I will go further and say that conditions in the Cagayan valley did not differ essentially from those which prevailed throughout all portions of the archipelago which fell under Insurgent control, except that in several provinces captured friars and other Spaniards were quickly murdered whereas in the Cagayan valley no friar was quite killed outright by torture. Those who ultimately died of their injuries lived for some time.

Let us now consider some of the actual occurrences in

[1] Blount, p. 111.

these other provinces, continuing to follow the route of our tourists until it brings us back to Manila.

South Ilocos

The first province visited by Messrs. Wilcox and Sargent after leaving Aparri was South Ilocos. The conditions which had prevailed at Vigan, the capital of the province, shortly before their arrival, are described in a letter signed "Mariano" and addressed under date of September 25, 1898, to Señor Don Mena Crisólogo, from which I quote extracts :—

"DEAR MENA: I read with a happy heart your letter of the 3rd instant, and in answer I have to say :—

"On the 22nd of August a mass meeting was held for the election of the local presidente of this town, and I was elected to the office; and on the 1st instant the Colonel appointed me Provisional Provincial President of this province, so that you can imagine the position I am in and the responsibilities which weigh on me.

"Your house is occupied by the Colonel, in view of the fact that it is not rented.

"I have here eleven friar prisoners and the damned priests who escaped from here have not as yet been returned, but it is known that they are prisoners in Cagayan, and as soon as they arrive here I will treat them as they deserve.

"It is with great regret that I have to relate the events and misfortunes which we have been suffering here since the arrival of the troops, as all the detachments are supported by the towns, and here in the capital where the commissary is established, our resources are exhausted, owing to the unreasonable demands of the commissary, because he never asks what is only just and necessary, but if he needs provisions for 200 men, he always asks enough for 1000. And notwithstanding this, the most lamentable and sad occurrences are taking place almost daily in the different barrios, and often in the town itself; the soldiers are guilty of many abuses and disorderly acts, such as rapes and murders, which usually remain unpunished by reason of the real authors thereof not being found, and when they are found and reported to their commanders, the latter do nothing. One night the house and estate of Sario Tinon in Anannam was sacked by six armed men, who threatened him and took his money, his wife's jewels and the best horses he had. Thank God that his family was at the time in the capital, and it appears that now the authors of this act are being discovered.

"I am at the present time working with Father Aglipay to have the forces stationed here replaced by our volunteers which I am recruiting, in order to prevent in so far as possible the frequent acts of barbarity which the former are committing in the province.

"When the friars from Lepanto arrived here, they were made to publish the following proclamation : —

"'*Proclamation.* — We, the friars, declare that all the acts committed by us against the honest Filipinos when we discharged our respective offices, were false and in contravention of the rights of the Holy Church, because we only wished to deceive and prejudice the honest inhabitants of the Philippines ; for which reason we now suffer what we are suffering, as you see, according to the old adage that "he who owes must pay." And now we inform all you honest Filipinos that we repent for the acts above referred to, which are in contravention of the laws and good customs, and ask your pardon. — VIGAN, September 13, 1898.'

"All of which I communicate to you in order that you may form an idea of what is taking place here, and take such steps as may be proper for the common good, and especially for the good of this town, hoping that with the aid of your valuable protection the abuses and disorders suffered by the residents will be stopped."[1]

The province of Abra, now a subprovince of South Ilocos, was evidently no exception to the general rule, for there is on file a letter to Aguinaldo with twenty-six signatures, protesting bitterly against the oppression of the poor, in the effort to compel them to contribute war taxes, complaining against the misuse of supplies gathered ostensibly for the soldiers, and stating that the petitioners will be obliged to take refuge with the Igorots and Negritos, if not granted relief.[2]

[1] P. I. R., 974. 3.

[2] "December 20, 1898.

"To the Honorable President of the Revolutionary Government.

"The undersigned residents of the *barangay* of D. Francisco Querubín and D. Melchor Balueg, of Bucay, of the province of Abra, appeal

BUILDING THE BENGUET ROAD.

In this, as in many other places, it proved necessary to blast the road out of the solid rock.

Apparently the trouble grew, for on December 27, 1898, the "Director of Diplomacy" telegraphed to Aguinaldo concerning it, saying : —

"Most urgent. The discontent in the provinces of Pangasinán, Tarlac and Yloco (Ilocos) is increasing. The town of Bangbang rose in revolt the 25th and 26th of this month, and killed all of the civil officials. It is impossible to describe the abuses committed by the military and civil authorities of the said provinces. I urge you to send a force of 100 men and a diplomatic officer to reëstablish order. The matter is urgent." [1]

I find nothing important in the Insurgent records concerning conditions in La Union at this time. Pangasinán,

to you with the utmost subjection from their place of residence and state: That their heads or representatives, D. Francisco Querubín and Melchor Balueg, respectively, force them to pay two *pesos* each as a war tax, your humble vassals above cited being hardly able to earn their own livelihood and support their families, and, notwithstanding their labor, some of them cannot get anything to eat without appealing to the charity of their richer neighbours; but notwithstanding this sad situation, they offer a *peseta* each as a mark of gratitude to the mother country, Filipinas, but said gentlemen, the representatives mentioned, have not the slightest pity and worry us to the extent of having kept us in our houses a day and a night without anything to eat, not even permitting us to go out to get a drink.

"We must inform you that the head of the *barangay*, D. Melchor Balueg, when he gathers the supplies for the troops stationed in his town, said supplies consisting of rice, pigs, chickens and eggs, uses one-half of what is gathered, and then again orders his assistants to save."

"In fact, the undersigned request you to direct that the *peseta* which they offer be accepted and that the said Don Francisco Querubín and Don Melchor Balueg be relieved of their duties, in order to put a stop to the abuses constantly committed by them; and if this be not done, the petitioners will be obliged to leave their homes and property in the town and take up their residences in the mountains with the Negritos and Igorots, in order that the others may remain in the town and live tranquilly.

"This is a grace which we do not doubt we will receive from you, whose life may God preserve for many years.

"BUCAY, November 12, 1898."　　　　　(26 signatures)

(In blue pencil in the handwriting of Aguinaldo :) "It will be approved.
"Dec. 20, 1898.

"E. A."
—P. I. R., 991. 4.

[1] P. I. R., 849.

Tarlac, Pampanga and Bulacan, which were now revisited by our tourists, have already been discussed.

The Province of Manila

Conditions in Manila Province, as distinguished from Manila City, left much to be desired.

Admiral Dewey made a statement applicable to the territory adjacent to the city and bay of Manila in a cablegram to Washington dated October 14, 1898, which reads as follows : —

"It is important that the disposition of the Philippine Islands should be decided as soon as possible. . . . General anarchy prevails without the limits of the city and bay of Manila. Natives appear unable to govern." [1]

Of it Blount says : —

"In this cablegram the Admiral most unfortunately repeated as true some wild rumours then currently accepted by the Europeans and Americans at Manila which, of course, were impossible of verification. I say 'unfortunately' with some earnestness, because it does not appear on the face of his message that they were mere rumours. And, that they were wholly erroneous, in point of fact, has already been cleared up in previous chapters, wherein the real state of peace, order, and tranquillity which prevailed throughout Luzón at that time has been, it is believed, put beyond all doubt." [2]

Blount seems here to have overlooked the fact that the admiral himself was in Manila Bay and in Manila City at the time he sent this cablegram. The statements in question were not rumours, they were deliberate expressions of opinion on the part of a man who had first-hand information and knew what he was saying.

They were not the Admiral's only allegations on this subject. When testifying before the Senate committee he said : —

"*Admiral Dewey.* I knew that there was no government in the whole of the Philippines. Our fleet had destroyed the

[1] Blount, p. 130.   [2] *Ibid.*, pp. 130–131.

only government there was, and there was no other government; there was a reign of terror throughout the Philippines, looting, robbing, murdering; a reign of terror throughout the islands."

La Laguna

Having brought our tourist friends safely back to Manila, we must now leave them there and strike out by ourselves if we are to see other provinces.

La Laguna lies just east of Manila. Of it we learn that:

"Laguna Province was so overrun by bands of robbers that the head of the pueblo of San Pablo ordered the people to concentrate in the town to avoid their attacks." [1]

Bataan

The province of Bataan lies just across the bay from Manila.

"On January 10, 1899, the secretary of the interior directed the governor of Bataan Province to ascertain the whereabouts of a number of men who had just deserted with their rifles from the commands there. He was to appeal to their patriotism and tell them that if they would but return to their companies their complaints would be attended to and they would be pardoned." [2]

Zambales

Zambales joins Bataan on the west and north. On November 13, 1898, Wenceslao Vinvegra wrote to Aguinaldo describing the state of affairs in this province. From his letter we learn that two brothers named Teodoro and Doroteo Pansacula, claiming to be governor and brigadier general respectively, who are charged with abandonment of their posts in the field, disobedience and attempts against the union of the Insurgents, had been committing all manner of abuses. They had organized a band of cut-throats, armed with rifles and bolos, and

[1] P. I. R., 1142. 4.   [2] *Ibid.*, 2002. 3.

were terrorizing the towns, committing robberies and murders and ordering that money be furnished for themselves and food for their men.

They were also encouraging the people to disobey the local authorities and refuse to pay taxes, and were promulgating a theory, popular with the masses, that the time had come for the rich to be poor and the poor rich.

They had furthermore induced regular Insurgent troops to rise up in arms.[1]

From this communication it would appear that the Insurgent government had not been entirely effective in Zambales up to November 13th, 1898.

From other communications we learn that the soldiers at Alaminos were about to desert on November 30th, 1898;[2] that it was deemed necessary to restrict travel between Tarlac, Pampanga, Bataan and Zambales in order to prevent robberies;[3] and that on January 9, 1899, the governor of the province found it impossible to continue the inspection of a number of towns, as many of their officials had fled to escape the abuses of the military.[4] Conditions were obviously very serious in Zambales at this time.

[1] P. I. R., 964. 3.

[2] "On November 30, 1898, the commander in Alaminos, Zambales Province, telegraphed that his soldiers were all about to desert as the head of the town would not furnish rations or pay without orders from the governor." — P. I. R., 2002. 3.

[3] "On December 22, Aguinaldo, in accordance with a request from the governor of Zambales Province, ordered the heads of the provinces of Pangasinán, Tarlac, Bataan, and Pampanga to prohibit the people of their provinces from going to Zambales without passports signed by them, stating the route they were to take in going and returning and the length of time to be spent in the journey. The governor of Zambales had asked for this regulation in order to prevent the commission of robberies in Zambales and to distinguish persons justly subject to suspicion from those of good conduct." — P. I. R., 266. 3.

[4] "On January 9, the governor of Zambales found it impossible to continue the inspection of certain towns of his province and to continue holding elections, as many of the officials had fled to escape the exactions and abuses of the military commanders."
— P. I. R., 988. 2.

Cavite

Cavite province lies immediately south of Manila province as the latter was then constituted. On August 24, 1898, the secretary of war wired Aguinaldo that two drunken Americans had been killed by Insurgent soldiers.[1] On the same day General Anderson advised the governor of Cavite that one American soldier had been killed and three wounded by his people, and demanded his immediate withdrawal, with his guard, from the town.[2] The governor asked Aguinaldo for instructions. Aguinaldo replied instructing the governor to deny that the American had been killed by Insurgent soldiers and to claim that he had met death at the hands of his own companions. The governor was further directed to give up his life before leaving the place.[3]

In view of the definite statement from one of his own officers that the soldier in question was killed by Filipino soldiers, Aguinaldo's instructions to say that he was killed by Americans are interesting as showing his methods.

Not only were the Insurgents obviously unable to control their own soldiers in Cavite town sufficiently to prevent them from committing murder, but conditions in the province of the same name left much to be desired.

---

[1] "The Governor of Cavite reports two drunken Americans have been killed by our soldiers. I tell him to have an investigation immediately and report the fact to the American commander." — P. I. R., 849.

[2] "Most urgent. Gen. Anderson informs me in a letter that, 'in order to avoid the very serious misfortune of an encounter between our troops, I demand your immediate withdrawal with your guard from Cavite. One of my men has been killed and three wounded by your people.' This is positive and does not admit of explanation or delay. I ask you to inform me of your decision." — P. I. R., 849.

[3] "Gen. Riego de Dios, Cavite: Telegram received. Do not leave the post, and say that you cannot abandon the city without my orders, and say that he was not killed by our soldiers, but by them themselves [the Americans. — D. C. W.], since they were drunk, according to your telegram. Give up your life before abandoning that place, and investigate matters." — P. I. R., 849.

On December 29, 1898, the governor wired Aguinaldo that the town of Marigondong had risen in arms.[1]

It is a well-known fact that land records were destroyed in Cavite. Of this matter Taylor says: —

"In Cavite, in Cavite Province, and probably in most of the other provinces, one of the first acts of the insurgents who gathered about Aguinaldo was to destroy all the land titles which had been recorded and filed in the Spanish administrative bureaus. In case the independence of the Philippines was won, the land of the friars, the land of the Spaniards and of those who still stood by Spain, would be in the gift of Aguinaldo or of any strong man who could impose his will upon the people. And the men who joined this leader would be rich in the chief riches of the country, and those who refused to do so would be ruined men." [2]

Sorsogón

"The native civil officials who took charge of the government of Sorsogón Province when the Spaniards abandoned it did not think it worth while to hoist the insurgent flag until a force of four companies arrived there to take station early in November, 1898. The officer in command promptly ordered the Chinamen in the town of Sorsogón, who are prosperous people, to contribute to the support of his troops. They at once gave him cloth for uniforms, provisions, and 10,000 pesos. This was not sufficient, for on November 8 Gen. Ignacio Paua, who seems to have been the insurgent agent in dealing with the Chinese, complained that the troops in Sorsogón were pillaging the Chinamen there. They had killed 13, wounded 19, and ruined a number of others." [3]

In January, 1899, a correspondent wrote Aguinaldo that it was very difficult to collect taxes as every one was taking what he could lay his hands on.[4]

---

[1] "Urgent. Gen. Alvarez telegraphed that Riego de Dios informed him that the town of Maragondong had risen in arms on account of abuses committed by the local President against Salvador Riego. This is the reason the town took up arms. Will go there to-morrow."
— P. I. R., 849.

[2] Taylor, 19 AJ.   [3] P. I. R., 1057. 4.   [4] Taylor, 95 HS.

Ambos Camarines

On September 18, 1898, Elias Angeles, a corporal of the *guardia civil*, headed an uprising against the Spaniards. The Spanish officer in command, and all of his family, were killed by shooting up through the floor of the room which they occupied. Angeles then assumed the title of Politico-Military-Governor.

When the Tagálog Vicente Lucban arrived on his way to Samar, he ordered Angeles to meet him at Magarao, with all his troops and arms, disarmed the troops, giving their rifles to his own followers, marched into Nueva Caceres and took possession of the entire government. Aguinaldo subsequently made Lucban a general, and sent him on his way to Samar.

Lucban was succeeded by another Tagálog, "General" Guevara, a very ignorant man, who displayed special ability in making collections, and is reported to have kept a large part of the funds which came into his possession.

Colonel Peña, who called himself "General," was one of the worst of the Tagálog invaders, for they were practically that. He threatened all who opposed him with death, and summarily shot at least one man in Tigaon. That town subsequently rose against him, and he was badly cut up by the Bicols.[1] On getting out of the hospital he was sent away.

The daughters of prominent families suffered at the hands of these villains. Peña abducted one, a son of Guevara another. Her brother followed young Guevara and killed him. If girls of the best families were so treated, how must those of the common people have fared?

Braganza ordered the killing of all Spaniards and Chinese at Minalabag. Some forty-eight Spaniards were murdered.

[1] The name applied to the Filipinos of Ambos Camarines, Albay and Sorsogón.

Many Chinese were killed at Pasacao; about thirty at Libmanan by order of Vicente Ursua a Tagálog; more than twenty at Calabanga.

Conditions became so unbearable that Faustino Santa Ana gathered around him all Bicols who were willing to fight the Tagálogs, but the troubles were finally patched up.

American troops had little difficulty in occupying Ambos Camarines and other Bicol provinces, owing to the hatred in which the Tagálogs were held.

Mindoro

Conditions in the important island of Mindoro may be inferred from the fact that it became necessary for its governor to issue a decree on November 10, 1898, which contained the following provisions among others : —

"2nd.   The local presidentes of the pueblos will not permit any one belonging to their jurisdiction to pass from one pueblo to another nor to another province without the corresponding pass, with a certificate upon its back that the taxes of its holder have been paid.

" 3rd.   That from this date no one will be allowed to absent himself from his pueblo without previously informing its head who will give him an authorization on which will be noted the approval of the presidente of the pueblo. . . .

" 5th.   Persons arriving from a neighboring town or province in any pueblo of this province will immediately present themselves before the presidente of said pueblo with their passes. He will without charge, stamp them with his official seal."[1]

These are peculiar regulations for a province which is at peace, and as Major Taylor has truly remarked : —

"The form of liberty contemplated by the founders of the Philippine Republic was not considered incompatible with a very considerable absence of personal freedom."[2]

Later, when travelling through Mindoro, I was told how an unfortunate legless Spaniard, who had been running a small shop in one of the towns and who was on good terms with his Filipino neighbors, was carried out into

[1] P. I. R., 262. 3.   [2] Taylor, 48 AJ.

FREIGHT AUTOS ON THE BENGUET ROAD.

This road has been correctly described as "an automobile boulevard," but the autos in use on it are not all pleasure machines.

the plaza, seated in a chair, and then cut to pieces with bolos in the presence of his wife and children who were compelled to witness the horrible spectacle!

On this same trip Captain R. G. Offley, then the American Governor of Mindoro, told me while I was at Pinamalayan that the people there were greatly alarmed because a murderer, liberated under the amnesty, had returned and was prowling about in that vicinity. This man had a rather unique record. He had captured one of his enemies, and after stripping him completely had caused the top of an immense ant-hill to be dug off. The unfortunate victim was then tied, laid on it, and the earth and ants which had been removed were shovelled back over his body until only his head projected. The ants did the rest! Another rather unusual achievement of this interesting individual was to tie the feet of one of his enemies to a tree, fasten a rope around his neck, hitch a carabao to the rope, and start up the carabao, thus pulling off the head of his victim. Yet this man and others like him were set at liberty under the amnesty proclamation, in spite of the vigorous protests of the Philippine Commission, who thought that murderers of this type ought to be hanged.

And now I wish to discuss briefly an interesting and highly characteristic statement of Judge Blount. In referring to conditions in the Visayan Islands, he says: —

"Of course the Southern Islands were a little slower. But as Luzón goes, so go the rest. The rest of the archipelago is but the tail to the Luzón kite. Luzón contains 4,000,000 of the 8,000,000 people out there, and Manila is to the Filipino people what Paris is to the French and to France. Luzón is about the size of Ohio, and the other six islands that really matter, are in size mere little Connecticuts and Rhode Islands, and in population mere Arizonas or New Mexicos."[1]

This paragraph is no exception to the general rule that the statements of this author will not bear analysis. One

[1] Blount, p. 116.

of the other six islands that he says really matters is
Samar. Its area is 5031 square miles. The area of
Rhode Island is 1250 square miles. The smallest of the
six islands named is Bohol, with an area of 1411 square
miles. It cannot be called a little Rhode Island.

As regards population, Arizona has 122,931. It is
hardly proper to call either Panay with a population of
743,646, Cebu with 592,247, Negros with 460,776, Leyte
with 357,641, Bohol with 243,148 or even Samar with
only 222,690, a mere Arizona, and New Mexico with
195,310 is also a bit behind.

Luzón really has an area of 40,969 square miles and a
population of 3,798,507.[1] What Blount is pleased to call
"the tail to the Luzón kite," is made up as follows: —

ISLAND	AREA (SQUARE MILES)	POPULATION
Samar	5,031	222,690
Negros	4,881	460,776
Panay	4,611	743,646
Leyte	2,722	357,641
Cebu	1,762	592,247
Bohol	1,411	243,148
Totals	20,419	2,620,148

Even so, the tail is a trifle long and heavy for the kite,
but if we are going to compare Luzón with "the Southern
Islands," by which Blount can presumably only mean the
rest of the archipelago, why not really do it? The process involves nothing more complicated than the subtrac-
tion of its area and population from those of the archipelago as a whole.

	AREA (SQUARE MILES)	POPULATION
Philippines . . .	115,026	7,635,426
Luzón	40,969	3,798,507
Difference . .	74,057	3,836,919

[1] Accepting the 1903 census figures.

Performing this operation, we discover that the tail would fly away with the kite, as Luzón has less than half of the total population and only a little more than a third of the total area.

To compare the area or the population of one large island with those of individual small ones, in determining the relative importance of the former in the country of which it makes up a part, is like comparing the area and population of a great state with those of the individual counties going to make up other states.

Blount resorts to a similar questionable procedure in trying to show the insignificance of Mindoro and Palawan. There are an island of Mindoro and a province of Mindoro; an island of Palawan and a province of Palawan. In each case the province, which includes numerous small islands, as well as the large one from which it takes its name, is much larger and more populous than is the main island, and obviously it is the province with which we are concerned.

Even if Blount wished to limit discussion to the Christian natives commonly called Filipinos, his procedure is still wholly unfair. Of these there are 3,575,001 in Luzón and 3,412,685 in the other islands. In other words, the Filipino population is almost equally divided between the two regions.

As he would not have found it convenient to discuss the conditions which arose in Mindanao under Insurgent rule, he attempts to show that no political importance attaches to them. In the passage above quoted he does not so much as mention either Mindoro or Palawan (Paragua). Elsewhere, however, he attempts to justify his action by making the following statements:—

"The political or governmental problem being now reduced from 3141 islands to eleven, the last three [1] of the nine

[1] Aguinaldo considered Mindanao important enough to form one of the three federal states into which he proposed to divide the Philippines.

contained in the above table may also be eliminated as follows : [1] —

"Mindoro, the large island just south of the main bulk of Luzón, pierced by the 121st meridian of longitude east of Greenwich, is thick with densely wooded mountains and jungle over a large part of its area, has a reputation of being very unhealthy (malarious), is also very sparsely settled, and does not now, nor has it ever, cut any figure politically as a disturbing factor." [2]

Apart from the fact that the political problem involved in the government of the important islands which Blount would thus leave out of consideration, is not solved by ignoring it, certain of his further statements cannot be allowed to go uncorrected.

The allegation that the island has never "cut any figure politically as a disturbing factor" is absurd. In the Spanish days its forests furnished a safe refuge for evil-doers who were from time to time driven out of Cavite and Batangas. A large proportion of its Filipino inhabitants were criminals who not infrequently organized regular piratical expeditions and raided towns in Masbate, Romblon and Palawan. The people of the Cuyos and Calamianes groups lived in constant terror of the Mindoro pirates, and *tulisanes*,[3] who paid them frequent visits. I myself have been at Calapan, the capital of the province, when the Spanish officials did not dare to go without armed escort as far as the outskirts of the town for fear of being captured and held for ransom. During considerable periods they did not really pretend to exercise control over the criminal Filipinos inhabiting the west coast of the island. Conditions as to public order were worse in Mindoro than anywhere else in the archipelago north of Mindanao and Joló.

No less absurd are Blount's suggestions as to the general worthlessness of the island. There are high mountains in its interior, and there are great stretches of the

---

[1] Blount, p. 228.   [2] *Ibid.*, p. 229.   [3] Bandits, or organized robbers.

most fertile land in the world along its coast. Its northern and eastern portions have a very heavy and evenly
distributed rainfall, and are admirably suited to the growing of cocoanuts, hemp, cacao, rubber and similar tropical products. In this region rice flourishes wonderfully
without irrigation. There was a time in the past when
Mindoro was known as "the granary of the Philippines."
Later its population was decimated by constant Moro
attacks, and cattle disease destroyed its draft animals,
with the result that the cultivated lands were abandoned
to a considerable extent and again grew up to jungle,
from which, however, it is easy to redeem them. The
west coast has strongly marked wet and dry seasons similar to those at Manila. There is abundant water available for irrigation, furnished by streams which never run
dry. Much of the soil is rich, and will grow the best of
sugar in large quantity. The forests, which now cover
extensive areas, abound in fine woods, and produce rubber
and other valuable gums. There are outcroppings of
lignite at numerous points on the island, and in the vicinity of Mt. Halcon is found the finest marble yet discovered in this part of the world. Gold is also present
in some quantity at various places. In short, Mindoro
is naturally one of the richest islands in the Archipelago.
If its tillable lands were under high cultivation, it would
support half the population of the Philippines.

Palawan

In endeavouring to show that Palawan is without political importance Blount has followed precisely the procedure which he adopted in the case of Mindoro. First,
he gives the area and the population of the island, when
he should concern himself with the province. The area
of the island is 4027 square miles; that of the province,
5238 square miles. According to the 1903 census, the
population of the island was 10,918, while that of the

province, which contains such thickly settled and fertile
islands as Cuyo and Agutaya, was 39,582. Of course, if
one wishes to emphasize the unimportance of Palawan,
it is more convenient to take the figures for the island.

Blount says : —

"Paragua,[1] the long narrow island seen at the extreme lower
left of any map of the archipelago, extending northeast-south-
west at an angle of about 45°, is practically worthless, being
fit for nothing much except a penal colony, for which purpose
it is in fact now used." [2]

I must deny the truthfulness of his statements, even
if we limit our consideration to the island of Palawan.
Only 159 of its 4027 square miles are utilized for a penal
colony. Its natural wealth is simply enormous. It is
covered throughout the greater part of its extent with
virgin forest containing magnificent stands of the best
timber. Damar, a very valuable varnish gum, is abundant in its mountains. Much of the so-called "Singapore
cane," so highly prized by makers of rattan and wicker
furniture, comes from its west coast. It is a well-watered
island, and its level plains, which receive the wash from
its heavily forested mountains, have a soil of unsurpassed
fertility in which cocoanuts come to bearing in five years
or even less. Incidentally, the greater part of the island
lies south of the typhoon belt. Malampaya Sound, situated near its northwestern extremity, is one of the world's
great harbors. But should we wish to rid ourselves of
this wonderful island, I may say, without violating any
official confidences, that there was a time when Germany
would have been more than pleased to take it off our
hands ; and indeed our British friends, who were sufficiently interested in it to survey it some decades ago,
might possibly be prevailed upon to accept it !

There are good reasons why Blount thought it convenient to make it appear that Palawan was politically un-

---

[1] The old Spanish name for Palawan.   [2] Blount, p. 228.

important. Shortly after the outbreak of hostilities with Spain the Filipino garrison at Puerto Princesa mutinied, and the things which they did were not nice. Among others, they liberated the convicts, Puerto Princesa being at the time a penal colony, and the latter, together with some of the soldiers, started up the east coast of the island, leaving a trail of devastation in their wake. The prosperous town of Tinitian was abandoned as they approached it, and was so thoroughly cleaned out by them that it has never since been reoccupied except by a few stragglers. Other towns, including Tay-Tay, were raided.

On November 27, 1899, Aguinaldo's representative in this province wrote him that the inhabitants were preparing to kill all the Tagálogs and revolt against Insurgent rule.[1] Later when some of the latter were anxious to get the people of one of the northern settlements to take them on a short boat journey, these Visayans consented to give them a lift only on condition that they first allow themselves to be bound, and then took them out to sea and threw them overboard.

Another thing which Blount would have found it inconvenient to discuss is the conduct of the people of Cuyo, at one time the capital of the province. On this island, which contains but twenty-one square miles, there were in 1903 no less than 7545 inhabitants. They hated and feared the people of Mindoro and sent messengers to Iloilo, after the Americans had occupied that place, to beg for a garrison of American troops, and to say that if furnished with an American flag they themselves would defend it. For some reason they were not given the flag, and the sending of a garrison was long delayed. Having grown weary of waiting, they made an American flag of their own, hoisted it, and when the Insurgents from Mindoro came intrenched themselves and defended it. They were actually being besieged when the American garrison finally arrived. Here is one more fact inconsistent with

[1] P. I. R., 944. 10.

the theory that the Filipino people were a unit at Aguinaldo's back, and of course the easiest way to get around such an occurrence is to forget to mention it!

Mindanao

And now we come to the great island of Mindanao, which all but equals Luzón in size, having an area of 36,292 square miles as against the 40,969 of Luzón. Blount's first mention of it is peculiar.

In connection with the words "the other six islands that really matter," in the passage above cited on page 116 of his book, he has inserted a foot-note reading as follows: —

"The six main Visayan Islands. Mohammedan Mindanao is always dealt with in this book as a separate and distinct problem." [1]

But it was hardly possible for him to dismiss this great island, which is a little continent by itself, quite so cavalierly and I will quote the more important of his further and later statements regarding it: —

"While the great Mohammedan island of Mindanao, near Borneo, with its 36,000 square miles of area, requires that the Philippine archipelago be described as stretching over more than one thousand miles from north to south, still, inasmuch as Mindanao only contains about 500,000 people all told, half of them semi-civilized, the governmental problem it presents has no more to do with the main problem of whether, if ever, we are to grant independence to the 7,000,000 Christians of the other islands, than the questions that have to be passed on by our Commissioner of Indian Affairs have to do with the tariff. Mindanao's 36,000 square miles constitute nearly a third of the total area of the Philippine archipelago, and more than that fraction of the 97,500 square miles of territory to a consideration of which our attention is reduced by the process of elimination above indicated. Turning over Mindanao to those crudely Mohammedan semi-civilized Moros would indeed be 'like granting self-government to an

[1] Blount, p. 116.

The Famous Zig-zag on the Benguet Road.

Apache reservation under some local chief,' as Mr. Roosevelt, in the campaign of 1900, ignorantly declared it would be to grant self-government to Luzón under Aguinaldo. Furthermore, the Moros, so far as they can think, would prefer to owe allegiance to, and be entitled to recognition as subjects of, some great nation. Again, because the Filipinos have no moral right to control the Moros, and could not if they would, the latter being fierce fighters and bitterly opposed to the thought of possible ultimate domination by the Filipinos, the most uncompromising advocate of the consent of the governed principles has not a leg to stand on with regard to Mohammedan Mindanao. Hence I affirm that as to it, we have a distinct separate problem, which cannot be solved in the lifetime of anybody now living. But it is a problem which need not in the least delay the advent of independence for the other four-teen fifteenths of the inhabitants of the archipelago — all Christians living on islands north of Mindanao. It is true that there are some Christian Filipinos on Mindanao, but in policing the Moros, our government would of course protect them from the Moros. If they did not like our government, they could move to such parts of the islands as we might permit to be incorporated in an ultimate Philippine republic. Inasmuch as the 300,000 or so Moros of the Mohammedan island of Mindanao and the adjacent islets called Jolo (the 'Sulu archipelago,' so called, 'reigned over' by the sultan of comic opera fame) originally presented, as they will always present, a distinct and separate problem, and never did have anything more to do with the Philippine insurrection against us than their cousins and co-religionists over in near-by Borneo, the task which confronted Mr. Root in the fall of 1899, to wit, the suppression of the Philippine insurrection, meant practically the subjugation of one big island, Luzón, containing half the population and one third of the total area of the archipelago, and six neighbouring small ones, the Visayan Islands." [1]

Now as a matter of fact Mindanao is by no means Mohammedan. The Mohammedan Malays, called Moros, are found here and there along the western coast of the Zamboanga peninsula and along the southern coast of the island as far as Davao. They also extend far up the Cotabato River and occupy the Lake Lanao region, but that

[1] Blount, p. 229.

is all. The interior of the island is for the most part occupied by the members of a number of non-Christian, non-Mohammedan tribes, while its northern and eastern coasts are inhabited by Visayan Filipinos, of whom there are many in Zamboanga itself.

While, as Blount says, the Moros took no part in the insurrection against the United States, the Visayans of Mindanao did, and we had some lively tussles with them in Misamis and in Surigao.

It is indeed unthinkable that we should turn Mindanao over to the Moros. Abandonment of it by us would in the end result in this, as they would take possession of the entire island in the course of time. Neither the other wild tribes nor the Filipinos could stand against them. I heartily agree with the conclusion that we must retain this island for many years before we can settle the problems which it presents. It is further true that we might retain it and still grant independence to the remainder of the Philippine Archipelago, but if we are to eliminate Mindanao from consideration because the Filipinos have no right to control the Moros, of whom there are in reality only about a hundred and fifty-four thousand[1] on the island, and could not if they would, what about Luzón, where there are in reality no less than four hundred and sixty thousand non-Christians,[2] many of whom, like the Ifugaos, Bontoc Igorots, Kalingas and wild Tingians, are fierce fighters and practically all of whom are bitterly opposed to the thought of possible ultimate domination by Filipinos, while most of them welcome American rule?

Have the Filipinos any more moral right to control them than they have to control the Moros? Could they control them if they would? And has the most uncompromising advocate of the consent of the governed principle "a leg to stand on" in the one case if he lacks it in the other?

The Filipino politicians are not ready to admit that

[1] According to the census of 1903, 154,706.   [2] See table on p. 651.

Filipinos could not satisfactorily govern Moros and have even alleged that they did so govern them during the period now under discussion. Let us examine the facts.

Aguinaldo attempted to enter into negotiations with the Sultan of Joló, addressing him as his "great and powerful brother," [1] but this brother does not seem to have received his advances with enthusiasm, and the other brothers proceeded to do things to the Filipinos at the first opportunity.

José Roa in writing Aguinaldo on January 26, 1899, of conditions in the province of Misamis says : [2] —

"Hardly had said evacuation of Iligan taken place on the 28th of last month, when the Moros or Mohammedans of the interior, our mortal enemies since times immemorial on account of their religious fanaticism which they carry to extremes, as do their co-religionists in Europe and Asia, and on account of their objection to leading a civilized life, began to harry the town of Iligan which is the nearest town to the lake around which is the densest Moro population. Due to the prestige of the local president of that town, Señor Carloto Sariol, and the energy that he showed, after some days of constant firing against groups who descended upon the suburbs of the town, he was successful in having them abandon their hostile attitude and promise to live in peace and harmony with said

[1] (Contemporary copy in Spanish. — P. I. R., Books C–L:)
"January 19, 1899.
"The President of the Philippine Republic very cordially greets his great and powerful brother, the Sultan of Jolo, and makes known : —
"That the Filipinos, after having thrown off the yoke of foreign domination cannot forget their brothers of Jolo to whom they are bound by the ties of race, interests, security and defense in this region of the Far East.
"The Philippine Republic has resolved to respect absolutely the beliefs and traditions of each island in order to establish on solid bases the bonds of fraternal unity demanded by our mutual interests.
"I therefore in the name of all the Filipinos very gladly offer to the powerful Sultan of Jolo and to all brothers who acknowledge his great authority, the highest assurance of friendship, consideration and esteem.
"MALOLOS, January 18, 1899."

(No signature.)

[2] P. I. R., 76. 1.

towns, this verbal agreement being participated in by the Dattos of some settlements who did not wish to treat with the Spanish Government.

"Being acquainted nevertheless with these people, we know by experience that the more friendly they appear, the more we must watch against them, because as soon as they find a good opportunity they do not fail to take advantage of it to enter the towns for the purpose of sacking them and kidnapping as many of their inhabitants as possible in order to reduce them to slavery."

Immediately after the abandonment of Cotabato by the Spaniards the Filipino residents set up a government there. A few days later the Moro datos, Piang, Ali and Djimbangan, dropped in with their followers, cut off the head of the Filipino *presidente,* served a few other leading officials and citizens in the same manner, and proceeded to set up a government of their own which was the only government that the place had prior to the arrival of the American troops.

Dato Djimbangan promptly caused the Filipina women of the place to be stripped and compelled to march before him on the public plaza in a state of nudity.

At Zamboanga the Moros could have taken the town at any time after the Spaniards left had they desired to do so. On the arrival of the Americans Dato Mandi offered to take it and turn it over to them, but his proposition was declined.

He subsequently swore to an affidavit relative to conditions under Insurgent rule. It reads as follows: —

"We always had peace in Zamboanga District, except during the revolution of the Filipinos in the year 1899, when for seven or eight months there was in existence the so-called Filipino Republic. During that time there was much robbing and killing; the life of a man was worth no more than that of a chicken; men killed one another for personal gain; enemies fought one another with the bolo instead of settling their differences before the law. It was a time of bloodshed and terror. There was no justice. Because of this the Moros were opposed to the Filipinos. There was conflict between the better class of Filipinos and the revolutionists, who had gained control of the local government." [1]

Elsewhere throughout the Moro territory those Filipinos who did not promptly make their escape were murdered or enslaved. In short, the lion and the lamb lay down together, with the lamb inside as usual.

Thus it will be seen that this first and last attempt of Filipinos to govern Moros did not result in complete success.

Baldomero Aguinaldo made a subsequent attempt to open communication with the Sultan of Joló, authorizing him to establish in all the *rancherias* of Mindanao and Joló a government in accordance with a decree duly transmitted. The Sultan was requested to report the result of his efforts and to give the number of his forces with their arms, and was advised that, "if in this war, which I consider to be the last, we secure our independence and with the opposition of our brothers in that region, with yourself at their head, we are successful in preventing the enemy from gaining a foothold, the grateful country will always render a tribute of homage and gratitude to your memory." [2] Curiously, the Sultan seems to have remained unmoved by the appeal.

[1] From an official document on file at Manila.

[2] "Being brothers, the descendants of the same race and of one soul, the same sun shines upon us and we breathe the same air, so that our sentiments are also one, and we aspire to the independence and liberty of our country in order to secure its progress and place it on a level with other civilized nations; and with this assurance I have taken the liberty to address you this letter, begging of you to accept the commission which in the name of our government I have the honour to confer upon you. You are authorized thereunder to establish in all the 'Rancherias' of Mindanao and Jolo, a civil and military economic-administrative organization, in accordance with the decrees which I enclose herewith, and after having established the same, I request that you make a report to our Honourable President of the Philippine Republic, Sr. Emilio Aguinaldo, of the result thereof and of the number of the force with their arms and ammunition, in order to ascertain whether they would be sufficient to prevent the invasion of the enemy and whether there is any necessity of sending reënforcements of arms to said Islands for this purpose. If in this war, which I consider to be

Masbate

This tight little island of 1236 square miles had in 1903 a Visayan population of 29,451. Its people are all Filipinos, and are on the whole rather an unusually orderly and worthy set. There is no reason why it should have been excluded in considering "the human problem in its broader governmental aspect," whatever that may be, nor can I understand why Blount should have desired to exclude it except that he seems to have been endeavouring to exclude everything possible outside of Luzón, in order to increase the apparent importance of the Christian provinces of that island. Masbate should of course be taken into account in connection with the Visayan Islands, of which it is one.

The islands ordinarily included in the group known as "The Visayas" from the ancient tribal name of the civilized Filipino people who inhabit them, who are called Visayans, are Samar, Panay, Negros, Leyte, Cebú, Bohol, Masbate, Tablas, Romblon, Ticao, Burias, Siquijor and numerous smaller islands adjacent to those named. Although their inhabitants are all rated as one people, they speak a number of more or less distinct dialects. Only Panay, Negros, Samar, Tablas and Sibuyan have non-Christian inhabitants, and in the three islands last named their number is so small as to be negligible. In the mountains of Panay and Negros, however, Negritos are to be found in considerable numbers, as are the representatives of a tribe sometimes called *Monteses* [1] and sometimes

the last, we secure our independence, and with the opposition of our brothers in that region, with yourself at their head, we are successful in preventing the enemy from gaining a foothold, the grateful country will always render a tribute of homage and gratitude to your memory.

"God preserve you many years.

"May 31, 1899.   "BALDOMERO AGUINALDO,
     "Lieut. Gen. Superior P. M. Commander of Southern Region.
"To the Honourable Sultan Raha Halon."

— P. I. R., 810–4.

[1] Spanish for "mountain people."

Bukidnon. The latter tribal designation I have thought it best to reserve for certain inhabitants of northern Mindanao.

In the Visayas, Palawan and Mindanao the government of Aguinaldo was established at various places and different times, without consulting or considering the will of the people. The men who went as his delegates were supported by armed forces, hence their authority was not at first questioned, but soon there arose murmurings which might easily have grown into a war cry.

The attitude of the Visayan Filipinos is clearly foreshadowed in the following extract from a letter dated January 14, 1899, in which Mabini discussed the advisability of putting the constitution in force : —

"And even if this change is made, I fear that Negros and Iloilo will form a federal Republic and not one in conformity with the centralized Republic provided for by the Constitution." [1]

The action later taken by Negros shows that there was abundant reason for this fear.

As late as February 26, 1899, the Insurgent government was still ignorant as to the real conditions in Negros and Mindanao.[2]

From a letter written on March 18, 1899, to Apacible at Hongkong, we learn that Aguinaldo and his followers were even then still uninformed as to events in the Vi-

[1] P. I. R., 512. A 5.

[2] Extract from a letter to Apacible of the Hongkong junta dated February 26, 1899 : —

"It is also said that the Cantonal Government of Negros has wished to make a treaty with the Americans, some members of that government having come in American transports to confer with General Otis. We are not aware of the conditions of the arrangement, because the Negros people have thus far not wished to put themselves in communication with us; we only know by news more or less reliable that the capital of that island has been occupied by the American forces without opposition.

"Of Mindanao we know absolutely nothing; we also are ignorant of what has been the lot of our agents in America."

sayan Islands.[1] In view of these facts, how ridiculous become the contentions of those who claim that the Malolos government represented the archipelago as a whole. And what shall we say of the following statement, remembering that the Treaty of Paris was signed December 10, 1899?

"When the Treaty of Paris was signed, General Otis was in possession of Cavite and Manila, with less than twenty thousand men under his command, and Aguinaldo was in possession of practically all of the rest of the archipelago with between 35,000 and 40,000 men under his command, armed with guns, and the whole Filipino population were in sympathy with the army of their country." [2]

Ultimately, by one means or another, and chiefly by the use of armed emissaries, the Visayan Islands, with the exception of Negros, were brought into the Insurgent fold.

Mabini's fear that Negros and Iloilo would form a federal republic was not realized, but Negros set up its own government, applied to the local commander of the United States forces for help, endeavoured with almost complete success to keep out Tagálog invaders, and presently settled down contentedly under American rule, facts of which Blount makes no mention. On the contrary, without just cause, he includes this great island, with its 4881 square miles of territory and its 560,776 inhabitants, in the area over which he claims that Aguinaldo exercised complete control.

At Iloilo the American troops encountered opposition when they planned to land. Negotiations had been en-

---

[1] "Of the Visayas and Mindanao we know nothing positive as yet, it is whispered that the Americans have succeeded in occupying Negros and Cebú against the will of the inhabitants. Iloílo continues the struggle energetically. It does not matter that they occupy temporarily those beautiful islands, because Luzón will know how to fight for herself and the rest of the islands, and will not lay down arms without the independence of the Philippine Archipelago."

[2] Blount, p. 140.

A Typical Baguio Road.

The roads in Baguio were originally built with money obtained from the sale of lots. Some insular government funds have been expended in surfacing them.

tered into with the local Filipino officers, but the latter, under the influence of representatives whom Aguinaldo had sent from Luzón, announced themselves as adherents of his government, and when the American troops finally disembarked fired the town ahead of them. It has been claimed that in doing this they were inspired by pure patriotism, but the facts shown by their own records present a very different picture.

In writing to Aguinaldo on April 8, 1899, Mabini says:

"We have received a communication forwarded from Iloílo, from General Martín Delgado and Francisco Soriano, your commissioner. Soriano states that the troops of Diocno have done nothing except commit excesses and steal money during the attack by the Americans upon the town of Iloílo, even going so far as to break their guns by using them as poles to carry the stolen money which they took to Cápiz. It is said that these forces, besides being unwilling to fight the Americans, refuse to give their guns to those who do wish to fight and do not want Cápiz to aid the people of Iloílo, who are the ones who support the entire forces, including the troops of Diocno who went there." [1]

This same letter contains the following brief reference to conditions in Cebu and Leyte: —

"Also a native priest, Señor Pascual Reyes, has arrived here from Cebú, and says that in Leyte General Lucban is committing many abuses and that Colonel Mójica is only a mere figurehead. In Cebú, he says, things are also in a chaotic condition, because the military chief, Magsilum [Maxilom, — Tr.], and the people are not in harmony."

Further details as to conditions in Cebu are given in a letter to Aguinaldo from the commissioner whom he put in charge of elections in that island, who on February 19, 1899, writes: [2] —

"Having arrived in this province the 8th of last month, I left on the 11th for the northern pueblos of this Island to hold the elections for the offices ordered by the Superior Decree of June 18, last.

*   *   *   *   *   *   *

[1] P. I. R., 62. 2.   [2] Ibid., 144. 1.

"The news spread like an electric spark, as in all the pueblos I visited later I found that almost all of the residents were in their homes, so that when the elections were held in the town hall, all the principal residents attended, requesting me to inform you that they were disposed to sacrifice even their dearest affections whenever necessary for our sacred cause; they only asked me to inform those who hold the reins of government at the present time in this province, that some steps be taken to put a stop to the arbitrary acts which had been and still are being committed by the so-called Captains, Majors, Colonels, Generals and Captains General, who abusing in the most barefaced manner the positions they claimed to hold, were depriving them of their horses and their carabaos, or cattle. I promised them that I would do this, as I do now, by sending a communication at once to Sres. Flores and Maxilom, who are at the head of the provincial government, impressing upon them the fact that if they continue to grant ranks and titles to persons of this character, as they have done, it would end in the utter ruin of this wealthy province."

He adds that these men did not remedy the evils complained of. It would be possible to cover in detail all of this and the remaining Insurgent territory, and to show that Judge Blount was quite right in stating that conditions similar to those encountered in Luzón arose there, but the limitations of time and space forbid, and I must ask my readers to accept on faith the statements of Blount and myself that such was the case!

Taylor thus summarizes the conditions which ultimately arose : —

"The Insurgent soldiers lived in their own land as they would have lived in a conquered country. They were quartered on the towns and the towns had to feed them whether they would or not.

"Peace there was where Aguinaldo's soldiers had not penetrated, but there does not seem to have been progress. Life went very well in a long siesta in the shady villages under the palm trees, but not only the structure of the State, its very foundations were falling apart. When Aguinaldo's soldiers came they brought cruelty and license with them. Proud of their victories and confident in themselves they felt that the labourers in the fields, the merchants in the towns, were for the purpose of administering to their necessities and their desires. Aguinaldo, having seen this force gather about him, was forced to entreat it, to appeal to it; he was never strong enough to enforce discipline, even if he cared to do it."

Aguinaldo himself finally became disheartened over his inability to maintain a decent state of public order in the territory which he claimed to govern, and in December, 1898, tendered his resignation, giving among other reasons odious favouritism on the part of some of the military chiefs, together with a desire to enrich themselves by improper means, such as accepting bribes, making prisoners a source of gain, and decreasing the allowance of the soldiers. He said that many soldiers had received sums of money as their share of booty, and intimated that officers must have done the same. He made charges against civil as well as military officers and ended by saying that he retained the evidence for presentation when called on.[1]

[1] "The second reason for my resignation is the pain caused me by having still to read among the reports of our military associates that in some of the chiefs, besides odious favouritism, is clearly seen a desire to enrich themselves, accepting bribes, making even prisoners a means of gain, and others there are, above all the commissaries, who dare to decrease the allowance of the soldier, little enough already; — I throw the blame of all this upon those who taught us such a custom; consequently I have reason to hope that they will change their methods.

"The same cause of complaint I have concerning some companions who are discharging civil offices, especially those who are far from the oversight of the government, who put their own welfare before the common good, and devise a thousand means to further their own ends, even to the extent of gambling. Where are the police? Are they, perchance, also bribed? Pity money is so ill spent! However, every one is obliged to know that falsehood will never prevail against truth, and as evidence hereof many soldiers have confessed to the government as to having received certain sums in the share of the booty, and if we consider that the latter who receive their share have told the truth, why should those who are present during the partition of the money and receive nothing, not do so? In this way the eyes of some that were blinded are gradually opened; I confess, moreover, that the latter are to be blamed less than those in authority who are so

Aguinaldo was later persuaded to withdraw his resignation. No wonder that he wished to tender it!

In referring to the report of Wilcox and Sargent, Blount has said : —

"This report was submitted by them to Admiral Dewey under date of November 23, 1898, and by him forwarded to the Navy Department for its information, with the comment that it 'in my opinion contains the most complete and reliable information obtainable in regard to the present state of the northern part of Luzon Island.' The Admiral's indorsement was not sent to the Senate along with the report." [1]

He thus gives it to be understood that the admiral believed that the report truthfully set forth the conditions which actually existed in these provinces, and that his indorsement was suppressed. Not only was it true that this report when rendered contained the most complete and reliable information then available in regard to the existing state of the northern part of Luzon Island, but it contained the only first-hand information available. The facts ultimately leaked out and led the admiral radically to change his opinion as to the conditions which arose under Insurgent rule. Of them he later said : —

"There was a sort of a reign of terror ; there was no government. These people had got power for the first time in their lives and they were riding roughshod over the community. The acts of cruelty which were brought to my notice were hardly credible. I sent word to Aguinaldo that he must treat his prisoners kindly, and he said he would."

I believe that I have fully demonstrated the truth of these statements. Blount was thoroughly familiar with

attached to the methods of the past administration, who, we may hope, will change their mode of conduct and exhibit true patriotism.

*   *   *   *   *   *   *

"I certify to the truth of all the above-mentioned evils, which must be eradicated. I retain the evidence for presentation when called on, so that if any of the readers hereof should consider themselves referred to and should resent it, I am ready to beg their pardon." — P. I. R., 8. 2.

[1] Blount, p. 108.

Dewey's testimony before the Senate Committee, in which they occur, but he did not mention them.

I cannot close this discussion of Insurgent rule without quoting extracts from a remarkable document written by Isabelo Artacho in October,[1] 1899. It was entitled "Declaration Letter and Proclamation" and was addressed to the Filipino people. While it is probable that Artacho was impelled to tell the truth by his hatred for Aguinaldo, tell the truth he did, and his rank and standing entitle his statements to consideration : —

"Study the work of the insurrection; see if it is, as is said, the faithful interpretation of your wishes and desires.

"Go through your towns, fields, and mountains. Wherever you see an insurgent gun or bolo you will find girls and faithful wives violated, parents and brothers crying for the murder of a son or of a brother; honest families robbed and in misery; villages burned and plundered for the benefit of a chief or a General; you will see fresh and living signs yet of those horrible crimes perpetrated with the greatest cynicism by those who call themselves your liberators! Liberators because they wear red pants, or a red shirt, or carry on their hats a piece of red cloth or a triangular figure!

"Here, a president stabs a man, perhaps the most honest of the village, simply for having implored mercy for a creature arbitrarily inflicted with the *cepo* [an oblong square piece of heavy wood divided into two parts, with a lock at each end and six or more holes in the middle to confine the feet of prisoners]; there, a dying man, suspended by the feet in a *cepo*, raised from the level of the ground, by another president who has charged him with an unproved crime; there a poor woman falsely charged and driven by petty officers with their bayonets for having objected to their invasion into her house, or shop, they being supposed to be, each, Justice itself, '*Justicia*,' and to be obeyed as images of the Gods; there, generals who murder without fear, for an insignificant motive, creatures whose members are being mutilated, or their flesh cut in slices and afterwards roasted and given them to eat; there, officers braining a girl who has refused to accede to their sensual wishes, the lifeless body of the victim, pierced with shots, after having been made use of, is thrown into the river. It is

[1] Senate Documents, Vol. 25, pp. 2928–2941.

not unusual to witness officers burying people alive in a tomb prepared by the victim, by order of the murderer; it is not unusual to see a *Puisne*-Judge pointing a revolver at a man who is about to give evidence, and threatening to brain him for having dared to ask: 'Why and to whom am I to declare?' And finally, on his tottering throne, you will see the Magistrate of the Philippines, so called by his worshippers, with his mephistophelian smile, disposing and directing the execution of a murder, of a plunder, of a robbery, or the execution of some other crimes against those who are indifferent or do not care to worship him, such indifference being considered a crime.

"Putting aside the many other murders, I may mention that one recently committed on the person of the renowned and by many called the worthy General, Antonio Luna, which took place just at the entrance of the palace of the Republic Presidency, and also the assassination at Kavite of the ever remembered martyr, Andrés Bonifacio, the founder of the 'Katipúnan' Society, and the one who initiated the Revolution of 1896; against the memory of whom it has been committed, in the proclamation of that falsely called Republic, the criminal and unjust omission to render the smallest manifestation of Filipinos' feelings towards him, to prevent that same might dislike his murderers!

"Study the ordinances and constitution of this so-called democratic Government of the Republic, that grand work of the wise Filipinos; admire with me that beautiful monument erected on a sheet of paper and consecrated to the conquest of reason and labour, especially in connection with human rights and property, the basis for the well-being of social life; but, lament and deplore with me its palpable nullity when brought to practice and you will again see that the laws were made for the people and not the people for the laws!

"Under this republic called democratic it is a crime to think, to wish, to say, anything which does not agree with what the said Gods think, wish and say. Nobody and nothing is attended to, whilst those who have your lives in their hands must be respected.

"Under this Goverment there cannot be the slightest notice taken of family, property, morality and justice, but confusion and disorder appear everywhere like a dreadful shadow, produced by the ignorance of the subordinate officers, and of the powers that be in the villages and provinces, who are supported by a special committee, or special commissioners empowered to impoverish and to ruin all and with the right of disposing, at their own accord, life, family and individual property without responsibility whatsoever on their part.

* * * * * * *

"Let the peaceful annexation of the whole of the Southern Islands of Joló, Mindanao, Iloílo, Negros, Cebú and others where now the American flag is hoisted and under whose shadow tranquillity and well-being are experienced, speak for itself.

"Let it speak for itself, the proceeding observed by the whole people of Imus, who were asking protection when the American troops took possession of the town of Bacoor, whilst the insurgent troops there located were hostile.

"Let them speak for themselves, the protests against the war made by the numerous persons of S. Francisco de Malabón, Sta. Cruz de Malabón, Perez Dasmariñas and other towns, before the Worthy Chief Mariano Trías, who ultimately refused, with dignity, the high position of Secretary of War, for which rank he was promoted for reasons which are not worth publishing here. In fine, let it speak for itself, the non-resistance shown by the people of Old Kavite [Kawit], Noveleta, and Rozario of the heroic province of Kavite, notwithstanding the many intrenchments and troops there located, as well as the identical behaviour observed by other towns of Luzon provinces who are ready to follow when the American troops are in them.

* * * * * * *

"In fact no one would believe it, and the Philippine people are tired of waiting for the day when Haring Gavino will shake a napkin to produce suddenly horses vomiting fire and lightning and troops of dangerous insects; that day in which they will witness the realization of that famous telegraphed dream to the effect that two hours after the commencement of the war the insurgents will take their breakfast in the Palace of ' Malacañang,' their tiffin in the Senate House, and their dinner on board the *Olympia* or in Kavite; that day in which the celebrated *Pequenines* army, with their invisible Chief-leader, will exterminate the American troops by means of handfuls of dust and sand thrown at them, which process, it is said, has caused the smallpox to the Americans; that day in which the *Colorum* army will capture the American fleet with the cords their troops are provided with, in combination with a grand intrenchment of Tayabas made of husks of paddy, by a Nazarene, who will then, by merely touching, convert each

husk into a Bee with a deadly sting; that day in which the
insurgents, like their leaders, provided with hosts of flour,
or of paper, pieces of candles of the holy-week matins, holy
water, pieces of consecrated stones; of vestments belonging
to a miraculous Saint or with some other Anting-Anting or
talisman or *amuletos*, will make themselves invulnerable to
bullets; also have power to convert into any of the four elements, like those personages of the Philippine legends and
comedies, — Ygmidio, Teñoso, Florante, Barnardo, Carpio,
etc.

"Yes, the people of the Philippines are quite tired of waiting
for the predicted European conflict, which it is said would
give them their independence; if not, perhaps, divide the
Islands as they are now amongst cousins, brothers, nephews,
uncles and godfathers.

"In the near future, when we have acquired the necessary
political and social education and the habit of behaving justly
towards ourselves and towards our fellow-brothers; when free
from all superstition, healthy, strong and vigorous, we find
ourselves capable of governing ourselves, without there being
the possibility of the preponderance of our passions in the
consideration, direction, and administration of the interests
of our country, then, and only then, we will be free! we will
be independent! [1]

"HONGKONG, 1st October, 1899."

Most of the men who perpetrated the outrages I have
detailed are alive to-day, and are powers in their respective
communities. Simeon Villa was recently elected a member of the municipal board from the south district of
Manila, but fortunately an American governor-general
prevented him from taking his seat. Just prior to my
departure from Manila he was appointed, by Speaker
Osmeña, a member of a committee on reception for
Governor-General Harrison.

The kind of independent "government" these men established is the kind that they would again establish if
they had the chance,[2] but among the persons to be tortured

[1] P. I. R., 838-2.

[2] In this connection note Blount's statement: —

"But we are considering how much of a government the Filipinos
had in 1898, because the answer is pertinent to what sort of a govern-

One of the First Benguet Government Cottages.

and murdered would now be those Americans who failed to escape seasonably. I do not mean to say that such a state of affairs would come about immediately, but it would certainly arise within a comparatively short time. Sooner yet "the united Filipino people" would split up on old tribal lines, and fly at each other's throats.

ment they could run if permitted now or at any time in the future."
— BLOUNT, p. 73.

CHAPTER VIII

Did We Destroy a Republic?

THE claim has frequently been made that the United States government destroyed a republic in the Philippine Islands,[1] but some of the critics seem to entertain peculiar ideas as to what a republic is. Blount states[2] that Aguinaldo declined to hear our declaration of independence read "because we would not recognize his right to assert the same truths," and then apparently forgetting the Insurgent chief's alleged adherence to the principles of this document, he lets the cat out of the bag by saying that "the war satisfied us all that Aguinaldo would have been a small edition of Porfirio Diaz," and would himself have been "The Republic."[3]

He would doubtless have set up just this sort of a government, if not assassinated too soon, but it would

[1] Blount refers to
"The death-warrant of the Philippine republic signed by Mr. McKinley on September 16th." — BLOUNT, p. 99.
Speaking of Mr. Roosevelt's opinion of the practicability of granting independence to the Filipinos, he says: —
"Yet it represented then one of the many current misapprehensions about the Filipinos which moved this great nation to destroy a young republic set up in a spirit of intelligent and generous emulation of our own." — BLOUNT, p. 230.

[2] "Here was a man claiming to be President of a newly established republic based on the principles set forth in our Declaration of Independence, which republic had just issued a like Declaration, and he was invited to come and hear our declaration read, and declined because we would not recognize his right to assert the same truths." — BLOUNT, p. 59.

[3] "The war satisfied us all that Aguinaldo would have been a small edition of Porfirio Diaz, and that the Filipino republic-that-might-have-been would have been, very decidedly, 'a going concern,' although Aguinaldo probably would have been able to say with a degree of accuracy, as Diaz might have said in Mexico for so many years, 'The Republic? I am the Republic.'" — BLOUNT, p. 292.

hardly have accorded with the principles of the declaration of independence, nor would it have been exactly "a government of the people, by the people, for the people."

Blount truly says[1] that the educated Filipinos, admittedly very few in number, absolutely control the masses. He adds[2] that *presidentes* of pueblos are as absolute bosses as is Murphy in Tammany Hall, and that the towns taken collectively constitute the provinces. The first statement is true, and the second, which is tantamount to a declaration that the *presidentes* control every square foot of the provinces and every man in them, is not so far from the truth as it might be. I have been old-fashioned enough to retain the idea that a republic is "a state in which the sovereign power resides in the whole body of the people, and is exercised by representatives elected by them."

Blount labored under no delusion as to the fitness of the common people to govern.[3]

[1] "The war demonstrated to the army, to a Q. E. D., that the Filipinos are 'capable of self-government,' unless the kind which happens to suit the genius of the American people is the only kind of government on earth that is respectable, and the one panacea for all the ills of government among men without regard to their temperament or historical antecedents. The educated patriotic Filipinos can control the masses of the people in their several districts as completely as a captain ever controlled a company." — BLOUNT, p. 292.

[2] "Even to-day the presidente of a pueblo is as absolute boss of his town as Charles F. Murphy is in Tammany Hall. And a town or pueblo in the Philippines is more than an area covered by more or less contiguous buildings and grounds. It is more like a township in Massachusetts, so that when you account governmentally for the pueblos of a given province, you account for every square foot of that province and for every man in it."

[3] "In there reviewing the Samar and other insurrections of 1905 in the Philippines, you find him (*i.e.* Roosevelt) dealing with the real root of the evil with perfect honesty, though adopting the view that the Filipino people were to blame therefor, because we had placed too much power in the hands of an ignorant electorate, which had elected rascally officials." — BLOUNT, p. 297.

Also: —

"But we proceeded to ram down their throats a preconceived theory that the only road to self-government was for an alien people to step in and make the ignorant masses the *sine qua non*." — BLOUNT, p. 546.

Not only did the Filipinos themselves understand perfectly well that they had no republic, but there were many of them who were fully aware of the fact that they could establish none. Fernando Acevedo, in writing to General Pío del Pilar on August 8, 1898, said : [1] —

"There could be no republic here, even though the Americans should consent, because, according to the treaties, the Filipinos are not in condition for a republic. Besides this, all Europe will oppose it, and if it should be that they divide our country as though it were a round cake, what would become of us and what would belong to us?"

I will now trace the evolution of the government which Aguinaldo did set up. In doing so I follow Taylor's argument very closely, drawing on his unpublished Ms., not only for ideas, but in some instances for the words in which they are clothed. I change his words in many cases, and do not mean to unload on him any responsibility for my statements, but do wish to acknowledge my indebtedness to him and at the same time to avoid the necessity for the continual use of quotation marks.

Aguinaldo's methods in establishing his republic are shown by his order [2] that "any person who fights for his country has absolute power to kill any one not friendly to our cause" and the further order [3] prescribing that twelve lashes should be given to a soldier who lost even a single cartridge, while if he continued to waste ammunition he should be severely punished. In March, 1899, workmen who had abandoned their work in the arsenal at Malolos were arrested, returned, given twenty-five lashes each and then ordered to work.[4]

Also : —
"Of course the ignorant electorate we perpetrated on Samar as an 'expression of our theoretical views' proved that we had 'gone too fast' in conferring self-government, or to quote Mr. Roosevelt, had been 'reposing too much confidence in the self-governing power of a people,' if to begin with the rankest material for constructing a government that there was at hand was to offer a fair test of capacity for self-government." — BLOUNT, p. 546.   [1] P. I. R., 499. 1 Ex. 134.
    [2] *Ibid.*, 206. 1.   [3] *Ibid.*, 1124. 2.   [4] *Ibid.*, 204. 6.

The news that an American expedition was about to sail for the Philippines made him realize that he had not much more than a month in which to place himself in a position in which he would have to be consulted and assisted, and this he tried to do. The arms he received from Hongkong on May 23 enabled him to begin an insurrection, not as an ally of the United States, but on his own account. From May 21 to May 24 he issued orders for the uprising against Spain. On May 24 he declared himself Dictator of the Philippines in a proclamation in which he promised to resign his power into the hands of a president and cabinet, to be appointed when a constitutional assembly was convened, which would be as soon as the islands had passed into his control. He further announced that the North American nation had given its disinterested protection in order that the liberty of the Philippines should be gained.[1] On May 25, 1898, the first American troops sailed from San Francisco for the Philippines.

Aguinaldo still had a month in which to seize enough Spanish territory to erect thereon what would appear to the Americans on their arrival to be a government of Luzón, of which he was the head. The Hongkong junta and Aguinaldo himself intended to ask for the recognition of their government, but they had first to create it. To obtain recognition it was necessary that the American commander on land should be able to report that wherever he or his troops had gone the country was ruled by Aguinaldo according to laws which showed that the people were capable of governing themselves.

As the United States is a republic it was natural that the directing group of insurgent leaders should decide upon a republican form of government. That form would appeal to the people of the United States; the first "Christian Asiatic Republic" was a description which would inevitably awaken sympathy in that mother of

[1] P. I. R., 206. 6.

republics. The idea was a wise and subtle one; but Aguinaldo's republic was merely an elaborate stage-setting, arranged for the contemplation of the people of the United States.

By June 5, 1898, the success of the insurgent arms had been such that Aguinaldo felt that he could throw down the mask. He would still be glad of American assistance, but he felt himself strong enough to do without it. He saw that "there can now be proclaimed before the Filipino people and the civilized nations its only aspiration, namely, the independence of this country, which proclamation should not be delayed for any ulterior object of this government" [1] and ordered that the independence of the Philippines should be proclaimed at his birthplace, Cavite Viejo, on June 12, 1898. On that date he formally proclaimed it. The provinces of Cavite, Bataan, Pampanga, Batangas, Bulacan, Laguna and Morong were about to fall into his hands, the Spanish troops in them being besieged, and about to surrender.

From the same place on June 18, 1898, Aguinaldo promulgated his decree for the creation and administration of municipalities. [2] In brief, this provided that as soon as the territory of the archipelago, or any portion thereof, had passed from the possession of Spanish forces, the people in the towns who were most conspicuous for their intelligence, social position and upright conduct were to meet and elect a town government. The heads of the towns in every province were to elect a head for the province and his three counsellors. The provincial council, composed of these four officials, with the presidente of the capital of the province, were to see to the execution in that province of the decrees of the central government and to advise and suggest.

This provincial council was to elect representatives for the revolutionary congress, which was to be charged with submitting suggestions to the central government

---

[1] P. I. R., 674. 1.   [2] *Ibid.*, 206. 3.

upon interior and exterior affairs, and was to be heard by the government upon serious matters which admitted of delay and discussion.

Before any person elected to office was permitted to discharge his functions, his election was to be approved by the central government. The military commanders, except in time of war, were to have no jurisdiction over the civil authorities. They could, however, demand such supplies as they might need, and these could not be refused. The government was to appoint commissioners to carry these regulations into effect.

On June 20 Aguinaldo issued his regulations for the government of provinces and municipalities [1] as supplemental to the decree of two days before. It went into the details of government, under the following heads: police, justice, taxation and registration of property.

On June 23 he proclaimed the establishment of a revolutionary government, with himself as "president." In this capacity he had all the powers of the Spanish governor-general, unhampered by any orders from Spain. It is true that the scheme provided for the eventual formation of a republic, but it is doubtful if the people who drew it up really knew what that word meant. What was provided for in practice was a strong and highly centralized military dictatorship, in which, under the form of election, provision was made for the filling of all offices by men devoted to the group which had seized control.

According to this decree the dictatorial government was in future to be entitled the revolutionary government. Its duty was to struggle for the independence of the Philippines in order to estabish a true republic. The dictator was to be known as the president of the revolutionary government. There were to be four secretaries — one of foreign affairs, commerce and marine; one of

[1] P. I. R., 206. 3.

war and public works; one of police and interior order, justice, education and hygiene; one of the treasury, agriculture and manufactures. The government could increase the number of secretaries if necessary. They were to assist the president in the despatch of business coming under their departments.

In addition to the president and his secretaries, there was to be a revolutionary congress composed of representatives from the provinces of the Philippine Archipelago, elected as provided by the decree of June 18. In case a province was not able to elect representatives, the government would appoint them for such province. The congress was to discuss and advise, to approve treaties and loans, and to examine and approve the accounts of the secretary of the treasury. If important matters admitted of delay, the congress would be heard concerning them; but if they did not admit of delay, the president of the government was to act at once. Projects of law could be presented by any representative, and by the secretaries of the government.

A permanent committee of congress presided over by the vice-president was to be chosen by that body. This was to serve as a court of appeal in criminal cases and as a court of final jurisdiction in cases arising between the secretaries of the government and provincial officials. The acts of congress were not to go into effect until the president of the government ordered their execution. He was also to have the right of veto.

This was a well-devised plan to secure control for the central group about Aguinaldo. His commissioners, under a form of election in which the electors were carefully selected men, established municipal governments devoted to the cause of the revolution. These were to choose provincial officials and members of the congress. All elections were subject to Aguinaldo's approval, and every province was under the command of a military representative of his, who could and did call upon the civil authorities for

TYPICAL COTTAGES AT BAGUIO.

Cottages of this type are used by officers of the government.

such supplies as he deemed fit. All real power was vested in the central group, and the central group was composed of Emilio Aguinaldo and his public and private advisers. By this time he had gathered about him men who were trained in the law, some of whom had served the Spanish government in various capacities. They were accustomed to the methods that had previously prevailed under the Spanish régime, and were now ready to draw up constitutions and regulations for the new government. Mabini wrote the three organic decrees. Copies of them were sent to the foreign consuls in Manila, and on July 15, 1898 to Admiral Dewey.

Although the title of "president" was assumed by Aguinaldo, as more likely to be favourably considered in the United States than "dictator," the tendency of his followers who had not been educated in Europe was to speak of and to regard him not as a president, but as an overlord holding all power in his hands. The people did not feel themselves citizens of a republic, copartners in an estate; they considered themselves subject to a ruler who sometimes called himself president, and sometimes dictator. Indeed, there is much to show that if Aguinaldo and his followers had succeeded in their plans, even the name "republic" would not have been long continued as the title of his government.[1]

[1] On July 7, 1898, the secretary of the revolutionary junta in Mindanao, in writing to Aguinaldo, closed his letter with the following formula: "Command this, your vassal, at all hours at the orders of his respected chief, on whom he will never turn his back, and whom he will never forswear. God preserve you, Captain General, many years." P. I. R., 1080. 1. Every now and then we find a queer use of the term "royal family." This seems to have been common among the mass of the people. Heads of towns and men of position often used the expression "royal orders" in speaking of the orders and decrees issued by Aguinaldo. For example, the officials of Tayug, a town of 19,000 people in Pangasinán Province, certified, on October 9, 1898, that they had carried out the instructions for "the establishment of the popular government in accordance with the royal decree of June 18, 1898." — P. I. R., 1188. 1.

In October certain of Aguinaldo's adherents in Tondo wrote to him

Aguinaldo's claim as to the effectiveness of his government on August 6, 1898, was as follows:[1] "The government of the revolution actually rules in the provinces of Cavite, Batangas, Mindoro, Tayabas, Laguna, Morong, Bulacan, Bataan, Pampanga, Infanta and besieges the capital, Manila. The most perfect order and tranquillity reign in these provinces, governed by authorities elected by the inhabitants in conformity with the organic decrees dated June 18 and 23 last. Moreover, the revolution has about nine thousand prisoners of war who are treated humanely and according to the rules of civilized warfare. We can muster more than thirty thousand men organized as a regular army."

It may have been that in the majority of these provinces municipal governments, formed in accordance with the provisions of the decree of June 18, had been established; but provincial governments had not been established in all of them, and tranquillity did not reign in any of them,

and protested against the acts of the local presidente, who, they held, had not been duly elected in accordance with the provisions of the "royal order" of June 18, 1898. They closed their respectful protest by requesting that said royal order should be obeyed.—Taylor, AJ., 63.

In 1899 an officer of the army in Union Province wrote: "In accordance with the orders of the secretary of war of our republican government of these islands, issued in compliance with royal decree, article 5, published on March 8." On September 1, 1898, the local presidente of the town of Mangatarem, writing to the head of the province, said that he had not furnished the estimates required because the elections provided for in "article 7 of the royal decree of the superior government, dated June 18 last," had not been approved. A young son of a member of Aguinaldo's cabinet, writing to his father in September, 1899, spoke of the "royal decree of June 18, 1898." — P. I. R., 1188. 3. In Romblon, in August, 1898, elections were held in compliance with the prescription of the "royal decree of June 18, 1898," and Aguinaldo approved them, apparently without considering that this was an anomalous way of describing a decree of the dictator of the so-called republic. On March 7, 1899, a general in the revolutionary service stated that an officer had been released from arrest by a "royal order." The attitude of mind which made men speak of Aguinaldo's "royal orders" in 1898 did not change when he fled before the advance of the United States army. His orders remained royal orders. They were again and again referred to in this way.

[1] P. I. R., Books C–1.

as they were the scene of operations against the Spaniards. There could not well have been nine thousand prisoners in his hands at this time, as that was claimed later when a large additional number of Spaniards had surrendered. As for the thirty thousand men organized as a regular army, there may be a certain difference of opinion as to what constitutes a regular army; the men who saw Aguinaldo's force then, and who have read the papers of its leaders, must be of the opinion that that force was not a regular army. Probably only Manila Province had a provincial government on August 6. Its local presidentes met at Cavite Viejo on August 3 and elected three members of congress from the province, and also the members of the provincial government. The election took place under the supervision of Colonel Teodoro Gonzales, whom Aguinaldo had appointed governor of Manila Province on August 1. He remained governor after the election was held. Not until August 17 did the local presidentes of Bulacan assemble under the presidency of the secretary of the interior and proceed to elect two members to congress and the members of the provincial government. Not until August 20 was there an election for the members of the provincial government of Cavite Province. This was held in the town of Cavite. Isaac Fernando Rios, who was afterwards a member of the Filipino junta in Madrid, was chosen a representative of the province; but as he wrote that he was in favour of coming to some agreement with Spain which would permit the development of the Philippines, without abandoning the sovereignty of that country, Aguinaldo promptly disapproved his election [1] and ordered a new one held for the office thus left vacant. On October 2, 1899, Aguinaldo approved the result of a new election held there because four of the five high officials of the province had absented themselves, while one of them had died. Of the men who had so absented themselves one had gone abroad,

[1] P. I. R., 1216. 1.

while the other three had remained in Manila or Cavite under the government of the United States.[1]

The people of the provinces obeyed the men who had arms in their hands. It is not probable that many of them had any conviction concerning the form of government which would be best for the Philippines. There were no signs of a spontaneous desire for a republic. Orders came from the group about Aguinaldo, and the people accepted a dictator and a republic as they accepted a president and a republic, without knowing, and probably without caring very much, what it all meant, except that they hoped that taxes would cease with the departure of the friars. A determined and well-organized minority had succeeded in imposing its will upon an unorganized, heterogeneous, and leaderless majority.

As soon as a province was occupied by the Insurgents it was divided into territorial zones within which command was exerted by military officers. On July 20, 1898, Cavite had been divided into four zones, and next day Brigadier-General Artemio Ricarte was placed in command of the province and the first zone.

By July 7 Bulacan Province had been divided into six zones, and Nueva Ecija into four zones, with a separate commander for each zone. These men established the government prescribed by Aguinaldo's decrees of the middle of June. Probably by the end of July Aguinaldo's municipal governments had been established in the greater part of the towns of Luzón. These governments were not established by the mass of the people. The mass of the people were not consulted, but they were not in the habit of being consulted in such matters and probably saw no necessity for it in this case. As an evidence of this we have the fact that from the beginning the acts of election were almost always drawn up in Spanish, although by far the greater portion of the people of the archipelago spoke only the native dialects.

[1] P. I. R., 1216. 1.

The method of establishing these municipal governments employed in Cavite in June, 1898, was continued to the end of Aguinaldo's rule. It was the same in different places and at different times. Data obtained from reports and documents written in towns far removed from each other follow. They must be considered together in order to obtain an idea of what this method really was.

When the Insurgent movement had progressed sufficiently far, the leaders collected their adherents and obtained recognition as the heads of their provinces or districts. For example, representatives of the towns of Pampanga assembled at San Fernando on June 26, 1898, and under the presidency of General Maximo Hizon agreed to yield him "complete obedience as military governor of the province and representative of the illustrious dictator of these Philippine Islands." [1] The town of Macabebe refused to send any delegates to this gathering. Commissioners, in almost every case officers of Aguinaldo's army, were empowered by him to establish the so-called republican government. They appointed delegates who proceeded to the smaller towns and held elections; but whenever possible the commissioner of Aguinaldo presided. In many cases these delegates were lieutenants of the army. The commissioners selected the electors, for they had all to be "marked out by their good conduct, their wealth, and their social position," and they had all to be in favour of independence. They then presided at the elections, which were *viva voce*. They apparently selected the people to be elected, and forwarded a record of the proceedings to the central government. The election had to be approved by the dictator or president before the successful candidates could assume the duties of their offices. Later on, the military commanders remote from the seat of government were authorized to approve elections and install the

[1] P. I. R., 223.

successful candidates, but the records of election had even then to be forwarded to the capital for approval, the action of the commissioner not being final.

The commissioners do not seem to have been able to find many men who had the necessary requisites for electors. In the town of Lipa, Batangas Province, with a population of forty thousand seven hundred forty-three, at the election held July 3, 1898, a presidente was chosen for whom twenty-five votes were cast. On November 23, 1898, an election was held at Vigan, Ilocos Sur, for a presidente to succeed one who had been elected representative in congress. One hundred and sixteen votes were cast. The population of Vigan is nineteen thousand. On October 5, 1898, at Echague, Isabela Province, a presidente was elected for whom fifty-four votes were cast. The population of Echague is fifty-four thousand. On October 2, 1898, at Cabagan Nuevo, Isabela, one hundred and eleven men voted out of a population of sixty-two hundred and forty. On January 29, 1899, the town of Hernani, in Samar, elected its municipal officials under the supervision of V. Lukban. Fifty-four men voted. The town has a population of twenty-five hundred and fifty-five.

The elections, so-called, were not always held without protest. For example, the town of San José, Batangas, protested unavailingly to Aguinaldo against the result of an election held at 10 P.M., in a storm of rain. Men who had been on friendly terms with the Spaniards were usually excluded from all participation. If in spite of the precautions taken men were elected who were disliked by the commissioner or his supporters, the election could be set aside on the ground that the person elected was not an adherent of the revolution.

The elections were often held in a singular manner, as in the following case : [1] —

" On August 20, 1898, four men of Tondo appeared before

[1] P. I. R. 1133. 1.

Aguinaldo on Bacoor and announced that they were representatives of the people of the district, who loved liberty. Then
in accordance with the directions of the president of the republic
under the supervision of the secretary of the interior, they drew
lots from a hat to decide how the offices of the head of the district, delegate of police, delegate of the treasury and delegate
of justice were to be distributed. The decision having been
made in this simple fashion, Aguinaldo gravely approved the
election as expressing the will of the people. Perhaps it did,
for they seem to have continued, at least for a time, to obey
them. On November 14, 1898, Aguinaldo again approved an
election for local officials in Tondo which since August 13 had
been within the American lines."

On August 23 San Carlos, in Pangasinán Province, a
town of twenty-three thousand people, elected its officials
under the new form of government. The presidente chosen
was a well-known member of the Katipúnan, and before
the election was held announced his intention of killing
any one who was chosen for the position for which he was
a candidate.[1] He was accordingly elected. In spite
of this grave informality, an informality which formed
one ground for a protest on the part of some of the people
of the town, Aguinaldo approved the election.

On October 21, 1898, an election was held under the
supervision of the military commander in Camarines for
the municipal officials of the town of Yriga.[2] The voting
was oral, and a secretary wrote down the votes for the
two candidates under direction of the commissioner,
who finally announced that the candidate whose friend
he was had been elected, but without stating how many
votes he had received. This newly elected head of the
town had the town crier on the following night publish
through the streets an address to the people, in which he
thanked those who had voted for him and warned those who
had not that it would be well for them to beware. The
Spanish law known as the Maura Law, which regulated the
elections in the municipalities under the Spanish government, provided for a limited electoral body, composed

[1] P. I. R., 1137. 4.   [2] *Ibid.*, R., 1165. 2.

largely of ex-officials of the municipalities. The choosing
of an electoral body by the military commander of a district probably did not seem strange to the people. The
provincial and municipal officials were established in office
by armed men, and they were obeyed because they had
been installed by armed men; but it was a form of election to which people, as a rule, saw no reason to object.
There were, however, in many cases bitter complaints of
the abuses committed by the officers thus "elected."

This form of government spread with the advance
of Aguinaldo's arms. Municipal elections were held
in Tarlac in July, in Ilocos Norte and Tayabas in August,
in Benguet and the Batanes Islands in September, 1898,
in Panay in December, 1898, and in Leyte and Samar in
January, 1899.

On December 27 Antonio Luna wrote that all the
provinces of Luzón, Mindoro, Marinduque, Masbate,
and Ticao, Romblón, part of Panay, the Batanes, and
Babuyanes Islands were under the jurisdiction of the
insurgent government.[1]

By October 7, 1898, 14 of the 36 provinces and districts into which Luzón had been divided by the Spanish
government had civil governors.[2] These 14 were Tagálog provinces or provinces which the Tagálogs controlled. The other provinces were still under military
rule, and, indeed, even the provinces under civilians were
dominated by their military commanders. With the
manner of holding elections which prevailed, the governors
must have been men who were in favour of the military
party in force, for otherwise they would not have been
elected.[3]

It is not probable that the number of provinces under
civil governors much increased. If in Pangasinán Province, where there are many Tagálogs, organizations
opposed to the rule of Aguinaldo could cause serious
disorders, as was the case, it must have been considered

[1] P. I. R., 319. 1.   [2] *Ibid.*, 3. 33.   [3] *Ibid.*, 1022. 3.

A BAGUIO HOME.

This is the residence of the author. Note the rose bushes climbing up to the second story.

expedient for the success of the attempt of the Tagálogs, who form only a fifth of the population, to dominate the archipelago, that all provinces in which an effective majority of the people were not of that tribe, should be kept under military rule. The municipal governments which had been established in Luzón were in the hands of Aguinaldo's adherents, or of men who it was hoped would prove loyal to him. They were men of the Spanish-speaking group, which has always dominated the people of the islands. They were probably not as a rule men of means. Many of them, perhaps most of them, had been clerks and employees under the Spanish government, and they saw no reason for changing the methods of town administration which had then been followed. The municipal taxes, the estimates for expenditures, and the regulations for town government, were but little modified from those they found in force. In many ways such changes as were made were for the worse.

Once installed in power, Aguinaldo's officials were required to exercise over the mass of the people about the same control that had always been exercised over them. The governing group considered that they were perfectly capable of providing for the welfare of the islands, and that it was the duty of the people to obey them without question.

When the insurgent force was increased in preparation for war with the Americans a large number of municipal officials resigned, or attempted to do so. It was not easy for a municipal official under Aguinaldo's government to resign. A resignation, to be accepted, had to be accompanied by the certificate of a physician that the person concerned was unfit to perform the duties of his office. Judging by the record,[1] an epidemic seems to have attacked the municipal officials in January, 1899. It is probable that they saw that war was inevitable and that they did not wish to remain in charge of the towns

[1] P. I. R., 1200.

and be responsible for providing for the necessities of
"the liberating army." In Pangasinán in that month
men could not leave their barrios without obtaining the
permission of the headman, and in one town men who had
attempted to sell their property for the purpose of going
to Manila were, on January 17, ordered to be arrested
and their conduct investigated.[1]

Aguinaldo, having established himself at Malolos, ordered the congress provided for in his decree of June 23,
1898, to assemble at the capital on September 15, 1898, and
appointed a number of provisional representatives for
provinces and islands not under his control.[2] It has often
been claimed that Aguinaldo's government controlled
at this time the whole archipelago, except the bay and
city of Manila and the town of Cavite.[3]

Blount quotes the following statement from the report
of the First Philippine Commission : —

"While the Spanish troops now remained quietly in Manila,
the Filipino forces made themselves masters of the entire
island except that city." [4]

I signed that statement, and signed it in good faith ;
nevertheless, it is untrue. The Filipino forces never con-

[1] P. I. R., 907. 6.   [2] P. I. R., 39. 7.
[3] The following memorandum to accompany a letter from Señor
Don Sixto Lopez, Secretary of Señor Don Felipe Agoncillo, to the
Honorable the Secretary of State, written January 5, 1899, clearly
sets forth this claim : —
   "Pursuant to the action of said congress a detailed system of government has been provided for and is actually maintained in all the portions of the Philippine Islands, except so much of the provinces of
Manila and Cavite as is now in the actual possession of the American
Army, such excepted part containing only about 3 per cent. of the population of the entire islands and an infinitely smaller proportion of their
area.
   " From the foregoing it will appear that the Philippine government
is now, as it has been practically ever since the 16th of June, 1898,
in substantially full possession of the territory of the people it represents." — Taylor Ex. 530 57 KU., Congressional Record, June 3, 1902,
Vol. 35, part 6, p. 6217.
   [4] Blount, p. 70.

trolled the territory now known as Ifugao, Bontoc, Kalinga or Apayao, much less that occupied by the Negritos on the east coast of Luzón, but this is not all. There exists among the Insurgent records a very important document, prepared by Mabini, showing that when the call for the first session of the Filipino congress was issued, there were no less than sixty-one provinces and *commandancias*, which the Insurgents, when talking among themselves, did not even claim to control, and twenty-one of these were in or immediately adjacent to Luzón.[1]

[1] "September, 1898.

"DECREE

"Although article 11, Chapter 2, of the Organic Decree of June 23 (1898) last, prescribes that the appointment of provisional representatives of Congress be given to persons who have been born or have resided in the provinces which they are to represent; taking into consideration the urgent necessity that said body enter upon its functions immediately, I hereby decree the following : —

"1. The following are appointed provisional Representatives . . .

"2. A meeting of Congress is called for the 15th instant, to be held in the town of Malolos, province of Bulacán.

"3. The Secretary of the Interior shall take steps to notify the persons appointed and those elected by the popular commanders in the provinces already occupied by the Revolution, of the call as soon as possible.

"Giv. . . ."

(Attached hereto is the following, with the names written in Mabini's handwriting :)

"September, 1898.

"Provinces not subject to the Revolutionary Government of the Philippines.

NAMES	CLASSES	
Albay	Highest class	2. Salvador V. del Rosario and Felipe Buencamino
Ilocos Norte	do	2. José, Antonio Luna
Ilocos Sur	do	2. Ignacio Villamor, José Aleji
Isabela de Luzón	Third class	1. Aristón Bautista
Sorsogón	do	1. José Albert
Cagayán	do	1. Pablo Tecson

The men who composed this congress were among the ablest natives of the archipelago; but representative

NAMES	CLASSES	
Abra	Pol.-Mil. Govt.	1. Isidro Paredes
Nueva Viscaya	do	1. Enrique Mendiola
Corregidor	do	
Catanduanes	do	
Batanes	do	
Masbate and Ticao	Pol.-Mil. Comandancia	1. Alberto Barreto
Amburayan	do	
Apayaos	do	
Benguet	do	1. Joaquín Luna
Binatanga	do	
Bontoc	do	1. Fernando Canon
Burias	do	
Cayapa	do	
Itaves	do	
Lepanto	do	1. León Apacible
Príncipe	do	1. Mariano Ocampo
Quiangan	do	
Tiagan	do	
Cabugauan	do	
Island of Cebú	Pol.-Mil. Govt. of highest class	2. Cayetano Arellano and Pardo de Tavera
Iloilo, Panay	do	2. Gregorio Araneta and Melecio Figueroa
Island of Leyte	do	1. León Guerrero
Negros Occidental	do	1. José María de la Viña
Island of Samar	do	Pablo Ocampo
Antique, Island of Panay	do	1. Hipólito Magsalin
Cápiz	Lowest class	1. Miguel Zaragoza
Negros Oriental	do	1. Aguedo Velarde
Island of Bohol	do	1. Juan Manday Gabriel
Romblón	Pol.-Mil. Comandancia	1. Vicente González Maninang
Concepión	do	1. Mariano V. del Rosario
Zamboanga	1st Dist. Pol.-Mil. Govt.	1. Pedro A. Paterno
Misamis	2d Dist. do	1. Maximino Paterno
Surigao	3d Dist. do	1. Benito Valdés
Davao	4th Dist. do	1. Telesforo Chuidian
Cotabato	5th Dist. do	1. Enrique Mercaida
Basilan	6th Dist. do	1. Juan Tuason

institutions mean nothing unless they represent the
people; if they do not, they are a conscious lie devised
either to deceive the people of the country or foreign
nations, and it is not possible for any system founded
upon a lie to endure. A real republic must be founded not
upon a few brilliant men to compose the governing group
but upon a people trained in self-restraint and accustomed to govern by compromise and concession, not

NAMES	CLASSES	
Lanao	7th Dist. do	1. Gonzalo Tuason
Dapitan	Pol.-Mil. Comandancia	1. Gonzalo Tuason
Butúan	do	
Barás is under Pol.-Mil. Govt. of Bahia Illana		
Levac is under Pol.-Mil. Comandancia of Cottabatto		
Matti	Pol.-Mil. Comandancia	
Malabang. This Comandancia is under the Military Comandancia of Bahia Illana.		
Reina Regente. This Comandancia is under the Pol.-Mil. Govt. of Cottabato		
Bay of Sarangani and adjacent islands	Pol.-Mil. Comandancia	
Tucuran	Pol.-Mil. Govt.	
Island of Joló	do	1. Benito Legarda
Siassi	Pol.-Mil. Com.	
Tataan	do	
Bongao	do	
Island of Paragua	Pol.-Mil. Govt.	1. Felipe Calderón.
Balabac	do	1. Manuel Jérez
Calamianes	do	1. Manuel Genato
Marianas Islands	do	
Oriental Carolines	do	
Camarines, North and South		Don Tomás del Rosario and Don Cecilio Hilario

Exhibit 226, 76 MG, E, Extract from original in Spanish, A. L. S.,
P. I. R., 416. 1.''

by force.   To endure it must be based upon a solid foundation of self-control, of self-respect and of respect for the rights of others upon the part of the great majority of the common people.   If it is not, the government which follows a period of tumult, confusion and civil war will be a government of the sword.   The record the Philippine republic has left behind it contains nothing to confirm the belief that it would have endured, even in name, if the destinies of the islands had been left in the hands of the men who set it up.

The national assembly met on the appointed day in the parish church of Barasoain, Malolos, which had been set aside for the meetings of congress.   This body probably had then more elected members than at its subsequent meetings, but even so it contained a large number of men who were appointed by Aguinaldo after consultation with his council to represent provinces which they had never even seen.

From a "list of representatives of the provinces and districts, selected by election and appointment by the government up to July 7, 1899, with incomplete list of October 6, 1899"[1] I find that there were 193 members, of whom forty-two were elected and one hundred fifty-one were appointed.   This congress was therefore not an elective body.   Was it in any sense representative?   The following table, showing the distribution of delegates between the several peoples, will enable us to answer this question.

In considering this table it must be remembered that the relationship given between the number of delegates assigned to a given people and the number of individuals composing it is only approximate, as no one of these peoples is strictly limited to the provinces where it predominates.

I have classified the provinces as Tagálog, Visayan, etc., according to census returns showing the people who form a majority of their inhabitants in each case.[2]

[1] P. I. R., 38. 3.
[2] The 1903 census returns are here used for each of the several peoples.

People	Number	Elected Delegates	Appointed Delegates
Visayans	3,219,030	0	68
Tagálogs	1,460,695	18	19
Ilocanos	803,942	7	11
Bicols	566,365	4	7
Pangasináns	343,686	2	2
Pampangans	280,984	2	2
Cagayans	159,648	4	6
Zambalans	48,823	1	2
Non-Christians	647,740	4	34
		42	151

It will be noted that the Tagálog provinces had eighteen out of a total of forty-two elected delegates. The Visayans, by far the most numerous people in the islands, did not have one. The non-Christian provinces had a very disproportionately large total of delegates, of whom four are put down as elected, but on examination we find that one of these is from Lepanto, the capital of which was an Ilocano town; one is from Nueva Vizcaya, where there is a considerable Cagayan-Ilocano population; one is from Benguet, the capital of which was an Ilocano town, and one from Tiagan, which was an Ilocano settlement. These delegates should therefore really be credited to the Ilocanos.

If the individual relationships of the several members are considered, the result is even more striking. Of the thirty-eight delegates assigned to the non-Christian provinces, one only, good old Lino Abaya of Tiagan, was a non-Christian. Many of the non-Christian *comandancias* were given a number of delegates wholly disproportionate to their population, and in this way the congress was stuffed full of Tagálogs.

Think of Filipe Buencamino, of Aguinaldo's cabinet, representing the Moros of Zamboanga; of the mild, scholarly botanist Leon Guerrero representing the Moros,

Bagobos, Mandayas and Manobos of Davao; of José M. Lerma, the unscrupulous politician of the province of Bataan, just across the bay from Manila, representing the wild Moros of Cotabato; of Juan Tuason, a timid Chinese *mestizo* Manila business man, representing the Yacan and Samal Moros of Basilan; of my good friend Benito Legarda, since a member of the Philippine Commission, and a resident delegate from the Philippines to the congress of the United States, representing the bloody Moros of Jolo! Yet they appear as representatives of these several regions.

Few, indeed, of the delegates from non-Christian territory had ever set foot in the provinces or *comandancias* from which they were appointed, or would have been able to so much as name the wild tribe or tribes inhabiting them.

I have been furnished a list, made up with all possible care by competent persons, from which it appears that there were eighty-five delegates actually present at the opening of congress, of whom fifty-nine were Tagálogs, five Bicols, three Pampangans, two Visayans, and one a Zambalan. For the others there are no data available. Yet it has been claimed that this was a representative body! It was a Tagálog body, without enough representatives of any other one of the numerous Philippine peoples to be worth mentioning.

With a congress thus organized, Aguinaldo should have had no difficulty in obtaining any legislation he desired.

The committee of congress appointed to draw up a constitution set to work promptly, and by October 16, 1898, had proceeded so far with their work that Buencamino was able to write to Aguinaldo that while he had been of the opinion that it would have been best for him to continue as a dictator aided by a committee of able men, yet it would now be a blow to the prestige of congress to suspend its sessions. Aguinaldo noted upon this letter the fact that he did not approve of a constitution.[1]

[1] P. I. R., 485. 1.

The Baguio Hospital.

This hospital, built on a picturesque site in the midst of imposing mountain scenery, where it gets the full sweep of the cool pine-scented breezes, has done wonderful work. Note the tuberculosis cottages on the crest of the ridge.

Apparently early in December the committee submitted their project. In presenting it to congress they said[1] that—

"The work whose results the commission has the honour to present for the consideration of congress has been largely a matter of selection; in executing it not only has the French constitution been used, but also those of Belgium, Mexico, Brazil, Nicaragua, Costa Rica, and Guatemala, as we have considered those nations as most resembling the Filipino people."

The most important difference between this project and the actual constitution adopted was that, although the project provided that the Dominican, Recollect, Franciscan and Augustinian friars should be expelled from the country and that their estates should become the property of the state, yet it recognized the Catholic religion as that of the state and forbade state contribution to the support of any other, although it permitted the practice in private of any religion not opposed to morality, which did not threaten the safety of the country. The government was authorized to negotiate a concordat with the Pope for the regulation of the relations between church and state. A strong party was in favour of this recognition, but it finally failed of adoption, and the constitution as promulgated provided for the freedom and equality of religion and for free and compulsory education which had not been provided for in the original project. The constitution as approved forbade the granting of titles of nobility, decorations or honorary titles by the state to any Filipino. This paragraph did not exist in the original project, which merely forbade any Filipino to accept them without the consent of the government.

Mabini, the ablest of all Aguinaldo's advisers, did not approve of the constitution. He himself had drawn up a project for a constitution during June, 1898, but it was not accepted by the committee, the greater part of whom were Catholics and for that reason opposed to

[1] P. I. R., 40. 1.

Mabini, who was a bitter antagonist of that church. And yet when separation of church and state was finally provided for it did not please Mabini, who, although he was opposed to church control, wrote to Aguinaldo [1] that the constitution as passed by congress was not acceptable and should not be promulgated because the constitutional guarantees of individual liberty could not be maintained, as the army had to be in control for the time being, and furthermore it was not expedient to separate church and state, as this separation would alienate many of their adherents. Indeed, there was not much in the constitution which he thought ought to take immediate effect, [2] and he wrote that congress was ill-disposed toward him because he had refused to agree to its promulgation. Existing conditions were such that he believed that all powers should be vested in one person. He warned Aguinaldo that if the constitution were put in force, he would be at the mercy of his secretaries. On January 1, 1899, Aguinaldo, probably at the suggestion of Mabini, proposed certain changes in it. [3]

Evidently the provisions of the constitution did not worry Aguinaldo much, as is shown by his reply to the request by some of his officers for information as to what reward those who were first in the attack on Manila should receive. He promised them such titles as marquis, duke, etc. [4]

On January 2, 1899, Aguinaldo announced the formation of a new cabinet made up as follows: Apolinario Mabini president and secretary of foreign affairs; Teodoro Sandico, secretary of the interior; Mariano Trias, secretary of the treasury; Baldomero Aguinaldo, secretary of war and navy, and Gracio Gonzaga, secretary of *fomento*. [5] On January 4 Mabini took the oath of office as the presi-

---

[1] P. I. R., 377. 13.
[2] *Ibid.*, 472. 9.
[3] *Ibid.*, 40. 8.
[4] *Ibid.*, 849. See p. 143.
[5] A general term covering education, public works, agriculture and commerce.

dent of the council of government. This body met twice a week at Malolos on set days, and at the close of its deliberations forwarded to Aguinaldo a statement of the subjects discussed and the conclusions reached for his decision. The president of the republic did not preside at, or take part in, its deliberations.

On January 4, 1899, General Otis issued a proclamation in which he announced that the United States had obtained possession of the Philippines and that its government would be extended over the islands of the archipelago. Aguinaldo replied next day with one which, if not intended to be a declaration of war, was at least a warning that hostilities were imminent. This proclamation was carried into Manila by his emissaries and posted up over the one issued by the American commander. It was a challenge to a trial of strength, and Aguinaldo and his advisers hastened their preparations for the coming combat.

The secretary of the interior on the same day sent an order to the heads of all provinces directing the organization of territorial militia to resist the American invasion, and ordering the heads of the towns to hold meetings of the people to protest against the aggression of the United States. They were held in accordance with these orders, and records of the proceedings were sent to Malolos and published in the official organ of the government as evidence of the feeling of the people. It was, however, not considered necessary in publishing them to mention the fact that they had been held in compliance with orders.

On January 14, 1899, Mabini wrote to Aguinaldo[1] recommending changes in the proposed constitution, which he still liked as little as ever. He was afraid that Negros and Panay would refuse to accept the form of government it prescribed. The worst thing about it was that the Americans would be less disposed to recognize Aguinaldo's government; for when they saw the constitution they would know, as it made no mention of them, that the

[1] P. I. R., 512. A 5.

Filipinos wanted independence. Mabini thought that it was possible that the wording of the constitution might have been deliberately planned by members of the congress in favour of annexation to the United States, so that that country would be warned, would become more mistrustful, and would refuse to recognize Aguinaldo's government. Whatever the president of the council may have thought about the theoretical advisability of a congress to represent the people, he found one much in the way when he had obtained it.

Buencamino advised that the constitution should be approved and promulgated; one argument was that the congress had been consulted in the matter of a national loan, and if it was dissolved, there could be no loan. This was apparently the only matter upon which it had been consulted.[1]

The constitution of the Philippine Republic was ratified at a session of the congress on January 20, 1899.

On January 21, 1899, Aguinaldo sanctioned it and ordered that it should be "kept, complied with and executed in all its parts because it is the sovereign will of the Philippine people." [2] The constitution provided for a government of three coördinate powers, executive, legislative and judicial. Whether it provided for a form of government which would have succeeded in the Philippines was not determined by actual experience. It was never really put in force for war with the United States began in two weeks and the constitution must stand as the expression of the ideas of a certain group of educated natives rather than as the working formula for the actual conduct of the political life of a nation. One proof of this is the fact that not until June 8, 1899, were Aguinaldo's decrees upon the registration of marriages and upon civil marriage, dated June 20, 1898, revoked, and the provisions of the constitution concerning marriage put in effect.[3]

[1] P. I. R., 485. 5.
[2] Senate Document 138, Fifty-sixth Congress, First Session.
[3] P. I. R., Books B–6.

Aguinaldo had approved the constitution; he had informed the foreign consuls and General Otis that it had been promulgated and become the law of the land. It was not promulgated. It had not become the law of the land. It served one important purpose. It passed into the hands of the Americans and showed them the ability and the aspirations of certain individuals of the archipelago, but Mabini and his followers did not believe in its form or in its provisions, and Mabini at least was emphatic in his declarations that the time had not yet come for it to be put into effect. On January 24, 1899, he wrote to Aguinaldo that if it should be promulgated it would be absolutely necessary to give the president the veto power, and replace the elected representatives by others appointed by the government. If this were not done the president would be at the mercy of congress, and the people, seeing that disagreement between the executive government and the congress was the cause of its misfortunes, would start another revolutionary movement to destroy both of them.[1]

As long as Mabini remained in power the constitution was mere paper. Its adoption was not indicative of the capacity of the people to maintain self-government. It expressed only the academic aspirations of the men who drafted it. There is not the slightest evidence from any previous or subsequent experience of the people that it would have worked in practice. It was enacted for the misleading of Americans rather than for the benefit of the Filipinos.

While the government of Aguinaldo was called a republic, it was in fact a Tagálog military oligarchy in which the great mass of the people had no share. Their duty was only to give soldiers for the army and labourers for the fields, and to obey without question the orders they received from the military heads of their provinces.

There is no cause for vain regrets. We did not destroy a republic in the Philippines. There never was anything there to destroy which even remotely resembled a republic.

[1] P. I. R., 472. 8.

CHAPTER IX

The Conduct of the War

It is not my intention to attempt to write a history of the war which began on February 4, 1899, nor to discuss any one of its several campaigns. I propose to limit myself to a statement of the conditions under which it was conducted, and a description of the two periods into which it may be divided.

From the outset the Insurgent soldiers were treated with marked severity by their leaders. On June 17, 1898, Aguinaldo issued an order to the military chiefs of certain towns in Cavite providing that a soldier wasting ammunition should be punished with twelve lashes for a first offence, twenty-four for a second, and court-martialled and "severely punished" for a third.[1]

[1] "To the Military Chiefs of the towns mentioned in the margin [there is nothing in the margin. — Tr.] : —

" As there are still many soldiers paying no notice to the order forbidding the waste of cartridges, you are required to give a certain amount of ammunition to each soldier and to see every day if there is any cartridge missing, and if so, inquire into the reason. In order that this may be successfully carried out, I have deemed it proper to prescribe the punishment for such offence, of which you will inform the soldiers under your command, and post this circular in a prominent place. Said punishments are as follows : —

"Art. 1. A soldier found wasting ammunition shall be punished with 12 lashes; in case he commits the same offence again he shall be punished with 24 lashes ; and on a further offence of like character by the same soldier, he shall be court-martialled and severely punished.

"Art. 2. A soldier who has been found short of even one cartridge out of the ammunition assigned to him, shall be punished with 12 lashes, provided that he has not previously been in any engagement.

"Art. 3. A soldier who has been found with no cartridges by reason of throwing them away during an engagement, shall be court-martialled, and severely punished.

" I most earnestly recommend you to carefully look after your soldiers and see that every one is complying with the foregoing order.

" This order should be transmitted from one town to another mentioned in the margin, and the last one should return it to this office

On November 16, 1900, General Lacuna ordered that any officer allowing his soldiers to load their rifles when not before the enemy should be liable to capital punishment,[1] which in practice was frequently inflicted on soldiers for very minor offences.

Men of means were drafted into the ranks and then excused from service on the payment of cash.

The soldiery, quartered on the towns, committed endless abuses. Conditions were bad enough before the outbreak of hostilities, as I have shown in the chapters dealing with Insurgent rule. They grew rapidly worse thereafter, and human life became cheap indeed.

" The documents of this period show that the insurgent troops driven from the front of Manila fell upon the people of the neighbouring towns and burnt, robbed, and murdered. Either their officers lost all control over them, or else they directed these outrages. It was not for some days that control was regained."[2]

with the information that the same has been received and complied with by all.

"May God guard you many years.

"CAVITE, June 17th, 1898."

"E. AGUINALDO, Dictator.
— P. I. R., 1124. 2.

[1] "November 16, 1900.

(Stamp) "LACUNA BRIGADE. HEADQUARTERS.

"MAJOR THOMAS TAGUNTON: Advise all officers of this brigade that he who allows his soldiers to load their rifles without being before the enemy, shall be liable to capital punishment. If the soldiers intentionally or otherwise fire their pieces, whether in the air or at any determined or undetermined person, said soldiers and the officers to whose command they belong shall also be liable to the same punishment as above, without further proceedings, for the reason that we are almost in front of the enemy, and all the more if the shots take effect upon any of the soldiers or chiefs.

"Sergeants and corporals shall also take heed of the present warnings, as they will also be given the same punishment if they by abandoning their squads allow them to commit certain outrages.

"You will report receipt of and compliance with this order.

"God preserve you many years.

"General Headquarters, November 16, 1900.

(Signed) "LACUNA, General, Political-Military Governor and Chief of Operations."
— P. I. R., 643. 1.

[2] Taylor, AJ. 85.

Endless orders were issued by Aguinaldo and other high Insurgent officers, prohibiting rape, brigandage and robbery, and there was grave need of them.   Unfortunately they could not be enforced.   Indeed it was often impossible to distinguish between Insurgent soldiers, who removed their uniforms or had none, and brigands pure and simple.[1]

Many men were soldiers at one time and brigands at another.   Unquestionably soldiers and brigands sometimes coöperated.   Garrisons were withdrawn from towns which did not promptly and fully comply with the demands of Insurgent commanders,[2] and armed bandits appeared and plundered them.

[1] "KABAT´AN, Oct. 14th, 1899.

"EDICT

"MARTÍN F. DELGADO, GENERAL AND POLITICO-MILITARY GOVERNOR OF THE PROVINCE OF ILOÍLO.

" As a consequence of the frequent assaults and robberies committed by persons wearing military uniforms, and with the determination to correct, with a firm hand, such scandalous conduct, which, besides causing such deeds to be laid at the door of the military, also makes it easier for evil-doers to commit their misdeeds, I have, at the suggestion of the Councillor of Police, ordered the following : —

" 1. From this date forward all private citizens are absolutely prohibited from wearing military uniforms.

" 2. All authorities, both civil and military, under this Government, are obliged to see to the strict enforcements of this edict.

" 3. All persons who, not being in the military service, are, after the publication of this edict, found wearing military uniforms, and who cannot show that they are in the military service, will be suspected as evil-doers and will be sent to this Government to be subjected to the corresponding corrective measures.

*   *   *   *   *   *

(Signed) " MARTÍN DELGADO,
" GOVERNOR-GENERAL-PRESIDENT."
—P. I. R., 881. 4.

[2] "On April 10, 1899, General Delgado wrote that, benignity having failed, rigorous methods would be used to enforce collections and that if the people did not pay —

" ' I shall, with great pain, see myself under the necessity of withdrawing all my forces to the mountains and leaving them [the pueblos] to the fate which God will decide upon,' which of course meant that he

GOVERNMENT CENTRE AT BAGUIO.

There were some Insurgent leaders, like Cailles, who suppressed brigandage with a heavy hand,[1] but many of them were indifferent, even if not in alliance with the evil doers.

THE VISAYAS

Feeling between Tagálog soldiers and Visayan people grew constantly more bitter, and before many months had passed they fell to killing each other. The highest officers of the "Regional Revolutionary Government of the Visayas" protested vigorously to Aguinaldo,[2]

would leave them to the mercy of the bandits who stood ready to descend upon them." — P. I. R., B., 4.
" This threat was not an idle one." — Taylor, 67 HS. E–L.

[1] "SANTA CRUZ, LAGUNA, July, 1899.
" HON. SR. EMILIO AGUINALDO. . . .
" There was a notorious bandit here who was the terror of the province with his gang; I had him arrested and shot and the robberies ceased. Murders were being committed; I had the murderers caught, shot one of them, and there were no more murders; officers of the reserve would consider themselves kings in their towns, they would shoot the local *presidentes* and commit other unlawful acts; I disarmed them, and tried the most celebrated one, called Arcadio Castillo, alias Bancucane, who attempted to escape and was killed. With the death of these persons order has been completely reëstablished in this province. Several had rifles that were used only for robbery and after two or three trials all turned over their rifles, and the arming of the battalion was completed.
 *   *   *   *   *   *   *
(Signed) "JUAN CAILLES."
— P. I. R., 7 & 8.

[2] "REGIONAL REVOLUTIONARY GOVERNMENT OF THE VISAYAS.
"OFFICE OF THE PRESIDENT.
"KABATÚAN, March 16, 1899.
" TO THE HONOURABLE PRESIDENT OF THE PHILIPPINE REPUBLIC,
"SEÑOR EMILIO AGUINALDO Y FAMY,
"MOST DISTINGUISHED PRESIDENT:
 *   *   *   *   *   *   *
" In order to avoid the distress which the knowledge of the abuses which are already unbearable, daily committed by the troops of Señor Diocno, will cause you, this government has hesitated to communicate them to you, but, as there is almost a reign of terror here, it feels that it must inform you of them in order to remedy them. The death of private individuals and assaults committed in the towns are daily

but without result. The situation was entirely beyond his control.

On April 20, 1899, General Delgado issued an order which tells a significant story of conditions, and of his own weakness in dealing with them.[1]

reported as having been committed by the troops of General Diocno. Of the numerous companies of Señor Diocno, only two under the orders of General Araneta fight against the enemy, the remainder are the terror of the town and it is a week since Sr. Diocno went to Capiz without telling any one what he was going to do.

"In view of the facts pointed out, the soldiers of this General constituting a constant danger to the town, this government asks you to order General Diocno to turn over his rifles to us to kill Americans with and to enable the towns to recover their former tranquillity; this government asks this of you, relying upon the well-known justice with which you act and it wishes for you many years of life for our liberty and our independence.

"KABATÚAN, March 16, 1899.

(Signed)   "JOVITO YUSAY,
"Temporary President.

(Signed)   "FRANCISCO SORIANO,
"General Secretary."
—P. I. R., 52. 5.

[1] "Martín Delgado y Bermejo, lieutenant general and general in chief of the republican army of the Visayan Islands.

"GENERAL HEADQUARTERS OF SANTA BARBARA,
"April 20, 1899.

"The existence of a state of war, and the trying circumstances through which the country is now passing have brought about a complete change in the order of nearly all the pueblos; and I have noticed with profound regret that sacking, robbery, sequestrations, and other crimes highly dishonourable to our noble cause, are of daily occurrence. With a view to preventing such conduct in the future, and in order to guarantee to the inhabitants of the military district under my command the most complete tranquillity, I hereby decree:

"1. That any person or persons who commit acts of brigandage, sequestration, incendiarism, rape, or other disturbances of a public nature calculated to excite the public, or which infringe individual or property rights, shall be severely punished in accordance with military law.

"2. That all offenders who present themselves to the Local or Military Authorities within the 30 days immediately following this date, and who turn over their arms and join our forces and help to fight other outlaws and to defend the nation, will be pardoned for the crimes they have committed.

"3. That when the period of 30 days above mentioned has passed,

In Luzón General Trias of Cavite accused the soldiers and citizens of his province of committing "robberies, assaults, kidnappings and crimes which are committed only by barbarous and savage tribes." [1]

That very serious conditions promptly became general is conclusively shown by the record of Aguinaldo's government for February 24, 1899, when it decided —

"that the president of the council shall study such measures as will put an end to the continual discord and friction between the civil and military authorities of every province, in order that fatal consequences may be avoided."

any person taken in the act of committing robbery, or who attempts to rob with an organized band of outlaws, or who steals, rapes, or performs acts of incendiarism, or any other criminal act, will be summarily condemned to death by a military tribunal.

"The Local Juntas of the various towns in conjunction with citizens of standing and the military authorities will organize a vigilance service to maintain public order and the authority of the law.

"M. Delgado."
—P. I. R., Books B 4.

[1] "February 13, 1899.
(In the margin: A stamp which says:) "Philippine Republic — Headquarters of operations of the provinces of Southern Luzón.

"It is with great regret that I have learned that robberies, assaults, kidnapping, and other crimes which are committed only by barbarous and savage tribes, are taking place in our towns, without taking into consideration that the purpose of the insurrection which has given origin to our social regeneration is true justice, for the reëstablishment of which the lives and property are being sacrificed of all who are proud of being called Filipinos. These acts are being committed without restriction by civilians as well as soldiers perhaps with the coöperation of their respective chiefs, to the shame of the authority vested in them and to the prejudice of the society to which they unworthily belong, and even to the integrity itself of the Republic. And in order that these barbarous and savage acts may disappear and that rigorous and exemplary punishment be meted out, I have deemed it proper to forward to you for general information the proclamation of these Headquarters of February 12th last, which is as follows:

*   *   *   *   *   *   *

(Signed) "Mariano Trias.
"Lieutenant-General.

"To the Politico-Military Chief of Infanta." — P. I. R., 896–9.

With such conditions prevailing among the Filipinos themselves, it was to be expected that the laws of civilized warfare would be violated and that American soldiers taken prisoners would sometimes be treated with barbarity. Flags of truce were deliberately violated.[1] American soldiers were trapped, poisoned [2] and murdered in other ways.[3]

It was promptly charged in the United States that American soldiers were committing barbarities, and Blount has revived these old tales.

I know personally that during the early days of the war Insurgent prisoners and wounded were treated with the greatest humanity and kindness.

A part of the Insurgent plan of campaign was the circulation of the most shocking statements concerning the abuses committed by American soldiers. I have

---

[1] "There does not seem to have been the faintest conception that there was any reason for not using the white flag to deceive people who were foolish enough to believe that Aguinaldo was going to adhere to the rules prescribed for its use. The writer in the early spring of 1899 once watched an insurgent party advance under a white flag upon an American line of trenches. When an officer and a bugler went forward to receive them they threw down the flag and immediately opened fire with the rifles which they were then seen to be dragging behind them." — TAYLOR, 48 HS.

[2] "Such ammunition was not effective unless fired from very close quarters, but even its possession made the guerrillas stronger than the people of the country and undoubtedly had much to do with securing their coöperation, not only as bolomen but also in the digging of the pits which were placed in the trails and also set about the towns. These were required to be constructed by the local authorities. In the bottom was set a sharp spike of bamboo, sometimes poisoned; and the pit was covered with leaves and soil upon a fragile framework; so that if a man stood upon it he would fall through upon the spike. Bows were set in the jungle with a string set across the trail so that any one stumbling over it would discharge a sharp bamboo shaft with a poisoned head. On September 18, 1900, Lukban congratulated the people of the town of Katubig upon the efficient use they had made of arrows with the heads dipped in 'dita,' a native poison.   (P. I. R., 502. 8.)" — TAYLOR, 83 HS.

[3] See also the chapter entitled "Murder as a Governmental Institution."

elsewhere described[1] the fate that overtook Colonel Arguelles, in part because he told the truth as to the humane treatment by the Americans of prisoners and wounded.

Not only did some of those who did this forfeit their lives, but newspaper articles, military orders, and proclamations issued by civil officers informed the people that the American soldiers stole, burned, robbed, raped and murdered. Especial stress was laid on their alleged wholesale violations of women, partly to turn the powerful influence of the women as a whole against them, and partly to show that they were no better than the Insurgents themselves, who frequently committed rape.[2]

[1] See p. 313.

[2] The following newspaper supplement printed in Tagálog for the benefit of the common people, is typical of this class of literature, with which the country was kept flooded:

(Circular printed in Tagálog. P. I. R., 17–6. Supplement to *Heraldo Filipino.*

"Friday, 24th February, 1899.

" COUNTRYMEN:

"We must consider ourselves fortunate that the bad intentions of North America were found out early. If we had not found them out by this time we should have been entrapped. And we should thank God that they commenced the war.

"You ought to know by this time that these people can teach us nothing good. What we can learn from them is all evil. You must admit the truth of what they are reported to do to our brothers in Manila where they rob the houses when the dwellers in them are out or busy. Their evil inclinations prevail over them to such an extent that the houses most worthy of consideration are not safe. They are worse than the wild people who live in the woods, they have not the slightest idea of looking at things from the point of view of a man of honour nor have they the slightest respect for reason, for this does not control their actions in the least. Without the slightest attention to civility they rush into houses and if they find the people eating, without saying a word, they take what they want from the table, put it into their mouths and go as they came.

"If they find people sleeping or resting, taking the siesta, it makes no difference to them ; they go into the most private parts of the house as though they were walking in the street.

"In the shops they take what pleases them and if the owner wants payment they threaten him with their rifles.

These horrible tales were at first believed even by some of the responsible Insurgent officers in remote regions,[1] but all such men soon learned the truth, which was known to most of them from the start.

In official correspondence between them, not intended for the public, orders were given to use women as bearers of despatches for the reason that Americans did not search them.[2] More significant yet, when conditions

" One can hardly believe and my pen refuses to write all of the perversity, and evil and bad habits of these people.

" Their habits and manners are a disgrace to the country where they were born.   In no history have such customs and manners been described even in that of the most ignorant people.

" They search women who pass, feeling all over their bodies, taking from them money and whatever else they carry and if they come on them in a lonely place they strip them naked after violating them and do not leave a rag on them.

" Are these those honest men of whom we have heard?   Are these the people who were going to teach us good habits?   Are these the people who were going to guide us?   The race which does these things is the most hated one in the world, it is the race which commits most cruelties, it is the race which does not treat its mother with respect; in this race there is not the slightest idea of personal dignity, it is a race which does not know what honour is, which does not possess the slightest vestige of regard for good manners.   Are these the people who are going to protect us?   It is better for us to die at once than fall into the power of these unequalled malefactors.

" ¡ Down with the bad men !

" ¡ Kill the Americans ! !

" ¡ Let the people of the United States be exterminated ! ! !

" ¡ Notice. — This sheet is distributed gratis."

[1] "A light upon the treatment of women by these people is given by the fact that after an American detachment had captured Lukban's papers and family on August 18, and came so close to taking him that he was able to recognize their guide, one of his correspondents wrote to him that to their surprise the women, who had fully expected to be abused, had been treated with respect and given a house to live in. (P. I. R., 1143. 4.)" — TAYLOR, 84 HS.

[2] In a letter to General Ambrosio Moxica from ———— dated March 2, 1900, occurs the following : —

"The guerillas quartered in the neighbourhood must render mutual assistance and keep up communication, so as to get the news as to where the enemy comes or goes, and the time at which they will pass certain points, endeavouring also to arrange that all the guerilla bands should have regular couriers, with you or with general headquarters, giving advice daily of any occurrence and carrying correspondence.   They became bad in the provinces, Insurgent officers sent their women and children to seek American protection in Manila or elsewhere. Cartload after cartload of them came in at Angeles, shortly after General Jacob H. Smith took that place. Aguinaldo himself followed this procedure, as is shown by the following extracts from Villa's famous diary : [1] —

"*December* 22. — It was 7 A.M. when we arrived in Ambayuan. Here we found the women worn out from the painful journey they had suffered. They were seated on the ground. In their faces were observed indications of the ravages of hunger; but they are always smiling, saying they would prefer suffering in these mountains to being under the dominion of the Americans, and that such sacrifices are the duties of every patriot who loves his country.

"We secured some camotes in this settlement, cooked them immediately, and everybody had breakfast. Our appetites were satisfied.

"The honorable president had already decided some days before to send all the women to Manila, including his family, and this was his motive in hurrying his family forward with him.

* * * * * * *

"*December* 24. — We find ourselves still in Talubin. About 8 o'clock this morning a report came saying the Americans had arrived at Bontoc, the provincial capital, the nearest town to Talubin, and distant from it two hours by the road. An immediate decision was made. The honourable president told his family and the other women that they should remain in the settlement and allow themselves to be caught by the Americans, and he named Señors Sytiar and Paez to remain also, with the obligation of conducting the women to Manila. As soon as the arrangement was effected, the honourable president prepared himself for the march. The parting was a very sad one for himself and for his family.

must select trustworthy women to carry correspondence, charging them to hide the letters underneath their skirts, bearing in mind that the Americans do not search them; and in sending to the towns for arms or food, the orders must be sent by women and for small quantities, so as not to attract attention." — P. I. R., 2035. 3.

[1] Simeon Villa, who accompanied Aguinaldo on his long flight, kept a somewhat detailed account of events in the form of a diary.

" The honourable president left Talubin at 11 o'clock in the morning, his family and the other women remaining behind with two gentlemen charged with conducting them to Manila."[1]

In this, as in all other similar cases, the women were kindly treated and safely conducted to their destination. Aguinaldo and his fellows knew the happy fate of the members of his own family, as is shown by a later entry : —

" *February* 6. — We have been informed that the mother and son of the honourable president are at Manila, living in the house of Don Benito Legarda, and that they reached that capital long before the wife and sister of the honourable president. We have also learned that Señor Buencamino, and Tirona, and Concepcion are prisoners of the American authorities in Manila. With reference to the wife and sister of the honourable president and the two Leyba sisters, it is said that they went to Vigan and from there went by steamer to Manila."[2]

The mother and son, accompanied by Buencamino, had allowed themselves to be captured at an earlier date. What shall we say of a leader who would turn his mother, wife, sister and son over to American soldiers for safe-keeping, and then continue to denounce the latter as murderers, and violaters of women? Aguinaldo did just this. That the Insurgent leaders were early and fully aware of the treatment accorded their wounded is shown by the following extract from a letter to General Moxica of Leyte, dated March 2, 1900, giving instructions as to what should be done with wounded men : —

" If by chance any of our men are wounded on the field or elsewhere, efforts must be made to take away the rifles and ammunition at once and carry them away as far as possible, so that they may not be captured by the enemy ; and if the wounded cannot be immediately removed elsewhere or retreat from the place, let them be left there, because it is better to save the arms than the men, as there are many Filipinos to fill up the ranks, but rifles are scarce and difficult to secure for battle ; and besides the Americans, coming upon any wounded, take good care of them, while the rifles are destroyed ; therefore,

[1] P. I. R., 869.   [2] *Ibid.*

A Scene in the Baguio Teachers' Camp.

The houses are for visiting lecturers and persons of similar rank. The tents are for the teachers.

I repeat, they must endeavour to save the arms rather than the men." [1]

There were some rare individual instances in which un-injured Filipinos were treated with severity, and even with cruelty, by American soldiers. They occurred for the most part late in the war when the "water cure" in mild form was sometimes employed in order to compel persons who had guilty knowledge of the whereabouts of firearms to tell what they knew, to the end that the perpetration of horrible barbarities on the common people, and the assassination of those who had sought American protection, might the more promptly cease. Usually the sufferers were themselves bloody murderers, who had only to tell the truth to escape punishment. The men who performed these cruel acts. knew what treatment was being commonly accorded to Filipinos, and in some instances to their own comrades. I mention these facts to explain, not to excuse, their conduct. Cruel acts cannot be excused, but those referred to seldom resulted in any permanent injury to the men who suffered them, and were the rare and inevitable exceptions to the general rule that the war was waged, so far as the Americans were concerned, with a degree of humanity hitherto unprec-edented under similar conditions. The Insurgents vio-lated every rule of civilized warfare, yet oathbreakers, spies and men fighting in citizens' clothes not only were not shot by the Americans, as they might very properly have been, but were often turned loose with a mere warn-ing not to offend again.

The false news circulated to aid the Insurgent cause was by no means limited to such matters. Every time their troops made a stand they were promptly defeated and driven back, but their faltering courage was bolstered up by glorious tidings of wonderful, but wholly imaginary, victories won elsewhere. It was often reported that many

[1] P. I. R., 2035. 3.

times more Americans had fallen in some insignificant skirmish than were actually killed in the whole war, while generals perished by the dozen and colonels by the thousand. Our losses on March 27, 1899, in fighting north of Manila, were said to be twenty-eight thousand. In reality only fifty-six Americans were killed in all northern Luzón during the entire month.

On April 26, 1899, the governor of Iloilo published the following remarkable news items among others : —

"PAVIA, April 6th, 1899.

"The Liberating Army of the Visayan Islands to the Local Presidents of the towns shown on the margin :

"*Towns:* Santa Barbara, Pavía, Leganes, Zárraga, Dumangas, Batac Viejo, Tuilao, Batac Nuevo, Banate.

*   *   *   *   *   *   *

"Santa Ana taken by Americans burning town our troops advancing to Rosario and Escolta Americans request parley account death General and officers and many soldiers.

*   *   *   *   *   *   *

"At 3 P.M. of the 14th battle at Santolan 500 American prisoners who are to be taken to Malolos.

"At 9.45 P.M. Commissioner Laguna details 6000 more Americans dead and 600 prisoners.

"Otis requests parley, and our representatives being present, he tells them to request peace and conditions, to which they replied that he, and not they, should see to that, so the parley accomplished nothing.

"To-day, Wednesday, a decisive battle will be fought.

"Among the 5000 prisoners there are two generals. To-morrow 7.15 Pasig in our power. Americans little by little leaving for Manila.

"General Malbar to Provincial Chief Batangas.

"According to reports by telegraph hostilities have commenced and all at Santa Mesa have fallen into our hands, also Pasay and Maytubig.

"American boat surrendered at Laguna de Bay many prisoners taken.

"General Ricarte to Provincial Chief of Batangas : Battle stopped by truce Japan and Germany intervene to learn who provoked war.

"Foreigners favor parley one American general and chiefs and officers dead." [1]

Santa Ana is a suburb of Manila. The Rosario and Escolta are the main business streets of the city.

Apparently the Insurgents must have thought that colonels were as numerous in our army as in theirs, for they reported two thousand of them killed on February 6, 1899, and threw in one general for good measure.[2]

We learn from the *Filipino Herald* for February 23, 1899, that on that day the Filipino army captured and occupied the suburbs of Manila, while American troops were besieged in the outskirts of the city, at La Loma, and in the neighbouring town of Caloocan.[3]

[1] P. I. R., 886. 13.

[2] Exhibit 1233
(Original in Spanish. Contemporary copy. P. I. R., Books B. 4.)
"GENERAL HEADQUARTERS, SANTA BARBARA, Feb. 28th, 1899."
(Literal copy of telegram.)

* * * * * *

"Casualties, Americans, on 6th, 2000 Colonels dead, one General; all churches converted into hospitals full American wounded; total American casualties 7000 confirmed by General Fullón just arrived from Malolos; says also Iloílo quiet and not taken.

* * * * * * *

"A true copy
"By order of Chief of Staff.   "JUAN BELOSO."

[3] (Supplement to the *Filipino Herald*.)

"Thursday, Feb. 23rd, 1899. — 4 P.M.
"The Filipino Army occupies the suburbs of Manila.

* * * * * * *

"The three columns commanded by Generals Pío del Pilar and Licerio and Col. Hizon now occupy the suburbs of Sampaloc, San Miguel, San Sebastián, Binondo, San Nicholás and Tondo.
"The Cavite battalion has possession of the Cuartel de Meisic and our flag is now flying there.

"SIX THOUSAND AMERICANS BESIEGED ! ! !

"The American troops now in Caloocan and La Loma to the number of over six thousand are besieged by the columns commanded by Generals Luna, Llanera and García.

But why continue. No tale concerning American losses in the Philippines was too fantastic to be told by the leaders and believed by the soldiery and the populace. The American soldiers were even said to be refusing to fight, and great prisons were being constructed in order properly to punish them.

General MacArthur and his entire staff were captured before March 2, 1900, according to a letter sent to General Moxica of Leyte on that date.[1]

And what of conditions in the United States during this troubled period? We learn from the Insurgent records that prior to January 15, 1900, "the Union Army" had met with a new disaster, as a result of which President McKinley tendered his resignation, being succeeded by Mr. Bryan. Philippine independence was to be proclaimed on February 4, 1899. On January 20, "General Otis's successor, John Waterly, of the democratic party," arrived at Manila with papers and instructions relative to proclaiming the Philippine Republic.[2] Things now

"THE HONOURABLE PRESIDENT

"This very moment the special train carrying the Honourable President has left for Caloocan.

"Viva the independent Philippines !!!

"Viva the unconquerable Philippine Army !!!

"Notice. This sheet is distributed gratis." — P. I. R., 70–6.

[1] "(News.) The American General, MacArthur, with his entire staff, was taken prisoner by our troops in Northern Luzón. Another American general died on the 5th of January last in the North, who was seriously wounded in an ambush or fight. When shot he was a colonel, but on account of said fight he was promoted to the rank of a general, so that later when he died, he had the benefit of that rank."

— P. I. R., 2035. 3.

[2] (Telegrams)

"WASHINGTON, January 15, 1900, 10 A.M.

" (Received, Cebú, January 16, 1900, 11 A.M.)

" Owing to a new disaster of the Union Army, MacKinley has tendered his resignation as President, Mr. Bryan succeeding him.

"Peace promulgated in the Philippines. Basis of the protectorate is being discussed.

"Philippine independence will be proclaimed February the 4th.

went from bad to worse. The trouble between democrats and republicans resulted in an insurrection. Before August, 1901, President McKinley had brought about strained relations between Germany and the United States by bribing an anarchist to assassinate the German Emperor.[1] Before September 15, 1901, he had been killed by a member of the Democratic party, and the Filipinos could acclaim their independence.[2]

The first period of the war, which we may term the period of organized armed resistance, drew rapidly to its close, and there followed the second period, characterized by guerrilla tactics on the part of the Insurgents.

On September 14, 1899, Aguinaldo accepted the advice of General Pío del Pilar, ex-bandit, if indeed he had ever ceased to rob and murder, and authorized this man, whom he had been again and again asked to remove, to begin guerrilla warfare in Bulacan. Guerrilla tactics were duly authorized for, and had been adopted by, Insurgent forces everywhere before the end of November.

Of this style of fighting Taylor has truly said : —

"If war in certain of its aspects is a temporary reversion to barbarism, guerrilla warfare is a temporary reversion to savagery. The man who orders it assumes a grave responsibility before the people whose fate is in his hands, for serious as is the material destruction which this method of warfare entails, the destruction to the orderly habits of mind and thought which, at bottom, are civilization, is even more serious. Robbery and brigandage, murder and arson follow in its wake.

"Remark. — The basis of a protectorate has been published in English."

"MANILA, January 20, 1900, 10 A.M.
"(Received at Cebú on the same day, at 11 A.M.)
"Otis' successor, John Waterly, of the democratic party, has just arrived. He brings with him papers and instructions in regard to proclamation of the Philippine Republic.

"It is believed that Rev. Martin, Bishop of Cebú, will be transferred to the Archbishopric of Manila, and Rev. Nozaleda to Spain." — P. I. R., Books B–10.

[1] P. I. R., 1193. 2.   [2] *Ibid.*, 2025.

Guerrilla warfare means a policy of destruction, a policy of terror, and never yet, however great may have been the injury caused by it, however much it may have prolonged the war in which it has been employed, has it secured a termination favorable to the people who have chosen it." [1]

The case under discussion furnished no exception to the general rule.

Such semblance of discipline as had previously existed among the Insurgent soldiers rapidly disappeared. Conditions had been very bad under the "Republic" and worse during the first period of the war. During the second period they rapidly became unendurable in many regions, and the common people were driven into the arms of the Americans, in spite of threats of death, barbarously carried out by Insurgent officers, soldiers and agents in thousands of cases. I have described at some length the conditions which now arose in the chapter on Murder as a Governmental Agency, to which the reader is referred for details. [2]

In the effort to protect the towns which showed themselves friendly, the American forces were divided, subdivided and subdivided again. On March 1, 1901, they were occupying no less than five hundred two stations. By December of the same year the number had increased to six hundred thirty-nine, with an average of less than sixty men to a post. As a result of the protection thus afforded and of the humane conduct of our troops, the people turned to us in constantly increasing numbers.

It remained to stamp out the dying embers of insurrection, while continuing to seek to protect those who put their trust in us. Further subdivision of the troops in order to garrison more points was hardly possible, but field operations were actively pushed. One after another the Insurgent leaders were captured or voluntarily surrendered. Most officers of importance issued explanatory statements to the people shortly after giving up active field operations,

[1] Taylor, 47 HS.   [2] Beginning on page 730.

whether they surrendered voluntarily or were taken prisoners. Aguinaldo himself was captured on March 23, 1901, at Palanan, the northernmost point on the east coast of Luzón inhabited by civilized people. No place in the islands, inhabited by Filipinos, is more completely isolated, and he had long been almost entirely cut off from his followers, many of whom believed him to be dead. On April 19, 1901, he issued an address to the Filipino people, in which he clearly recognized the fact that they wanted peace. He said : —

"MANILA, April 19, 1901.

" To the Filipino People : —

" I believe that I am not in error in presuming that the unhappy fate to which my adverse fortune has led me is not a surprise to those who have been familiar day by day with the progress of the war. The lessons thus taught, the full meaning of which has recently come to my knowledge, suggested to me with irresistible force that the complete termination of hostilities and a lasting peace are not only desirable but absolutely essential to the welfare of the Philippines.

" The Filipinos have never been dismayed by their weakness, nor have they faltered in following the path pointed out by their fortitude and courage. The time has come, however, in which they find their advance along the path impeded by an irresistible force — a force which, while it restrains them, yet enlightens the mind and opens another course by presenting to them the cause of peace. This cause has been joyfully embraced by a majority of our fellow-countrymen, who have already united around the glorious and sovereign banner of the United States. In this banner they repose their trust in the belief that under its protection our people will attain all the promised liberties which they are even now beginning to enjoy.

" The country has declared unmistakably in favor of peace; so be it. Enough of blood; enough of tears and desolation. This wish cannot be ignored by the men still in arms if they are animated by no other desire than to serve this noble people which has thus clearly manifested its will.

" So also do I respect this will now that it is known to me, and after mature deliberation resolutely proclaim to the world that I cannot refuse to heed the voice of a people longing for peace, nor the lamentations of thousands of families yearning to see their dear ones in the enjoyment of the liberty promised by the generosity of the great American nation.

"By acknowledging and accepting the sovereignty of the United States throughout the entire Archipelago, as I now do without any reservation whatsoever, I believe that I am serving thee, my beloved country. May happiness be theirs.

"EMILIO AGUINALDO.[1]

"MANILA, April 19, 1901."

This announcement of Aguinaldo, published in Spanish, Tagálog and English, undoubtedly hastened the end of the war, but it did not lead to immediate general surrender, for as Taylor has very truly said : —

"A force like Aguinaldo's could not be surrendered. It had been torn by internal dissensions and the bonds of discipline had always been very lax. It had originally been held together by a lively expectation of the advantages to be obtained from the pillage of Manila. That hope had disappeared, and the leaders had become the lords of life and property each in his own province. It was a force which could disintegrate, but which could not surrender. Only armies can do that. Forces over which their leaders have lost all except nominal control when beaten do not surrender. They disintegrate by passing through the stages of guerrilla warfare, of armed bands of highwaymen, of prowling groups of thieves, of sturdy beggars who at opportune moments resort to petty larceny."[2]

Aguinaldo's forces now passed through these several stages. Some of his more important subordinates had previously been captured or had surrendered. Others, still remaining in the field, now acted on his advice, more or less promptly. A few remained obdurate for a time, but as a rule not for long, and soon there remained in the field only a very limited number of real military leaders, like General Malvar in Batangas and General Lukban in Samar, and a very considerable number of bandit chiefs, some of whom had posed as Insurgents. The forces of the latter were now materially and rapidly augmented by men who had been Insurgent officers or soldiers and

[1] Taylor, 36 GV, Exhibit 1017.   [2] Taylor, 28 HS.

THE BAGUIO COUNTRY CLUB.

erving in this capacity had become so enamoured
wless life that they were now unwilling to settle
and work for their daily bread, preferring to con-
to live off their long-suffering fellow-countrymen,
n they robbed and murdered more mercilessly than

he war was practically over. The insurrection had
ed. In my opinion no Filipino who held out to the
d for independence compared in intellectual power with
abini, and I deem his views as to why it failed worthy
special attention. At the time of his death, he left
ehind a memoir from which I quote the following : —

"The revolution failed because it was poorly led, because
its head conquered his place, not by meritorious, but by repre-
hensible actions, because in place of supporting the men most
useful to the people, he rendered them useless because he was
jealous of them. Believing that the aggrandizement of the
people was nothing more than his own personal aggrandizement, he did not judge the merits of men by their capacity,
character, or patriotism, but by the degree of friendship and
relationship which bound them to him; and wishing to have
his favorites always ready to sacrifice themselves for him,
he showed himself complaisant to their faults. Having thus
secured the people, the people deserted him. And the people
having deserted him, he had to fall like a wax idol melted by
the heat of adversity. God forbid that we should forget so
terrible a lesson learned at the cost of unspeakable sufferings."[1]

These are by no means the only reasons why the revolution failed, but they foredoomed it to failure.

The surrender or capture of the more respectable
military element left the unsurrendered firearms in the
hands of men most of whom were ignorant, many of
whom were criminal, and nearly all of whom were irresponsible and unscrupulous.

Strict enforcement of the rules of civilized warfare
against them was threatened, but not actually resorted to.

[1] P. I. R., 1021. 6.

The situation was particularly bad in Batangas. General J. F. Bell was put in charge there, and he found a humane and satisfactory solution of the existing difficulties in reconcentration—not the kind of reconcentration which made the Spaniards hated in Cuba, but a measure of a wholly different sort. This measure and its results have been concisely described by Taylor, as follows : —

"General Bell said he was as anxious as any one could be to avoid making war against those who really wanted the termination of hostilities, and it was his duty to protect them against the vengeance of others. Over and above all these considerations in importance, however, was the absolute necessity of making it impossible for insurgents to procure food by levying contributions. Therefore, in order to give those who were pacifically inclined an opportunity to escape hardship, as far as possible, and preserve their food supply for themselves and their families, it was determined to establish zones of protection with limits sufficiently near all towns to enable the small garrisons thereof to give the people living within these zones efficient protection against ruinous exactions by insurgents. He accordingly, 'in order to put an end to enforced contributions now levied by insurgents upon the inhabitants of sparsely settled and outlying barrios and districts by means of intimidation and assassination,' ordered the commanding officers of all towns in the provinces of Batangas and Laguna to 'immediately specify and establish plainly marked limits surrounding each town bounding a zone within which it may be practicable, with an average-sized garrison, to exercise sufficient supervision over and furnish protection to inhabitants (who desire to be peaceful) against the depredation of armed insurgents. The limits may include the barrios which exist sufficiently near the town to be given protection and supervision by the garrison, and should include some ground on which live stock could graze, but so situated that it can be patrolled and watched. All ungarrisoned towns will be garrisoned as soon as troops become available.

"'Commanding officers will also see that orders are at once given and distributed to all the inhabitants within the jurisdiction of towns over which they exercise supervision, informing them of the danger of remaining outside of these limits, and that unless they move by December 25 from outlying barrios and districts, with all their movable food supplies, including rice, *palay*,[1] chickens, live stock, etc., to within the limits of the zone established at their own or nearest town, their property (found outside of said zone at said date) will become liable to confiscation or destruction. The people will be permitted to move houses from outlying districts should they desire to do so, or to construct temporary shelter for themselves on any vacant land without compensation to the owner, and no owner will be permitted to deprive them of the privilege of doing so. In the discretion of commanding officers the prices of necessities of existence may also be regulated in the interest of those thus seeking protection. As soon as peaceful conditions have been reëstablished in the brigade these persons will be encouraged to return to their homes, and such assistance be rendered them as may be found practicable.'

" It was deemed best not to compel the people to enter these zones; but they were warned that unless they accepted that protection their property, which consisted almost entirely of food supplies, would become liable to confiscation or destruction, because it might be impossible to determine whether it belonged to hostile or peaceful people. To put an end to vengeance by assassination, it was determined to make use of the right of retaliation conferred by General Order 100 issued by President Lincoln in 1863. A circular telegram was published announcing an intention to retaliate by the execution of prisoners of war in case any more were assassinated by insurgents for political reasons. It was not found necessary to do this. Assassinations stopped at once.

"As the campaign progressed it became more and more apparent that a large number of poor people had contributed through fear, for the power of the insurgents to collect came to an end after they had lost their power of intimidation. The efficiency of the protection afforded in such zones was the determining factor in forming the decision and attitude of many of the natives. The protection afforded was efficient, and from time to time many additional families entered the zones. The sentiment for peace grew stronger steadily and natives volunteered assistance to Americans at every hand and in every town. When these volunteers were trustworthy they were armed and sent out into the mountains from which they brought back guns, and insurgents, and hundreds of half-famished men, women, and children who, released from the intimidating influence of the insurgents, entered the zones of protection.

[1] Unhusked rice.

"The most serious discomfort experienced by any one within these areas was caused to the *mestizo* ruling group, whose members bitterly resented the blow to their prestige in being treated like every one else. They had been accustomed to have others work for them and obey them blindly. To a man who could speak Spanish and who had always been the lord of his *barrio*,[1] the possibility of having to cultivate a field with his own hands was an unthinkable and scandalous thing. These men suffered and suffered acutely; but it was not their bodies which suffered — it was their pride.

"Malvar surrendered on April 16, 1902. Most of the people had turned against their once highly respected chief, and toward the end several thousand natives of Batangas joined the Americans in their determined hunt for the fugitive leader. Realization of the fact that the people were against him materially aided in forcing his surrender.

"General Bell had captured or forced to surrender some 8000 to 10,000 persons actively engaged, in one capacity or another, in the insurrection. These prisoners were rapidly released when they had taken the oath of allegiance. By the first week of July no political prisoners were held in this region. They had returned to their homes.

"The policy of concentrating the people in protected zones and destroying the food which was used for the maintenance of guerrilla bands was not new. There had been precedents even in the United States. One of these is the order issued on August 25, 1863, by Brigadier-General Ewing, commanding the district of the border, with headquarters at Kansas City, Mo., in which he ordered the inhabitants of a large part of three counties of that State to remove from their residences within fifteen days to the protection of the military stations which he had established. All grain and hay in that district was ordered to be taken to those military stations. If it was not convenient to so dispose of it, it would be burned (Rebellion Records, Series I, Vol. XXII, Part II, p. 473). The American commanders in the Philippines had adopted no new method of procedure in dealing with war traitors; they had, however, effectively employed an old one.

"The insurrection had originated among the Tagálogs and had spread like a conflagration from the territory occupied by them. The fire had been quenched everywhere else. General Bell had now stamped out the embers in the Tagálog provinces.

[1] Village.

" On July 2 the Secretary of War telegraphed that the insurrection against the sovereign authority of the United States in the Philippines having come to an end, and provincial civil governments having been established throughout the entire territory of the archipelago not inhabited by Moro tribes, the office of military governor in the archipelago was terminated. On July 4, 1902, the President of the United States issued a proclamation of amnesty proclaiming, with certain reservations, a full and complete pardon and amnesty to all persons in the Philippine Archipelago who had participated in the insurrection."

General Bell's motives and methods in reconcentrating the inhabitants of this troubled region have been grossly misrepresented, and he himself has been sadly maligned. He is the most humane of men, and the plan which he adopted resulted in the reëstablishment of law and order at a minimum cost of human suffering.

Many of the occupants of his reconcentration camps received there their first lessons in hygienic living. Many of them were reluctant to leave the camps and return to their homes when normal conditions again prevailed.

The number of Filipinos killed during the Batangas campaign was very small.[1] Blount has sought to make it appear that partly as an indirect consequence of war there was dreadful mortality there, citing by way of proof the fact that the Coast and Geodetic Atlas, published as a part of the report of the first Philippine Commission, gave the population of Batangas as 312,192, while the census of 1903 gave it as 257,715.[2]

The report of the United States Philippine Commission for 1903 gives the population of Manila as 221,000, while in 1900 it had been 260,000. Does this mean that there had been a holocaust in Manila? Not at all. It means

[1] 153, according to Blount himself.

[2] "Nor can the ultimate responsibility before the bar of history for the awful fact that, according to the United States Coast and Geodetic Survey Atlas of the Philippines of 1899, the population of Batangas province was 312,192, and according to the American Census of the Philippines of 1903, it was 257,715, rest entirely on military shoulders." —BLOUNT, pp. 383–384.

only that the thousands of Filipinos who had sought the protection of the American forces there during the period when they feared their own soldiers in the provinces had mostly returned to their homes. During the disturbed period in Batangas great numbers of people took refuge in other and more peaceful regions. Some of them returned later; others did not.

Blount further quotes a statement in the 1901 report of the Provincial Secretary of Batangas to the effect that:

"The mortality, caused no longer by the war, but by disease, such as malaria and dysentery, has reduced to a little over 200,000 the more than 300,000 inhabitants which in former years the province had." [1]

Apart from the fact that these figures, showing a mortality of a hundred thousand from disease alone, are hardly consistent with those quoted by Blount as showing a decrease in population during a longer period of only fifty-four thousand four hundred and forty-seven, it is not apparent why Americans should be charged with deaths due to malaria or dysentery, since no systematic effort to rid Batangas of these ills had ever previously been made, and the very thing which then prevented the adoption of the measures subsequently so successfully put forth to this end was the disorderly conduct of the people themselves. As a simple matter of fact, however, there was no such dreadful mortality from these diseases at this time. Malaria has never been especially bad in this province, and even cholera, which swept it during the period in question and is far more readily communicated than is dysentery, caused only twenty-three hundred and ninety-nine known deaths.

In the end peace was established and prosperity followed in its wake.

This result was brought about in part by the efficient activity of the armed forces of the United States and in part by the efforts of the first and second Philippine Commissions. [2]

[1] Blount, p. 597.   [2] See Chapters XI and XII.

CHAPTER X

MR. BRYAN AND INDEPENDENCE

IN order to bring home to some of my Democratic and Anti-Imperialist friends the unreliable character of the testimony of even the very high officers of the so-called Philippine Republic, I here quote certain extracts from the Insurgent records, showing the important part played, doubtless unwittingly, by Mr. William Jennings Bryan in Philippine politics during the war. The first of these might properly have been considered in the chapter entitled "Was Independence Promised?" Others are instructive in that they show the use made of false news in bolstering up the Insurgent cause, and might with propriety have been included in the chapter on "The Conduct of the War." I have thought it best to keep them by themselves. Further comment on them would seem to be superfluous.

"On May 1, 1900 (P. I. R., 516. 6), I. de los Santos wrote a long letter in Tagálog and cipher to Aguinaldo, in which he reported upon the progress of what he would have probably called the diplomatic campaign. If this letter is to be believed, the agents in the United States of the junta had been able to form relations which might be of great value to them. Santos said in part: —

"'Commissioners . . . Señores Kant (G. Apacible) and Raff (Sixto López) duly carried out your last instructions given at Tárlac. Señor Del Pan, sailing by way of Japan, about the middle of October, and Señor Caney (G. Apacible), sailing by way of Europe about the 1st of November, met in Toronto about the middle of February following. But before the arrival of Kant, Raff had already come from Hayti (United States) and was able to pry in upon our political friends and enemies. When they met each other they continued the voyage incognito, as Raff had done previously, making themselves

295

known to a very few people; but later on, and according to the instructions carried by Caney, they made themselves known to a greater number of people, and have succeeded in interviewing Bryan who happened to be in New York. Señor Raff said that Bryan feared being present at a conference, lest he might be called a traitor by members of his own party, and also by those of the opposite or "imperialist" party, who are quite proud over the victories they have gained against our people over there. Nevertheless, Raff was able to be present and talk at some of the anti-imperialist meetings, our political friends introducing him as a friend from the committee (at Hong-kong) and as an advocate of the cessation of the war over there in order that our sacred rights may be given consideration by them. And as Bryan could not personally take part in the conference, he sent a most trusted person, his right-hand man, Dr. Gardner. The results of the conference between Señor Raff and Dr. Gardner, the latter acting in the name of Mr. Bryan, are as follows: —

"'1st. That we may fight on, and Bryan will never cease to defend our sacred rights. 2nd. That we must never mention Bryan's name in our manifestos and proclamations, lest the opposite party might say he is a traitor. 3rd. That we are in the right; and hence he promised in the name of Bryan that if this Señor Bryan is victorious in the presidential campaign, he will recognize our independence without delay. Your honored self can easily conclude from all the foregoing that Señor Del Pan, after the receipt of these promises, concurred with him; and he returned to inform Señor Apacible about the results of the conference. So these two studied over the plan of the policy to be adopted and carried out. I write you what their opinions are, viz.: 1st, that they will reside there, pending the outcome of the presidential contest, aiding the propaganda and enlivening it until November, the date set for the desired thing. Owing to what Dr. Gardner said and promised in the name of Bryan, some one ought to stay there in order that Bryan may be approached, if he is elected, so he can sign the recognition of our independence; and this should be done at once, lest in his excitement over the victory he should forget his promise. 3rd. For carrying out the two propositions just mentioned, they request 2000 pounds sterling, that is $20,000 in silver, to be used for the propaganda, for paying newspapers and for bribing senators — this last clause is somewhat dangerous and impossible. And 4th, that the money must be sent immediately, and that you should be informed not to mention the name of Bryan in the manifestos and proclamations.

"'In order to answer quickly and decisively that proposition, and as I did not have the desired money here, I answered as follows: "Plan approved; for the sake of economy we have decided that one of the two retire, but before doing so make arrangements, establish communications with leaders of Bryan's party, and he who remains should thus cultivate the relations; he who is to retire will locate himself in Paris near Señor Katipalad (Agoncillo) with whom he will secretly discuss political problems that may arise. So he will watch for the opportune moment of Bryan's election, in order to go immediately to Hayti and formally arrange the contract with Bryan." [1]

*   *   *   *   *   *   *

"'By the end of 1899, by the time guerrilla warfare was well under way, by the time that any Filipino government, unless an expression of the unfettered will of the nearest bandit who can muster a dozen rifles may be called a government, had ceased to exist, a strong opposition to the policy of the administration had arisen in the United States and a demand for the recognition of the independence of the Philippines. The junta in Hongkong were assured that the Democratic party would come into power in the next elections and that this would mean the success of the patriotic efforts of Aguinaldo and his followers. The news was good and was forthwith spread abroad in "Extracts from our correspondence with America," "News from our foreign agents," "News from America," and "Translations from the foreign press" — circulars and handbills printed on thin paper which were smuggled into the Philippines and passed into the hands of the guerrilla leaders who could read Spanish. They gathered their followers about them and told them that a powerful party had arisen in America which was going to give them all they had ever asked for. They had only to fight on, for success was certain. In America the "Anti-imperialists" were hanging the "Imperialists," and they should continue to harry the American adherents among the natives of the Philippines.

"'There are a number of these publications among the papers captured from the insurgents, and the adoption of this method of propaganda seems to have been nearly coincident with Aguinaldo's orders declaring guerrilla warfare. It does not

[1] Taylor, 13 KK, E.

seem likely that the matter contained in them was supplied by a Filipino, for if it was he assumed a general acquaintance among the people with American politics and American methods which they were far from possessing.

"'In these publications the Filipinos were assured that the Imperialists were kept in power only by the lavish contributions of the "truts," whatever they may have been; but the people of the United States were growing weary of their domination and were about to return to the true principles of Washington and Jefferson. The illustrious Americans " Crosvy Sticcney, and Vartridge" were all laboring for the cause of Philippine independence. Long lists of American cities were given in which the illustrious orators Mr. Croshy and Mr. Schurts had addressed applauding crowds upon the necessity of throttling the "truts" because they opposed recognition of the rights of the Filipinos. In August, 1900, "News from our agents in America" informed its readers that —

"'"W. J. Bryan has stated in a speech that his first act upon being elected President will be to declare the independence of the Philippines."

"'On June 16, 1900, Gen. Riego de Dios, acting head of the Hongkong junta, wrote to Gen. I. Torres (P. I. R., 530), the guerrilla commander in Bulacán Province, and assured him that a little more endurance, a little more constancy, was all that was needed to secure the attainment of their ends. According to their advices the Democratic party would win in the approaching elections in the United States, and — "it is certain that Bryan is the incarnation of our independence."

"'The number of men opposed to the policy of the administration was said to be continually increasing.

"'The attitude of those who protect us cannot be more manly and resolute : " Continue the struggle until you conquer or die." Mr. Beecher of the League in Cincinnati writes us : "I shall always be the champion of the cause of justice and of truth," says Mr. Winslow of the Boston League. "Not even threats of imprisonment will make me cease in my undertaking," Doctor Denziger assures us. "I shall accept every risk and responsibility," says Doctor Leverson. "If it is necessary, I shall go so far as to provoke a revolution in my own country," repeats Mr. Udell. "It is necessary to save the Republic and democracy from the abyss of imperialism and save the worthy Filipinos from oppression and extermination" is cried by all, and the sound of this cry is ever rising louder and louder.' "[1]

[1] Taylor, 15 and 16 KK, E.

Extract from a letter of Papa Isio[1] dated March 4, 1901 :—

"I have received from Luzón an order to proceed more rapidly with my operations this month, as Bryan ordered Emilío to keep the war going vigorously until April, and he also said that if independence was not given the Philippines by that time, he, Bryan, and his followers would rise in arms against the oppressors."[2]

"TARLAC, Oct. 26, 1899.
" To the Military Governor of This City, and
To the Secretary of the Interior.
"As a meeting shall be held on the morning of Sunday next in the Presidential Palace of this Republic in return for that held in the United States by Mr. Bryan, who drank to the name of our Honourable President as one of the heroes of the world, and for the purpose of celebrating it with more pomp and contributing to it the greater splendor with your personnel, I will be obliged to you if you will please call at this office to confer with me on the matter.
"God preserve you, etc.

(Signed) " F. BUENCAMINO." [3]

In a letter written by A. Flores, acting secretary of war, to the military governor of Tarlac on October 27, 1899, there occurs the following : —

"In the United States meetings and banquets have been held in honor of our Honourable President, Don Emilio Aguinaldo, who was pronounced one of the heroes of the world by Mr. Bryan, future president of the United States. The Masonic Society, therefore, interpreting the unanimous desires of the people, and with the approval of the government, will on Sunday the 29th instant, organize a meeting or popular assembly in the interest of national independence and in honor of Mr. Bryan of the anti-imperialist party, the defenders of our cause in the United States. The meeting will consist of two functions; first — at nine A.M. of the 29th the assembly will convene in a suitable place, a national hymn will inaugurate

---

[1] "Pope" Isio was the last of a series of bandit leaders, claiming for themselves miraculous powers, who long infested the mountains of Negros.
[2] P. I. R., 970. 7.   [3] P. I. R., 1134–1.

the exercises, after which appropriate addresses will be delivered; and second — at four P.M. a popular demonstration will take place throughout the town, with bands of music parading the streets; residents will decorate and illuminate their houses.

"Which I have the pleasure of transmitting to you for your information and guidance and for that of the troops under your command." [1]

[1] P. I. R., 17. 9.

CHAPTER XI

THE FIRST PHILIPPINE COMMISSION

I HAVE elsewhere mentioned the appointment of the First Philippine Commission.

On January 18, 1899, its civilian members met at Washington and received the President's instructions.

We were to aid in "the most humane, pacific and effective extension of authority throughout these islands, and to secure, with the least possible delay, the benefits of a wise and generous protection of life and property to the inhabitants."

We were directed to meet at the earliest possible day in the city of Manila and to announce by a public proclamation our presence and the mission intrusted to us, carefully setting forth that while the established military government would be continued as long as necessity might require, efforts would be made to alleviate the burden of taxation, to establish industrial and commercial prosperity and to provide for the safety of persons and property by such means as might be found conducive to those ends.

We were to endeavour, without interfering with the military authorities, to ascertain what amelioration in the condition of the inhabitants and what improvements in public order were practicable, and for this purpose were to study attentively the existing social and political state of the several populations, particularly as regarded the forms of local government, the administration of justice, the collection of customs and other taxes, the means of transportation and the need of public improvements, reporting through the Department of State the results of our observations and reflections, and recommending such executive action as might, from time to time, seem to us wise and useful.

301

We were authorized to recommend suitable persons for appointment to offices, made necessary by personal changes in the existing civil administration, from among the inhabitants who had previously acknowledged their allegiance to the American government.

We were to "ever use due respect for all the ideals, customs and institutions of the tribes which compose the population, emphasizing upon all occasions the just and beneficent intentions of the United States," and were commissioned on account of our "knowledge, skill, and integrity as bearers of the good-will, the protection and the richest blessings of a liberating rather than a conquering nation." [1]

Nothing could be more false than Blount's insinuation that we were sent out to help Otis run the war. [2] There was no war when we started, and we were expressly enjoined from interfering with the military government or its officers. We were sent to deliver a message of good-will, to investigate, and to recommend, and there our powers ended.

Mr. Schurman and I, with a small clerical force, sailed from Vancouver, January 31, 1899. On our arrival at Yokohama we learned with keen regret of the outbreak of hostilities at Manila.

Blount has incorrectly stated that President McKinley had sent the commission out when the dogs of war were already let loose. [3] The dogs of war had not been loosed

---

[1] For the full text of these instructions, see appendix, p. 975.

[2] "Mr. McKinley sent Mr. Taft out, in the spring preceding the election of 1900, to help General MacArthur run the war." — BLOUNT, p. 281.

"The Taft Commission was sent out, to 'aid' General MacArthur, as the Schurman Commission had 'aided' General Otis." — BLOUNT, p. 289.

[3] "In February, 1899, the dogs of war being already let loose, President McKinley had resumed his now wholly impossible Benevolent Assimilation programme, by sending out the Schurman Commission, which was the prototype of the Taft Commission, to yearningly explain our intentions to the insurgents, and to make clear to them how unqualifiedly benevolent those intentions were. The scheme was like trying to put salt on a bird's tail after you have flushed him." — BLOUNT, p. 217.

when we started, and one of the main purposes in sending us was to keep them in their kennels if possible.

Aguinaldo has made the following statements in his "Reseña Verídica" : —

". . . We, the Filipinos, would have received said commission, as honourable agents of the great America, with demonstrations of true kindness and entire adhesion. The commissioners would have toured over all our provinces, seeing and observing at close range order and tranquillity, in the whole of our territory. They would have seen the fields tilled and planted. They would have examined our Constitution and public administration, in perfect peace, and they would have experienced and enjoyed that ineffable charm of our Oriental manner, a mixture of abandon and solicitude, of warmth and of frigidity, of confidence and of suspiciousness, which makes our relations with foreigners change into a thousand colours, agreeable to the utmost.

"Ah ! but this landscape suited neither General Otis nor the Imperialists ! For their criminal intention it was better that the American commissioners should find war and desolation in the Philippines, perceiving from the day of their arrival the fetid stench emitted by the mingled corpses of Americans and Filipinos. For their purposes it was better that that gentleman, Mr. Schurman, President of the Commission, could not leave Manila, limiting himself to listen to the few Filipinos, who, having yielded to the reasonings of gold, were partisans of the Imperialists. It was better that the commission should contemplate the Philippine problem through conflagrations, to the whiz of bullets, on the transverse light of all the unchained passions, in order that it might not form any exact or complete opinion of the natural and proper limits of said problem. Ah ! it was better, in short, that the commission should leave defeated in not having secured peace, and would blame me and the other Filipinos, when I and the whole Filipino people anxiously desired that peace should have been secured before rather than now, but an honourable and worthy peace for the United States and for the Philippine Republic." [1]

These statements, made to deceive the public, make interesting reading in the light of our present knowledge as to the purposes and plans of Aguinaldo and his associates.

[1] P. I. R., 1300. 2.

On our arrival at Yokohama we were promptly informed by a secretary from the United States Legation that no less a personage than Marquis Ito had been in frequent communication with the Filipinos since 1894, that they had been looking to him for advice and support, and that he had interested himself in the present situation sufficiently to come to the American minister and offer to go to the Philippines, not in any sense as an agent of the United States, but as a private individual, and to use his influence in our behalf. His contention was that the then existing conditions resulted from misunderstandings.

He said that Americans did not understand Asiatics, but he was an Asiatic himself and did understand the Filipinos, and thought that he could settle the whole affair. The minister had cabled to Washington for instructions. Naturally the offer was not accepted.

I was reminded, by this extraordinary incident, of a previous occurrence. I spent the month of March, 1893, in Tokio when returning from my second visit to the Philippines, and was kindly invited to inspect the zoölogical work at the Imperial University. When I visited the institution for that purpose, I was questioned very closely on the islands, their people and their resources. The gentlemen who interrogated me may have been connected with the university, but I doubt it.

We reached Hongkong on February 22. Here I had an interview with Dr. Apacible of the junta, while Mr. Schurman visited Canton. Apacible told me that the Filipinos wanted an independent republic under an American protectorate. Pressed for the details of their desires, he said that "the function of a protector is to protect." Further than that he could not go. I tried to convince him of the hopelessness of the course the Filipinos were then pursuing and of the kindly intentions of my government, but felt that I made no impression on him.

We arrived at Manila on March 4, 1899, too late to

land. Firebugs were abroad. We watched a number of houses burn, and heard the occasional crackle of rifle fire along the line of the defences around the city. The next morning there was artillery fire for a time at San Pedro Macáti. Everywhere were abundant evidences that the war was on.

This left little for us to do at the moment except to inform ourselves as to conditions, especially as Colonel Denby had not yet arrived, and General Otis was overwhelmed with work and anxiety.

I renewed my acquaintance with many old Filipino and Spanish friends and improved the opportunity, not likely to recur in my experience, to see as much as possible of the fighting in the field.

One day when I was at San Pedro Macáti, Captain Dyer, who commanded a battery of 3.2-inch guns there, suggested that if I wished to investigate the effect of shrapnel fire I could do so by visiting a place on a neighbouring hillside which he indicated. Acting upon his suggestion, I set out, accompanied by my private secretary, who, like myself, was clad in white duck. The Insurgent sharpshooters on the other side of the river devoted some attention to us, but we knew that so long as they aimed at us we were quite safe. Few of their bullets came within hearing distance.

We were hunting about on the hillside for the place indicated by Captain Dyer, when suddenly we heard ourselves cursed loudly and fluently in extremely plain American, and there emerged from a neighbouring thicket a very angry infantry officer. On venturing to inquire the cause of his most uncomplimentary remarks, I found that he was in command of skirmishers who were going through the brush to see whether there was anything left there which needed shooting up. As many of the Insurgent soldiers dressed in white, and as American civilians were not commonly to be met in Insurgent territory, these men had been just about to fire on us when they discovered their mistake. We went back to Manila and bought some khaki clothes.

At first my interest in military matters was not appreciated by my army friends, who could not see what business I had to be wandering around without a gun in places where guns were in use. I had, however, long since discovered that reliable first-hand information on any subject is likely to be useful sooner or later, and so it proved in this case.

For several weeks after we reached Manila there was no active military movement; then came the inauguration of the short, sharp campaign which ended for the moment with the taking of Malolos. For long, tedious weeks our soldiers had sweltered in muddy trenches, shot at by an always invisible foe whom they were not allowed to attack. It was anticipated that when the forward movement began, it would be active. Close secrecy was maintained with regard to it. Captain Hedworth Lambton, of the British cruiser *Powerful*, then lying in Manila Bay, exacted a promise from me that I would tell him if I found out when the advance was to begin, so that we might go to Caloocan together and watch the fighting from the church tower, which commanded a magnificent view of the field of operations.

I finally heard a fairly definite statement that our troops would move the following morning. I rushed to General Otis's office and after some parleying had it confirmed by him. It was then too late to advise Lambton, and in fact I could not properly have done so, as the information had been given me under pledge of secrecy. Accompanied by my private secretary, Dr. P. L. Sherman, I hastened to Caloocan, where we arrived just at dusk, having had to run the gantlet of numerous inquisitive sentries *en route*.

We spent the night in the church, where General Wheaton and his staff had their headquarters, and long before daylight were perched in a convenient opening in

The Bureau of Science Building, Manila.

This is one of the best equipped laboratory buildings in the world.

its galvanized iron roof, made on a former occasion by a shell from Dewey's fleet.

From this vantage point we could see the entire length of the line of battle. The attack began shortly after daylight. Near Caloocan the Insurgent works were close in, but further off toward La Loma they were in some places distant a mile or more from the trenches of the Americans.

The general plan of attack was that the whole American line should rotate to the north and west on Caloocan as a pivot, driving the Insurgents in toward Malabon if possible. The latter began to fire as soon as the American troops showed themselves, regardless of the fact that their enemies were quite out of range. As most of them were using black-powder cartridges, their four or five miles of trenches were instantly outlined. The ground was very dry so that the bullets threw up puffs of dust where they struck, and it was possible to judge the accuracy of the fire of each of the opposing forces.

Rather heavy resistance was encountered on the extreme right, and the turning movement did not materialize as rapidly as had been hoped. General Wheaton, who was in command of the forces about the church, finally moved to the front, and as we were directly in the rear of his line and the Insurgents, as usual, overshot badly, we found ourselves in an uncomfortably hot corner. Bullets rattled on the church roof like hail, and presently one passed through the opening through which Major Bourns, Colonel Potter, of the engineer corps, and I were sticking our heads. Immediately thereafter we were observed by Dr. Sherman making record time on all fours along one of the framing timbers of the church toward its tower. There we took up our station, and thereafter observed the fighting by peeping through windows partially closed with blocks of volcanic tuff. We had a beautiful opportunity to see the artillery fire. The guns were directly in front of and below us and we could watch the laying of the several pieces and then turn our field-glasses on the particular portions of the Insurgent trenches where the projectiles were likely to strike. Again and again we caught bursting shells in the fields of our glasses and could thus see their effect as accurately as if we had been standing close by, without any danger of being perforated by shrapnel.

After the Insurgent position had been carried we walked forward to their line of trenches and followed it east to a point beyond the La Loma Church, counting the dead and wounded, as I had heard wild stories of tremendous slaughter and wanted to see just how much damage the fire of our troops had really done. On our way we passed the Caloocan railroad station which had been converted into a temporary field hospital. Here I saw good Father McKinnon, the chaplain of the First California Volunteers, assisting a surgeon and soaked with the blood of wounded men. He was one chaplain in a thousand. It was always easy to find him. One had only to look where trouble threatened and help was needed. He was sure to be there.

On my way from the railway station to the trenches I met a very much excited officer returning from the front. He had evidently had a long and recent interview with Cyrus Noble,[1] and was determined to tell me all about the fighting. I escaped from him after some delay, and with much difficulty. Later he remembered having met me, but made a grievous mistake as to the scene of our encounter, insisting that we had been together in "Wheaton's Hole," an uncommonly hot position where numerous people got hurt. He persisted in giving a graphic account of our experiences, and in paying high tribute to my coolness and courage under heavy fire. My efforts to persuade him that I had not been with him there proved futile, and I finally gave up the attempt. I wonder how many other military reputations rest upon so slender

---

[1] A brand of whiskey then much in use.

a foundation! This experience was unique. I never saw another officer under the influence of liquor when in the field.

At the time that we visited the Insurgent trenches, not all of our own killed and wounded had been removed, yet every wounded Insurgent whom we found had a United States army canteen of water at his side, obviously left by some kindly American soldier. Not a few of the injured had been furnished hardtack as well. All were ultimately taken to Manila and there given the best of care by army surgeons.

Sometime later a most extraordinary account of this fight, written by a soldier, was published in the *Springfield Republican*. It was charged that our men had murdered prisoners in cold blood, and had committed all manner of barbarities, the writer saying among other things: —

"We first bombarded a town called Malabon and then entered it and killed every man, woman and child in the place."

The facts were briefly as follows: There was an Insurgent regiment in and near a mangrove swamp to the right of this town. When it became obstreperous it was shelled for a short time until it quieted down again. None of the shells entered the town. Indeed, most of them struck in the water. Our troops did not enter Malabon that day, but passed to the northward, leaving behind a small guard to keep the Insurgents from coming out of Malabon in their rear. Had they then entered the town, they would not have found any women, children or non-combatant men to kill for the reason that all such persons had been sent away some time before. The town was burned, in part, but by the Insurgents themselves. They fired the church and a great orphan asylum, and did much other wanton damage.

Being able to speak from personal observation as to the occurrences of that day, I sent a long cablegram direct to the *Chicago Times-Herald* stating the facts.

After my return to the United States, President McKinley was kind enough to say to me that if there had been no other result from the visit of the first Philippine Commission to the islands than the sending of that cablegram, he should have considered the expense involved more than justified. He added that the country was being flooded at the time with false and slanderous rumours, and people at home did not know what to believe. The statements of army officers were discounted in advance, and other testimony from some unprejudiced source was badly needed.

On April 2, 1899, Colonel Denby arrived, and our serious work began. The fighting continued and there was little that we could do save earnestly to strive to promote friendly relations with the conservative element among the Filipinos, and to gather the information we had been instructed to obtain.

On April 4, 1899, we issued a proclamation setting forth in clear and simple language the purposes of the American government.[1] It was translated into Tagálog and other dialects and widely circulated. The Insurgent leaders were alert to keep the common people and the soldiers from learning of the kindly purposes of the United States. They were forbidden to read the document and we were reliably informed that the imposition of the death penalty was threatened if this order was violated. In Manila crowds of Filipinos gathered about copies of the proclamation which were posted in public places. Many of them were soon effaced by Insurgent agents or sympathizers.

This document unquestionably served a very useful purpose.[2] For one thing, it promptly brought us into much closer touch with the more conservative Filipinos.

[1] For the text of this document see the Appendix, p. 977.

[2] In view of the alleged attitude of General Otis toward the work of the Commission, the following statement by him as to the effect of this proclamation is of interest : —

General Otis said : "It was unanimously decided to print, publish,

We soon established relations of friendliness and confidence with men like Arellano, Torres, Legarda and Tavera, who had left the Malolos government when it demonstrated its futility, and were ready to turn to the United States for help. Insurgent sympathizers also conferred freely with us. We were invited to a beautiful function given in our honour at the home of a wealthy family, and were impressed, as no one can fail to be, with the dignified bearing of our Filipino hosts, a thing which is always in evidence on such occasions. We gave a return function which was largely attended and greatly aided in the establishment of relations of confidence and friendship with leading Filipino residents of Manila.

The Filipinos were much impressed with Colonel Denby. He was a handsome man, of imposing presence, with one of the kindest hearts that ever beat. They felt instinctively that they could have confidence in him, and showed it on all occasions.

Meanwhile we lost no opportunity to inform ourselves as to conditions and events, conferring with Filipinos from various parts of the archipelago and with Chinese, Germans, Frenchmen, Belgians, Austrians, Englishmen, Spaniards and Americans. Among the witnesses who

post, and disseminate as much as possible among the inhabitants under insurgent domination this address, printing the same in the English, Spanish, and Tagálog languages. This was done, but scarcely had it been posted in Manila twenty-four hours before it was so torn and mutilated as to be unrecognizable. It suffered the same fate as the proclamation of January 4, set out in pages 113 and 114 of this report, but it produced a marked beneficial influence on the people, especially those outside our lines, as it carried with it a conviction of the United States' intentions, on account of the source from which it emanated, it being an expression from a committee of gentlemen especially appointed to proclaim the policy which the United States would pursue."
— TAYLOR, 90 AJ.

Taylor adds: "The commander of one of the regiments of sandatahan in Manila reported that he had forced the people of the city to destroy the proclamations issued by the commission (P. I. R., 73. 9). As he found this necessary, the action of the people could hardly have reflected their real feelings in the matter."

came before us were farmers, bankers, brokers, merchants, lawyers, physicians, railroad men, shipowners, educators and public officials. Certainly all classes of opinion were represented, and when we were called upon by the President, a little later, for a statement of the situation we felt fully prepared to make it.

Blount has charged that the commission attempted to interfere with the conduct of the war, and cites a cablegram from General Otis stating that conferences with Insurgents cost soldiers' lives in support of this contention. No conference with Insurgent leaders was ever held without the previous knowledge and approval of the general, who was himself a member of the commission.

Late in April General Luna sent Colonel Arguelles of his staff to ask for a fifteen days' suspension of hostilities under the pretext of enabling the Insurgent congress to meet at San Fernando, Pampanga, on May 1, to discuss the situation and decide what it wanted to do. He called on the commission and urged us to ask Otis to grant this request, but we declined to intervene, and General Otis refused to grant it.

Mabini continued Luna's effort, sending Arguelles back with letters to Otis and to the commission. In the latter he asked for "an armistice and a suspension of hostilities as an indispensable means of arriving at peace," stating explicitly that the Philippine government "does not solicit the armistice to gain a space of time in which to reënforce itself."

The commission again referred Arguelles to General Otis on the matter of armistice and suspension of hostilities. We suspected that the statement that these things were not asked for in order to gain time was false, and this has since been definitely established.

Taylor says : —

"On April 11 Mabini wrote to General Luna (Exhibit 719) that Aguinaldo's council was of the opinion that no negotiations for the release of the Spanish prisoners should be considered unless the American Commission agreed to a suspension of hostilities for the purpose of treating, not only in regard to the prisoners, but for the purpose of opening negotiations between Aguinaldo's government and the American authorities.

"'In arriving at this decision we have been actuated by the desire to gain time for our arsenals to produce sufficient cartridges, if, as would seem to be probable, they persist in not even recognizing our belligerency, as means for furthering the recognition of our independence.'" [1]

Arguelles, on his return, was instructed to ask Otis for a —

"general armistice and suspension of hostilities in all the archipelago for the short space of three months, in order to enable it to consult the opinion of the people concerning the government which would be the most advantageous, and the intervention in it which should be given to the North American Government, and to appoint an extraordinary commission with full powers, to act in the name of the Philippine people." [2]

General Otis naturally again declined to grant the request for a suspension of hostilities.

Little came of the conference between Arguelles and the commission, except that we really succeeded in convincing him of the good intentions of our government, and this promptly got him into very serious trouble, as we shall soon see. I took him to a tent hospital on the First Reserve Hospital grounds where wounded Insurgents were receiving the best of treatment at the hands of American surgeons, and he was amazed. He had been taught to believe that the Americans murdered prisoners, raped women, and committed similar barbarities whenever they got a chance. As we have seen, stories of this sort were industriously spread by many of the Insurgent leaders among their soldiers, and among the common people as well. They served to arouse the passions of the former, and stirred them up to acts of devilish brutality which they might perhaps not otherwise have perpetrated.

[1] Taylor, 96 AJ.   [2] *Ibid.*

Arguelles told the truth upon his return, and this, together
with his suggestion that it might be well to consider the
acceptance of the form of government offered by the
United States, nearly cost him his life.   Relative to this
matter Taylor says : —

"When Arguelles returned to the insurgent lines, it must
have been considered that he had said too much in Manila.
While he had been sent there to persuade the Americans to
agree to a suspension of hostilities to be consumed in endless
discussion under cover of which Luna's army could be reorganized, he had not only failed to secure the desired armistice, but
had come back with the opinion that it might after all be
advisable to accept the government proposed by the United
States. On May 22 General Luna ordered his arrest and
trial for being in favour of the autonomy of the United States
in the Philippine Islands. He was tried promptly, the prosecuting witness being another officer of Luna's staff who had
accompanied him to Manila and acted as a spy upon his movements (P. I. R., 285. 2). The court sentenced him to dismissal
and confinement at hard labor for twelve years. This did not
satisfy Luna's thirst for vengeance, and he was imprisoned in
Bautista on the first floor of a building whose second story
was occupied by that officer. One night Luna came alone
into the room where he was confined and told him that although
he was a traitor, yet he had done good service to the cause ;
and it was not proper that a man who had been a colonel in the
army should be seen working on the roads under a guard. He
told him that the proper thing for him to do was to blow his
brains out, and that if he did not do it within a reasonable time
the sentinel at his door would shoot him. He gave him a
pistol and left the room. Arguelles decided not to kill himself, but fully expected that the guard would kill him. Shortly
afterwards Luna was summoned to meet Aguinaldo, and never
returned. On September 29, 1899, his sentence was declared
null and void and he was reinstated in his former rank (P. I. R.,
285. 3, and 2030. 2)." [1]

Colonel Arguelles has told me exactly the same story.
For a time it seemed as if the views expressed by him
might prevail.

[1] Taylor, 97 AJ.

THE PHILIPPINE GENERAL HOSPITAL.

This photograph shows the administration building, to the right and left of which may be seen portions of two ward pavilions. These latter structures extend backward in a double row, while in the centre, back of the administration building, come the building containing the surgical amphitheatres, private operating room and electrical apparatus and that containing the kitchen and the subsistence storerooms. The several buildings are connected by corridors.

"According to Felipe Buencamino and some others, the majority of the members of congress had been in favour of absolute independence until they saw the demoralization of the officers and soldiers which resulted in the American occupation of Malolos. In the middle of April, 1899, they remembered Arellano's advice, and all of the intelligent men in Aguinaldo's government, except Antonio Luna and the officers who had no desire to lay down their military rank, decided to accept the sovereignty of the United States. At about the same time copies of the proclamation issued by the American Commission in Manila reached them and still further influenced them toward the adoption of this purpose. By the time congress met in San Isidro on May 1, 1899, all of the members had accepted it except a few partisans of Mabini, then president of the council of government. At its first meeting the congress resolved to change the policy of war with the United States to one of peace, and this change of policy in congress led to the fall of Mabini and his succession by Paterno. The first act of the new council was the appointment of a commission headed by Felipe Buencamino which was to go to Manila and there negotiate with the American authorities for an honourable surrender." [1]

"Although Mabini had fallen from power, Luna and his powerful faction had still to be reckoned with. He was less moderate than Mabini, and had armed adherents, which Mabini did not, and when Paterno declared his policy of moderation and diplomacy he answered it on the day the new council of government was proclaimed by an order that all foreigners living in the Philippines except Chinese and Spaniards, should leave for Manila within forty-eight hours." [2]

Unfortunately Luna intercepted the Buencamino commission. Its head he kicked, cuffed and threatened with a revolver. One of its members was General Gregorio del Pilar. He was allowed to proceed, as he commanded a brigade of troops which might have deserted had he been badly treated, but Luna named three other men to go with him in place of those who had been originally appointed.[3] They were Gracio Gonzaga, Captain Zialcita, and Alberto Baretto. They reached Manila on May 19,

[1] Taylor, 97 AJ.   [2] *Ibid.*
[3] Nominally they were named by Aguinaldo.

1899, and during their stay there had two long interviews with the commission.

They said that they had come, with larger powers than
had been conferred on Arguelles, to discuss the possibility
of peace, the form of ultimate government which might
be proposed in future, and the attitude of the United
States government toward needed reforms.

Meanwhile, on May 4, we had laid before the President
a plan of government informally discussed with Arguelles,
and had received the following reply, authorizing, in substance, what we had suggested : —

"WASHINGTON, May 5, 1899, 10.20 P.M.

"SCHURMAN, MANILA :
    "Yours 4th received. You are authorized to propose that
under the military power of the President, pending action of
Congress, government of the Philippine Islands shall consist
of a governor-general, appointed by the President; cabinet,
appointed by the governor-general; a general advisory council
elected by the people; the qualifications of electors to be carefully considered and determined; the governor-general to have
absolute veto. Judiciary strong and independent; principal
judges appointed by the President. The cabinet and judges
to be chosen from natives or Americans, or both, having regard
to fitness. The President earnestly desires the cessation of
bloodshed, and that the people of the Philippine Islands at an
early date shall have the largest measure of local self-government consistent with peace and good order.

                                                 "HAY." [1]

Our proclamation of April 4, 1899, was also taken up
at their request and was gone over minutely, sentence by
sentence. We were asked to explain certain expressions
which they did not fully understand.

They told us that it would be hard for their army to
lay down its arms when it had accomplished nothing, and
asked if it could be taken into the service of the United
States. We answered that some of the regiments might

[1] Report of the Philippine Commission to the President, Vol. I,
1900, p. 9.

be taken over and employment on public works be found for the soldiers of others.

We endeavoured to arrange for an interview with Aguinaldo, either going to meet him or assuring him safe conduct should he desire to confer with us at Manila.

They left, promising to return in three weeks when they had had time to consider the matters under discussion, but they never came back.

Shortly thereafter there was an odd occurrence. Soon after our arrival we had learned that Mr. Schurman was a man of very variable opinions. He was rather readily convinced by plausible arguments, but sometimes very suddenly reversed his views on an important subject.

At the outset Archbishop Nozaleda made a great impression upon him. The Archbishop was a thoroughgoing Spaniard of the old school, and entertained somewhat radical opinions as to what should be done to end the distressing situation which existed. After talking with him Mr. Schurman seemed to be convinced that we ought to adopt a stern and bloody policy, a conclusion to which Colonel Denby and I decidedly objected.

A little later he made a trip up the Pasig River with Admiral Dewey and others and had a chance to see something of the aftermath of war. It was not at all pretty. It never is. I was waiting for him with a carriage at the river landing on his return and had hard work to keep him away from the cable office. His feelings had undergone a complete revulsion. He insisted that if the American people knew what we were doing they would demand that the war be terminated immediately at any cost and by whatsoever means, and he wanted to tell them all about it at once. By the next morning, however, things fortunately looked rather differently to him.

Mr. Schurman acquired a working knowledge of the Spanish language with extraordinary promptness. Shortly thereafter Colonel Denby and I discovered that when

Filipinos came to see the commission in order to impart information or to seek it, he was conferring with them privately and sending them away without our seeing them at all.

Soon after we had made our formal statement of the situation to the President, Mr. Schurman had an interview with an Englishman who had been living in Insurgent territory north of Manila, from which he had just been ejected, in accordance with Luna's order. This man told him all about the mistakes of the Americans and evidently greatly impressed him, for shortly thereafter he read to us at a commission meeting a draft of a proposed cablegram which he said he hoped we would approve. It would have stultified us, had we signed it, as it involved in effect the abandonment of the position we had so recently taken and a radical change in the policy we had recommended. Mr. Schurman told us that if we did not care to sign it, he would send it as an expression of his personal opinion. Colonel Denby asked him if his personal opinion differed from his official opinion, and received an affirmative reply. We declined to approve the proposed cablegram, whereupon he informed us that if his policy were adopted, he and General Aguinaldo would settle things without assistance from us, and that otherwise he would resign. He inquired whether we, too, would send a cable, and we told him certainly not, unless further information from us was requested. He sent his proposed message, in somewhat modified form, and received a prompt reply instructing him to submit it to the full commission and cable their views.

He did submit it to Colonel Denby and myself at a regularly called commission meeting, argued that in doing this he had obeyed the President's instructions, and vowed that he would not show it to General Otis. I showed it to the General myself, allowing him to believe that I did so with Mr. Schurman's approval, and thus avoided serious trouble, as he had been personally advised from Washington of the instructions to Mr. Schurman. The General then joined with Colonel Denby and myself in a cablegram setting forth our views, and so this incident ended.

Mr. Schurman did not resign, but thereafter we saw very little of him. He made a hasty trip to the Visayas and the Southern Islands and sailed for the United States shortly after his return to Manila, being anxious to get back in time for the opening of the college year at Cornell.

Colonel Denby and I were instructed to remain at Manila, where we rendered such assistance as we could give, and continued to gather information relative to the situation, the country and the people. In this latter work we were given invaluable help by Jesuit priests, who prepared for us a comprehensive monograph embodying a very large amount of valuable information, and furnished us a series of new maps as well. The latter were subsequently published by the United States Coast and Geodetic Survey in the form of an Atlas of the Philippines.

Early in September we had a most interesting interview with Sr. José de Luzuriaga, a distinguished and patriotic Filipino from western Negros, where American sovereignty had been accepted without resistance. Up to that time it had been possible for the people of Negros to keep out Tagálog invaders. Sr. Luzuriaga assured us that so long as this condition continued, there would be no trouble, and he was quite right.

Aguinaldo's agents eventually gained a foothold there for a short time, and did some mischief, but it did not result very seriously.

We felt an especial interest in this island, as General Otis had asked us carefully to study and to criticise a scheme for its government which had been drafted by General James F. Smith, who afterward became justice of the Supreme Court of the Philippines, secretary of public instruction and governor-general of the islands, and was then in command of the troops in Negros.

General Lawton arrived in the Philippines during our stay. His coming had been eagerly looked forward to by the army. He had sailed with the understanding that he was to be put in charge of field operations. While he was at sea, influences were brought to bear which changed this plan.

It is my firm conviction that if Lawton had been put in command, the war would have ended promptly. He was a wonderful man in the field. He possessed the faculty of instilling his own tremendous energy into his officers and men, whose privations and dangers he shared, thereby arousing an unfaltering loyalty which stood him in good stead in time of need. If there was fighting to be done, he promptly and thoroughly whipped everything in sight. He punished looting and disorder with a heavy hand, treated prisoners and noncombatants with the utmost kindness, and won the good-will of all Filipinos with whom he came in contact.

General MacArthur was always declaring that the Filipinos were a unit against us and that he could never get information from them. General Lawton never lacked for such information as he needed, and constantly and successfully used the Filipinos themselves as messengers and for other purposes. I came to know him intimately, and learned to admire and love him as did all those who had that great privilege.

For some time I had charge of his spies. Never have men taken longer chances than did the faithful few who at this time furnished us with information as to events in Insurgent territory. Discovery meant prompt and cruel death. For a long time Major F. S. Bourns had performed the uncongenial task of directing the spies. He was then the chief health officer of Manila, and as all sorts of people were compelled to consult him on sanitary matters, visits to his office aroused no suspicion. He spoke Spanish, and this was imperatively necessary. Our spies simply would not communicate results through interpreters. The facts revealed by the Insurgent records show how right they were in refusing to do so.

Major Bourns eventually returned to the United States. His work was taken over by an army officer, with the result that two of our best men died very suddenly in that gentleman's back yard. As I spoke Spanish, and as all sorts of people came to see the commission, I was the logical candidate for this job, which I thereupon inherited.

Each morning, if there was news, I myself laboriously thumped out my notes on the typewriter, making an original and one copy. The copy I took at once to General Lawton. The original I took, later, to General Otis.

General Lawton was firmly convinced that most army officers were unfitted by their training to perform civil functions. He organized municipal governments with all possible promptness in the towns occupied by his troops, and in this work he requested my assistance, which I was of course glad to give. Sr. Felipe Calderon drafted a simple provisional scheme of municipal government which I submitted for criticism to that most distinguished and able of Filipinos, Sr. Cayetano Arellano.[1] When the final changes in it had been made, I accompanied General Lawton on a trip to try putting it into effect. We held elections and established municipal governments in a number of the towns just south of Manila, and in some of those along the Pasig River.

General Otis watched our operations and their results narrowly, and was sufficiently well pleased with the latter to order General Kobbé to follow a similar course in various towns on or near the railroad north of Manila. Kobbé did not profess to know much about municipal government, and asked me to go with him and help until he got the hang of the thing, which I did.

Thus it happened that the first Philippine Commission had a sort of left-handed interest in the first municipal governments established in the islands under American rule.

[1] Now chief justice of the Philippine Supreme Court.

In his endeavour to show that the Commission interfered with military operations, Blount has ascribed certain statements to Major Starr. He says: " . . . at San Isidro on or about November 8, Major Starr said: 'We took this town last spring,' stating how much our loss had been in so doing, 'but partly as a result of the Schurman commission parleying with the Insurgents, General Otis had us fall back. We have just had to take it again.'" [1]

If Major Starr ever made such a statement he was sadly misinformed. General Lawton was the best friend I ever had in the United States Army. I saw him almost daily when he was in Manila, and he showed me the whole telegraphic correspondence which passed between him and General Otis on the subject of the withdrawal from San Isidro and Nueva Ecija, which was certainly one of the most ill advised moves that any military commander was ever compelled to make. General Lawton's unremitting attacks had absolutely demoralized the Insurgent force, and my information is that when he finally turned back, Aguinaldo and several members of his cabinet were waiting, ten miles away, to surrender to him when he next advanced, believing that they could never escape from him. I have not the telegraphic correspondence before me, but I remember its salient features. Otis ordered Lawton to withdraw, and Lawton, convinced of the inadvisability of the measure, objected. Otis replied that, with the rainy season coming on, he could neither provision him nor furnish him ammunition. Lawton answered that he had provisions enough to last three weeks and ammunition enough to finish the war, whereupon Otis peremptorily ordered him to withdraw. The Philippine Commission had no more to do with this matter than they had to do with the similar order against advancing which Otis sent Lawton on the day the latter won the Zapote River fight, when the Insurgents were running all over the

[1] Blount, p. 235.

The College of Medicine and Surgery, Manila.

Province of Cavite. Lawton wanted to push forward and clean the whole place up. The reply to his request to be allowed to do so ran, if memory serves me well, as follows : —

"Do nothing. You have accomplished all that was expected of you."

Later on, Lawton and his devoted officers and men had to duplicate the fierce campaign which had resulted in the taking of San Isidro. This made possible the movement that Lawton had had in mind in the first instance, which was made with the result that organized armed resistance to the authority of the United States promptly ceased in northern Luzón.

While on this subject I wish to record the fact that shortly after his return from the San Isidro campaign General Lawton asked me to accompany him on a visit to General Otis and act as a witness. I did so. In my presence Lawton said to Otis that if the latter would give him two regiments, would allow him to arm, equip and provision them to suit himself, and would turn him loose, he would stake his reputation as a soldier, and his position in the United States Army, on the claim that within sixty days he would end the insurrection and would deliver to General Otis one Emilio Aguinaldo, dead or alive. The general laughed at his offer. General Lawton asked me some day to make these facts public. As life is an uncertain thing, I deem it proper to do so now. Personally I am convinced that if his offer had been accepted he would have kept his promise.

On September 15, 1899, Colonel Denby and I sailed for the United States, having been recalled to Washington. Shortly after our arrival there the commission issued a brief preliminary report. The winter was spent in the preparation of our final report, which constituted a full and authoritative treatise on the islands, the people and their resources. Father José Algué, the distinguished head of the Philippine Weather Bureau, was called to Washington to help us, and gave us invaluable assistance.

Our preliminary report, dated November 2, 1899, and the first volume of our final report, published on January 31, 1900, contained our observations and recommendations relative to political matters.

Mr. Schurman has been credited with saying in an address made on January 11, 1902: "Any decent kind of government of Filipinos by Filipinos is better than the best possible government of Filipinos by Americans." [1]

On November 2, 1900, he signed the following statement: [2] —

"Should our power by any fatality be withdrawn, the commission believe that the government of the Philippines would speedily lapse into anarchy, which would excuse, if it did not necessitate, the intervention of other powers and the eventual division of the islands among them. Only through American occupation, therefore, is the idea of a free, self-governing, and united Philippine commonwealth at all conceivable. And the indispensable need from the Filipino point of view of maintaining American sovereignty over the archipelago is recognized by all intelligent Filipinos and even by those insurgents who desire an American protectorate. The latter, it is true, would take the revenues and leave us the responsibilities. Nevertheless, they recognize the indubitable fact that the Filipinos cannot stand alone. Thus the welfare of the Filipinos coincides with the dictates of national honour in forbidding our abandonment of the archipelago. We cannot from any point of view escape the responsibilities of government which our sovereignty entails; and the commission is strongly persuaded that the performance of our national duty will prove the greatest blessing to the peoples of the Philippine Islands."

More than fourteen years' experience in governmental work in the Philippines has profoundly impressed me with the fundamental soundness of these conclusions of the first Philippine Commission. Every statement then made still holds true.

[1] Blount, p. 105.   [2] Report Philippine Commission, Vol. I, p. 183.

CHAPTER XII

The Establishment of Civil Government

THE first Philippine Commission did not complete its work until March, 1900. By this time conditions had so far improved in the archipelago that President McKinley was prepared to initiate a movement looking toward the establishment of civil government there. With this end in view he appointed the following commission of five civilians; William H. Taft of Ohio, Dean C. Worcester of Michigan, Luke E. Wright of Tennessee, Henry C. Ide of Vermont and Bernard Moses of California. Our appointments were dated March 16, 1900. Our instructions which were full, are given in the appendix.[1] I was the only member of the first commission to be reappointed. Neither General Otis nor Admiral Dewey cared to serve, and indeed the professional duties of each of them rendered his appointment to the new commission difficult, if not impossible. Mr. Schurman had at one time expressed himself as vigorously opposed to the idea of a new commission, maintaining that the best results could be obtained by the appointment of a civil governor with wide powers. It was therefore taken for granted that he would not desire reappointment. Colonel Denby was keenly interested in the work and would have been glad to continue it, but he was past seventy and with his good wife had then spent some fifteen years in the Far East. He doubted whether his strength would be adequate to bear the strain of the arduous task which obviously lay before the new commission, and Mrs. Denby desired to remain in the United States where she

[1] P. 981.

could be near her children from whom she had been long separated, so her husband felt constrained to say that he did not wish to return to the Philippines.

I separated from him with the keenest regret. He was an amiable, tactful man of commanding ability and unimpeachable integrity, actuated by the best of motives and loyal to the highest ideals. He constantly sought to avoid not only evil but the appearance of evil. I count it one of the great privileges of my life to have been associated with him. The one thing in the book written by James H. Blount which aroused my ire was his characterization of Colonel Denby as a hypocrite. No falser, meaner, more utterly contemptible statement was ever made, and when I read it the temptation rose hot within me to make public Blount's personal Philippine record, but after the first heat of anger had passed I remembered what the good old Colonel would have wished me to do in such a case, and forbore.

The second Philippine commission, hereinafter referred to as "the commission," received its instructions on April 7, 1900.

They covered a most delicate and complicated subject, namely, the gradual transfer of control from military to civil authority in a country extensive regions of which were still in open rebellion.

In the opinion of President McKinley there was no reason why steps should not be taken, from time to time, to inaugurate governments essentially popular in their form as fast as territory came under the permanent control of our troops, and indeed, as we have seen, this had already been done by the army. It was provided that we should continue and perfect the work of organizing and establishing civil governments already commenced by the military authorities. In doing this we were to act as a board of which Mr. Taft was designated president. It was contemplated that the transfer of authority from military commanders to civil officers would be gradual, and full and complete coöperation between these authorities was enjoined. Having familiarized ourselves with the conditions then prevailing in the islands, we were to devote our attention first to the establishment of municipal governments, in which the natives should be given the opportunity to manage their local affairs to the fullest extent and with the least supervision and control found to be practicable. We were then to consider the organization of larger administrative divisions, and when of the opinion that the condition of affairs in the islands was such that the central administration could safely be transferred from military to civil control were to report this conclusion to the secretary of war with our recommendations as to the form of central government which should be established.

Beginning with September 1, 1900, we were authorized to exercise, subject to the approval of the President and the secretary of war, the legislative power, which was then to be transferred from the military governor to us until the establishment of civil central government, or until Congress should otherwise provide. We were authorized during a like period to appoint to office such officers under the judicial, educational, and civil service systems, and in the municipal and departmental governments, as were duly provided for. Until the complete transfer of control the military governor was to remain the chief executive head of the government and to exercise the executive authority previously possessed by him and not expressly assigned to the commission by the president in his instructions. In establishing municipal governments we were to take as the basis of our work those established by the military governor, under the order of August 8, 1899, which I had helped to set up, as well as those established under the report of a board constituted by the military governor by his order of January 29, 1900, of which Señor Cayetano Arellano was the president.

In the establishment of departmental or provincial

governments we were to give special attention to the then-existing government of the island of Negros, established with the approval of the people of that island under the order of the military governor of July 22, 1899.

We were instructed to investigate troubles growing out of large land holdings, including those of the religious orders, and to promote, extend and improve the system of education already inaugurated by the military authorities, giving first importance to the extension of a system of primary education free to all, which would tend to fit the people for the duties of citizenship and the ordinary avocations of a civilized community. Instruction was to be given at first in the native dialects, but full opportunity for all of the people to acquire English was to be provided as soon as possible. If necessity demanded, we were authorized to make changes in the existing system of taxation and in the body of the laws under which the people were governed, although such changes were to be relegated to the civil government which we were to establish later, so far as might be. Our instructions contained the following important passages : —

" In all the forms of government and administrative provisions which they are authorized to prescribe, the commission should bear in mind that the government which they are establishing is designed not for our satisfaction, or for the expression of our theoretical views, but for the happiness, peace and prosperity of the people of the Philippine Islands, and the measures adopted should be made to conform to their customs, their habits, and even their prejudices, to the fullest extent consistent with the accomplishment of the indispensable requisites of just and effective government.

" At the same time the commission should bear in mind, and the people of the islands should be made plainly to understand, that there are certain great principles of government which have been made the basis of our governmental system which we deem essential to the rule of law and the maintenance of individual freedom, and of which they have, unfortunately, been denied the experience possessed by us ; that there are also certain practical rules of government which we have found to be essential to the preservation of these great principles of liberty and law, and that these principles and these rules of government must be established and maintained in their islands for the sake of their liberty and happiness, however much they may conflict with the customs or laws of procedure with which they are familiar.

"It is evident that the most enlightened thought of the Philippine Islands fully appreciates the importance of these principles and rules, and they will inevitably within a short time command universal assent. Upon every division and branch of the government of the Philippines, therefore, must be imposed these inviolable rules : —

"That no person shall be deprived of life, liberty, or property without due process of law; that private property shall not be taken for public use without just compensation; that in all criminal prosecutions the accused shall enjoy the right to a speedy and public trial, to be informed of the nature and cause of the accusation, to be confronted with the witnesses against him, to have compulsory process for obtaining witnesses in his favour, and to have the assistance of counsel for his defence; that excessive bail shall not be required, nor excessive fines imposed, nor cruel and unusual punishment inflicted; that no person shall be put twice in jeopardy for the same offence, or be compelled in any criminal case to be a witness against himself; that the right to be secure against unreasonable searches and seizures shall not be violated; that neither slavery nor involuntary servitude shall exist except as a punishment for crime; that no bill of attainder or ex-post-facto law shall be passed; that no law shall be passed abridging the freedom of speech or of the press, or the rights of the people to peaceably assemble and petition the Government for a redress of grievances; that no law shall be made respecting the establishment of religion, or prohibiting the free exercise thereof, and that the free exercise and enjoyment of religious profession and worship without discrimination or preference shall forever be allowed."

It has been the fashion in some quarters to sneer at the last of these paragraphs, and to insinuate, if not to charge, that President McKinley in his policy toward the Philippine Islands was actuated by unworthy motives. Nothing could be further from the truth. From the beginning to the end the real good of the several peoples of the archipelago came first with him, and no one who had the privilege of knowing him well doubts it.   Thoroughly imbued with the lofty sentiments expressed by him in our instructions, we set forth on our long pilgrimage to a country where we were to undertake a heavy task essentially different from that which had ever before fallen to the lot of any five citizens of the United States.

On April 17, 1900, we sailed from San Francisco on the United States army transport *Hancock*.   We were forty-five strong.   Of this goodly company only four remain in the Philippines to-day,[1] — Mr. and Mrs. Branagan, Mrs. Worcester and myself.   Singularly enough, with two exceptions, all of the others are still alive and at work. Arthur W. Ferguson, prince of interpreters, who was later appointed Executive Secretary, died in the service after more than six years of extraordinarily faithful and efficient work.   James A. LeRoy, my faithful, able and efficient private secretary, contracted tuberculosis, and fell a victim to it after a long and gallant fight.

At Honolulu we met with a severe disappointment.   It was of course our duty to call on Governor Dole.   We were advised that silk hats and frock coats must be donned for this visit, and it was perishing hot.   We reached the palace in a reeking perspiration and had a long wait in a suffocating room.   When Mr. Dole appeared, he was closely followed by an attendant bearing a large and most attractive-looking bottle carefully wrapped in a napkin, and our spirits rose.   But, alas!   It contained Poland water.

At Tokio we had an audience with the Emperor and were received by the Empress as well.   In the high official who had charge of the palace where these events took place, I discovered an old University of Michigan graduate who made the occasion especially pleasant for me.

We finally reached Manila on the morning of June 3. Although the thermometer was in the nineties, a certain

[1] September 15, 1913.

An Old-style Schoolhouse, with Teachers and Pupils.

frigidity pervaded the atmosphere on our arrival, which General MacArthur, the military governor, seemed to regard in the light of an intrusion.

He had been directed to provide suitable office quarters for us.   To our amazement and amusement we found desks for five commissioners and five private secretaries placed in one little room in the Ayuntamiento.[1]   While it was possible to get through the room without scrambling over them, it would have been equally possible to circle it, walking on them, without stepping on the floor.   In the course of our first long official interview with the General, he informed us that we were "an injection into an otherwise normal situation."

He added that we had already mediatized the volume of work that flowed over his desk.   At the moment none of us were quite sure what he meant, but we found the word in the dictionary.   How often in the weary years that were to follow I wished that some one would materially mediatize the task which fell to my lot !   It was General MacArthur's honestly held and frankly expressed opinion that what the Filipinos needed was "military government pinned to their backs for ten years with bayonets." He later changed that view very radically, and when civil provincial governments were finally established it was with his approval, and, in many instances, upon his specific recommendation.

At the outset some effort was made to keep the public away from us.   Word was passed that we had no authority, which was true enough, as our legislative activities were not to begin until September 1.   The ninety days which intervened were very advantageously spent in gaining familiarity with the situation, which we had no difficulty in doing.   Plenty of people were already weary of military rule and flocked to us.   None of my companions had ever before set foot in the Philippines, and

---

[1] The building where the executive offices of the insular government have been located since the American occupation.

although I had spent more than four years there, I still had plenty to learn.

In this connection I am reminded of an event which occurred somewhat later. While the commission was en route from Iloilo to Catbalogan when we were establishing civil provincial governments, General Hughes and Mr. Taft became involved in a somewhat animated discussion. The General displayed an accurate knowledge of facts which were of such a nature that one would hardly have expected an army officer to be familiar with them. Mr. Taft said: "General, how do you do it? You have always been a busy man, devoted to your profession. How have you managed to accumulate such a remarkable fund of information?" The General smiled his rare smile and replied: "Governor, I will tell you. I always try to go to bed at night knowing a little more than I did when I got up in the morning." It is a wise plan to follow.

On September 1 we assumed the legislative power, our first official act being to appropriate $2,000,000 Mexican for the construction and repair of highways and bridges.

We were impressed with the fundamental necessity of promptly opening up lines of land communication in a country which almost completely lacked them, and there were many poor people in dire need of employment who would be relieved by the opportunity to earn an honest living which the inauguration of road construction would afford them.

Our second act appropriated $5000 Mexican for the purpose of making a survey to ascertain the most advantageous route for a railroad into the mountains of Benguet, where we wished to establish a much-needed health resort for the people of the archipelago.

Seven days later we passed an act for the establishment and maintenance of an efficient and honest civil service in the Philippine Islands. This measure was of basic importance. We had stipulated before leaving Washington that no political appointees should be forced upon us under any circumstances. The members of the second commission, like their predecessors of the first, were firm in the belief that national politics should, if possible, be kept out of the administration of Philippine affairs, and we endeavoured to insure this result.

Our tenth act appropriated $1500 Mexican to be paid to the widow of Salvador Reyes, vice-president of Santa Cruz in Laguna Province, assassinated because of his loyalty to the established government.

Our fifteenth act increased the monthly salaries of Filipino public school teachers in Manila.

Our sixteenth and seventeenth acts reorganized the Forestry Bureau and the Mining Bureau.

On October 15 we appropriated $1,000,000 United States currency, for improving the port of Manila, where there was urgent need of protection for shipping during the typhoon season.

On December 12 we passed an act authorizing the establishment of local police in cities and towns in the Philippine Islands and appropriating $150,000 United States currency for their maintenance.

Two days later we passed a much-needed act regulating the sale of intoxicating liquors within the city of Manila and its attached barrios.

On December 21, we appropriated $75,000 United States currency for the construction of the Benguet Road, little dreaming how much time would elapse and how many more dollars would be appropriated, before a vehicle passed over it.

It will be sufficiently evident that I cannot here give an account of the several acts which we passed when I say that they number four hundred forty-nine during the first year. We created the administrative bureaus of a well-organized government, established civil rule in numerous municipalities and provinces, provided for the necessary expenses of government, organized courts and reformed the judiciary. So important were the results following the establishment of the Civil Service Act and the act providing for the organization of courts for the Philippine Islands that I have devoted a chapter to each.

Although there were no limits on our power to enact legislation other than those imposed by our instructions hereinbefore referred to, nothing was further from our desire than to exercise too arbitrarily the authority conferred upon us.

Taylor has correctly described our method of procedure in the following words : —

"On September 1, 1900, the Commission began its legislative and executive duties. In performing them it adopted the policy of passing no laws, except in cases of emergency, without publishing them in the daily press, nor until after they had passed a second reading and the public had been given an opportunity to come before the Commission and suggest objections or amendments to the bills. Before enacting them they were submitted to the military governor for his consideration and comment." [1]

The other especially important events of our first legislative year were the establishment of civil rule in the municipalities as well as in thirty-eight provinces and the substitution of the military central government by the gradual creation of bureaus and the ultimate appointment of a civil governor and of five heads of executive departments.

On November 23, 1900, we passed an act providing for the establishment of a civil government in the province of Benguet, and thus it happened that a province practically all of whose inhabitants were members of a non-Christian tribe was the first to enjoy the benefits of civil rule. This action grew out of investigations by General Wright and myself made when visiting Baguio during the latter part of July, which led us to the conclusion that civil government could be established in Benguet at any time and

[1] Taylor, 18 HS.

should be established as soon as possible. In view of the rather primitive state of civilization of the people for whom we were legislating, a special act adapted to local conditions was passed providing for a provincial government and fixing a form of government for the several settlements.

On January 31, 1901, we passed an act for the organization of municipal governments in the Philippine Islands which, with various amendments, is still in effect and has been made applicable to all municipal corporations of the Philippines inhabited chiefly by Filipinos, except the city of Manila, the city of Baguio and a few small settlements in the so-called special government provinces.[1]

On February 6, 1901, we passed a general act for the organization of provincial governments in the Philippine Islands. A special act was required to make it applicable to any given province.

Having thus prepared for the serious work of establishing civil government throughout the archipelago so fast and so far as conditions might seem to justify, we determined to visit the several provinces and to familiarize ourselves with conditions on the ground in each case before taking action. We invariably sought the opinion of the military authorities as to the fitness of the provinces under consideration for civil rule, and never established it except with their approval. Indeed, in several cases we yielded to their judgment and organized provinces which we ourselves thought might better wait for a time.

Our first trip was to the northward along the line of the Manila-Dagupan railway, and in the course of it we organized the provinces of Bulacan, Pampanga, Tarlac and Pangasinán.

On the 2d of March we crossed Manila Bay to Bataan and established a civil provincial government there.

[1] This name is applied to certain provinces organized under special acts because the majority of their inhabitants are non-Christians.

The first provincial officers were necessarily appointed, not elected. I well remember the consternation which Mr. Taft created on this trip, when in announcing the appointment of a man of strong character who was much disliked by some of the people present, he said that if the appointee did not behave well his official head would be promptly removed. Surprise showed on almost every face in the audience. They had become sufficiently accustomed to the idea of being beheaded or otherwise sent out of the world by their own people, but had been led to believe that the Americans were a humane nation, and it took Mr. Taft at least five minutes to explain his joke.

During the second week in March the commission transferred its officers bodily to the United States Army Transport *Sumner* and started on a long journey in the course of which it visited and established provincial governments in eighteen provinces,[1] returning to Manila on the 3d of May.

This trip was most interesting but dreadfully wearing. Everywhere we were overwhelmed by the hospitality of our Filipino friends. We arrived at some new place nearly every morning, and the programme in each was much the same. After an early breakfast we hurried ashore, drove or walked about for a short time to see what the town was like, and then attended a popular meeting in its largest building, where we held long and frank converse with the people on local conditions, giving them every opportunity to air their views, with the result that the local orators, of whom there were usually more than a sufficiency, had an opportunity to bring their heavy guns into action. Then followed a recess in the course of which we partook of a very elaborate lunch, and when possible conferred privately with in-

[1] Tayabas, Romblon, Masbate, Iloilo, Antique, Capiz, Cebú, Bohol, Occidental Negros, Oriental Negros, Leyte, Albay, Ambos, Camarines, Sorsogon, Marinduque, Batangas, Surigao, and Misamis.

fluential men, often learning things which they did not care to tell us in public. Then came another open meeting at which the actual organization of the province was effected and the officials were appointed and sworn in. After this there was a long formal dinner, with the endless courses which characterize such functions in the Philippines, and then came a ball which lasted till the wee small hours. When at last we got on board, tired out, our steamer sailed, and often brought us to some new place by sunrise.

In several instances we did not pass the act organizing a given province at the time of our visit, but for one reason or another postponed action until a later date. We visited a number of places like Joló, Basilan, Zamboanga, Cotabato, Davao and Samar, where we had no intention of establishing civil government, in order to observe local conditions.

We touched at Marinduque on our trip south, and found that nothing could then be done there, but the better element were anxious for a change, and we promised them that if they would bring about certain specified results before our return we would give them a provincial government. They undertook to do so, and kept their word. Needless to say we also kept ours.

We had grave doubts as to the advisability of establishing civil governments in Cebú, Bohol and Batangas. In the first of these places the people were sullen and ugly. In the second there was a marked disinclination on the part of leading citizens to accept public office. There had been a little scattering rifle fire on the outskirts of the capital of the third very shortly before our arrival there, but the organization of all these provinces was recommended by the military authorities, and we decided to try an experiment which could do little harm, as we could return any one of them to military control in short order should such a course seem necessary.

An effort has been made to make it appear that in

organizing Cebú, Bohol and Batangas, we acted prematurely and upon our own initiative, thus complicating the situation for the military authorities. I will let Blount voice this complaint. He says in part : —

"In his report for 1901 Governor Taft says that the four principal provinces, including Batangas, which gave trouble shortly after the civil government was set up in that year, and had to be returned to military control, were organized under civil rule 'on the recommendation' of the then commanding general (MacArthur). It certainly seems unlikely that the haste to change from military rule to civil rule came on the motion of the military. If the Commission ever got, *in writing*, from General MacArthur, a 'recommendation' that any provinces be placed under civil rule while still in insurrection, the text of the writing will show a mere soldierly acquiescence in the will of Mr. McKinley, the commander-in-chief. Parol[1] contemporaneous evidence will show that General MacArthur told them, substantially, that they were 'riding for a fall.' In fact, whenever an insurrection would break out in a province after Governor Taft's inauguration as governor, the whole attitude of the army in the Philippines, from the commanding general down was 'I told you so.' They did not say this where Governor Taft could hear it, but it was common knowledge that they were much addicted to damning 'politics' as the cause of all the trouble."[2]

Prophecy is always dangerous and when unnecessary seems rather inexcusable. I submit the essential portions of the record to show exactly what we did get from General MacArthur, and add the suggestion that it was really hardly essential that he should make his recommendations in writing, as he did, for the reason that he was a gentleman and would not have repudiated a verbal recommendation once made.

On February 5, 1901, Governor Taft wrote General MacArthur a letter closing with the following paragraph : —

"As already communicated to you the purpose of the Commission is to make a Southern trip on the 23rd of February, or as soon thereafter as practicable, with the idea of arranging

[1] Obviously a misprint, perhaps, for " perusal of."   [2] Blount, p. 380.

A MODERN PRIMARY SCHOOL BUILDING.

Contrast this structure with the native houses near it.

for provincial governments there, and I am directed by the Commission to request your opinion as to the provinces in which provincial governments may be safely established. It is understood that Panay, Romblon, Tayabas, and possibly one or two of the Camarines are ready for this. What has been said with reference to the Northern provinces applies to these, but we shall communicate with you further as to the Southern provinces when we have been advised as to the possibility of securing a steamer."

On February 9, General MacArthur gave the following instructions to the Commanding General, Department of the Visayas:—

"The Military Governor desires that you report to this office at the earliest date practicable the provinces in your department that may be considered ready for the establishment of civil governments therein and in this connection directs me to say that it should not be considered as necessary that complete pacification has been brought about in a province before reporting it as ready for such government; that the provincial civil governments to be established will doubtless prove useful agents in the further work of pacification."

On February 27, that officer reported that in his opinion Iloilo, Capiz, Oriental Negros and Occidental Negros were ready; that Antique might be in a few days, and that Cebú, Bohol and Leyte were not. These facts were reported to Governor Taft by General MacArthur on March 4, and on the same day Lieutenant-Colonel Crowder wrote to the commanding general of the Visayas:—

"The Military Governor directs me to say that he regards the initiation of provincial civil government as an aid in the work of pacification, in which view it is not necessary that a province should be completely pacified as a condition to the initiation of such government. He has expressed to the Commission the opinion that you may be able, upon their arrival at Iloilo, to submit a supplementary list of provinces in which it would be advisable to establish at once these governments."

Meanwhile General MacArthur wrote on February 13, to Governor Taft:—

"In partial reply to your letter of the 5th instant I have the honor to inform you that the Commanding General, Department of Southern Luzon, reports but one province, Tayabas, as ready at the present time for civil government. I add the provinces of Laguna, Batangas and Cavite, believing that the institution of civil government in all these provinces will be in assistance of the military authorities in the work of pacification."

General MacArthur's communications seem to me to show something more than "a mere soldierly acquiescence in the will of Mr. McKinley," especially as the President had no knowledge of these provinces, and never made any recommendation whatsoever relative to the establishment of civil government there.

Similarly, in establishing civil government in Cebu and Bohol, the commission acted on the specific recommendation of the military, and rather against its own judgment. There seemed no very good reason for refusing to try civil government, if the commanding general wanted it tried, and when it failed, as it promptly did, in Cebu, Bohol and Batangas, these provinces were immediately returned to the full control of the military, and left there until conditions became satisfactory.

Having escaped the perils of the deep, and the much graver perils of the dinner table, during our southern trip, we returned to Manila, wearier, wiser and sadder men than when we started, for we had learned much of the superstitions, the ignorance and the obsessions which prevailed among the Filipinos, and we knew that many of the men who from love of country had accepted office under us had done so at the peril of their lives. We had all had an excellent opportunity to come to know the Filipinos. Their dignity of bearing, their courtesy, their friendly hospitality, their love of imposing functions, and of *fiestas* and display, their childishness and irresponsibility in many matters, their passion for gambling, for litigation and for political intrigue, even the loves and the hatreds of some of them, had been spread before us like an open book.   It is a fact that except for the inhabitants of Cebu, Bohol and Batangas, the people wanted what we had to give them and were grateful for it.   Never before had they had their day in court, and they appreciated it.

The establishment of civil government throughout so large a proportion of the provinces in the islands would have been impossible at this time had it not been for the helpful activities of the Federal Party organized on December 23, 1900, by many of the best and most influential Filipinos in the archipelago for the purpose of aiding in the establishment of peace and order.   Its members were tireless in their activities.   They succeeded in persuading many Insurgent leaders to lay down their arms, so that a normal condition could be restored in territory which the latter had previously harried.   They convinced many of the common people of the true purposes of the American government, and in numerous other ways rendered invaluable services.

The officers and many of the members and agents of this party were promptly sentenced to death by Aguinaldo, and many of them were assassinated ;[1] but the party persisted in its efforts until success was attained.

During June of 1901 Professor Moses and I made a horseback trip through Pangasinán, La Union, Benguet, Lepanto and Ilocos Sur, accompanied by our private secretaries.   Professor Moses was in wretched health as the result of overwork and confinement, and needed out-of-door exercise.

I had been intrusted with the drafting of legislation for the government of the non-Christian tribes, and wanted to learn as much about them as possible, so that I could act intelligently.

We started from Dagupan mounted on horses kindly furnished us by the army, and escorted by four mounted infantrymen.   None of us had ridden for years, and

[1] For further details see pp. 746; 753.

army officers were offering wagers that we would not get as far as Baguio. At Mangaldan a cavalry outfit replaced our mounted infantrymen, and while the members of our new escort were resting under the shade of a tree in the cemetery, I heard them voicing joyful anticipations of the easy time they were to have travelling with tenderfeet. I made up my mind to give them some healthful exercise on the trip.

Having first visited the work at the lower end of the Benguet Road and then travelled across country in a driving storm over wretched trails, we reached Bauáng, our point of departure for the interior. Here I called the sergeant in charge and asked him where were the extra shoes for our horses. In some confusion he confessed that he had brought none, whereupon I read him a homily on the duties of a cavalryman, and sent the whole outfit to San Fernando to get the horses reshod and provided with extra shoes for the trip.

We arrived at Baguio in a howling typhoon. When we emerged from the hills into the open, and our horses got the full sweep of the storm, they at first refused to face it. We forced them into it, however, and a few moments later had found refuge in the house of Mr. Otto Scheerer, a hospitable German. The cavalrymen and the horses got in under the building. It gave me great joy to hear through the floor the voice of the sergeant remarking, with much emphasis of the sort best represented in print by dashes, that if he had known the sort of a trip he was starting on he would have been on sick report the morning of his departure.

We waited in vain three days for the storm to end and then rode on. Mr. Scheerer, who accompanied us, had sent ahead to arrange for lunch at the house of a rich Igorot named Acop, but when we arrived at this man's place, soaked, cold, and hungry, we found it shut up. He had not received the message and was away from home. Investigation showed that our only resource in the commissary line were some wads of sticky, unsalted, boiled rice which our Igorot carriers had inside their hats, in contact with their frowsy hair. We bolted as much of this as the Igorots could spare, killing its rather high flavour with cayenne peppers picked beside the trail, and continued our journey. In descending a steep hill my horse stumbled and while attempting to recover himself drove a sharp stone into his hoof and turned a complete somersault, throwing me over his head on to the rocks. When I got him up he was dead lame, and I walked the rest of the way to Ambuklao, where we arrived just at sunset.

This once prosperous little Igorot hamlet had been burned by the Spaniards, for no apparent reason, during their flight from the province in 1906, and we found only two houses standing. They were naturally crowded. I was so dead with fatigue that I threw my saddle on the ground, and using it as a pillow, lay down in a couple of inches of water and fell sound asleep. Later the Igorots vacated one of the houses, and placed it at our disposal. I spent the greater part of the night in a contest with an old Igorot woman, who for the commendable purpose of keeping us warm tended a smoky pitch-pine fire, and shut the door, which afforded our only means of ventilation, every time I dropped asleep. Awakened by the stifling smoke I would open it again, but as soon as I dozed she would shut it. I finally solved the problem by lying down with my head sticking out of the door.

The next day was bright and clear. We rested until noon, drying out our belongings meanwhile, and then continued our journey, visiting the Igorot settlements on the Agno River and those in southern Lepanto and finally reaching Cervantes, the capital of that sub-province. The Igorots of Benguet and Lepanto received us with the utmost friendliness, and when not in danger of breaking our necks by falling over the edges of the wretched trails, we greatly enjoyed our trip.

At Cervantes we were met by a delegation of Bontoc Igorots, who begged us to visit their country, and we were just preparing to do so when we received a telegram recalling us to Manila to be present at the inauguration of Mr. Taft as civil governor. During our absence the commission had established provincial governments in Rizal, Cavite and Nueva Ecija. Mr. Taft was inaugurated on July 4, 1901. Thenceforth he exercised control over the provinces where civil government had been established, while the military governor continued in charge of each of the remaining provinces until it was duly organized and transferred to civil control.

In August, 1901, the commission sailed on a tour of the remaining northern provinces, visiting La Union, Ilocos Sur, Abra, Ilocos Norte, Cagayan, Isabela and Zambales in the order named, and establishing a government in each. On the trip to Abra those members of the commission not previously accustomed to roughing it in the islands were given a novel experience, for we went up the Abra River on bamboo rafts. However, a veritable ship of state had been prepared for Governor Taft, and no one suffered any great discomfort.

At Vigan, the capital of Ilocos, we narrowly escaped drowning in the surf when returning to our steamer. For a time our good *viray* [1] with some twenty oarsmen was unable to make headway through the rolling waves. It broached to, nearly filled with water, and struck the bottom heavily several times. Some of the men quit rowing and began to pray, whereupon General J. F. Bell, who was sitting in the stern, rose to his feet, and shouted at them until they became more afraid of him than of the sea, and pulled for dear life until we were out of danger. Upon arrival at the ship we watched with interest the progress of other boats through the surf, and were alarmed to see the men in one madly divesting themselves of their clothing. When it finally came alongside its occupants

[1] A native surf boat.

made flying leaps for the gangway, and we discovered that a great hole had been knocked in its bottom, and that raincoats, ordinary coats, and trousers had been jammed into this opening in order to keep the rapidly sinking craft afloat for a few moments.

In the Cagayan valley we had a taste of real tropical heat. Never have I seen a man suffer more than did Mr. Taft at Ilagan on the day when we established a provincial government for Isabela, and the night that followed still lingers in my memory. The air was suffocating. My bed was in a corner. I dragged it out between a window and a door and threw both wide open. Still I could not sleep. Slipping off my pajamas, I seated myself on the broad window sill. The heat was intolerable. I poured water over myself and resumed my seat in the window. The water would not evaporate. I sat there until morning, as I could not endure the heat lying down.

Such conditions are unknown throughout the greater part of the archipelago, where cool sea breezes temper the heat at all times. In the Cagayan valley an immense plain is bordered by ranges of high mountains to the east and the west. They seem to shut off both monsoons to a considerable extent, and there very trying heat is by no means unusual.

On September 1, 1901, the first day of the second year of actual service of the commission, a complete central civil government was established. Commissioner Wright was appointed secretary of commerce and police; Commissioner Ide, secretary of finance and justice; Commissioner Moses, secretary of public instruction, and I myself secretary of the interior. The commission was strengthened by the addition of three Filipino members: Señor Benito Legarda, Señor José R. de Luzuriaga, and Dr. T. H. Pardo de Tavera, all of whom were men of exceptional ability and had rendered distinguished service in the establishment of peace and order.

Except for the addition of one more Filipino on July

6, 1908, the organization of the commission has remained unchanged up to the present time, although there have been numerous changes in its personnel. The task which lay before it was to enact a code of laws adapted to the peculiar conditions existing in the Philippines, and this was indeed a herculean undertaking. Its members laboured unremittingly. Governor Taft and General Wright were towers of strength in the early days. The rest of us did what we could, and I, for one, am very proud of the result. Certainly no one can ever claim that the commission was not industrious. Before it finally ceased to be the legislative body of the islands it had passed some eighteen hundred acts. Obviously, as it is not my purpose to write an encyclopedia of law, I cannot discuss them in detail, and must content myself with here barely mentioning a few of the more important results obtained, leaving the more detailed discussion of some of them for later chapters.

In general, it may be said that the additional bureaus necessary for the work of the Insular government were created, and given proper powers. Civil government was gradually extended to the entire archipelago.[1] The criminal code was amended and supplemented by the passage of new laws. The administration of justice was reorganized and reformed.[2] An efficient native insular police force was organized, and an admirable state of public order brought about.[3] The health service was extended to the provinces, and health conditions were greatly improved throughout the islands.[4] Baguio was made accessible and became both the summer capital and a health resort for the people of the islands.[5] The scientific work of the government was coördinated, and efficiency and economy in its performance were insured.[6]

Primary and secondary schools were established throughout the islands, supplemented by trade schools, and

[1] See Chapters XXI–XXIV.   [2] Chap. XV.   [3] Chap. XIV.
[4] Chap. XVI.   [5] Chap. XVII.   [6] Chap. XVIII.

OLD-STYLE CENTRAL SCHOOL BUILDING.
This structure is typical of the better-class school-houses constructed by the Spaniards.

MODERN CENTRAL SCHOOL BUILDING.
This structure is typical of the better-class school-houses constructed under American rule.

a normal school at Manila.[1] Legislation was enacted,
and submitted to the President and to Congress, covering
the disposition of public lands.[2] The purchase of extensive estates belonging to certain religious orders, and
the sale of their holdings therein to tenants, was provided for.[3] Fairly adequate legislation for the protection
and development of the forest resources of the islands
was enacted.[4] Means of communication by land and
sea were greatly improved, and the development of commerce was thus stimulated.[5]

It is a noteworthy fact that all of these things were
done with a per capita taxation of about $2.24!

Another fundamentally important aid to the commercial
development of the islands was afforded by a radical ref-
ormation of the currency.

The islands under the sovereignty of Spain had their
own distinct silver coinage in peso, media peso, peseta
and media peseta pieces.

In 1878 the Spanish government, hoping to check the
heavy exportation of gold currency from the Philippines,
passed a law prohibiting the importation of Mexican
dollars, but allowed the Mexican dollars then in the islands
to continue to circulate as legal tender.

When the American troops arrived, there were in circulation the Spanish-Philippine peso and subsidiary
silver coins; Spanish pesos of different mintings; Mexican
pesos of different mintings; Hongkong dollars, fractional
silver coins from different Chinese countries, and copper
coins from nearly every country in the Orient. Although
a law had been passed prohibiting the introduction
of Mexican dollars into the islands, they were being
constantly smuggled in. Fluctuations in the price of
silver affected the value of the silver coins, and the money
in common use was in reality a commodity, worth on any
given day what one could get for it. These conditions

[1] See Chapter XIX.   [2] Chap. XXX.   [3] Chap. XXX.
    [4] Chap. XXXI.   [5] Chap. XXXII.

affected most disastrously the business interests of the islands. Merchants were forced to allow very wide margins in commercial transactions, because they did not know what their goods would actually cost them in local currency upon arrival. The most important business of the local banks was in reality that of exchange brokers and note shavers. They hammered the exchange rate down and bought silver, then boosted the rate skyward and sold.

The American army brought in a large amount of gold, but this did not remain in circulation long, as it was exported by the different business concerns, or hoarded.

United States silver money had a limited circulation during the early days of American occupation, but it passed at less than its true value. An effort was made under the military administration to keep the ratio of exchange at two to one by the purchase from the public of all United States currency offered at that rate to the banks.

For a long time the banks refused to carry private accounts in United States currency, but when it was offered for deposit it was changed into Mexicans with a heavy charge for the transaction, and an account opened in Mexican currency to the credit of the depositor. If the depositor afterward desired to get United States currency, he gave a check for it at the then existing rate of exchange. Such conditions were intolerable, and the commission passed an act making it an offence to refuse to accept for deposit the currency of the sovereign power, but this did not remedy the fundamental difficulty. There came a heavy slump in the price of silver. The Insular government lost a very large sum because of the decrease in value of its silver coin.

Mr. Charles A. Conant had been brought from the United States to make a report on the feasibility of providing an American coinage for the islands. He recommended that the unit of value should be a peso, equivalent to fifty cents United States currency. Congress, by an act passed July 1, 1902, vested general authority over the coinage in the Philippine government, but the commission decided not to take action until more specific authority could be obtained from Congress, as the proposed reform was radical, and it was very important that the new currency should at the outset command the confidence so essential to its success.

After long discussion, Congress authorized, by an act passed March 2, 1903, a new currency system based on a theoretical peso of 12.9 grains of gold 900 fine, equivalent to one-half of a United States gold dollar. The circulating medium was to be the Philippine silver peso, which was to be legal tender for all debts, public and private, and its value was to be maintained on a parity with the theoretical gold peso. For this purpose the creation of a gold standard, or gold reserve fund, was provided for, and this fund was to be maintained and could be used for no other purpose.

Considerable difficulty was experienced in introducing the new currency into the islands. The banks at first failed to give any assistance to the government. The business men of Manila, and especially the Chinese, discounted the new Philippine peso, because it did not contain as much silver as did the Mexican dollar. They were quickly brought to time, and given to understand where they stood if they discredited the currency of the country.

The Spanish Philippine coins and the Mexican coins in circulation were collected by the treasury and exported to the San Francisco mint, where they were reminted into new coins of the weight and fineness prescribed by law.

The establishment of a gold standard fund to maintain the parity between the gold and silver dollar was quickly effected by the sale of exchange on the United States in accordance with the established law, at a cost estimated to be the same as the transportation of the gold coin itself.

The army, by direction of the secretary of war, ceased to pay in United States money, and its paymasters were given credit at the Insular Treasury, where they obtained the necessary funds in Philippine currency.

The government also authorized, in addition to the coinage of silver, the issuance of paper money in two, five, and ten peso notes. All of the coins and bills were readily interchangeable with the United States coins in common use, the dollar being worth two pesos, the half dollar one peso, the twenty-five cent piece a half peso, the ten-cent piece a peseta, the five-cent piece a media peseta and the cent two centavos.

Unfortunately the silver value of the new peso was such that when the price of silver again rose, its bullion value was greater than its money value, and in consequence coins of this denomination were hoarded and exported. It proved necessary to prohibit their exportation, and to issue new coins of less bullion value, but this was the only really serious difficulty attending a fundamental reform which put the currency on a sound basis. The original pesos were recoined and a handsome profit made on the transaction.

No one who has not lived in a country where the circulating medium is constantly fluctuating in value can fully appreciate the enormous benefit conferred on the Philippine Islands by this important reform.

Another reform of far-reaching importance was the readjustment of the burden of taxation so that it should bear lightly on the necessities of life, and heavily on its luxuries. This was a complete reversal of the scheme which we found in force, under which wheat flour and kerosene oil paid very heavy import duties while cigars and champagne were lightly taxed.

We imposed export taxes on certain products of the country. Such taxes are objected to by many political economists, but were approved of by the Filipinos, who strongly opposed the imposition of a logical and very necessary personal tax to provide funds for the construction and maintenance of highways and bridges. It is usually wise, when practicable, to obtain funds for necessary governmental purposes by the imposition of taxes which are willingly paid.

Mr. Taft resigned the governorship of the Philippines to become secretary of war, his resignation taking effect January 31, 1904. He had performed a monumental work for the Filipinos, and for humanity at large, during his years of service in the islands, and carried with him the good will of most of the people whom he had so faithfully, efficiently and self-sacrificingly served. He had at one time very gravely impaired his health by hard work, and when the opportunity came to satisfy a lifelong ambition by accepting appointment as a Justice of the Supreme Court of the United States, he had passed it by, in order to perform his duty to the people of the Philippine Islands. As secretary of war, and as President of the United States, he availed himself of every opportunity which these high offices afforded to help the Filipinos, and to increase the prosperity of their country. They have had no better friend, and no other friend whom they have ever had has been so useful to them. One more proof of his real greatness is afforded by the fact that to-day, after being reviled by many Filipino politicians whom he befriended, who have succeeded to a large degree in making the common people of the Philippines consider him their enemy, his interest in the people of the Islands is as keen, and his eagerness to help them is as great, as in the early days when they acclaimed him their deliverer.

General Luke E. Wright, a democrat of Memphis, Tennessee, was appointed by President Roosevelt civil governor in Mr. Taft's place. He rendered his country and the Filipinos most distinguished service. It is one thing to build up a great government, with numerous political appointments at one's disposal, and another to stand by and keep it running smoothly and efficiently, when a lot of disappointed politicians, who have seen their last hope of political preferment go a-glimmering, are throwing sand into the bearings of the machine. This latter class had begun to plot against Governor Taft before his resignation took effect, but their machinations were rendered fruitless by the wave of regret raised by his coming departure.

They now devoted themselves, with a good deal of success, to injuring Governor Wright, who declined to be dictated to, in the matter of appointments, by the Federal Party, and aroused the ire of many politicians by occasionally telling the Filipinos unpalatable but wholesome and necessary truths relative to their fitness for immediate independence.

General Wright, whose title had been changed from governor to governor-general on February 6, 1905, went on leave during the latter part of that year, fully expecting to return and resume his work in the Philippines, but the islands were not to see him again. He resigned, effective April 1, 1906, to become United States Ambassador to Japan. In my opinion, the acceptance of his resignation at this time was one of the gravest mistakes ever made in the Philippine policy of the United States. The islands were deprived of the services of a very able and distinguished man, thoroughly conversant with their needs, who had the courage of his convictions, and whose convictions were thoroughly sound.

Certain Filipino politicians openly boasted that they had secured his removal, and they and their ilk were encouraged to put forth new and pernicious efforts. Had General Wright returned to the islands much of the political unrest from which they have since suffered would have been avoided. He was beloved by his associates, who felt a sense of personal loss when they learned that the places which had known him in The Philippines would know him no more.

He was succeeded for the brief period of five and a half months by Judge Henry C. Ide, vice-governor and secretary of finance and justice, who had performed his duties while he was on leave. Judge Ide was a republican, from Vermont. He resigned on September 19, 1906.

He was succeeded by General James F. Smith, a democrat from California, who had come to the islands as a colonel of volunteers, and had won promotion because of his valuable services in the Visayas, and more especially in the island of Negros, where he had earned the good will of the Filipinos by his tact and kindness. Later he had served, unwillingly, as head of the Manila custom house.

He was subsequently made a justice of the supreme court of the Philippines. A lawyer by profession, he had resigned this position with regret to accept appointment, on January 1, 1903, as secretary of public instruction. He did not desire the governor-generalship and made a strong but unsuccessful effort to avoid accepting the position, which he finally took from a sense of duty. He was a good lawyer, with a big heart, and a keen insight into human nature. He thoroughly understood the Filipinos, and he made an excellent governor-general. It was during his term of office that the Philippine Legislature, composed of an upper appointive house, the Philippine Commission, and a lower elective house, the Philippine Assembly, met for the first time on October 16, 1907.

I devote a separate chapter[1] to the Philippine Legislature and its work, so need not discuss it here. Suffice it to say that such success as attended the work of this body during its inaugural, first and special sessions, was very largely due to the tactful influence of Governor-General Smith, who gave the speaker of the assembly much valuable, friendly counsel, and kept the two houses

[1] Chapter XXVII.

working in comparative harmony. Having struggled through one session of the legislature, Governor-General Smith felt at liberty to resign. He greatly desired to leave the Philippine government service and return to the practice of his profession. His resignation was reluctantly accepted, about a year after he had tendered it, and he left the service on November 10, 1909.

He was succeeded by Vice-Governor W. Cameron Forbes, a republican from Massachusetts, who had accepted appointment as secretary of commerce and police on June 15, 1904. A man of independent means, Mr. Forbes entered the public service only because of the opportunity for greater usefulness which was thus afforded him. He brought to bear on the problems which confronted him as secretary of commerce and police intelligence and ability of a very high order. Wide practical experience in the management of large business interests had admirably fitted him to improve the organization and increase the efficiency of the insular police force, and to mature and carry out plans for bettering means of communication and otherwise facilitating and stimulating the normal, healthful commercial development of the islands. I have devoted several chapters to the discussion of the results accomplished along these lines,[1] and will not attempt here to enumerate them.

Like all of his predecessors, he brought to the office of governor-general mature experience gained on the ground, having been in the service more than five years at the time of his promotion.

As governor-general, he not only retained his keen interest in the large problems which had previously engaged his attention, and laboured unceasingly and most successfully in the performance of the duties of his new office, but took an especial interest in the development of the summer capital, and in the work for the non-

---

[1] Chapters XIV, XXII, XXIII and XXIV.

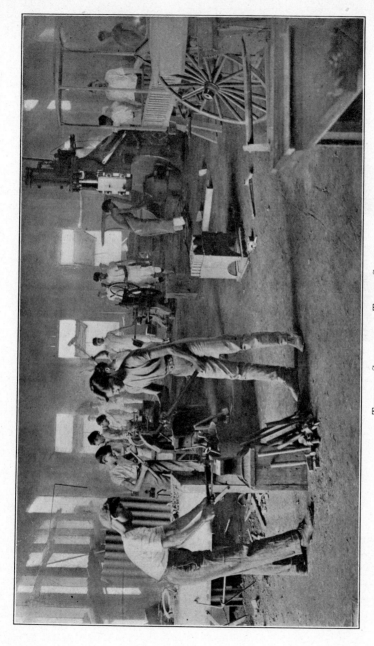

TYPICAL SCENE IN A TRADE SCHOOL.

In institutions like this, young Filipinos are being taught the dignity of labor and are learning useful trades.

Christian peoples of the islands, devoting a much greater amount of time and attention to familiarizing himself with the needs of this portion of the population than had ever previously been given to it by any governor-general. He visited the Moros and the Bukidnons in the south, and the Negritos, the Benguet Igorots, the Lepanto Igorots, the Bontoc Igorots, the Ilongots, the Ifugaos, the Kalingas, and both the wild and the civilized Tingians, in the north, repeatedly inspecting the several subprovinces of the Mountain Province.

Through his generosity in making proper grounds available, public interest in outdoor sports was greatly stimulated at Manila and at Baguio, while his own participation in polo, baseball and golf was a good example to Americans and Filipinos alike, in a country where vigorous outdoor exercise is very necessary to the physical development of the young and the preservation of the health of the mature.   He was a true friend of the Filipinos, whom he genuinely liked and was always ready to assist. His personal influence was a powerful factor in the success of the very important work carried on at the Philippine Normal School and the Philippine Training School for Nurses.

During his term of office the prosperity of the islands increased by leaps and bounds, public order became better than ever before in their history, and the efficiency of the civil service reached its maximum.   No other governor-general ever drew so heavily on his private means in promoting the public good, and it was the irony of fate that he should have been accused, by certain irresponsible anti-imperialists, of using his public office to promote his private interests.   Near the end of his administration grossly and absurdly false charges were made against him on the floor of the House by Representative William A. Jones.   As their falsity has been conclusively and finally shown,[1] I will not here lend importance to them by repeating them.   No official

[1] Reply to Jones, Pamphlet, Manila, 1913.

has ever given any country a cleaner administration than Governor-General Forbes gave the Philippines.

It was his fortune to be in office at the time of the change in the national administration of the United States. After continuing to serve for months with no sign from Washington as to whether his resignation was desired, he was advised by the Chief of the bureau of insular affairs that the appointment of Mr. Francis Burton Harrison, who is a Tammany Hall democrat, as his successor had been sent to the Senate,[1] and three days after its confirmation received a curt request for his resignation to be effected in a week and a day. He was also requested to employ servants for Mr. Harrison. Spaniards who read on the public streets newspapers which printed this message were seen to tear them up and stamp on the pieces ! Our Spanish friends are accustomed to expect courtesy in connection with the removal of faithful and efficient public servants.

All other governors-general had taken the oath of office at Manila. Mr. Harrison took it at Washington on September 2, 1913. He is the first American governor of the islands who has entered upon his high duties without previous experience in the country which he is to govern, and he has as yet displayed little inclination to profit by the experience of either Filipino or American administrative insular officials of high rank. It is too soon to discuss any feature of his administration other than his attitude toward the civil service, which I take up elsewhere,[1] and I can only express the hope that when he has gained that knowledge which can come only through personal observation on the ground, he will grow to be a wise, strong, conservative official.

The establishment of civil government in the Philippine Islands under American rule was a gradual evolution up to the time of the assumption of control by Governor-General Harrison.

[1] See pp. 375–77.

I will not attempt to follow in detail all of its successive stages, but in closing this chapter will endeavour briefly to summarize the results obtained up to that time.

The Philippines now have two delegates to the Congress of the United States appointed by the legislature in accordance with the provision of Section 8 of the Act of Congress of July 1, 1902. Both are Filipinos.

The ranking executive officials of the insular government are a governor-general, a secretary of the interior, a secretary of finance and justice, a secretary of commerce and police and a secretary of public instruction. All of these officers are appointed by the President, subject to confirmation by the Senate. The secretary of finance and justice is a Filipino; the other secretaries of departments are Americans.

There is a legislature composed of two houses known respectively as the Philippine Commission and the Philippine Assembly. The Philippine Commission is composed of nine members; five are the governor-general and the four secretaries of department *ex officio*, and four are appointed by the President subject to confirmation by the Senate. Four of the members are Filipinos and five are Americans.[1]

The Philippine Assembly is composed of eight-one elected members, all of whom are Filipinos. They represent thirty-four of the thirty-nine provinces into which the archipelago is divided. The two houses of the legislature have equal powers. Neither has any special privilege in the matter of initiating legislation, and affirmative action by both is required in order to pass it. The Moro Province, the Mountain Province and the provinces of Nueva Vizcaya and Agusan are not represented in the assembly, nor are they subject to the jurisdiction of the Philippine Legislature. The Philippine Commission alone has legislative jurisdiction over them, their population being largely com-

[1] Under the new regime these figures have been reversed.

posed of Moros, or members of other non-Christian tribes.

The provinces may be divided into regularly organized provinces governed under the provincial government act, and specially organized provinces, which include the Moro Province, the Mountain Province and the provinces of Mindoro, Palawan, Agusan and Nueva Vizcaya, of which the first is governed under a special law and the remaining four are governed under a different one known as "The Special Provincial Government Act."

Regularly organized provinces have a governor and a treasurer. The governor is elected, and the treasurer is appointed by the governor-general with the approval of the commission. These two officials, with another known as the third member, constitute a provincial board. The third member is elected. As the Filipinos usually elect to office men from among their own people, practically all of the elective provincial officers are Filipinos, as are ten of the appointive officers, it having been the policy to appoint Filipinos whenever possible.

Regularly organized provinces are divided into municipalities which elect their own officers and control their own affairs for the most part. Provincial treasurers have intervention in municipal expenditures, which are approved in advance for each fiscal year, and municipal officers may be removed for misconduct by the governor-general.

All officers of the six special government provinces are appointed by the governor-general with the approval of the commission.

There are four regularly organized municipalities in these provinces, but the remainder of their territory is divided into townships, which elect their own officers, except their secretary-treasurers, who are appointed by the provincial governor; and into *rancherias* or settlements, with all of their officials appointed by the provincial governor. This latter form of local government is confined to the more primitive wild people.

The judiciary is independent. The details of its organization will be found in Chapter XV.

Three of the seven justices of the supreme court, including the chief justice, are Filipinos, as are approximately half of the judges of the courts of first instance and practically all justices of the peace.

At the close of the fiscal year ending June 30, 1913, 71 per cent of the employees in the classified civil service of the islands were Filipinos painstakingly trained for the positions to which they had been appointed.

Prior to the American occupation, the Filipinos had practically no intervention in the government of their country.

The changes introduced in the twelve years since the establishment of civil government began are of a sweeping and radical nature. For reasons hereinafter fully set forth, I believe they have been somewhat too sweeping, and too radical. At all events, it is now certainly the part of wisdom carefully to analyze their results before going further.

I deem the subject of the establishment of civil governmental control over the non-Christian tribes of the Philippines worthy of special consideration.[1]

[1] See Chapters XX–XXIV.

CHAPTER XIII

The Philippine Civil Service

BEFORE the Philippine Commission left Washington, a clear understanding was reached with the President and secretary of war to the effect that no political appointee whatsoever should under any circumstances be forced upon us. After arrival at Manila early attention was given to the drafting of a civil service act by Mr. Taft, who was fortunate in having the assistance of Mr. Frank M. Kiggins, chief of the examining division of the United States Civil Service Commission. The passage of this act and its strict enforcement led to very favourable comment in the United States. In his first annual message President Roosevelt said : —

"It is important to have this system obtain at home, but it is even more important to have it rigidly applied in our insular possessions. . . .

"The merit system is simply one method of securing honest and efficient administration of the government, and in the long run the sole justification of any type of government lies in its proving itself both honest and efficient."

Secretary Root also gave us his fullest support, calling attention to the fact that the law which we had passed was of a very advanced type, and that under such circumstances as confronted us, the securing of the best men available should outweigh, and indeed practically exclude, all other considerations.

Our action met with the unqualified approval of organizations which especially interest themselves in the maintenance of clean and efficient public service, such as the Cambridge (Massachusetts) Civil Service Reform

Association [1] and the National Civil Service Reform League, whose committee on civil service in dependencies spoke in very high terms of existing conditions in the Philippines.[2]

In its first annual report the Civil Service Board called attention to some of the more important provisions of the Act in the following words : —

"Competitive examinations must, whenever practicable, be held for original entrance to the service, and promotions of employees must also be based upon competitive examinations, in which the previous experience and efficiency of employees shall be given due consideration. The examinations for entrance to the service must be held in the United States and in the Philippine Islands, and applicants are required to be tested in both English and Spanish.

"Disloyalty to the United States of America as the supreme authority in the Islands is made a complete disqualification for holding office, and every applicant for admission to the service must, before being admitted to examination, take the oath of loyalty. By an amendment to the Civil Service Act on January 26, 1901, it is further declared that all persons in arms against the authority of the United States in the Philippine Islands, and all persons aiding or abetting them, on the first day of April, 1901, shall be ineligible to hold office.

"A minimum age limit of eighteen years and a maximum age limit of forty years are fixed for those who enter the lowest grades in the service. This avoids the difficulty and embarrass-

[1] "The merit system has received renewed support from President Roosevelt in his administration, and by the extension of civil service throughout the nation, as well as in our new possessions. The Philippine service is reported to be very satisfactory, and efforts are being made for the extension and larger development of regulations in Porto Rico."

[2] "From the President down, every official charged with a duty touching the government of our dependencies is imbued with a profound sense of duty, and adequate realization of the situation and the imperative necessity of an unselfish, patriotic execution of the laws and regulations in the interest of the highest welfare of the inhabitants of the dependencies. With this state of affairs, the establishment of the merit system in them on an enduring basis should follow as a matter of course. It will be the aim of this Committee to aid in every possible way in extending and improving the system, and to that end to give to the whole subject careful and detailed study."

ment that would result from the admission of men advanced in years to positions where the duties can be better performed by younger and more energetic persons.

"The Board is given authority to investigate matters relative to the enforcement of the act and the rules, and is empowered to administer oaths, to summon witnesses, and to require the production of office books and records in making such investigations. Without such a provision it would be very difficult, if not impossible, to conduct satisfactory investigations, but with the authority conferred by the act, the Board can make a rigid inquiry into the facts of every case arising under the act and the rules.

"The act provides for the ultimate classification of all positions in the service, from laborers to heads of bureaus and offices, and the Board may, in its discretion, determine the efficiency of those now in the service as well as those who may enter hereafter through its examinations. This authority will enable the Board to ascertain the fitness of all employees so that only the most competent will be retained in the service.

"As a check upon the illegal payment of salaries the act provides that whenever the Board finds that a person has been appointed in violation of its provisions or of the rules of the Board, and so certifies to the disbursing and auditing officers, such payments shall be illegal, and if payment is continued the disbursing officer shall not receive credit for the same and the auditing officer who authorizes the payment shall be liable on his official bond for the loss to the government."

In its third annual report the Civil Service Board mentioned the following among its distinctive duties: —

"All appointments to classified positions are required to be made on a form prescribed by the Board, and the Board's attestation is required in each case before the Civil Governor or Secretary of Department will approve the appointment and before the disbursing officer will pay any salary.

"The papers in all cases of reduction, removal and enforced resignation are required to be submitted to the Board for recommendation before transmission to the Civil Governor or Secretary of Department for final action.

"The Board is required to keep a record of all unclassified as well as classified employees in the Philippine civil service, showing among other things date of appointment, original position and salary, place of employment, all changes in status and grade, and all accrued and sick leave granted.

AN EMBROIDERY CLASS.

This is a typical scene in the Manila School of Household Industries, where Filipina women are taught useful and profitable employments.

"From its service records the Board is required to compile annually, for publication on January 1, a roster of the officers and employees under the Philippine Government.

"Applications from employees, classified and unclassified, for accrued and sick leave for more than two days must be made on a form prescribed by the Board and forwarded to it for verification of service record and previous leave granted and for recommendation before final action is taken by the Civil Governor or Secretary of Department."

These extracts from official reports clearly show that the act was indeed of a very advanced type, and if honestly enforced would of necessity lead to the establishment and maintenance of "an efficient and honest civil service," for which purpose it was enacted.

In 1905 the insular government dispensed with boards as administrative agencies, and in accordance with this general policy, a bureau of civil service with a director at its head was substituted for the Civil Service Board, thus securing greater administrative efficiency and increased economy.

At first the Civil Service Act applied to comparatively few positions, as only a few bureaus and offices had been created, but as the government was organized and grew, the different bureaus and offices were placed in the classified service, the acts organizing them leaving in the unclassified service positions to which in the judgment of the commission the examination requirements of the act should not apply. Ultimately these requirements were made applicable to the treasurers of all municipalities and to all positions, including teachers, in the executive and judicial branches of the central government, the provincial governments, and the governments of the cities of Manila and Baguio, except a few specifically excepted by law, which for the most part are unclassified or exempt in almost all governments, national, state and municipal, having civil service laws. None of the states of the Union has such a widely extended classification of its civil service.

With the exception of the positions specifically placed in the unclassified service by law and of appointments made by the Philippine Commission, all positions in the Philippine civil service are classified and must be filled by appointees who have passed civil service examinations. Neither the governor-general nor the Bureau of Civil Service can, by the promulgation of civil service rules, or in any other manner whatever, transfer any position from the classified to the unclassified service or except from examination any position in the classified service. Under most of the civil service laws of the United States the President or the governor of the state has authority to transfer positions from the non-classified or exempted class to the competitive classified civil service or *vice versa*, these powers sometimes leading to manipulation of the civil service rules for political purposes.

In the Philippines, where emergencies, such as cholera epidemics, sometimes lead to the employment of large bodies of temporary employees without examination, when the emergency has passed the temporary employees have always been discharged; and no employee has ever received classification without examination on account of temporary service. This is in marked contrast to the practice in the United States, where large bodies of employees taken on for temporary service due to emergencies, such as the war with Spain, are not infrequently blanketed into the classified service without examination.

In its last annual report the board recommended that a number of official positions in the unclassified service be placed in the classified service, and gave as a reason therefor that such action would "add to the attractiveness of the classified service by increasing the opportunities therein for promotion to responsible positions." This recommendation was adopted by providing that all vacancies in the positions of heads and assistant heads of bureaus or offices and of superintendents shall be filled by promotion, with or without examination, in the discretion of the civil governor or proper head of a department, of persons in the classified civil service, if competent persons are found therein.

This provision is an important and distinguishing feature of the Philippine Civil Service Act. The federal civil service has none comparable with it. It is of special value in that it induces young men of exceptional ability and training to enter the lower grades, for they have the certainty that faithful and efficient work will in the end earn for them the highest positions.

On February 25, 1909, the director of civil service made the following statement with respect to the observance of the law : —

"A careful study of Act 5 and all acts amendatory thereof will show that there has been no change in the policy adopted by the Commission at the outset to extend the classified service as widely as possible and to fill by promotion all the higher positions so far as practicable. The provision requiring the higher positions to be filled by promotion so far as practicable has always been regarded by the Philippine Commission, by this Bureau, and by others interested in obtaining the best possible government service in the Philippines as one of the most important provisions of the Civil Service Act. It has been faithfully observed by all Governors-General. . . . With the exception of the positions of Governor-General and Secretaries of Departments, the Philippine Civil Service Act requires the highest positions in the executive civil service, namely, chiefs and assistant chiefs of Bureaus and Offices, to be filled by promotion from the entire service in all cases except when in the opinion of the appointing power there is no person competent and available who possesses the qualifications required, and this provision has been faithfully observed heretofore."

The enforcement of the law by the commission has received the following commendation from the executive committee of the National Civil Service Reform League :—

"We have further to note with satisfaction the course of the Philippine Commission, by which, if it be persevered in, the merit system will be established in the Islands of that archipelago at least as thoroughly and consistently as in any department of government, Federal, State, or Municipal, in the Union. This must be, in any case, regarded as a gratifying recognition of sound principles of administration on the part of the Commission, and justifies the hope that, within the limits of their jurisdiction at least, no repetition of the scandals of post-bellum days will be tolerated."

Up to the time of the appointment of Governor-General Harrison the provisions of the Civil Service Act and rules were firmly supported by all of the governors-general and secretaries of departments, and the annual reports of the governor-general uniformly expressed satisfaction with their practical operation. Mr. Taft was always an enthusiastic supporter of the merit system.

Governor-General Forbes in his inaugural address made the following statements : —

"It is necessary that the civil service should be rigidly maintained and its rules carefully observed. One very distinguished Filipino has recently been appointed to administrative control of one of the most important departments of the Government, equal in rank to any executive position in the Islands with the exception of the Executive head. In the executive branch of the Government, the Filipinization of the service must steadily continue. As vacancies occur Filipinos will be gradually substituted for Americans as rapidly as can be done without positive detriment to the service. At the same time, care will be taken to provide a suitable career for honest and capable Americans who have come out here in good faith. They should know that during good behavior and efficient performance of their duty they are secure in their positions, and that when they desire to return to the United States an effort will be made to place them in the civil service at home.

"I want no better men than the present officers and employees of the Government, Americans and Filipinos. They compare favorably with any set of men I have ever seen both as regards ability and fidelity to duty."

Under the operation of the Civil Service Act the proportion of Filipinos employed has increased from 49 per cent, in 1903, to 71 per cent in 1913, as is shown by the following table : —

Comparison of Percentages of Americans and Filipinos in the Service

Year	Number of Employees	
	Americans	Filipinos
1903	51%	49%
1904	49	51
1905	45	55
1906 [1]	—	—
1907	40	60
1908	38	62
1909	38	62
1910	36	64
1911	35	65
1912	31	69
1913	29	71

For the first few years after the establishment of the government large numbers of Americans were appointed, as there were comparatively few Filipino candidates with the necessary educational qualifications. During the last two years, 89 per cent of the persons appointed in the islands have been Filipinos.

There has been a great increase in the number of Filipinos entering the civil service examinations in English. Ten years ago 97 per cent of those examined took their examinations in Spanish, while during last year 89 per cent of those examined took examinations in English, the total number so examined being 7755. Almost all appointees for ordinary clerical work are now Filipinos, but the supply of bookkeepers, stenographers, civil engineers, physicians, veterinarians, surveyors, chemists, bacteriologists, agriculturists, horticulturists, constabulary officers, nurses, electricians, mechanical engineers, and other scientific employees is still insufficient to meet the demands of the service. Only one Filipino has passed

[1] No data for 1906 available.

the stenographer examination in English since the organization of the government, and it is necessary each year to bring many American stenographers from the United States. A few Filipinos pass each year the junior stenographer examination [1] and are able to fill some of the positions which would formerly have required the appointment of Americans.

The salaries paid to executive officials, chiefs of bureaus and offices, chief clerks, and chiefs of divisions equal in many instances those paid to officials occupying similar positions in the service of the United States government.

In the legislative branch the speaker receives $8000 per annum. Members of the Philippine Commission without portfolios receive $7500 per annum. Members of the Philippine Assembly receive $15 a day for each day in which the assembly is in session.

In the executive branch secretaries of departments receive $15,500 per annum each, including $5000 received by them as members of the Philippine Commission. The executive secretary receives $9000 per annum. The salaries of other bureau chiefs range from $2500 per annum to $7500.

The justices of the Philippine Supreme Court receive $10,000 per annum. Judges of courts of first instance receive from $4500 to $5500.

The following extracts from an article by the chairman of the Philippine Civil Service Board give information with respect to salaries in the Philippine Islands, as compared with salaries paid in surrounding British and Dutch colonies : —

"The salaries paid officials in all branches of the service of the Straits Settlements are generally lower than those paid in the Philippine civil service. In this connection, however, it is only just to state that the population and extent of the territory under British control, and the expenses of living, are less than in the Philippines, while the difficulty of the prob-

[1] Eight passed last year.

lems to be solved is not so great. The salaries paid to natives who fill the lower grade positions in the civil service of the Philippine Islands are three and four times as great as the salaries paid to natives in similar classes of work in the civil service of the British Malay colonies.

"A study of the colonial civil service of the Dutch in the islands of Java and Madura gives us somewhat different results. . . .

"The matter of salaries is peculiarly interesting. The comparison made above of the compensations received by the high officials in the civil service of the English colonies and by those in the Philippines does not hold good when applied to the Dutch in Java. In fact, the salary of the Governor-General of Java is somewhat remarkable in contrast with that of the Civil Governor of the Philippines. As is well known, the latter receives $20,000, while the salary of the Governor-General of Java amounts to 132,000 gulden or something over $53,000. The American official is given, in addition, free transportation on all official investigations and free use of the governor's palace, but not the cost of maintenance. On the other hand, the Dutch governor is granted 51,000 gulden (about $21,500) as personal and household expenses and travel pay.

"The general secretary of the government receives 24,000 gulden ($9648), as compared with the executive secretary of the Philippine government, whose salary is $7500.[1] The seven heads of departments in the Javanese service each receive a like compensation of 24000 gulden. The Raad, or Council, of the Dutch colonial government is composed of a vice-president and four members — the former receiving about $14,500, the latter slightly over $11,500 each. In the Philippine government the executive functions of heads of departments are exercised by four members of the legislative body, each of whom receives $10,500 for his executive services and $5000 for his legislative duties. Without going further into detail, the conclusion is evident that all officials of high rank are much better paid in the Dutch service. When a comparison is made between the chief clerks and other office employees of middle grades — not natives — the salaries are seen to be about the same in the two countries.

"All natives in positions of lower grades, however, in the Philippine Islands fare better than their Malay brethren, either in the Straits Settlements or in the East Indies." — (Second Annual Report of the Philippine Civil Service Board, pp. 60, 61.)

[1] He now receives $9000.

"Difference in salaries for subordinate positions in the British and Dutch colonial services and the Philippine service are distinctly in favour of subordinate employees in the Philippine service; only the higher officials, after long experience, in the British colonial service receive larger salaries than corresponding officials in the Philippine service; the leave of absence and other privileges for the Philippine service are not less liberal than for other colonial services." — (Report of the Philippine Commission for 1905, p. 74.)

The entrance salaries of Americans brought to the islands are considerably in excess of the entrance salaries received on appointment to the civil service in the United States.

The following table shows the minimum entrance salaries given to Americans appointed in the United States to the United States civil service, as shown by the manual of examinations of the United States Civil Service Commission for the fall of 1913, and to Americans appointed in the United States to the Philippine Civil Service: —

	PHILIPPINES	UNITED STATES
Aid (Surveyor) . . .	$1400	$ 900
Civil Engineer	1400	1200
Forester, assistant . .	1400	1200
Scientific Assistant, (Agricultural Inspector).	1400	600
Physician	1600	1320
Printer	2000	.50 per hour
Stenographer	1200	700
Trained Nurse	600 Board, quarters and laundry	600 and laundry
Teacher	1000	540
Veterinarian	1600	1200

The following cases taken from the official rosters show some promotions to the higher positions in the service of employees who entered the lower ranks of the classified service: —

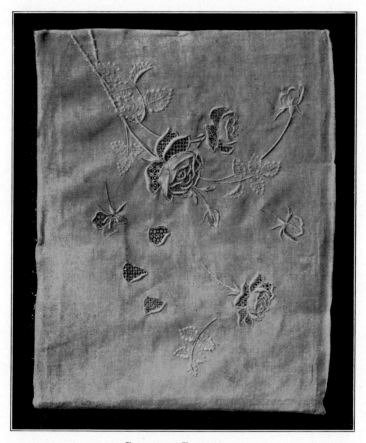

PHILIPPINE EMBROIDERY.

This work was done by a pupil in one of the Manila city schools.

A clerk who entered the service in 1899 at $1800 per annum was appointed in 1903 an assistant chief of bureau at $3000 per annum and in 1908 executive secretary at $9000 per annum. A teacher appointed in 1899 at $720 per annum was appointed a chief of an office at $4000 per annum and in 1912 a judge at $4500 per annum. A teacher who entered the service in 1901 at $1200 per annum was in 1909 appointed a chief of a bureau at $6000 per annum. A teacher who entered the service in 1904 at $1000 per annum was appointed in 1911 an assistant chief of a bureau at $6000 per annum. A clerk who entered the service in 1901 at $1200 per annum was appointed in 1909 an assistant chief of the executive bureau at $3750 per annum and in 1912 a chief of a bureau at $6000 per annum. A stenographer who entered the service in 1902 at $1400 per annum was in 1908 appointed an assistant chief of a bureau at $5000 per annum. A transitman who entered the service in 1905 at $1400 per annum was in 1913 appointed an assistant chief of a bureau at $4500 per annum. An accountant who entered the service in 1901 at $1800 per annum was in 1907 appointed an assistant chief of a bureau at $3750 per annum and in 1909 a chief of a bureau at $6000 per annum. A law clerk who entered the service in 1904 at $1800 per annum was in 1913 appointed judge at $4500 per annum. In no service anywhere has promotion depended more directly on demonstrated ability, and in many instances it has been rapid.

Young men living two in a room may obtain room and board in boarding houses in Manila at a rate as low as $35 per month each. In the Young Men's Christian Association building, a large reënforced concrete structure with reading room, gymnasium, and a good restaurant, the charge for two in a room is $10.25 each. Board costs $27.50, a total of $37.75. The expenses for clothing in Manila are less than in the United States, as white clothing is worn the whole year and white duck suits may be obtained for about $3 each. The expenses for laundry amount to about $5 a month. The necessity of employing a *muchacho* [1] is *nil*, in the case of an unmarried employee who boards. Servants are far cheaper and better in the Philippines than in the United States.

In a discussion of the salaries paid in the Philippine civil service the question of the leave allowed should be considered. Classified employees who receive an annual salary of $1000 or more per annum may be granted twenty-eight days' leave per annum to cover absences from duty due to illness or other causes. If not taken during the calendar year in which it is earned or in January or February of the succeeding year, it is forfeited. Employees taking vacation leave during the months of December, January, February and March may take fifty-six days, corresponding to two years of service, at one time, and may thus get time to visit Australia, Japan, China, and neighbouring countries.

In addition to vacation leave an employee whose salary is $1000 or more but less than $1800 per annum is entitled to thirty days' accrued leave per annum, and an employee whose salary is $1800 per annum or more is entitled to thirty-five days' accrued leave per annum. Accrued leave may accumulate for not more than five years of service.

All classified employees are entitled to visit the United States or foreign countries once in every three years, receiving in addition to their accrued leave, one year's vacation leave, allowance of actual travel time at half pay not to exceed sixty days, and return travel expenses from place of residence in the United States, or from port of embarkation in a foreign country to Manila, on the completion of two years of service after date of return. An employee entitled to thirty-five days' accrued leave per annum who visits the United States after having rendered three years of service receives a total of two hundred thirteen days' accrued leave, vacation leave, and half-pay travel time. If he postpones his visit till he has com-

[1] Male servant.

pleted five years of service, he receives a total of two hundred ninety-one days' accrued leave, vacation leave and travel time. An employee entitled to thirty days' accrued leave per annum who visits the United States after three years of service receives a total of one hundred ninety-four days' leave and half-pay travel time, and if he postpones his visit until he has rendered five years of service, he receives a total of two hundred fifty-nine days' leave and travel time.

It will be seen that these are very liberal allowances. An employee receiving $1200 at the end of two years of service may spend eight weeks of vacation leave visiting Japan or other surrounding countries, and at the end of an additional year's service he may visit his home in the United States with six and a third months' absence on full and half pay and with his expenses from his home to Manila payable two years after his return, and during every three years of his service he may have the same privileges.

The law also provides that if an employee is wounded or injured in the performance of duty, he may have a total of six months' leave on full pay in addition to any accrued leave to his credit.

Employees who have rendered satisfactory service and resign after three or more years receive in a lump sum all accrued leave due and thirty days' half salary. For example, an employee who has received $1800 per annum and has served five years without taking any leave in excess of the four weeks' vacation leave allowable annually would draw $1025 were he to resign.

The school sessions amount to forty weeks per annum and the school vacations to twelve weeks per annum.[1] Teachers receive an annual salary and draw full pay during vacations as well as during school sessions. Every third year they are allowed to visit the United States or foreign countries with an allowance of sixty days' half-pay travel time in addition to the ten weeks' long vacation,

[1] Two weeks at Christmas and ten weeks in April, May and June.

and on completing two years of service after return to the islands they are entitled to their travelling expenses from place of residence in the United States to Manila or from port of embarkation in a foreign country to Manila.

It is interesting to compare these provisions with the regulations governing leave of absence in the British colonial service:—

(1) There is no distinction between sick leave and ordinary leave, the leave of absence on account of sickness being charged against the ordinary leave allowable.

(2) There are two classes of leave: vacation leave on full pay and half-pay leave.

(3) The vacation leave amounts to three months every two years, and must be taken during the two years, as it does not accumulate.

(4) The half-pay leave amounts to two months for each year of service, but cannot be taken until after a period of six years' resident service in the Colony, except in cases of serious indisposition supported by medical certificate, or of "urgent private affairs," the nature of which must be stated to the governor. In either case, the governor and council must be satisfied that the indulgence is indispensable.

Half pay in African and Asiatic colonies may accumulate for twelve years' service —*i.e.* twenty-four months' half-pay leave.

(5) After the exhaustion of all vacation leave and half-pay leave, an advance of six months' half-pay leave may be made on special grounds ("urgent private affairs" or illness supported by a medical certificate), the advance being charged against leave accruing subsequently.

(6) For the purpose of visiting home, an officer may be granted the vacation leave due him (which is never more than three months) on full pay, and his accumulated half-pay leave, to commence at the expiration of his vacation leave.

(7) Judicial and education officers do not receive the vacation leave described in paragraph 3 above, the vacation of courts and schools being considered equal to this, but they do receive the half-pay leave described in paragraph 4, and may, when visiting home on half-pay leave, receive full pay during any ordinary vacation of the court or school.

It will be noted that although officers in the British colonial service are allowed much longer periods of absence, the greater part of their absence is on half pay and the total money value of the leave allowable in the British colonial service and in the Philippine civil service is about the same. As officers naturally prefer to be on full pay instead of half pay while on leave, the provision of the Philippine law is in their interest; it is also in the interest of the service, as the periods of the absence from duty are not so prolonged.

The Philippine Civil Service Law is now about to be put to its first really severe test as a result of the change in the national administration. Heretofore those whose duty and privilege it has been to enforce it have been in the most full and hearty sympathy with its purposes. President McKinley was from the outset definitely committed to the widest application of the merit system to appointments in the Philippines. Mr. Roosevelt and Mr. Taft firmly supported that system, as has each succeeding governor-general up to, but not including, Mr. Harrison, who is as yet an unknown quantity.

It is interesting, however, to note that on the day following his arrival there was a demand for the instant resignation of Mr. Thomas Cary Welch, a faithful and efficient employee of the government, who had been for nearly ten years in the service, whose position was desired for, and immediately given to, Mr. Stephen Bonsal. That gentleman had been appointed at Washington a member of the Municipal Board of Manila immediately after Mr. Harrison's confirmation as governor-general. It is not recorded that Mr. Bonsal rendered any valuable service to the city on the voyage, or during the twenty-four hours of his occupancy of his municipal post subsequent to his arrival! Nor does it appear that he passed any examination before his early promotion.

Following closely upon the removal of Mr. Welch came a demand for the resignation of Captain Charles H. Sleeper, Director of Lands, who was unquestionably one of the ablest and most efficient of the bureau chiefs.

He had earned the ill-will of the *politicos* by insisting that persons authorized to make public land surveys, or other surveys on which claims of title as against the government were to be based, should know enough about surveying to make one correct survey when given an opportunity practically to demonstrate their abilities under very favourable conditions. He had also incurred the dislike of influential *caciques* by defending the occupants of small holdings on friar estates from the rapacity of their rich neighbours, and by protecting free-patent applicants and homesteaders when large landowners opposed their applications in order to prevent their securing land, so that they might the more easily be held as peon labourers.

He had started in his bureau a practical school for Filipino surveyors which was training really well-qualified candidates for positions desired by the politicians for themselves or their incompetent friends.

Last, but not least, he had helped to upset the plans of the men primarily responsible for the so-called "friar lands investigation" conducted by the House Committee on Insular Affairs, which cost the United States government a very large sum, and resulted in demonstrating his uprightness and the efficiency of his administration.

Mr. John R. Wilson, the assistant director of lands, was absent at the moment, but his resignation was demanded on the day of his return. He too was an active, efficient, upright man.

Both of these removals were political acts, pure and simple. Sr. Manuel Tinio was appointed Director of Lands. He is a bright young Ilocano of good character, who had become a "general" in the Insurgent army at twenty-one years of age. He is unfit to hold the place, because, as he has himself frankly said, he knows nothing about the work. He is charged with the duty of administering $7,000,000 worth of friar lands, and the whole public domain of the Philippine Islands, and with such minor duties as the checkmating of the machinations of numerous wealthy Filipinos who seek fraudulently to acquire great tracts through fraudulent claims to unperfected titles and by other improper means.

While in Honolulu, *en route* to Manila, Mr. Harrison gave out an interview, which I am credibly informed he has since confirmed in substance. It contained the following statement: —

"For years I have been of the minority in Congress and have seen the Democrats kicked about, trampled upon, and otherwise manhandled by Republicans, so that I must confess it now gives me a saturnine pleasure to see the Democrats in a position to do the same thing to the Republicans."

His early official acts after arrival at Manila confirmed the belief that this was indeed the spirit in which he was facing the grave responsibilities which there confronted him.

It is beyond doubt or cavil that high ideals heretofore have prevailed in the Philippine Civil Service. Are they now to be substituted by the methods of the ward politician?

In its report for 1901 the Philippine Commission said: —

"The civil service law has been in operation since our last report, and we see no reason to change our conclusion as to the absolute necessity for its existence, and strict enforcement. Without this law American government in these Islands is, in our opinion, foredoomed to humiliating failure."

I signed that report. I have not since seen any reason to change my mind.

CHAPTER XIV

The Philippine Constabulary and Public Order

During the last thirty years of Spanish rule in the Philippines evil-doers were pursued and apprehended and public order was maintained chiefly by the *guardia civil*. At the time of its organization in 1868 this body had a single division. By 1880 the number had been increased to three, two for Luzón and one for the Visayan Islands.

The *guardia civil* was organized upon a military basis, its officers and soldiers being drawn from the regular army of Spain by selection or upon recommendation. Detachments were distributed throughout the provinces and were commanded according to their size by commissioned or non-commissioned officers. Central offices were located in district capitals; company headquarters were stationed in provincial capitals, and detachments were sent to places where they were deemed to be necessary.

Under ordinary conditions they rendered service as patrols of two men each, but for the purpose of attacking large bands of outlaws one or several companies were employed as occasion required.

The *guardia civil* had jurisdiction over all sorts of violations of laws and municipal ordinances. They made reports upon which were based the appointments of municipal officers, the granting of licenses to carry firearms, and the determination of the loyalty or the disloyalty of individuals.

They were vested with extraordinary powers. Offences against them were tried by courts-martial, and were construed as offences against sentinels on duty. Penalties were therefore extremely severe.

378

Officers of the *guardia civil* on leave could by their own initiative assume a status of duty with the full powers and responsibilities that go with command. This is contrary to American practice, under which only dire emergency justifies an officer in assuming an official status unless he is duly assigned thereto by competent authority.

The *guardia civil* could arrest on suspicion, and while the Spanish Government did not directly authorize or sanction the use of force to extort confessions, it was not scrupulous in the matter of accepting confessions so obtained as evidence of crime, nor was it quick to punish members of the *guardia civil* charged with mistreatment of prisoners.

Reports made by the *guardia civil* were not questioned, but were accepted without support even in cases of the killing of prisoners alleged to have attempted to escape, or of men evading arrest.

This method of eliminating without trial citizens deemed to be undesirable was applied with especial frequency in the suppression of active brigandage, and latterly during the revolution against Spain. Prisoners in charge of the *guardia civil* were always tied elbow to elbow. They knew full well that resistance or flight was an invitation to their guards to kill them, and that this invitation was likely to be promptly accepted.

In the investigation of crime the members of this organization arrested persons on suspicion and compelled them to make revelations, true or false. Eye-witnesses to the commission of crime were not needed in the Spanish courts of that day. The confession of an accused person secured his conviction, even though not made in the presence of a judge. Indirect and hearsay evidence were accepted, and such things as writs of habeas corpus and the plea of double jeopardy were unknown in Spanish procedure.

The *guardia civil* could rearrest individuals and again

charge them with crimes of which they had already been acquitted. I have been assured by reliable Filipino witnesses that it was common during the latter days of Spanish sovereignty for persons who had made themselves obnoxious to the government to be invited by non-commissioned officers to take a walk, which was followed either by their complete disappearance or by the subsequent discovery of their dead bodies.

It naturally resulted that the members of the *guardia civil* were regarded with detestation and terror by the people, but their power was so absolute that protest rarely became public. The one notable exception was furnished by Dr. Rizal's book entitled "Noli Me Tangere," which voiced the complaints of the Filipinos against them. There is not a vestige of doubt that hatred of them was one of the principal causes of the insurrection against Spain.

In 1901 the American government organized a rural police force in the Philippines. It was called the Philippine constabulary. The insurrection was then drawing to a close, but there were left in the field many guerilla bands armed and uniformed. Their members sought to excuse their lawless acts under the plea of patriotism and opposition to the forces of the United States. In many provinces they combined with professional bandits or with religious fanatics. Various "popes" arose, like Papa Isio in Negros. The Filipinos had become accustomed to a state of war which had continued for nearly six years. Habits of peace had been abandoned. The once prosperous haciendas were in ruins. War and pestilence had destroyed many of the work animals, and those which remained continued to perish from disease. Asiatic cholera was sweeping through the archipelago, and consternation and disorder followed in its wake.

Under such circumstances the organization of a rural police force was imperatively necessary. Unfortunately the most critical situation which it was to be called upon

FILIPINO TRAINED NURSES.

to meet had to be faced at the very outset, when both officers and men were inexperienced and before adequate discipline could be established.

The law providing for its establishment was drawn by the Honourable Luke E. Wright, at that time secretary of commerce and police and later destined to become governor-general of the Philippines and secretary of war of the United States.

It was intended that the constabulary should accomplish its ends by force when necessary but by sympathetic supervision when possible, suppressing brigandage and turning the people towards habits of peace. The fact was clearly borne in mind that the abuses of the *guardia civil* had not been forgotten and the new force was designed to meet existing conditions, to allay as rapidly as possible the existing just rancour against the similar organization established under the Spanish régime, and to avoid the evils which had contributed so much toward causing the downfall of Spanish sovereignty. The law was admirably framed to achieve these ends.

The officers of the constabulary were selected chiefly from American volunteers recently mustered out and from honourably discharged soldiers of the United States army. Some few Filipinos, whose loyalty was above suspicion, were appointed to the lower grades. This number has since been materially augumented, and some of the original Filipino appointees have risen to the rank of captain.

It was inevitable that at the outset there should be abuses. The organization was necessarily born at work; there was no time to instruct, to formulate regulations, to wait until a satisfactory state of discipline had been brought about. There were not barracks for housing the soldiers; there were neither uniforms, nor arms, nor ammunition. There was no system for rationing the men. All of these things had to be provided, and they were provided through a natural evolution of practical processes, crystallizing into form, tested by the duties of the day. The organization which grew up was a true survival of the fittest, both in personnel and in methods. The wonder is not that some abuses occurred, but that they were so few ; not that there were occasional evidences of lack of efficiency, but that efficiency was on the whole so high from the beginning.

The several provinces were made administrative units, the commanding officer in each being designated as "senior inspector." The men who were to serve in a given province were by preference recruited there, and a departure was thus made from the usual foreign colonial practice.

In 1905 the total force was fixed at one hundred companies with a nominal strength of two officers and fifty men each. Under special conditions this rule may be departed from, and the size of the companies or the number of officers increased.

Each province is divided by the senior inspector into sections, and the responsibility for patrol work and general policing rests on the senior company officer in each station. The provinces are grouped into five districts, each commanded by an assistant chief who exercises therein the authority, and performs the duties appropriate to the chief for the entire Philippines. The higher administrative positions have always been filled by detailing regular officers of the United States army.

The constabulary soldiers are now neatly uniformed, armed with Krag carbines and well disciplined. They show the effect of good and regular food and of systematic exercise, their physical condition being vastly superior to that of the average Filipino. They are given regular instruction in their military duties. It is conducted in English.

The Philippine constabulary may be defined as a body of armed men with a military organization, recruited from among the people of the islands, officered in part by Americans and in part by Filipinos, and employed primarily for police duty in connection with the establishment and maintenance of public order.

Blount's chapters on the administrations of Taft, Wright and Smith embody one prolonged plaint to the effect that the organization of the constabulary was premature, and that after the war proper ended, the last smouldering embers of armed and organized insurrection should have been stamped out, and the brigandage which had existed in the Philippines for centuries should have been dealt with, by the United States army rather than by the constabulary.

Even if it were true that the army could have rendered more effective service to this end than could have been expected at the outset from a newly organized body of Filipino soldiers, the argument against the organization and use of the constabulary would in my opinion have been by no means conclusive. It is our declared policy to prepare the Filipinos to establish and maintain a stable government of their own. The proper exercise of police powers is obviously necessary to such an end.

From the outset we have sacrificed efficiency in order that our wards might gain practical experience, and might demonstrate their ability, or lack of ability, to perform necessary governmental functions. Does any one cognizant of the situation doubt for a moment that provincial and municipal affairs in the Philippine Islands would to-day be more efficiently administered if provincial and municipal officers were appointed instead of being elected? Is any one so foolish as to imagine that the sanitary regeneration of the islands would not have progressed much more rapidly had highly trained American health officers been used in place of many of the badly educated and comparatively inexperienced Filipino physicians whose services have been utilized?

Nevertheless, in the concrete case under discussion I dissent from the claim that more satisfactory results could have been obtained by the use of American troops.

The army had long been supreme in the Philippines. Every function of government had been performed by its officers and men, if performed at all. Our troops had been combating an elusive and cruel enemy. If they were human it is to be presumed that they still harbored animosities, born of these conditions, toward the people with whom they had so recently been fighting. Had the work of pacification been then turned over to them it would have meant that often in the localities in which they had been fighting, and in dealing with the men to whom they had very recently been actively opposed in armed conflict, they would have been called upon to perform tasks and to entertain feelings radically different from those of the preceding two or three years.

A detachment, marching through Leyte, found an American who had disappeared a short time before crucified, head down. His abdominal wall had been carefully opened so that his intestines might hang down in his face.

Another American prisoner, found on the same trip, had been buried in the ground with only his head projecting. His mouth had been propped open with a stick, a trail of sugar laid to it through the forest, and a handful thrown into it.

Millions of ants had done the rest.

Officers and men who saw such things were thereby fitted for war, rather than for ordinary police duty.

The truth is that they had seen so many of them that they continued to see them in imagination when they no longer existed. I well remember when a general officer, directed by his superior to attend a banquet at Manila in which Americans and Filipinos joined, came to it wearing a big revolver!

Long after Manila was quiet I was obliged to get out of my carriage in the rain and darkness half a dozen times while driving the length of Calle Real, and "approach to be recognized" by raw "rookies," each of whom pointed a loaded rifle at me while I did it. I know that this did not tend to make me feel peaceable or happy. In my opinion it was wholly unnecessary, and yet I did not blame the army for thinking otherwise.

After the war was over, when my private secretary, Mr. James H. LeRoy, was one day approaching Malolos, he was sternly commanded by a sentry to halt, the command being emphasized as usual by presenting to his attention a most unattractive view down the muzzle of a Krag. He was next ordered to "salute the flag," which he finally discovered with difficulty in the distance, after being told where to look. The army way is right and necessary in war, but it makes a lot of bother in time of peace!

This was not the only reason for failing to make more extensive use of American soldiers in police duty. A veteran colonel of United States cavalry who had just read Judge Blount's book was asked what he thought of the claim therein made that the army should have done the police and pacification work of the Philippines. His reply was: —

"How long would it take a regiment of Filipinos to catch an American outlaw in the United States? Impossible!"

Another army officer said: —

"Catching Filipino outlaws with the Army is like catching a flea in a twenty-acre field with a traction engine."

There is perhaps nothing so demoralizing to regular troops as employment on police duty which requires them to work singly or in small squads. Discipline speedily goes to the dogs and instruction becomes impossible.

Successful prosecution of the work of chasing *ladrones* in the Philippines requires a thorough knowledge of local topography and of local native dialects. Spanish is of use, but only in dealing with educated Filipinos. A

VOL. I — 2 c

knowledge of the Filipino himself; of his habits of thought; of his attitude toward the white man; and toward the *illustrado*, or educated man, of his own race; ability to enter a town and speedily to determine the relative importance of its leading citizens, finally centring on the one man, always to be found, who runs it, whether he holds political office or not, and also to enlist the sympathy and coöperation of its people; all of these things are essential to the successful handling of brigandage in the Philippines, whether such brigandage has, or lacks, political significance.

The following parallel will make clear some of the reasons why it was determined to use constabulary instead of American soldiers in policing the Philippines from the time the insurrection officially ended: —

UNITED STATES ARMY	PHILIPPINE CONSTABULARY
Soldier costs per annum $1400. (Authority: Adjutant General Heistand in 1910.)	Soldier costs per annum $363.50.
American soldiers come from America.	Constabulary soldiers are enlisted in the province where they are to serve.
Few American soldiers speak the local dialects.	All constabulary soldiers speak local dialects.
Few American soldiers speak any Spanish.	All educated constabulary soldiers speak Spanish.
American soldiers usually have but a slight knowledge of local geography and topography.	Constabulary soldiers, native to the country, know the geography and topography of their respective provinces.
Few American soldiers have had enough contact with Filipinos to understand them.	The Filipino soldier certainly knows his own kind better than the American does.

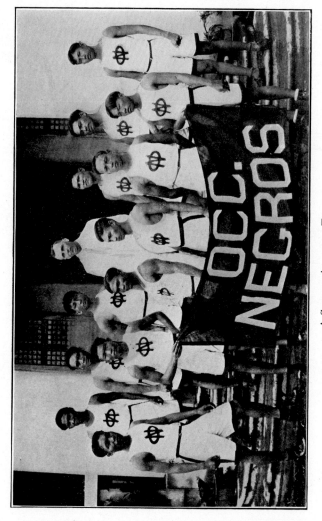

A SCHOOL ATHLETIC TEAM.

Calisthenic exercises taught in the public schools are converting puny youths into vigorous athletes.

The American soldier uses a ration of certain fixed components imported over sea. (A ration is the day's allowance of food for one soldier.)

The constabulary soldier is rationed in cash and buys the food of the country where he happens to be.

The American ration costs 24.3 cents United States currency (exclusive of cost of transportation and handling). Fresh meat requiring ice to keep it is a principal part of the American ration. To supply it requires a regular system of transport from the United States to Manila and from thence to local ports, and wagon transportation from ports to inland stations.

The constabulary cash ration is 10.5 cents United States currency. (No freight or handling charges.) The constabulary soldier knows not ice. His food grows in the islands. He buys it on the ground and needs no transportation to bring it to him.

The American soldier is at no pains to enlist the sympathy and coöperation of the people; and his methods of discipline, habits of life, etc., make it practically impossible for him to gain them.

The idea of enlisting the sympathy and coöperation of the local population is the strongest tenet in the constabulary creed.

Before preparing the foregoing statement relative to the reasons for using Philippine constabulary soldiers instead of soldiers of the United States army for police work during the period in question, I asked Colonel J. G. Harbord, assistant director of the constabulary, who has served with that body nine years, has been its acting director and is an officer of the United States army, to give me a memorandum on the subject. It is only fair to him to say that I have not only followed very closely the line of argument embodied in the memorandum which he was good enough to prepare for me, but have in many instances used his very words. The parallel columns are his.

The constabulary soldier, thoroughly familiar with the topography of the country in which he operates; speaking the local dialect and acquainted with the persons most likely to be able and willing to furnish accurate information; familiar with the characteristics of his own people; able to live off the country and keep well, is under all ordinary circumstances a more efficient and vastly less expensive police officer than the American soldier, no matter how brave and energetic the latter may be. Furthermore, his activities are much less likely to arouse animosity.

Incidentally, the army is pretty consistently unwilling to take the field unless the constitutional guarantees are temporarily suspended, and it particularly objects to writs of habeas corpus. The suspension of such guarantees is obviously undesirable unless really very necessary.

Let us now consider some of the specific instances of alleged inefficiency of the constabulary in suppressing public disorder, cited by Blount.

On page 403 of his book he says, speaking of Governor Taft and disorder in the province of Albay which arose in 1902–1903 : —

"He did not want to order out the military again if he could help it, and this relegated him to his native municipal police and constabulary, experimental outfits of doubtful loyalty, and, at best, wholly inadequate, as it afterwards turned out, for the maintenance of public order and for affording to the peaceably inclined people that sort of security for life and property, and that protection against semi-political as well as unmitigated brigandage, which would comport with the dignity of this nation."

The facts as to these disorders are briefly as follows :—

In 1902 an outlaw in Tayabas Province who made his living by organizing political conspiracies and collecting contributions in the name of patriotism, who was known as José Roldan when operating in adjoining provinces, but had an alias in Tayabas, found his life made so uncomfortable by the constabulary of that province that he transferred his operations to Albay. There he affiliated himself with a few ex-Insurgent officers who had turned outlaws instead of surrendering, and with oath violators, and began the same kind of political operations which he had carried out in Tayabas, the principal feature of his work being the collection of "contributions."

The troubles in Albay were encouraged by wealthy Filipinos who saw in them a probable opportunity to acquire valuable hemp lands at bottom prices, for people dependent on their hemp fields, if prevented from working them, might in the end be forced to sell them. Roldan soon lost standing with his new organization because it was found that he was using for his personal benefit the money which he collected.

About this time one Simeon Ola joined his organization. Ola was a native of Albay, where he had been an Insurgent major under the command of the Tagálog general, Belarmino. His temporary rank had gone to his head, and he is reported to have shown considerable severity and hauteur in his treatment of his former neighbours in Guinobatan, to which place he had returned at the close of the insurrection. Meanwhile, a wealthy Chinese *mestizo* named Don Circilio Jaucian, on whom Ola, during his brief career as an Insurgent officer, had laid a heavy hand, had become *presidente* of the town.

Smarting under the indignities which he had suffered, Jaucian made it very uncomfortable for the former major, and in ways well understood in Malay countries brought it home to the latter that their positions had been reversed. Ola's house was mysteriously burned, and his life in Guinobatan was made so unbearable that he took to the hills.

Ola had held higher military rank than had any of his outlaw associates, and he became their dominating spirit. He had no grievance against the Americans, but took every opportunity to avenge himself on the *caciques* of Guinobatan, his native town.

Three assistant chiefs of constabulary, Garwood, Baker and Bandholtz, were successively sent to Albay to deal with this situation. Baker and Bandholtz were regular army officers. The latter ended the disturbances, employing first and last some twelve companies of Philippine scouts, armed, officered, paid, equipped and disciplined as are the regular soldiers of the United States army, and a similar number of constabulary soldiers. Eleven stations in the restricted field of operations of this outlaw were occupied by scouts. There were few armed conflicts in force between Ola's men and these troops. In fact, it was only with the greatest difficulty that this band, which from time to time dissolved into the population only to reappear again, could be located even by the native soldiers. It would have been impracticable successfully to use American troops for such work.

Referring to the statement made by Blount [1] that Vice-Governor Wright made a visit to Albay in 1903 in the interest "of the peace-at-any-price policy that the Manila Government was bent on," and the implication that he went there to conduct peace negotiations, General Bandholtz, who suppressed outlawry in Albay, has said that Vice-Governor Wright and Commissioner Pardo de Tavera came there at his request to look into conditions with reference to certain allegations which had been made.

Colonel Bandholtz and the then chief of constabulary, General Allen, were supported by the civil governor and the commission in their recommendations that no terms should be made with the outlaws. The following statement occurs in a letter from General Bandholtz dated September 21, 1903 : —

"No one is more anxious to terminate this business than I am, nevertheless I think it would be a mistake to offer any

[1] Blount, p. 425.

such inducements, and that more lasting benefits would result by hammering away as we have been doing."

And General Allen said in an indorsement to the Philippine Commission : —

". . . in my opinion the judgment of Colonel Bandholtz in matters connected with the pacification of Albay should receive favourable consideration. Halfway measures are always misinterpreted and used to the detriment of the Government among the ignorant followers of the outlaws."

These views prevailed.

Blount has claimed that the death rate in the Albay jail at this time was very excessive, and cites it as an instance of the result of American maladministration.

Assuming that his tabulation[1] of the dead who died in the Albay jail between May 30 and September, 1903, amounting to 120, is correct, the following statements should be made : —

Only recently has it been demonstrated that beri-beri is due to the use of polished rice, which was up to the time of this discovery regarded as far superior to unpolished rice as an article of food, and is still much better liked by the Filipinos than is the unpolished article. Many of these deaths were from beri-beri, and were due to a misguided effort to give the prisoners the best possible food.

Cholera was raging in the province of Albay throughout the period in question, and the people outside of the jail suffered no less than did those within it. The same is true of malarial infection. In other words, conditions inside the jail were quite similar to those then prevailing outside, except that the prisoners got polished rice which was given them with the best intentions in the world, and was by them considered a superior article of food.

With the present knowledge of the methods of dissemination of Asiatic cholera gained as a result of the

[1] Blount, p. 430.

American occupation of the Philippines, we should probably be able to exclude it from a jail under such circumstances, as the part played by "germ carriers" who show no outward manifestations of infection is now understood, but it was not then dreamed of. One of the greatest reforms effected by Americans in the Philippines is the sanitation of the jails and penitentiaries, and we cannot be fairly blamed for not knowing in 1903 what nobody then knew.

The troubles in Albay ended with the surrender of Ola on September 25, 1903. Blount gives the impression that he had a knowledge of them which was gained by personal observation. He arrived in the province in the middle of November, seven weeks after normal conditions had been reëstablished.

On October 5, 1903, General Bandholtz telegraphed with reference to the final surrender of Ola's band : —

"The towns are splitting themselves wide open celebrating pacification and Ramon Santos (later elected governor) is going to give a record-breaking fiesta at Ligao. Everybody invited. Scouts and Constabulary have done superb work."

Blount makes much of disorders in Samar and Leyte. Let us consider the facts.

In all countries feuds between highlanders and low-landers have been common. Although the inhabitants of the hills and those of the lowlands in the two islands under discussion are probably of identical blood and origin, they long since became separated in thought and feeling, and grew to be mutually antagonistic. The ignorant people of the interior have always been oppressed by their supposedly more highly civilized brethren living on or near the coast.

The killing of Otoy by the constabulary in 1911 marked the passing of the last of a series of mountain chiefs who had exercised a very powerful influence over the hill people and had claimed for themselves supernatural powers.

Manila hemp is the principal product upon which these mountaineers depend in bartering for cloth and other supplies. The cleaning of hemp involves very severe exertion, and when it is cleaned it must usually, in Samar, be carried to the seashore on the backs of the men who raise it. Under the most favourable circumstances, it may be transported thither in small *bancas* [1] down the streams.

The lowland people of Samar and Leyte had long been holding up the hill people when they brought in their hemp for sale in precisely the way that Filipinos in other islands are accustomed to hold up members of the non-Christian tribes. They played the part of middlemen, purchasing the hemp of the ignorant hill people at low prices and often reselling it, without giving it even a day's storage, at a very much higher figure. This system was carried so far that conditions became unbearable and finally resulted in so-called *pulájanism* which began in the year 1904.

The term *pulájan* is derived from a native word meaning "red" and was given to the mountain people because in their attacks upon the lowlanders they wore, as a distinguishing mark, red trousers or a dash of red colour elsewhere about their sparse clothing. They raided coast towns and did immense damage before they were finally brought under control. It should be remembered that these conditions were allowed to arise by a Filipino provincial governor, and by Filipino municipal officials. It is altogether probable that a good American governor would have prevented them, but as it was, neither their cause nor their importance were understood at the outset. The *pulájan* movement was directed primarily against Filipinos.

The first outbreak occurred on July 10, 1904, in the Gandara River valley where a settlement of the lowlanders was burned and some of its inhabitants were killed.

[1] Native dugouts.

Eventually disorder spread to many places on the coast, and one scout garrison of a single company was surprised and overwhelmed by superior numbers. Officers and men were massacred and their rifles taken.

In point of area Samar is the third island in the Philippines. In its interior are many rugged peaks and heavily forested mountains. It was here that a detachment of United States marines under the command of Major Waller, while attempting to cross the island, were lost for nearly two weeks, going without food for days and enduring terrible hardships.

At the time in question there were not five miles of road on the island passable for a vehicle, nor were there trails through the mountains over which horses could be ridden. The only interior lines of communication were a few footpaths over which the natives were accustomed to make their way from the mountains to the coast.

Troops have perhaps never attempted a campaign in a country more difficult than the interior of Samar. The traditional needle in the haystack would be easy to find compared with an outlaw, or band of outlaws, in such a rugged wilderness.

Upon the outbreak of trouble troops were hurried to Samar, and by December, 1904, according to Blount himself, there were some 1800 native soldiers on the island who were left free for active operations in the field by the garrisoning of various coast towns with sixteen companies of United States infantry.

If the nature of the feuds between the Samar lowlanders and highlanders had then been better understood, the ensuing troubles, which were more or less continuous for nearly two years, might perhaps have been avoided. As soon as it became evident that the situation was such as to demand the use of the army it was employed to supplement the operations of the constabulary.

About the time that trouble ended in Samar it began in Leyte. There was no real connection between the

Filipina Girls playing Basket-ball.

disorders in the two islands. No leader on either island is known to have communicated with any leader on the other; no fanatical follower ever left Samar for Leyte or Leyte for Samar so far as we are informed.

For convenience of administration the two islands were grouped in a single command after the army was requested to take over the handling of the disturbances there, in coöperation with the constabulary. The trouble ended in 1907 and both islands have remained quiet ever since. The same causes would again produce the same results now or at any time in the future, and they would be then, as in the past, the outcome of the oppression of the weak by the strong and without other political significance. Under a good government they should never recur.

Many circumstances which did not exist in 1902 and 1904 made it feasible to use the army in Samar and Leyte during 1905 and 1906. The high officers who had exercised such sweeping powers during the insurrection had meanwhile given way to other commanders. Indeed, a practically new Philippine army had come into existence. The policy of the insular government as to the treatment of individual Filipinos had been recognized and indorsed by Americans generally, but many of the objections to the use of the troops, including the heavy expense involved, still existed and I affirm without fear of successful contradiction that had it been possible to place in Samar and Leyte a number of constabulary soldiers equal to that of the scouts and American troops actually employed, disorder would have been terminated much more quickly and at very greatly less cost.

With the final breaking up of organized brigandage in 1905 law and order may be said to have been established throughout the islands. It has since been the business of the constabulary to maintain it. The value of the coöperation of the law-abiding portion of the population has been fully recognized. The newly appointed constabulary officer has impressed upon him the necessity of manifesting an interest in the people with whom he comes in contact; of cultivating the acquaintance of Filipinos of all social grades, and of assisting to settle their disagreements and harmonize their differences whenever possible. He is taught a native dialect.

The constabulary have to a high degree merited and secured the confidence and good-will of the people, whose rights they respect. There is a complete absence of the old arbitrary procedure followed by the *guardia civil* and as a result there are frequent requests from Filipino officials for additional detachments, while the removal of a company from a given community is almost invariably followed by vigorous protests. The power of human sympathy is very great, and as the attitude of constabulary officers and men is usually one of sympathy, conciliation and affection, that body has earned and deserved popularity.

The success of the constabulary in apprehending criminals has been both praiseworthy and noteworthy. The courage and efficiency which have often been displayed by its officers and men in hard-fought engagements with Moro outlaws or with organized bands of thieves and brigands have been beyond praise. Many of its officers have rendered invaluable service in bringing the people of the more unruly non-Christian tribes under governmental control, not only bravely and efficiently performing their duty as police officers, but assisting in trail construction or discharging, in effect, the duties of lieutenant-governors in very remote places which could be visited by the actual lieutenant-governors only infrequently. I later take occasion to mention the valuable work done by Lieutenant Case in the early days of Ifugao, and to dwell at length on the splendid service rendered there by Lieutenant Jeff D. Gallman, who was for many years lieutenant-governor of the subprovince while continuing to serve as a constabulary officer. Lieutenant Maimban at Quiangan, and Lieutenant Dosser at Mayoyao, have been and are most useful, though they do not hold official positions under the Mountain Province or receive any additional compensation for the special services which they render. Captain Guy O. Fort served most acceptably as governor of the province of Agusan during the interim between the resignation of Governor Lewis and the appointment of Governor Bryant and Lieutenants Atkins and Zapanta have also rendered valuable service as assistants to the provincial governor. Lieutenant Turnbull is now assistant to the governor of Nueva Vizcaya for work among the Ilongots on the Pacific coast of northern Luzón. Other constabulary officers, who have not been called upon for special service of this kind, have performed their ordinary duties in such a way as to demonstrate that they were actuated by the spirit of coöperation and have been of great help.

But the work of the constabulary has not been confined to police duty. They have been of the greatest assistance to the Director of Health in effectively maintaining quarantine, and making possible the isolation of victims of dangerous communicable diseases like cholera and smallpox, when inefficient municipal policemen have utterly failed to do their duty. They have given similar assistance to the Director of Agriculture in the maintenance of quarantine in connection with efforts to combat diseases of domestic animals. In great emergencies such as those presented by the recent eruption of Taal volcano, and the devastation caused by great typhoons, they have been quick to respond to the call of duty and have rendered efficient and heroic service. They assist internal revenue officers. Except in a few of the largest cities they are the firemen of the islands and by their effective work have repeatedly checked conflagrations, which are of frequent occurrence and tend to be very destructive in this country, where most of the houses are built of bamboo and nipa palm, and where roofs become dry as tinder during the long period when there is little or no rain. They have aided in combating pests of locusts, and, in short, have been ready to meet almost any kind of an emergency which has arisen.

The importance of having such a body of alert, industrious, disciplined, efficient men inspired by a high sense of duty, and physically so well developed that they can continue to perform that duty in the face of long-continued privations and hardships, is beyond dispute. The results which have been obtained by the Philippine constabulary have abundantly justified the policy which led to its organization.

Its task has been no sinecure. Eleven officers and one hundred ninety-seven enlisted men have been killed in action. Forty-eight officers and nine hundred ninety-one men have died of disease. Forty-six officers have been wounded in action. Seven hundred sixty-eight men have been discharged for disability. Seven thousand four hundred twenty-four firearms and 45,018 rounds of ammunition have been captured by, or surrendered to, the constabulary. Four thousand eight hundred sixty-two outlaws have been killed and 11,977 taken prisoners. Twelve thousand two hundred sixty-two stolen animals have been recovered.

There are many things which are not brought home to the reader by such statistics. The weary days and nights on tropical trails; the weakness and pain of dysentery; the freezing and the burning of pernicious malaria; the heavy weight of responsibility when one must act, in matters of life and death, with no superior to consult; the disappointment when carefully laid plans go wrong; the discouragement caused by indifference; the danger of infection with loathsome diseases; ingratitude; deadly peril; aching wounds; sudden death, and, worse yet, death after suffering long drawn out, when one meets one's end knowing that it is coming and that one's family will be left without means or resources, — these are some of the things that the officers and men of this gallant corps have faced unflinchingly.

The work of the constabulary and of the Philippine scouts has conclusively demonstrated the courage and efficiency of the Filipino as a soldier when well disciplined and well led.

The establishment and maintenance of order in the Philippines have afforded opportunity for some of the bravest deeds in the annals of any race, and the opportunity has been nobly met. The head-hunters of the Mountain Province, the Mohammedan Moros of Mindanao, Joló and Palawan, the bloody *pulájanes* of Samar and Leyte, the wily *tulisanes* of Luzón, all unrestrained by any regard for the rules of civilized warfare, have for twelve years matched their fanatical bravery against the gallantry of the khaki-clad Filipino soldiers. Time and again a single officer and a handful of men have taken chances that in almost any other land would have won them the Victoria cross, the legion of honor, or some similar decoration. Here their only reward has been the sense of duty well done.

The force known as the Philippine constabulary was organized for the purpose of establishing and maintaining order. It has established and is maintaining a condition of order never before equalled or approached in the history of the islands. The policy which led to its organization has been a thousand times justified.

CHAPTER XV

THE ADMINISTRATION OF JUSTICE

In no branch of the public administration have there been more numerous or more beneficial reforms than in the administration of justice. They have resulted in simplifying organization, in decreasing the possibility of corruption and partiality, and in diminishing the cost of litigation and the time which it requires.

For the benefit of those especially interested I give in the appendix the past and present organization of the courts.[1] The subject is too technical to interest the average layman.

The slender salaries paid to judges, the fact that in the majority of cases their appointment and promotion were due to influence and suggestion, their liability to be transferred from one court to another or from the Philippines to the Antilles, as frequently happened, and the further fact that the subordinate personnel of the courts was not a salaried one, caused the administration of justice in the Philippine Islands to be looked upon askance. There was a general belief, well founded in many instances, that lawsuits were won through influence or bribery. Clerks and the subordinate personnel of the courts were readily bribed. Indeed, they frequently demanded bribes from litigants, or from defendants in criminal cases, under promise to expedite the trials if paid to do so, or under threat to commit some injustice if payment was not forthcoming. For many years after the American occupation justices of the peace received no salaries and had to

[1] See p. 998.

look to fees for their compensation. This system worked wretchedly. The positions were only too often filled by very incompetent and unworthy men, who stimulated litigation in order to make more money. Now all justices of the peace receive reasonable salaries.

The paying of regular salaries and the furnishing of necessary offices and supplies have done much to improve the work of justice of the peace courts, which are now presided over by men who average far better than even their immediate predecessors.

Until they were put on a salary basis the work of the Filipino justices of the peace left much more to be desired than is lacking at present. In many instances they allowed gross brutalities, perpetrated by the rich on the poor, or by the strong on the weak, to go unpunished. The following case furnished me by an American teacher is typical of what has occurred only too often : —

"On another occasion, I met the brother of my house *muchacha*,[1] a boy about eight. He had a sort of protuberance on one side caused by broken ribs which had not been set. I questioned my *muchacha*. She said her step-father had kicked the child across the room some weeks before and broken his ribs. The next day, I took the child together with Señora Bayot, the wife of the Governor's secretary, before the local Justice of the Peace. Señora Bayot translated and the child told the same story as had his sister. The Justice of the Peace issued an order for the step-father to report to him on the next day. That night my *muchacha* told me that her step-father had threatened to kill the child if he did not tell the Justice that he got the hurt by falling out of an orange tree. The child did as ordered, and the step-father was dismissed. When I questioned the Justice of the Peace as to why he credited the second tale, he said the child was under oath then, and was not under oath in the first statements."

It was not deemed wise at the outset to appoint a Filipino judge for the city of Manila, as it was feared that there would be a lack of confidence in a Filipino who had occasion to decide cases involving large sums of money

[1] Female servant.

in which Americans or foreigners on the one hand and Filipinos on the other were interested ; but a few years after the establishment of the new judicial system Filipino judges had won such a reputation for justice and fairness as to gain the confidence of Americans and foreigners and the appointment of a Filipino judge for the court of the city of Manila did not arouse any opposition.

Filipino judges of courts of first instance seem usually to have been actuated by a desire to do full justice. The instances in which complaints have been made against them because of partiality to party or to race are few. Some of them have been justly criticised for tardiness in cleaning up their dockets, and it is undoubtedly true that their capacity for turning out work is on the average below that of their Americans associates.

The fact must not be forgotten that Americans are in the majority in the Supreme Court, which reviews the decisions of courts of first instance, and this undoubtedly exercises a restraining influence. It is not possible accurately to judge what would be the actions of a body of men now subject to such control if it did not exist. It is furthermore true that the Filipinos are more inclined to be suspicious of their own countrymen than of Americans, and there have been from time to time specific requests from them that judges in certain provinces be Americans.

Under the Spanish régime the fees paid by litigants were excessive and the use of stamped paper was compulsory. Its value ranged from twenty-five centavos to two pesos for a folio of two sheets according to the amount involved in the suit. Now there are fixed fees of $8 in civil suits, except in probate matters, where the fee is $12.

It was in the power of an unscrupulous litigant to make a lawsuit almost eternal. In matters involving an amount exceeding $250 it was lawful to institute proceedings in the action whereby the decision of the main issue was suspended pending decision of the proceedings, and as a decision was appealable to the *audiencia*, this was often done

UNIVERSITY HALL, MANILA.

by attorneys who had an interest in delaying the suit. By instituting one proceeding after another a suit could be indefinitely prolonged.

Another method of securing delay was to object to the judge. In case the judge denied the ground of the objection, a proceeding was instituted against him and the trial of the main issue was turned over to another judge; although the proceeding arising out of the objection did not suspend the trial of the main issue, when the time came to decide the latter the decision was withheld until the proceeding arising out of the objection was settled, and as this latter was one in connection with which other proceedings could be instituted which might delay the decision and consequently the decision of the main issue, there was no end to the matter.

To-day all this has been stopped by the procedure in court. The challenging of judges is not allowed, although they must refrain from the trial of any matter when they are disqualified in any way as regards it. Proceedings which suspend the trial of the main issue cannot be instituted. The procedure itself is more expeditious, the time allowances and formalities have been reduced, and all the long Spanish civil procedure regarding the presentation of evidence has been shortened. Suits are settled with a speediness previously unknown. In order to avoid delay on the part of judges in rendering decisions, an act has been passed prohibiting the payment of their salaries without a certificate that they have no matter which has been awaiting decision for more than three months.

Owing to the inquisitorial procedure which obtained under Spanish rule, the disposition of criminal cases was even slower than that of civil cases. The cause would be commenced, either *de officio*, by the judge who had a knowledge of the crime, or by the prosecuting attorney, or by virtue of private accusation on the part of the person aggrieved. The case once started, the investigations made during the period known as the *sumario* were conducted in

the absence of the accused. The latter had no hand in
the case, as it was thought that the reserve and secrecy
of the procedure ought not to be violated to the end that
the accused might not frustrate the evidence of the prosecution by preparing his defence. Owing many times
to the inactivity of the judge or of the prosecuting attorney, to the great amount of work which weighed down
the courts — for actions were begun when there was
knowledge of the commission of the crime, although the
perpetrators were not known — and by the manipulations
at other times of the private accuser to whose interest
it was to harm the accused by delaying the *sumario*, this
period was often made to extend over years and years.
Meanwhile the defendant was confined in prison, as no
bail was allowed in any case in which the penalty was that
of *presidio correccional* (from six months and one day to
six years' imprisonment) or greater. In addition to this
the circumstance that all criminal causes in the islands
had to be sent for review to the proper *audiencia*, caused
a large accumulation of old cases in these higher courts,
and this alone made their disposition a matter of some
years.

To-day the procedure is rapid. Information having
been brought against the defendant, the trial is had in
the same term or at most during the next term of court.
Sometimes the trial is suspended owing to the non-appear-
ance of witnesses, but it can be said that cases are rare
where causes are pending in the docket of the court for
a longer period than two terms. Causes appealed to the
Supreme Court are disposed of promptly, and as a general
rule it does not take over six months to get a decision.

Defendants in criminal cases have now been granted
by the Philippine Bill certain fundamentally important
rights which they did not formerly enjoy; namely, to
appear and defend in person or by counsel at every stage
of the proceedings; to be informed of the nature and
cause of the accusation; to testify as witnesses in their

own behalf; to be exempt from testifying against themselves; to be confronted at the trial by, and to cross-examine, the witnesses against them; to have compulsory process issue for obtaining witnesses in their own favour; to have speedy and public trials; to be admitted to bail with sufficient sureties in all cases, except for capital offences. None of these rights were enjoyed under the procedure in effect during the Spanish régime. A man was prosecuted without being notified of the charges against him, and he was only made aware of the case against him after the *sumario*. When all of the evidence of the prosecution had been taken the accused was heard in his own defence. He was compelled to testify, and was subjected to a very inquisitorial examination, including questions which incriminated him. Although he had the right to compel witnesses for the prosecution to ratify over their signatures the evidence against him given during the *sumario*, as the defence of the majority of the accused was in the hands of attorneys *de officio* they nearly always renounced this privilege of the defendant, and, as has already been said, bail was not admitted in any grave offence during the trial.

No sentence of acquittal in a criminal case can now be appealed from by the government. Under the Spanish system sentences of acquittal of courts of first instance had to be referred for review to the proper *audiencia* and the fiscal of the latter could appeal from a sentence of acquittal by it.

The Philippine Bill grants to the inhabitants of the islands other important individual rights which they did not formerly possess.

The Spanish constitution was not in force here, and although the Penal Code contained provisions for punishing, in a way, officials who violated certain rights granted by the Spanish constitution, citizens had no expeditious method of securing their punishment. Now the Code of Civil Procedure grants them certain special remedies by which their

rights can be made good.   To illustrate : Under the Spanish
régime the only remedy for a man illegally detained was to
bring a criminal action against the person illegally detain-
ing him.   He did not have the remedy of the writ of habeas
corpus nor the writ of prohibition against an official who
attempted to make him the victim of some unlawful act.
His only remedy was to bring a criminal action against
such official, or to sue him for damages.   He could not
compel public officials to perform their ministerial duties
by mandamus proceedings.

The individual rights conferred by the Philippine Bill,
and the special remedies granted by the Code of Civil
Procedure, assure to the inhabitants of the islands liberties and privileges entirely unknown to them during
the days of Spanish sovereignty, and these liberties and
privileges are adequately safeguarded.

Two things still greatly complicate the administration
of justice in the Philippines.

The first is the dense ignorance of the people of the
working class who for the most part have failed to learn
of their new rights, and even if they know them are afraid
to attempt to assert them in opposition to the will of the
caciques, whose power for evil they know only too well.

The other is the unreliability of many witnesses and
their shocking readiness to perjure themselves.   It is always possible to manufacture testimony at small expense.
While the criminal libel suit brought against certain
members of the staff of the newspaper *El Renacimiento,*
which libelled me, was in progress the judge showed
me the opinion of the two Filipino assessors [1] in one of
the cases and told me that it was written by an attorney
for the defence.   I could not believe this, but a few
days later an assessor in another of the cases called at
my house, bringing a draft of the opinion of himself
and his associate which he sought to submit to me for

[1] Men appointed to assist the judge in deciding questions of fact.
Their decision is not binding on him.

criticism or modification, saying that I knew much more about the case than they did! He was nonplussed at my refusal to read the document, and left saying "*acqui tiene V. nuevo servidor.*" [1] Had I redrafted the opinion, as I might have done, my "new servant" would have called later for a *quid pro quo*.

Some of the Filipino judges of first instance have proved weak in matters affecting the integrity of public domain and the protection of the public forests, but on the whole these officers have done rather surprisingly well. It must be remembered that the best men in the islands have now been appointed, and that another generation must come on before there will be available any considerable number of new candidates who are up to the standard of the present appointees.

[1] Here [*i.e.* in me] you have a new servant.

CHAPTER XVI

HEALTH CONDITIONS

I HAD abundant opportunity to observe health conditions in the Philippines during the Spanish régime and they were shocking in the extreme. There were no provisions for the sanitary disposal of human waste even in Manila. If one had occasion to be out on foot at night, it was wise to keep in the middle of the street and still wiser to carry a raised umbrella.

Immediately after the American occupation some five hundred barrels of caked excrement were taken from a single tower in one of the old Manila monasteries. The moat around the city wall, and the *esteros,* or tidal creeks, reeked with filth, and the smells which assailed one's nostrils, especially at night, were disgusting.

Distilled water was not to be had for drinking purposes. The city water supply came from the Mariquina River, and some fifteen thousand Filipinos lived on or near the banks of that stream above the intake. The water was often so thick with sediment that one could not see through a glass of it, and it was out of the question to attempt to get it boiled unless one had facilities of one's own.

Conditions in the provinces were proportionately worse. As a rule, there was no evidence of any effort to put provincial towns into decent sanitary conditions. I must, however, note one striking exception. Brigadier General Juan Arolas, long the governor of Joló, had a thorough knowledge of modern sanitary methods and a keen appreciation of the benefits derivable from their application. When he was sent to Joló, practically in banishment, the town was a plague spot to which were assigned Spaniards whose early demise would have been

looked upon with favour by those in power. He converted it into a healthy place the death rate of which
compared favourably with that of European cities, thereby
demonstrating conclusively what could be done even
under very unfavourable conditions. No troops in the
islands were kept in anything like such physical condition
as were the regiments assigned to him, and he bore a
lasting grudge against any one inconsiderate enough to
die in Joló.

Everywhere I saw people dying of curable ailments.
Malaria was prevalent in many regions in which it was
impossible to secure good quinine. The stuff on sale
usually consisted largely of cornstarch, or plaster of Paris.
Fortunately we had brought with us from the United
States a great quantity of quinine and we made friends
with the Filipinos in many a town by giving this drug
gratis to their sick.

Smallpox was generally regarded as a necessary ailment
of childhood. It was a common thing to see children
covered with the eruption of this disease watching, or
joining in, the play of groups of healthy little ones.

The clothing of people who had died of smallpox was
handed on to other members of the family, sometimes
without even being washed. The victims of the disease
often immersed themselves in cold water when their fever
was high, and paid the penalty for their ignorance with
their lives.

The average Spaniard was a firm believer in the noxiousness of night air, which he said produced *paludismo*.[1]
Most Filipinos were afraid of an imaginary spirit, devil
or mythical creature known as *asuáng*, and closed their
windows and doors after dark as a protection against it.
Thus it came about that in a country where fresh air is
especially necessary at night no one got it.

Tuberculosis was dreadfully common, and its victims
were conveying it to others without let or hindrance.

[1] Malaria.

A distressingly large percentage of native-born infants died before reaching one year of age on account of infection at birth, insufficient clothing, or improper food. I have many times seen a native mother thrust boiled rice into the mouth of a child only a few days old, and I have seen babies taught to smoke tobacco before they could walk.

Before our party left the islands in 1888, cholera had broken out at a remote and isolated place. A little later it spead over a considerable part of the archipelago. On my return in 1890 I heard the most shocking stories of what had occurred. Victims of this disease were regarded with such fear and horror by their friends that they were not infrequently carried out while in a state of coma, and buried alive. It became necessary to issue orders to have shelters prepared in cemeteries under which bodies were required to be deposited and left for a certain number of hours before burial, in order to prevent this result.

In Siquijor an unfortunate, carried to the cemetery after he had lost consciousness, came to himself, crawled out from under a mass of corpses which had been piled on top of him, got up and walked home. When he entered his house, his assembled friends and relatives vacated it through the windows, believing him to be his own ghost. They did not return until morning, when they found him dead on the floor.

I heard a well-authenticated story of a case in which all the members of a family died except a creeping infant who subsisted for some time by sucking a breeding sow which was being kept in the kitchen.

During the great cholera epidemic in 1882 it is said that the approaches to the Manila cemeteries were blocked with vehicles of every description loaded with corpses, and that the stench from unburied bodies in the San Lazaro district was so dreadful that one could hardly go through it.

Beri-beri was common among the occupants of jails,

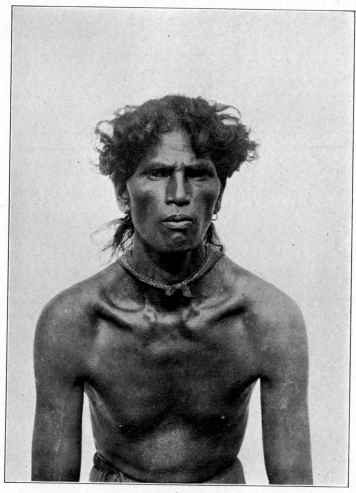

BAKÍDAN.

This Kalinga chief saved the lives of Colonel Blas Villamor, Mr. Samuel E.
Kane, and the author during the first trip ever made through the Kalinga
country by outsiders.

lighthouses and other government institutions, as well as in certain garrisoned towns like Balabac.

In 1892 I found the wife of a very dear Spanish friend dying from an ailment which in the United States could have been promptly and certainly remedied by a surgical operation. I begged him to take her to Manila, telling him of the ease with which any fairly good surgeon would relieve her, and promising to interest myself in her case on my arrival there. To my utter amazement I found that there was not a surgeon in the Philippine Islands who would venture to open the human abdomen. The one man who had sometimes done this in Spain stated that it would be impossible for him to undertake it in Manila, on account of the lack of a suitable operating room, of instruments and of the necessary anæsthetist and other professional assistants. In fact, at the time of the American occupation there was not a modern operating room, much less a modern hospital, in the Philippines. Thousands upon thousands of people were perishing needlessly every year for the lack of surgical intervention. A common procedure in dealing with wounds was to cover them with poultices of chewed tobacco, ashes, and leaves.

In many provinces the people were without medical assistance of any sort, and fell into the hands of native quacks who were little, if at all, better than witch doctors.

The most fantastic views were entertained relative to the causation of disease. In some towns it was vigorously asserted that after a peculiar looking black dog ran down the street cholera appeared. In other places cholera was generally ascribed to the poisoning of wells by Spaniards or foreigners.

Cemeteries were not infrequently situated in the very midst of towns, or near the local supplies of drinking water. Conditions within their walls were often shocking from an æsthetic view point. As the area available for burials was limited, and the graves were usually unmarked, parts of decomposed bodies were constantly being dug up. It was the custom to throw such remains about the foot of the cross at the centre of the cemetery.

Military sanitation was also very bad. I was at Zamboanga when the wreck of General Weyler's expedition to Lake Lanoa began to return. There had been no adequate provision for the medical care of the force in the field, and the condition of many of the soldiers was pitiable in the extreme. Disabled men were brought in by the shipload, and the hospitals at Zamboanga, Isabela de Basilan and Joló were soon filled to overflowing.

The lack of adequate sanitary measures was equally in evidence in dealing with cattle disease. Rinderpest, a highly contagious and very destructive disease of horned cattle, was introduced in 1888 and spread like fire in prairie grass. No real effort was made to check it prior to the American occupation, and it caused enormous losses, both directly by killing large numbers of beef cattle and indirectly by depriving farmers of draft animals.

When I first visited the islands every member of our party fell ill within a few weeks. All of us suffered intensely from tropical ulcers. Two had malaria; one had dysentery; one, acute inflammation of the liver, possibly of amœbic origin; and so on to the end of the chapter. I myself got so loaded up with malaria in Mindoro that it took me fifteen years to get rid of it.

Fortunately the American army of occupation brought with it numerous competent physicians and surgeons, and abundant hospital equipment and supplies, for the soldiers promptly contracted about all the different ailments to be acquired in the islands.

When I arrived in Manila on the 5th of March, 1899, I found that a great army hospital, called the "First Reserve," had been established in the old rice market. There was another sizable one on the Bagumbayan drive. A third occupied a large building belonging to French sisters of charity which was ordinarily used for school purposes.

In immediate connection with the First Reserve Hospital was a tent hospital where sick and wounded Insurgents were being given the best of care.

Field hospitals were promptly established as the troops moved out from Manila, and in connection with many of these Filipinos were given much needed medical and surgical help. The recipients of such kindly treatment were, however, prohibited by Insurgent officers from telling others of their experiences lest the hatred of Americans diminish as a result.

Smallpox had broken out among the Spanish soldiers in the walled city and was spreading badly when my friend, Major Frank S. Bourns of the army medical corps, was given the task of eradicating it, which he promptly accomplished. A little later the use of the Santa Ana church as a smallpox hospital was authorized, and sick Filipinos were carefully tended there.

The army promptly set about cleaning up Manila and waging war upon the more serious ailments which threatened the health of the soldiers and that of the public. The work was at the outset put under the direction of Major Edie, a very capable and efficient medical officer. Subsequently it was turned over to Major Bourns, who, on account of his intimate knowledge of Spanish, and his wide acquaintance with the Filipinos, was able to carry out many much-needed reforms, and in doing so aroused a minimum of public antagonism.

Upon the establishment of civil government Governor Taft was very desirous of retaining Major Bourns's services, but this did not prove practicable, as he desired to give up government work and engage in private business.

There was promptly created an efficient board of health made up of men of recognized ability and large practical experience. Its chairman was Major Louis M. Maus, commissioner of public health. The other members were Mr. H. D. Osgood, sanitary engineer; Dr. Franklin H. Meacham, chief sanitary inspector; Dr.

Paul C. Freer, superintendent of government laboratories; and Dr. Manuel Gomez, secretary.

This board was promptly put upon its mettle. It had inherited from the army an incipient epidemic of bubonic plague in Manila, and the disease soon spread to Cavite and also to Cebú, then the second port of the Philippines in commercial importance. It also appeared in several provincial towns near Cavite. An effective campaign against it, inaugurated at this time, was never abandoned until it was completely eradicated in 1906,—a noteworthy result to achieve in a country like the Philippines.

On March 21, 1902, I was advised that two patients at San Juan de Dios hospital were developing symptoms of Asiatic cholera, and on the following day a positive laboratory diagnosis was made. Other cases followed in quick succession, and we soon found ourselves facing a virulent epidemic of this highly dangerous disease. At the outset the mortality was practically 100 per cent. Unfortunately, there was no one connected with the medical service of the islands who had had practical experience in dealing with cholera, and we had to get this as we went along.

At the time of the outbreak, Governor Taft was in the United States, Acting Governor Wright was in Leyte, the secretary of finance and justice was in Japan, and there were present in Manila only the secretary of public instruction and the secretary of the interior. As the executive head of the government was absent, and there was no quorum of the legislative body, I of necessity arrogated to myself powers which I did not lawfully possess, appointing employees and incurring expenses without the usual formalities.

On the morning of March 22 I informed General Chaffee that four cases of cholera had occurred in Manila, and requested that an adequate military force be despatched to the valley of the Mariquina River to protect the city water supply from possible contamination.

This request was promptly acceded to, and the guard thereafter maintained proved adequate to prevent infection of the city water, although there are three towns on the river above the intake, and it was the custom of their people to bathe and wash their clothing in this stream. Many of the filthy surface wells of the city were filled as rapidly as possible, and those that could not be filled were closed.

The people, entirely unaccustomed as they were to any sanitary restrictions, believing that the disease was not cholera, and firm in their conviction that they had a right to do whatever they liked so long as they kept on their own premises, bitterly resented the burning or disinfection of their houses and effects, and the restriction of their liberty to go and come as they pleased, and in spite of the fact that the number of cases was kept down in a manner never before dreamed of at Manila, there arose an increasingly bitter feeling of hostility toward the work of the board of health. In fact, the very success of the campaign proved an obstacle, and we were assured that the disease could not be cholera, as, if it were, there would be a thousand deaths a day!

An educational campaign was immediately begun, and simple directions for avoiding infection were published and scattered broadcast. Distilled water was furnished gratis to all who would drink it, stations for its distribution being established through the city and supplemented by large water wagons driven through the streets. The sale of foods likely to convey the disease was prohibited. Large numbers of emergency sanitary inspectors were immediately appointed, and every effort was made to detect all cases as soon as possible. A land quarantine was established around the city, to protect the provinces.

In anticipation of a possible extensive outbreak of contagious disease a detention camp capable of accommodating some twenty-five hundred people had been established previously on the San Lazaro grounds, and to this place were taken the cholera "contacts." A cholera hospital was opened near this camp, and the stricken were removed to it from their homes as speedily as possible, the buildings which they had occupied being thoroughly disinfected, or burned if disinfection was impracticable.

The bodies of the dead were at the outset either buried in hermetically sealed coffins or cremated. When the detention camp and hospital at San Lazaro threatened to become crowded, a second camp and hospital were established at Santa Mesa. At this latter place both "contacts" and the sick were obliged to live in tents.

The Spanish residents were allowed to establish a private cholera hospital in a large and well-ventilated *convento* on Calle Herran. As the number of sick Spaniards was nothing like sufficient to fill this building, they were asked to turn over the unoccupied space in it to the board of health, which they most generously did.

In response to popular clamour a hospital under strictly Filipino management was opened in a nipa building in Tondo. Interest in it soon flagged, and the government found itself with this institution on its hands.

The epidemic came soon after the close of a long-continued war, and there were at that time in Manila not a few evil-intentioned persons, both foreign and native, who welcomed every opportunity to make trouble. The difficulties arising from the claim advanced by a number of reputable but ignorant medical men that the disease was not cholera at all were sufficiently great. They were enormously increased by false and malicious stories to the effect that "contacts" were killed at the detention camp; that patients on arrival at the cholera hospital were given a drink of poisoned *vino* [1] and instantly dropped dead; that the distilled water distributed free of charge was poisoned, and that the Americans were poisoning the wells.

---

[1] A strong alcoholic drink commonly made by diluting low-grade alcohol with water and flavouring it.

The necessary use of strychnine as a heart stimulant at the cholera hospital was made the basis for a story that the sick were being poisoned with this drug.

These silly tales were widely circulated and quite generally believed, and as a result of the fear thus engendered, and of the desire on the part of relatives and neighbours of stricken persons to escape disinfection and quarantine, strong efforts were often made to conceal the sick and the dead, and when this was not possible the "contacts" usually ran away. There were not wanting instances of the driving of cholera victims into the streets.

In spite of the generally hostile attitude of the public and some grave mistakes in policy, the measures adopted sufficed at the outset to hold the disease in check to an extent which surprised even the health officers themselves.

On May 15 there began a rapid and quite steady decline in the number of cases.

In June, however, it increased. During July it grew steadily larger, and on the 25th of that month there were ninety-one cases, the largest number which has ever occurred in Manila on any day since the American occupation.

Throughout the early months of the epidemic Major Maus had laboured unceasingly to check it, displaying an energy and an indifference to fatigue and personal discomfort which were highly commendable. The long-continued strain ultimately began to tell on him severely. On May 17 orders were received from the Adjutant-General's Office providing for his relief on or about July 30, and stating that Major E. C. Carter, of the United States Army Medical Corps, would be available for detail as commissioner of public health on that date, if his services were desired. Arrangements were accordingly made to have Major Carter proceed to the Philippines. Major Maus's resignation was accepted, effective July 31. Dr. Frank S. Bourns was urged to take temporary charge of the situation, and consented to do so.

On the 8th of August Major Carter arrived and announced his readiness to assume his duties, but it was suggested to him that he ought first to have some time to familiarize himself with them, and Dr. Bourns was left free to carry out the special work for which he had been appointed.

This he did with promptness and despatch, the number of cases for August being but seven hundred twenty as against thirteen hundred sixty-eight for the previous month. On the 8th of September, having brought the disease under control at Manila, he insisted on resigning in order to attend to his private affairs, which were suffering from neglect, and his resignation was reluctantly accepted.

Dr. Bourns's remarkable success in dealing with a very difficult situation was largely due to his ability to devise measures which, while thoroughly effective, were less irritating to the public than were those which had been previously employed.

The policy which he had inaugurated was followed by his successor with the result that the cases fell to two hundred seventy-five in September and eighty-eight in October. In November there was a slight recrudescence, but the disease did not again threaten to escape control and in February practically disappeared, there being but two cases during the entire month.

The return of hot, damp weather again produced a slight recrudescence, and scattering cases continued to occur until March, when the epidemic of 1902–1904 ended in Manila.

In view of the conditions which then prevailed and of the extreme risk of a general infection of the city water supply, which, had it occurred, would doubtless have resulted in the death of a third of the population, this is a record of which the Bureau of Health may well be proud.

The effort to prevent the spread of infection by maintaining a land quarantine around Manila proved entirely

In Hostile Country.

Colonel Villamor and the author at Bakidan's place in the Kalinga country. The four chiefs were not as yet ready to lay down their shields or head-axes.

ineffective.   The disease promptly appeared in the provinces where the campaign against it was from the outset in charge of newly appointed Filipino presidents of provincial boards of health, aided, when practicable, by medical inspectors from Manila.

Before it was finally checked in Manila there were 5581 cases with 4386 deaths; while in the provinces, in many of which it necessarily long ran its course practically unhindered, there were 160,671 cases, with 105,075 deaths.

On the 27th of April, 1904, the Board of Health passed the following resolutions : —

" Whereas cases of Asiatic cholera have occurred in but three provincial towns of the Philippine Islands since February 8, 1904; and

" Whereas only one case of Asiatic cholera has been reported as occurring any place in the Philippine Islands since March 8, 1904; and

" Whereas the city of Manila was declared on March 23 to be free from the infection of Asiatic cholera; On motion

" Resolved, That the islands composing the Philippine Archipelago are, and are hereby declared to be, free from the infection of Asiatic cholera; and

" Be it further resolved, That the Commissioner of Public Health be directed to send a copy of these resolutions to the honourable the Secretary of the Interior, the Municipal Board, the United States Marine-Hospital Service, and the Collector of Customs."

As a matter of fact, however, it later proved that cholera was endemic in certain swampy regions near Manila, and in 1905 we found ourselves with a new epidemic on our hands.

At the end of the second week, beginning August 23, there had been one hundred thirty-seven cases, as compared with one hundred twenty-five for the same period during the epidemic of 1902–1904.

However, the conditions for combating cholera were now far more favourable than in 1902. Major E. C. Carter had at his own request been relieved from duty as commissioner of public health, and Dr. Victor G. Heiser, passed assistant surgeon of the United States public health and marine hospital service, had been appointed to succeed him on April 5, 1905. Dr. Heiser was a highly trained officer of one of the most efficient services which has ever been organized for the combating of contagious and infectious diseases.

He had under him in the city of Manila a small but thoroughly trained body of twenty-four medical inspectors, of whom nineteen were Americans and five Filipinos. Profiting by his previous experience and that of his predecessors in the Philippine service, he inaugurated a campaign which practically terminated the epidemic in Manila on February 21, 1906,[1] with a total of two hundred eighty-three cases and two hundred forty-three deaths.

This brief and decisive campaign reflects the greatest credit on all concerned with it.

The board of health had one great advantage in the fact that the San Lazaro contagious disease hospital had been completed. This building, with its cool wards and attractive surroundings, made it possible to give cholera victims the best of care.

There was at the outset little or no fear of this hospital, but apparently this condition of things was not satisfactory to that small but dangerous element of the Manila public which from the time of the American occupation has never let pass any opportunity to make trouble. As usual, the medium of attack was the local press. *Soberania Nacional* published a most extraordinary article painting in vivid colours the alleged horrors of the San Lazaro Hospital, and stating among other things that the naked bodies of the dead, tagged and with their feet tied together, lay about the entrance of that institution. A more false statement was never published.

Within twenty-four hours after its appearance terror

[1] There was one stray case in March.

reigned among the lower classes, and living and dead cholera victims were being smuggled out of the city to neighbouring towns.

Feeling that the vicious attitude of a certain section of the press had cost lives enough, I sent the editor of this paper a courteous invitation to call at my office. He made no response. I then wrote him, demanding a retraction, and sending him a correct statement to publish.[1]

He was at first disposed to argue the matter, but finding that I meant business published the article which I sent to him and made the following retraction : —

[1] "To THE EDITOR OF EL SOBERANÍA NACIONAL, MANILA, P.I.

"SIR: In your issue of the 7th of July there appeared a paragraph embodying a shameful libel of the administration of the San Lazaro Hospital, which reads as follows :

"'*Un cuadro verdaderamente aterrador es el que presenta el patio del Hospital de San Lazaro. Los fallecidos por la enfermedad del colera, son expuestos desnudos en el atrio de dicho Hospital con un cartel atado en los pies con la inscripción de sus respectivos nombres.*'

"This statement was so grossly and ridiculously false and at the same time so extremely harmful in its effect as to bring you fairly and squarely within the reach of the law.

"Yesterday morning I sent you a courteous letter requesting you to come to my office, purposing to discuss the affair with you in a friendly manner, and hoping to find that the statement referred to had been prepared by some irresponsible subordinate and published through oversight.

"As, however, you have neither acceded to my request for a conference nor had the courtesy to reply to my letter, I now have the honour to forward you herewith a communication which embodies a reply to the false statement above referred to and at the same time conveys information as to what is actually being done at the San Lazaro Hospital. I request that you give this letter immediate publicity through your paper, and in the editorial columns or elsewhere in some conspicuous place retract immediately and fully the libellous statement relative to the exposure of the dead, above referred to.

"Kindly advise me of your intention in the matter. The bearer of this communication has instructions to wait for your reply. I shall interpret failure to hear from you by return messenger as refusal to retract this slander and to publish the enclosed communication, and shall act accordingly.

"Very respectfully,
"DEAN C. WORCESTER,
"*Secretary of the Interior.*"

"We are exceedingly glad to affirm in the honour of truth and justice, that the news given by us on the seventh instant under the title 'Painful Scenes,' and 'Naked Dead,' is absolutely absurd, false and unreasonable.

"We have investigated the truth of the said notice, and can affirm to our readers that it is entirely inaccurate, as in the court-yard of the said hospital the naked dead that we have spoken of are not now exposed, nor have they ever been so exposed.

"The truth is above all things, and to rectify a baseless piece of news should not be a doubtful action on the part of the person who gave the news, but rather something in his favour that the public should appreciate it at its full value.

"To conclude, we must record our gratitude to the Secretary of the Interior, the Hon. Dean C. Worcester, for the investigations made in the premises with the purpose of ascertaining the truth of the alleged facts, and for the courteous way in which he received us this morning when interviewed by one of our reporters."

In the provinces the results of the campaign against cholera were far less satisfactory than in Manila as was to be anticipated, owing to lack of adequate personnel, but the cases, which numbered 34,238 and deaths which numbered 22,938, were far fewer than during the previous epidemic.

I shall not attempt here to trace the course of the subsequent epidemics which have occurred from time to time, but shall content myself with giving the deaths by years. In 1908, they numbered 18,811; in 1909, 7306; in 1910, 6940; in 1911, 203. In 1912, there were none, and thus far in 1913 there have been none.[1]

The superstitious practices which were formerly employed by the Filipinos to combat this scourge have given way to simple and inexpensive hygienic measures, and we can safely count on sufficient coöperation from the people to make an effective campaign possible when it next appears.

Never shall I forget the strain of the early days of the first epidemic. Two of my best men, Dr. Meacham and

[1] Just before I left Manila in October, 1913, cholera reappeared there.

Mr. Mudge, literally worked themselves to death, remaining on duty when they knew that they were in imminent danger, and in the end laying down their lives willingly for an alien and hostile people. Such things make one proud of being an American.

At times the situation was not devoid of amusing features. I had occasion to visit one of the northern provinces, where the epidemic was especially severe, in an effort to calm the panic-stricken populace. I stayed with the governor, a very intelligent Filipino. For obvious reasons I investigated his domestic arrangements, finding that he was boiling drinking water, thoroughly cooking all food, and taking all usual and necessary precautions to prevent infection.

On returning to his house the first evening, after a short absence, I found the grounds decorated with lighted Japanese lanterns. Supposing that the proverbial Filipino hospitality had risen above even such untoward circumstances as those which then existed, I asked the governor what the entertainment was to be. In evident perplexity he replied that he had not planned to have any entertainment, and on my inquiring what the lanterns were for, said he had heard that they were good to keep away cholera germs !

I have referred to the fact that the civil government inherited a fairly well developed epidemic of bubonic plague. In 1901 this disease caused four hundred twenty-seven deaths, in 1902 it caused ten only, but the demands made on the sanitary force by the cholera epidemic which began in that year rendered it impossible to give to plague the attention which it otherwise would have had, with the result that in 1903 we had one hundred seventy-four deaths. In 1904 there were seventy-eight; in 1905, forty-three; in 1906, seven; in 1907, none; and from 1907 until 1912, none. In the latter year the disease was reintroduced.

Rats become infected with it, and fleas transmit it from them to human beings. It was probably brought in by pestiferous rodents hidden inside packages of vegetables, as it appeared in a district where crates of vegetables are opened in large numbers, and did not appear in the vicinity of the piers, although shore rats are abundant there, and if diseased rodents had landed from shipping, would promptly have become infected, — a thing which did not occur.

At about the same time plague also appeared at Iloilo, where it was eradicated with a total of nine deaths. At Manila there have been up to the present time [1] fifty-nine deaths, and scattering cases continue to occur at considerable intervals.

Had plague not been promptly and effectively combated, it would unquestionably have spread rapidly, causing untold misery and heavy property losses.

As I have previously stated, at the time of the American occupation smallpox was by many people regarded as an almost inevitable ailment of childhood. It proved necessary to secure the passage of legislation forbidding the inoculation of human beings with it to prevent misguided Filipinos from deliberately communicating it to their children, not because they did not dearly love them, but because they regarded infection with it as a calamity sure to come sooner or later, and desired to have it over with once for all.

We have performed more than ten million vaccinations, with the result that the annual deaths from this disease have decreased from forty thousand at the outset to seven hundred for the year just ended. There is now less smallpox in Manila than in Washington.

In the six provinces nearest Manila it was killing, on the average, six thousand persons annually. For a year after we finished vaccinating the inhabitants of these provinces it did not cause a death among them ; nor has it since caused such a death except among new-born children or newly arrived unvaccinated persons.

[1] Sept. 15, 1913.

These extraordinary results have been achieved without the loss of a life or a limb so far as we know. The vaccine used was prepared by our own Bureau of Science with extraordinary care, and has proved to be remarkably pure and active.

We at first endeavoured to have vaccinations performed by local Filipino health officers, but, after spending large sums without obtaining satisfactory results, gave up this plan and substituted therefor a method of procedure by which the work was carried on under the very immediate supervision of the director of health. We then made substantial progress. However, under the law as it at present stands, succeeding annual vaccination, intended to insure the immunization of children soon after they are born and of unvaccinated persons who may come into a given territory, are intrusted to the local Filipino authorities, with the result that in very many cases they are not attended to. We get elaborate returns showing the number of persons vaccinated. Then comes an outbreak of smallpox, and on investigation we learn that the vaccinations so fully reported were made on paper only ! In other words, the continuance of this work, of such vital importance to the Filipino people, is still directly dependent upon continued control by American health officers.

Another great problem now in a fair way to final solution is the eradication of leprosy. At the outset we were told by the church authorities that there were thirty thousand lepers in the islands. In 1905 we began to isolate and care for all supposed victims of this disease, only to find that many outcasts believed to be suffering from it were really afflicted with curable ailments. We were able to restore a very large number of them to society, to their great joy and that of their friends.

A few hundreds of true lepers were being humanely cared for in Manila and elsewhere. Many others had been driven out of the towns into forests or waste places on the larger islands, where they were perishing miserably from fever and other diseases. Still others had been isolated on sand quays, where they were in danger of dying from thirst during the dry season. Not a few wandered through the towns at will, spreading the disease broadcast.

All known lepers are now cared for at Culion, a healthful, sanitary town with good streets, excellent water and sewer systems, many modern concrete buildings and a first-class hospital.

They are not confined to the limits of the town, but wander at will, except that they are excluded from the immediate vicinity of the houses of the officers and employees of the colony.

They may have their little farms, and raise pigs, chickens, vegetables, etc., if they wish. They may, and do, float about over the waters of the neighbouring bay in boats or on rafts, and fish to their hearts' content. They are well fed and well cared for, and their physical condition improves to a marked degree promptly after their arrival at the colony. The only hardship which they suffer is that necessarily involved in separation from their relatives and friends, and this is mitigated by occasional visits which the latter may make them.

Since we began to isolate lepers, their number has decreased to approximately three thousand, and with a continuance of the present policy the disease should soon disappear from the Philippines.

During the period immediately subsequent to the American occupation, amœbic dysentery wrought sad havoc both among our soldiers and among civil government officers and employees. Four of my own family of five had it, and one had it twice, in spite of the fact that we took all known precautions; and the experience of my family was by no means exceptional. This disease then annually cost the lives of a large number of American men and women, and a considerable additional number went home invalids for life as a result of infection

TRAVEL UNDER DIFFICULTIES.

One of our bamboo rafts, loaded with baggage, on the Mabáca River.

with it. We seemed to hear almost daily of some new case.

Careful scientific investigation carried on at the bureau of science taught us the best methods of combating this type of dysentery, and the proper disposal of human feces, the regulation of methods used in fertilizing vegetables, improvement in supplies of drinking water, and other simple, hygienic measures have reduced the deaths from it among Americans to an almost negligible minimum. Such cases as occur are almost without exception detected early, and readily yield to treatment.

The belief that Filipinos do not suffer from this disease has proved to be without foundation. It kills thousands of them every year. Those who are willing to adopt the simple precautions which experience has shown to be necessary may enjoy the large degree of immunity from it which Americans now have.

The chief cause of amœbic dysentery in the Philippines has undoubtedly been infected drinking water. From time immemorial the people have been obtaining their water for drinking purposes from flowing streams, open springs or shallow surface wells.

The wells were especially dangerous, as it was the common custom to wash clothing around them so that water containing disease germs frequently seeped into wells used by whole villages. The results of such conditions during a cholera epidemic can readily be imagined.

The drinking supplies of many provincial towns have now been radically improved by the sinking of 853 successful artesian wells.

In many places there has been a resulting reduction of more than fifty per cent in the annual death rate. Large sums are spent yearly by the government in drilling additional wells, — a policy which is warmly approved by the common people. The recent appropriations for this purpose have been $255,000 for the fiscal year 1912, $60,000 for 1913 and $200,000 for 1914.

When we came to the islands, malaria was killing as many persons as was smallpox. The mortality caused by it is now being greatly reduced by giving away annually millions of doses of quinine, and by draining or spraying with petroleum places where mosquitoes breed, as well as by teaching the people the importance of sleeping under mosquito nets and the necessity of keeping patients suffering from active attacks of malaria where mosquitoes cannot get at them. Only quinine of established quality is allowed in the market.

The results obtained in combating malaria are often very striking. Calapan, the capital of Mindoro, was in Spanish days known as "the white man's grave" on account of the prevalence of "pernicious fever" there. To-day it is an exceptionally healthy provincial town.

At Iwahig, in Palawan, the Spaniards attempted to conduct a penal colony. They were compelled to abandon it on account of pernicious malaria, which caused continued serious mortality when the American government attempted to establish a similar institution there. Application of the usual sanitary measures has made it a healthful place.

Old jails throughout the islands have been rendered sanitary, or replaced by new ones. The loathsome skin diseases from which prisoners formerly suffered have in consequence disappeared. The practical results obtained in Bilibid, the insular penitentiary, are worthy of special note. The annual death rate at this institution was 78.25 per thousand for the calendar year 1904. It increased steadily each month from January, 1904, to September, 1905, when it reached its maximum, deaths occurring at the rate of 241.15 per thousand per year. At this time the director of health was given charge of the sanitation of this prison.

By remedying overcrowding, improving drainage, installing sewers and regulating diet along scientific lines, the rate was reduced in six months to 70 per 1000, and there it stuck.

A systematic examination of the stools of prisoners was then made. Eighty-four per cent were found to be afflicted with at least one intestinal parasite. Fifty per cent had two or more, and twenty per cent had three or more. Fifty-two per cent of the total had hookworm. Active treatment for the elimination of these parasites was begun in one barrack, and after the work was completed it was noted that there was much less disease there than in the remainder. All of the thirty-five hundred prisoners were ultimately examined, and intestinal parasites eradicated if present. The death rate then dropped to thirteen to the thousand, and has remained at or near this figure up to the present time.

I have already referred to the discovery of the cause of beri-beri, and to the effect of the governor-general's order forbidding the use of polished rice in government institutions or by government organizations.

I subsequently made a strong effort to secure legislation imposing a heavy internal revenue tax on polished rice, thus penalizing its use. I failed, but such effort will be renewed by some one, let us hope with ultimate success.

In Spanish days cholera, leprosy, smallpox and other dangerous communicable diseases were constantly reintroduced from without. This is no longer the case. The United States public health and marine hospital service has stretched an effective defensive line around the archipelago and has sent its outposts to Hongkong, Shanghai and Amoy, to prevent, so far as possible, the embarkation for Manila of persons suffering from such ailments. We now have the most effective quarantine system in the tropics, and one of the best in the world. At Mariveles there is a very large and complete disinfecting plant, and vessels may also be satisfactorily disinfected at Cebú and Iloilo.

This quarantine service kept the Philippines free from bubonic plague for seven years, and has repeatedly prevented the entry of pneumonic plague, that most deadly of all known diseases.

A peculiar and shockingly disfiguring disease known as yaws occurs somewhat infrequently in the Philippine lowlands and is very prevalent in a number of places in the highlands. In many ways it resembles syphilis, and indeed at one time was considered to be syphilitic in its origin. Doctor Richard P. Strong, of the Bureau of Science, made the very important discovery that salvarsan is an absolute specific for it. The effect of an injection of this remedy closely approaches a miracle in medicine. In five or six days the condition of the patient begins to improve rapidly. By the end of the second week his horrible sores have healed.

It was with this remedy that we began our health work among some of the wilder head-hunters of northern Luzón. Think of the advantage of being absolutely certain of curing such an ailment in every case, and think of the gratitude of poor wretches, undergoing untold suffering, when they were almost immediately relieved!

Soon after this use for salvarsan was discovered, I caused a liberal supply of it to be sent to the Bontoc Hospital. For some time we were unable to persuade any victims of yaws to undergo treatment, but finally we found one at Barlig who was guilty of a minor criminal offence, arrested him, and took him to Bontoc. Instead of putting him in jail there, we sent him to the hospital for treatment.

At first he complained bitterly that we were putting no medicine on his sores. Then the remedy began to work and he decided it was "strong medicine." By the tenth day he was running around town joyfully exhibiting his rapidly healing body to every one who would look at it. On the fourteenth day he suddenly disappeared, to the deep regret of the medical men, who had hoped that they might keep him as an example of what could be done, and thus persuade others to undergo treatment. A few days later, however, he reappeared with thirteen victims of yaws from his home town, having meanwhile twice covered on foot the great distance which separates Barlig from Bontoc, and assembled and brought in his fellow-sufferers.

As we have seen, the people of Manila were formerly supplied with impure drinking water from the Mariquina River, and were therefore in constant danger of infection with cholera and other deadly diseases. At a cost of some $1,500,000 we have given the city a modern water system, the intake of which is far up in the hills above the last village. The annual deaths from ordinary water-borne diseases exclusive of cholera have fallen from 3558 — the average number at the time the new system was introduced — to 1195. Recently a leak in the dam, which necessitated temporary resumption of the use of the Mariquina River water, was immediately followed by a marked increase in the number of deaths from such diseases, thus conclusively demonstrating the fact that we were right in ascribing the previous reduction in deaths to a better water supply.

This annual saving of lives is an important result, but more important yet is the fact that when Asiatic cholera reappears in the Mariquina valley, as it inevitably will sooner or later, we shall not live in constant fear of a general infection of the Manila water supply, which, judging from the experience of other cities where modern sanitary methods have been introduced, might result in the death of a third of the population. In every country a very considerable part of the population always fails to boil its drinking water, no matter how great the resulting danger may be.

Manila lacked any facilities for the proper disposal of human waste, and the conditions which resulted were unspeakable, especially in the little *barrios*, or groups of houses, placed close together, helter-skelter, on wet, swampy ground and reached by means of runways not worthy even of the name of alleys, as one often had to crouch to pass along them.

A modern sewer system costing $2,000,000, supplemented by a pail system, has very effectively solved this problem, while thousands of homes closely crowded on disease-infected, mosquito-breeding ground have been removed to high, dry, sanitary sites. The regions thus vacated have in many instances been drained, filled, provided with city water and good streets, and made fit for human occupancy.

The old moat around the city walls was a veritable incubator of disease. It has been converted into an athletic field where crowds of people take healthful exercise. The *esteros*, or tidal creeks, reeked with filth. More than twenty miles of such creeks have been cleaned out, although much still remains to be done to put them in really satisfactory condition.

There were no regulations covering the construction of buildings, and it was not unusual to find six or eight persons sleeping in a closed and unventilated room $10 \times 8 \times 8$ feet. Manila now has an excellent sanitary code, and such conditions have been made unlawful.

The previous woeful lack of hospital facilities has been effectively remedied. At a cost of approximately a million and quarter pesos we have built and equipped the great Philippine General Hospital, one of the most modern institutions of its kind in the world, and by far the best in the Far East. In it we have very satisfactorily solved the question of getting sufficient light and air in the tropics without getting excessive heat. Its buildings are certainly among the very coolest in the city of Manila, and "the hospital smell" is everywhere conspicuously absent.

It is called a three-hundred-bed institution, but as a matter of fact the ventilation is so admirable that nearly two hundred additional beds can safely be put in as an emergency measure.

Two hundred and twenty of its beds are free. In them a very large number of persons are annually given the best of medical and surgical care. At its free clinic some eighty thousand patients find relief in the course of a year.

The increase in private hospital facilities has also been noteworthy. Among the new institutions doing admirable work should be mentioned the University Hospital, an Episcopal institution; the Mary J. Johnston Hospital, a Methodist institution; and St. Paul's Hospital, a Catholic institution. Patients are admitted to all of them without regard to their religious belief, a policy the liberality of which must commend itself to all broadminded persons.

In enumerating the hospitals of Manila, the old Spanish institution, San Juan de Dios, should not be forgotten, for it has been improved and modernized until it offers good facilities for the treatment of the sick and the injured.

All of the above mentioned institutions are in effect acute-case hospitals designed for the treatment of curable ailments. Cases of dangerous communicable disease are excluded from them, but are adequately provided for at San Lazaro where the insular government has established modern and adequate hospitals for plague, smallpox, cholera, diphtheria, scarlet fever, measles, etc., as well as a detention hospital for lepers, pending their departure for Culion.

An insane hospital capable of comfortably accommodating 300 inmates has also been provided. A few years since the insane were commonly chained to floors, or tied to stakes under houses or in yards, and were not infrequently burned alive during conflagrations. Such conditions no longer exist, but the government is not yet able to provide for nearly all of the insane who need institutional care.

The several institutions above mentioned have a very important function apart from the relief of human suffering, in that they afford unexcelled opportunities for giving practical instruction in nursing and in the practice of medicine and surgery.

A few years ago there was not such a thing as a Filipina trained nurse in the islands. I was firmly convinced that the Filipinas of this country could learn to be good nurses, and made earnest efforts to have included among the first students sent at government expense to the United States several young women of good family who should attend nurses' training schools and then return to assist in our hospital work.

I failed to secure the adoption of this plan, but later the training of nurses was inaugurated in connection with hospital work at the old Civil Hospital, St. Paul's, the University Hospital, the Mary J. Johnston Hospital and the Philippine General Hospital. At the latter institution there is now conducted an admirable school where more than two hundred young men and women are being trained. Three classes have already graduated from it, and Filipina nurses have long since proved themselves to be exceptionally efficient, capable and faithful. It will be some time before we can educate as many as are needed in the government hospitals, and after that has been accomplished a vast field opens before others in the provincial towns, where the need of trained assistants in caring for the sick is very great.

We found exceedingly few competent Filipino physicians or surgeons in the islands. This condition was due not to natural incompetence on the part of the Filipinos but to the previous lack of adequate educational facilities. The government has established a thoroughly modern college of medicine and surgery, well housed, and provided with all necessary laboratory facilities. It furnishes the best of theoretical instruction, while its students have every opportunity for practical work at the bedsides of patients in the government hospitals, all patients in free beds being admitted subject to the condition that they will allow their cases to be studied.

DANGEROUS NAVIGATION.

This photograph shows one of our rafts passing a point on the Abulug River which we named the "Needle's Eye." The current was very swift, and the water forty feet deep. Many persons have been drowned, or killed by being thrown against the rocks, while trying to make this passage.

While there is still an evident tendency on the part of graduates of this school to feel that they know enough, and to desire to get to making money without delay, we are nevertheless managing to attract an increasingly large number of the more competent to the intern service of the Philippine General Hospital, where as the result of additional years of practical experience they become exceptionally proficient.

This institution, with its great free clinic, offers very exceptional facilities for practical instruction, and we have already trained some extremely competent Filipino physicians and surgeons.

As funds permit, hospital work is being extended to the provinces. At Cebú a thoroughly up-to-date sixty-bed institution is now open. A smaller one was established years ago at Baguio, where surgical work may be performed with great advantage on account of the rapidity with which convalescence occurs in the cool, pure mountain air, which also expedites the recovery of persons recuperating from wasting diseases.

A little more than a year ago a hospital was opened at Bontoc, the demand for accommodations being so great from the start that we did not even await the arrival of beds. Sick Igorots were only too glad to lie on the floor if their needs could be ministered to.

It had previously been the custom of the wild men to kill chickens, pigs or carabaos in case of illness, in order to propitiate evil spirits, the kind and number of animals killed being of course determined by the wealth of the patients. They have now satisfied themselves that quinine for malaria, salvarsan for yaws, and other effective remedies for common ailments are more useful and more readily obtained than was the helpful intervention of the *anitos*, or spirits of the dead, while the methods and results of modern surgery are a source of unending amazement and satisfaction to them.

The first surgeon to anæsthetize a Kalinga became

promptly and widely known as "the man who kills people and brings them to life again," and the individual on whom he operated successfully, who chanced to be the most influential chief of the tribe, became his friend for life. Indeed, the results of medical and surgical work for the wild men have been an important factor in bringing about and maintaining friendly relations with them.

Their gratitude is at times very touching. At Atok, in Benguet, there lives an Igorot chief named Palasi. When he was already old a son was born to him. This boy, who was the delight of his declining years, became deathly ill with confluent smallpox, and the Igorots considered him as good as dead. At this time Sanitary Inspector Baron appeared on the scene. He promptly turned every one else out of the house and himself nursed the boy, saving his life. Palasi wished to pay him for his services, but was informed by Mr. Baron that the government paid him, and he could not accept additional compensation. Palasi promptly made the long journey to Baguio to ascertain whether Baron had told him the truth, and was informed by Governor Pack that this was the case. The old man retired to Atok, quite disgusted with the strange ways of Americans.

Six months later he again appeared at Baguio to ask the governor about a *fiesta* which he had just heard it was customary to celebrate on the 25th of December. He had been told that Americans were in the habit of giving presents to each other at this time, and asked if this was the case. Governor Pack said yes. Palasi then inquired if the feast was a *good* feast, and the custom a *good* custom, and was assured that both of these things were true. He next asked if it would be a good feast for Igorots as well as for Americans, and receiving an affirmative reply from the unsuspecting governor, triumphantly declared that he was going to give Baron his best horse. Under the circumstances the governor allowed him to do so.

In connection with the Bontoc Hospital we use two men, one of whom travels from settlement to settlement, relieving minor ailments on the spot and sending to the hospital only those patients who need to go there, while the other stays at home and receives them. From time to time these two doctors "change works." Pages from their daily journals, written in the field, often read like romance.

Were I a young man, and possessed of adequate knowledge of medicine and surgery, I would ask nothing better than to minister to the wants of these people. One might not, and indeed would not, acquire great wealth, but he would be rich in friends. Here lies a great field for practical missionary work.

In connection with the health work there have been many occurrences which were both amusing and sad. At one time there was great excitement over a sacred spring which had appeared in Manila Bay off the district of Tondo. It was duly blessed by Aglipay, the head of the so-called Aglipayano church. Coincidently with its discovery there was a sharp little outbreak of Asiatic cholera. Investigation revealed the fact that the "spring" had its origin in a broken sewer pipe. We were obliged to prevent the faithful from further partaking of its waters, and thus insuring themselves a speedy trip to the better world.

At one time cases of cholera appeared scattered generally throughout the Mariquina valley and without apparent connection. For some days we were unable to make a guess as to their origin. Then we heard that a "Queen" had arisen at the town of Taytay near the Laguna de Bay. An investigation of the Queen and her activities resulted in rather astonishing revelations. She was a very ordinary looking Tagálog girl who had secured the body of an old bull-cart, stopped the cracks with clay, partially filled it with water and decaying vegetable matter, and at rather frequent intervals had bathed in the fermenting mass thus concocted. In due time she announced herself a healer of all the ills to which flesh is heir, and the sick flocked to her. Cholera was then prevalent in some of the towns near Taytay, and there were persons suffering from it among those seeking relief. Some of them were directed to wash their hands in the extemporized tank, while others bathed their bodies in it. As a result it soon contained a cholera culture of unprecedented richness. This was given to patients applying for treatment, and was bottled and sent to those who were too ill to come in person. Hence numerous scattering cases of cholera which did not bear any relationship to other known cases.

It proved quite an undertaking to put the Queen of Taytay out of business. We first asked the local authorities to have her sent to Manila, but the presidente and the police declined to act. We then applied for a warrant to the Filipino judge of the court of first instance having jurisdiction over Taytay, but that worthy official found it convenient to be suddenly called out of the province. At last we prevailed upon soldiers of the Philippine constabulary to arrest the queen and bring her to Manila.

We had anticipated that she might prove insane, but she showed herself to be a very keen-witted young woman. We employed her at the San Lazaro Hospital to look after cholera patients. The people of Taytay were not satisfied, and a few days later a large delegation of them came to Manila and demanded the Queen. I was at my wits' end to know what to do, but old Spanish law can usually be relied upon in emergencies, and the attorney-general discovered a provision couched in very general terms, which provided against disobedience to the authorities. It was only necessary for an "authority" to have read to an ordinary person a statement setting forth what that person must not do; then if the order was violated, such person could be made to suffer pains and penalties.

I accordingly prepared a most impressive order prohibiting the Queen of Taytay from further engaging in the practice of medicine, had her followers drawn up in battalion formation, placed myself at the front and centre, caused the Queen to be brought before me, and read her my communication, at the same time charging the good people of Taytay not to tempt her again to try her hand at healing, for the reason that if they did she would surely get into serious trouble. They marched away with the Queen and I have not heard of her since.

Hardly a year goes by that some similar miraculous healer does not set up in business, and the supply of dupes seems to be unending.

While it is comparatively easy to combat disease in a place like Manila, what of the provinces, where in many cases there is not one physician to two hundred thousand inhabitants?

To meet this difficulty we have an organization of district and municipal health officers. A district may include a single province or several provinces. A district health officer is invariably a physician who has had reasonably thorough practical training in the work of public sanitation, usually at Manila.

He is supposed to spend his time in sanitary work rather than in treating sick individuals, but it is, of course, impossible for him always to refuse to treat such persons, and we encourage gratuitous work for the poor when it can be carried on without interfering too seriously with more important duties.

Presidents of municipal boards of health may exercise jurisdiction over a single municipality or over several. They are supposed to maintain good sanitary conditions in their respective towns, under the general supervision of district health officers, and to instruct their people in sanitary methods and their results, as well as to devote a certain amount of their time to the relief of the suffering poor.

On the whole it must be admitted that while this

system has accomplished much, it has fallen far short of accomplishing what it should.

Men like Dr. Arlington Pond of Cebú have wrought marvels, and have conclusively demonstrated the fact that it is not the system that is at fault. Of our thirteen district health officers, ten are Filipinos. They are, with few exceptions, letter-perfect. They know what they ought to do, but as a rule lack the initiative and the courage to do it.

Recently after discovering exceptionally bad sanitary conditions in several towns of the province of Misamis, I demanded an explanation of the district health officer, an exceptionally well-educated and intelligent Filipino physician. I found, as I had anticipated, that the sanitary regulations of his towns left little to be desired, but that they were absolutely ignored.

I asked him what sense there was in paying his salary if he failed to remedy such conditions as I had discovered. He replied that if he were really going to compel people to clean up, it would be necessary to begin with the provincial governor, whose premises were in a bad state. When I suggested that in my opinion the provincial governor would be the best possible man to begin with, the doctor evidently thought me crazy!

It is as yet impossible for the average intelligent Filipino to understand that the rich and the poor, the powerful and the weak, should be treated alike.

It often happens that a province asks for an American health officer, or a Filipino demands the services of an American physician. My invariable procedure in such cases has been to request that the application be made in writing. For some mysterious reason the petitioners are seldom willing to go on record.

A short time since we had a strong demand from Iloilo for an American district health officer. I made the usual suggestion and got a written request that there be sent to Iloilo a district health officer " after the style of the district health officer of Cebú." If Dr. Pond's nationality may be considered a part of his style, then this was a request for an American, otherwise not !

With rather shocking frequency, Filipinos who must be examined for leprosy or some other dangerous communicable disease strongly insist that the examination be made by an American bacteriologist rather than by one of their own countrymen.

In connection with recent election troubles two men were wrongfully denounced as lepers. In several instances perfectly sound people have been thrust among lepers who were being taken on board steamer for transfer to Culion. This grievous wrong was committed by their enemies under cover of darkness, and in the confusion which attends the embarking of a number of people in a heavy sea. The reason why the services of Americans are often specially requested for diagnostic work is not far to seek !

It is a significant fact that our greatest success in establishing satisfactory provincial sanitary conditions has been achieved in certain of the "special government provinces," where the people are under the very direct control of American officials.

There is not a regularly organized province in the Philippines in which the towns are as clean as are those of Mindoro, where, until recently, we have never had a resident district health officer.

I believe that nowhere in the tropics can there be found native towns which are cleaner or more healthful than are those of Bukidnon, inhabited in some instances by people who have literally been brought down out of the tree-tops within the last two or three years. We have never had a resident health officer in this subprovince.

I mention these facts not as an argument against health officers, but as a proof of what can be done without them by intelligent Americans vested with proper authority.

It has given me especial pleasure to see the fundamental change which has come about in public sentiment relative to medical, surgical and sanitary work. At the outset sanitary inspectors and vaccinators carried on their work at serious risk of personal violence. Indeed, several of them were killed. Incredible tales were believed by the populace, with the result that cholera victims sometimes had to be taken to the hospital by force. In later years it has been by no means unusual for them to come in voluntarily and request treatment.

General hospitals were in the old days regarded as places where people so unfortunate as to have no homes to die in might go to end their days. It was almost impossible to get any other class of persons into them.

Now we constantly turn away deserving patients from the Philippine General Hospital because of lack of room. The common people are flocking to it in rapidly increasing numbers. We even have "repeaters," and persons who drop in just to get a comfortable bed and a bath while waiting for an examination which will inevitably show that there is nothing wrong with them.

Our difficulties were increased at the outset by the fact that many foreign medical men working in the Far East good-naturedly ridiculed our efforts to better conditions, claiming that in tropical colonies it was customary to take only such steps as would safeguard the health of European residents, and that it was really best to let the masses live as they would, since orientals were incapable of sanitary reform, and the attempt to bring it about involved a waste of effort that might be more profitably directed elsewhere. Furthermore these men were, in their several countries, practising what they preached.

It has been very interesting to note the reaction of American methods upon those previously in vogue in neighbouring colonies. At first our efforts to make Asiatics clean up, and to eliminate diseases like leprosy, cholera and plague, were viewed with mild amusement,

A Negrito Family and their "House."

not unmixed with contempt; but the results which we obtained soon aroused lively interest.

Foreign governments began to send representatives to the annual meetings of the " Philippine Island Medical Association," [1] in order to learn more of our methods. From these small beginnings sprang "The Far Eastern Association of Tropical Medicine," the biennial meetings of which bring together the most experienced, skilful and widely known physicians and sanitarians in the East for an interchange of views and experiences which is invaluable, and greatly facilitates concerted action between the various governments concerned in dealing with what may be termed "international health problems."

The first meeting of this Association was held at Manila, the second at Hongkong. The third will take place at Saigon.

The results of a rigid enforcement of the "Pure Food and Drugs Act" are worthy of more than passing notice. Such enforcement has been comparatively easy as the officials concerned are not hampered by politics. The Philippines were at one time a dumping-ground for products that could not be sold elsewhere, but it is now possible for Filipinos to obtain wholesome preserved foods and unadulterated drugs, except in very remote places where none of any sort are available.

The cost of our medical and sanitary work has been comparatively small. The per capita rate of taxation here is lower than in any other civilized country. What we have done has been accomplished without spending vast sums of money or resorting to military measures.

The results obtained are very largely due to the faithfulness and efficiency of Dr. Victor G. Heiser, who was chief quarantine officer of the Philippines when he succeeded Major E. C. Carter as commissioner of public

[1] The first organization of American physicians in the Philippines was the Manila Medical Association, from which the Philippine Island Medical Association ultimately developed.

health on April 5, 1905, and was later made director of health when the original board of health was abolished as an administrative entity. He has continued to hold the office of chief quarantine officer, and thus has been in complete executive control of the health situation for eight years.

Through good report and ill, mostly ill, he has given unsparingly of his time, his skill and his wisdom, always treating the government money as if it were his own.

His tenure of office has been long enough to enable him to inaugurate and carry out policies, and thus get results.

Seldom, if ever, have health officials been more viciously and persistently attacked than have Dr. Heiser and myself. The assaults on us have been the direct result of a firm stand for a new sanitary order of things, established in the interest of the whole body of inhabitants of these islands, civilized and uncivilized. We both welcome the profound change in public sentiment, which has slowly but surely come about as a result of practical accomplishment.

Many very grave health problems still confront the insular administration. Of these the most serious are the eradication of tuberculosis and the reduction of the very high infant mortality rate.

It is believed that about one Filipino in five suffers from tuberculosis in some form during his life and the work we have thus far accomplished in many fields must be considered as in a way a clearing of the decks for action against this, the greatest enemy of all. However, the Philippines do not differ essentially from other civilized countries, in all of which tuberculosis is a very serious factor in the death rate.

As regards infant mortality the situation is different. More than fifty per cent of the babes die before completing their first year of life. The causes which lead to this appalling result have been made the subject of careful investigation which still continues. Popular interest has been aroused, but it is undoubtedly true that many years of patient work will be necessary before anything approaching satisfactory results can be brought about.

The physical condition of the average Filipino is undoubtedly bad. Of one hundred seventy-eight university students recently examined sixty-nine were found to be suffering from serious organic troubles. Unquestionably the great mass of the people are underfed. This is largely due to the poor quality of the rice which they consume, and to the fact that rice forms too large a part of their diet. I am firmly convinced that much of the so-called laziness of the Filipinos is the direct result of physical weakness due to improper and insufficient food.

Since the American occupation a large amount of time has been successfully devoted to the working out of a good all-around diet made up of local products the cost of which comes within the means of the poor. The next thing will be to get them to adopt it, and there comes the rub. Incalculable good would result, if we could only persuade the people of these islands to sleep with their windows open. Thousands upon thousands of infant lives would be saved annually, if mothers could be persuaded not to give solid food to their little ones during the early months of their existence.

In the educational campaign which we have thus far conducted with some considerable degree of success, two agencies have proved invaluable, namely the Catholic Church and the public schools. Again and again I have begged Apostolic Delegate Monsignor Agius and Archbishop Harty to bring to bear the influence of the Church in favour of simple sanitary regulations, the general adoption of which was imperatively necessary in combating some epidemic of disease. They have invariably given me invaluable assistance.

Through the public schools we reach more than half a million children, and they take the information which we convey to them home to their parents. Simple rules for the prevention of cholera have been universally taught in the schools. When the use of English has become generalized the difficulty now encountered in reaching the common people will largely disappear. The truth is that they are singularly tractable and docile when their reason can be effectively appealed to. The readiness with which they have submitted to the rigorous measures necessary for the elimination of leprosy is a lasting honour to them.

Would the sanitary campaign so vitally important to the people of the Philippines be effectively continued if American authority were withdrawn at this time? With regret I must answer this question emphatically in the negative. We have succeeded in training a few good physicians and surgeons. We have thus far failed to train really efficient sanitary officers. What is lacking is not so much knowledge as to what should be done as initiative and courage to do it. Until this condition changes radically for the better, Filipinos cannot safely be intrusted with the sanitary regeneration of their country. Under American control the population of the islands is steadily and rapidly increasing. It is my firm conviction that if Filipinos were at this time placed in control of the health work, the population would steadily and rapidly decrease.

The present attitude of the Filipino press toward sanitary work is both interesting and important. I quote the following editorial from the March 27, 1913, issue of *El Ideal*, a paper generally believed to be controlled by Speaker Osmeña : —

"Some persons, who, because of being ignorant of many things, do not sympathize with the Filipino people, who are in the habit of frequently throwing up to them the violent opposition of our masses to strict sanitary measures in cases of epidemics, and the lively protests which are provoked here on some occasions by other provisions tending to end some public calam-

A Typical Negrito.

The people of this tribe of woolly-headed blacks are believed to be the aborigines of the Philippines. Only about twenty-five thousand of them remain.

ity, thinking they see in this disposition of mind an indication of our incapacity to govern ourselves. . . .

"To be more expressive, we shall say that the sanitary agents and veterinarians of the government, swollen with power and overly zealous of their prestige, quickly become, when an occasion like those cited by us presents itself, cunning czars, whose sphere of influence is in direct ratio to the peaceful character and ignorance of the people intrusted to their care, and whose excesses and abuses recognize no limits but the natural ones established by the greater or lesser honour of those public servants, their greater or lesser cynicism, and their greater or lesser degree of temerity.

"This, and nothing else, is the logical and natural explanation of the hostility of our people toward those measures of good government which are sincerely esteemed for what they are worth, but for which they have veritable terror because of the nameless abuses to which they give rise.

"These comments are of palpitating current interest at this moment, when reports are made almost daily to the press and the proper authorities of misbehaviour and excesses befitting soulless people who live without the law committed by persons who should be examples of prudence, honesty and good manners, for it is in this concept that the people are compelled to furnish them their daily bread."

It is deeply to be regretted that the public press of the islands has not yet become sufficiently enlightened to join in the great sanitary campaign which has already relieved an enormous amount of human suffering and has greatly increased the expectancy of life of the people of the Philippines.

The Philippine Assembly has repeatedly passed acts providing for the creation of a sort of sanitary council of numerous members authorized to pass on public health measures proposed by the director of health and instructed to disapprove them if not in accordance with the beliefs and customs of the Filipinos.

In protecting the public health in the Philippine Islands emergencies constantly arise which must be instantly and effectively met. It would be as logical to place a commanding general directing a battle under the control of an advisory board as it would thus to tie the hands of the director of health, and it is difficult to see how any competent and self-respecting sanitarian could be willing to continue to hold this position if so hampered.

The Philippine Commission has heretofore invariably tabled the acts designed to accomplish this end, but that body has now been "Filipinized" and its future attitude on this very important question is therefore in doubt. Hardly had the legislative session opened in October, 1913, when the assembly again passed the same old bill. Should it become a law, there will be occasion to watch, with especial interest, the death rate of Manila and that of the archipelago as a whole.

CHAPTER XVII

Baguio and the Benguet Road

In June, 1892, when sitting in a native house on a hill overlooking Naujan Lake in Mindoro, and anxiously awaiting the boats which were to make it possible for my party to return to the coast, I saw a small flotilla approaching.

To my surprise and regret I found that it was not coming for us, but brought a number of Spanish officers who had heard that we had some mysterious procedure for killing the tamarau, an extraordinarily wild and vicious little buffalo peculiar to this island. They had come to get us to tell them how we did it, if possible, and if not to watch us and find out for themselves.

We described to them our method, which was easily understood. It consisted in picking up a likely trail along some water course, following it until the tamarau was overtaken, and then shooting him. This looked suspiciously simple to our Spanish friends before they had tried it, and they shook their heads. After trying it they became convinced that more than a few days of experience would be necessary before satisfactory results could be obtained. They profited little by the best information we could give them, and by the services of the expert tracker whom we loaned to them. Meanwhile I obtained from one of them, Señor Domingo Sanchez, information destined to become of great importance in the development of the Philippines.

Señor Sanchez, who was an employee of the Spanish forestry bureau, told me that in the highlands of Northern Luzón at an elevation of about five thousand feet, there was a region of pines and oaks blessed with a perpetually temperate climate and even with occasional frosts. I confess that I did not believe all of his statements. I was then experienced in climbing Philippine mountains, and at five thousand feet had invariably found a hopeless tangle of the rankest tropical vegetation, with humidity so high that trees were draped with ferns, orchids, and thick moss, and dripping with moisture. However, I knew that the mere presence of pine and oak trees would mean the occurrence of special bird species feeding upon their seeds, and so determined to investigate.

A severe attack of typhoid fever necessitated my leaving the islands before I could carry out this plan, but upon my return with the first Philippine Commission in 1899 I remembered Señor Sanchez's story. In view of the probability that American occupation would continue for a long period, the existence or non-existence near Manila of an extensive highland region with a temperate climate became a question of great practical importance. I therefore caused search to be made in the Spanish archives to see what, if any, reliable information was available, and to my great satisfaction unearthed a detailed report made by a committee of three distinguished and competent Spanish officers who had spent some weeks at Baguio in the *comandancia* of Benguet, during which period they had made six temperature observations daily, had tramped over the neighbouring country very thoroughly, had located a number of springs of potable water and determined their approximate flow, and in short had gathered a large series of very valuable data which more than bore out the statements of Señor Sanchez.

I found, furthermore, that Spanish engineers had made a survey for a carriage road into this country, and had prepared a profile of it with estimates of the amount and cost of the necessary excavation and other work.

While in Washington during the winter of 1899–1900, I brought this matter to the attention of Secretary Root.

Just as the second Philippine Commission was filing out of his office, after receiving its instructions, he called out to us directing that we look into that Benguet matter, and if the facts proved to be as stated open up the country.

Mindful of these instructions the commission delegated General Luke E. Wright and myself to visit Benguet and familiarize ourselves with conditions by investigation on the ground. General MacArthur was dubious when we expressed a desire to carry out the instructions of the secretary of war. He told us that the country was very dangerous, doubtless confusing it with Bangued, the capital of Abra, near which there was at that time a strong and active Insurgent force.

We insisted on going, so he said that he would send a troop of cavalry with us, and he kept his word. During the last week of July we finally sailed from Manila on a naval vessel for San Fernando in the province of Union. From this place we expected to go by road as far as Naguilian, in the same province, and thence on horseback to Trinidad and Baguio, in Benguet.

In order to expedite investigations as much as possible we took with us Mr. Horace L. Higgins, president of the Manila and Dagupan Railway Company, who was an engineer of experience, to report on the practicability of constructing a railway to Baguio. We also took Major L. M. Maus, of the army medical corps, and Dr. Frank S. Bourns, who then held the volunteer rank of major in the same corps, to report on the possibilities of the place as a health resort. Two young naval officers went along just for the trip.

Major Maus accompanied us only because requested to do so. Taking the latitude and altitude as a basis for his calculations, he had already determined with a lead pencil and piece of paper just what the climate of Baguio must be, and had demonstrated to his own complete satisfaction that the statements of the members of the Spanish committee above referred to were necessarily false.

His first rude shock came when we were met at San Fernando by a young aide to Colonel [1] Duval, who was in command of the local garrison at that place.   This lieutenant told us that some negro soldiers were stationed at Trinidad and were being kept supplied by an army pack train.   I asked him how they were getting on.   He said very well, except that they could not keep warm.   They had called for all the spare blankets available, but still complained of the cold !

The trail proved to be in execrable condition.   No repair work had been done on it since 1896, and its constant use during the then-existing rainy season by a pack train had completed its destruction.   Much of the way it was a mere V in the earth, with deep mud at the bottom.

We left Naguilian early in the morning and stopped for lunch at a little place properly called Sablán, but unofficially known as "The Bells."   Aguinaldo had thought at one time of establishing his headquarters in Benguet and had planned to have a gun foundry at Sablán.   His troops accordingly stole most of the church bells in the neighbouring lowland towns, meaning to use them for gun metal, and compelled the unfortunate Benguet Igorots to carry them up the steep trail.   Boiler pipes, which had been used in lieu of carrying poles, had in several instances been badly bent out of shape.   There was even an old vertical boiler which had been lugged up entire for some unknown reason.

The labour involved must have been enormous, and we were assured that when the Igorot bearers, prostrated with fatigue, had refused to continue their titanic task without rest, they had been driven to it at the muzzles of Insurgent rifles, and that some of them had been shot as a lesson to the others.   At all events, the boiler and the bells were there, and there the boiler and the larger bells have remained ever since !

It was still steaming hot at Sablán, and the whole

[1] Now a major-general.

TYPICAL KALINGAS.

The people of this tribe, until recently fierce head-hunters, have been brought under effective control largely through the individual efforts of Lieutenant-Governor Walter F. Hale.

countryside was buried in the densest tropical vegetation. Major Maus was triumphant. Things were working out just as he had predicted. However, as we were already halfway up, we thought that we might as well continue the journey. I had expected to find pines and oaks, but had anticipated that they would grow amidst a dense tangle of damp tropical vegetation.

We were all literally dumfounded when within the space of a hundred yards we suddenly left the tropics behind us and came out into a wonderful region of pine parks. Trees stood on the rounded knolls at comparatively wide intervals, and there were scores of places where, in order to have a beautiful house lot, one needed only to construct driveways and go to work with a lawn-mower. At the same moment, a delightful cold breeze swept down from the heights above us.

Just at sunset we experienced a second surprise, coming out on the knife-sharp crest of a ridge, and seeing spread before us the Trinidad Valley, which is shaped like a huge wash-basin. Its floor was vividly green with growing rice, Igorot houses were dotted here and there over its surface, and the whole peaceful, beautiful scene was illuminated by the rays of the setting sun. The air had been washed clean by the heavy rain which had poured down on us throughout the afternoon, and the sight was one never to be forgotten.

Just at dusk we reached the little settlement of Trinidad, which had been the capital of the Spanish *comandancia* of Benguet, finding that its inhabitants were in part Ilocanos and in part Igorots.

Here we were hospitably entertained by the officers of the military post. It was so cold that one's breath showed. Major Maus improved the opportunity to indulge in a severe chill. Finding him buried under blankets, we asked his views as to the Benguet climate. They were radical! It is only fair to the Major to say that the report which he ultimately made set forth the facts fully and fairly.

It did not suit General MacArthur. Years afterward,
when discussing the climate of Benguet with Surgeon-
General Sternberg, I referred to this report and found to
my amazement that he had never seen it. He caused an
investigation to be made, and it was at last resurrected
from a dusty pigeonhole.

On our arrival at Trinidad we received a letter from
Mr. Otto Scheerer, the one white resident of Benguet,
inviting us to make our headquarters at his house when
we visited Baguio. Bright and early the next morning
Mr. Scheerer himself appeared on the scene and guided us
to his home, where he entertained us most hospitably
during our entire stay. The trip from Trinidad, a
distance of four miles, was made over a wretched pony
trail.

We found conditions exactly as described in the Spanish
report. The country was gently rolling, its elevation
ranging from forty-five hundred to fifty-two hundred feet.
The hills were covered with short, thick grass, and with
magnificent pine trees, which for the most part grew at
considerable distance from each other, while along the
streams there were wonderful tree ferns and luxuriant
tangles of beautiful tropical vegetation. It took us but a
short time to decide that here was an ideal site for a future
city, if water could be found in sufficient quantity.

We revisited each of the several springs discovered and
described by the Spanish committee, but decided that they
would be inadequate to supply a town of any great size.
Mr. Scheerer now came to the front and guided us to the
very thing that we were looking for, but had hardly dared
hope to find; namely, a magnificent spring of crystal-clear
water. At that time it was flowing nearly a million
gallons per day. It burst forth from a hillside in such a
manner as to make its protection from surface drainage
easy, and we decided that there was nothing lacking to
make Baguio an admirable site for the future summer
capital and health resort of the Philippines.

It was obvious that the construction of a highway from San Fernando, in Union, to Baguio would involve considerable expense, and we asked Mr. Scheerer about other possible lines of communication. A study of the Spanish maps had led us to consider two : one up the valley of the Agno River, and the other up that of the Bued River. The latter route had the great advantage of affording direct communication with the end of the railway line at Dagupan.

Mr. Scheerer took us to a point which commanded a view for some distance down the Bued River valley, and conditions looked rather favourable. Mr. Higgins undertook to make a trip down this valley to the plains of Pangasinán, reporting to us on his arrival at Manila, so we returned to that place and awaited advices from him. He was furnished with a guard of soldiers from Trinidad, and attempted to go down the river bed, but encountered unexpected difficulties, and his progress was finally checked by a box cañon from which he escaped with difficulty, spending a night without food or water on a chilly mountain top known as "Thumb Peak." The following morning he managed to cross to a high mountain called Santo Tomás, whence he returned to Baguio. He was, however, of the opinion that the trip down the cañon could be made without special difficulty by a party suitably provided with food and tentage.

Convinced by our report that active measures should be taken to establish communication with this wonderful region, the commission, on September 12, 1900, appropriated $5000 Mexican, "for the purpose of making a survey to ascertain the most advantageous route for a railway into the mountains of Benguet, Island of Luzon, and the probable cost thereof."

Captain Charles W. Meade, then serving as city engineer of Manila, was selected to make the survey. There was every theoretical reason to believe him competent, and we did not question either his integrity or his ability.

After being absent from Manila for some time, he reported in favour of the Bued River valley route, saying that it was entirely feasible to build a railway along it.

He suggested that, as the construction of a wagon road would be necessary in building the railroad, we might as well undertake that first, and so be able to go to Baguio in wheeled vehicles before the railroad was completed. He asked for $75,000 United States currency, with which to build this road, stating that he expected to be able to do it for $65,000, but would like $10,000 as a margin of safety.

On December 21, 1901, the commission passed an act authorizing the construction of a highway from Pozorubio, in Pangasinán, to Baguio, "the same to be built under the general supervision of the military governor and the immediate direction of Captain Charles W. Meade, Thirty-sixth Infantry, United States Volunteers, who has been detailed by the military governor for that purpose, along the general line of survey recently made by Captain Meade for a railway between said towns." The $75,000 asked for were appropriated by this act.

Work began promptly at both ends of the line. In June, 1901, I set out on my first trip through the wild man's territory in northern Luzón. Incidentally, and for my personal satisfaction only, I inspected the work on the road. We had been rather disappointed by Captain Meade's failure to make more rapid progress. At the lower end I found that delay was being caused by a huge cliff necessitating a very heavy rock cut. I was assured by Captain Meade that from this point on the line ran through dirt most of the way, so that the road could be completed very rapidly. This statement proved to be grossly in error. It took years of hard work to open up the road.

Its cost when finally ready for traffic was $1,961,847.05. Its length was forty-five kilometers eight hundred ninety-one meters,[1] of which thirty-four kilometers were in non-

---

[1] About 28.7 miles.

Christian territory. Some ten kilometers of the remainder have since been incorporated in the first-class road system of the province of Pangasinán, as this part is chiefly used by the people of that province in shipping their agricultural products to Benguet, and in maintaining communication between their towns.

The additional cost of the road to date [1] since it was first opened is $792,434, making its total cost to date $2,754,281.05. This includes not only the actual cost of maintenance, but very extensive improvements, such as the metalling of the road from the so-called zigzag to Baguio, the construction of five steel bridges, and the replacing of all the original bridges on the road and of all the original culverts except those made of concrete or masonry.

On my arrival in Benguet in 1901, I found that good progress had been made on the upper end of the road, which had penetrated for a short distance into the cañon proper without encountering any considerable obstacles.

On October 15, 1901, the commission stated in its annual report to the secretary of war, "He [2] has been much delayed by the difficulty of procuring the labour necessary for its early completion, and several months will yet elapse before it is finished!" They did!

On August 20, 1901, Captain Meade was relieved, and Mr. N. M. Holmes was made engineer of the road.

On February 3, 1902, a little sanitarium was opened in a small native house at Baguio. During the following July I was sent to it as a patient, and while in Benguet again inspected the road which had been continued high up on the cañon wall to a point where, on a very steep mountain side, a peculiar rock formation had been encountered at the very grass roots. This rock disintegrated rapidly under the action of the sun when exposed to it. Comparatively solid in the morning, it would crack to pieces and slide down the mountain side before

[1] May 1, 1913.   [2] Captain Meade.

night.   A sixty-foot cut had already been made into the precipitous mountain side, and the result was an unstable road-bed, hardly four feet in width, which threatened to go out at any moment.

My trip to Baguio promptly relieved a severe attack of acute intestinal trouble from which I had been suffering, and when Governor Taft fell ill the following year with a similar ailment, and his physicians recommended his return to the United States, I did my best to persuade him to try Baguio instead.   He decided to do so.

Five rough cottages had meanwhile been constructed for the use of the commissioners, the lumber for them being sawed by hand on the ground.   Boards had been nailed to frames as rapidly as they fell from the logs, and had shrunk to such an extent that a reasonably expert marksman might almost have thrown a cat by the tail through any one of the houses.   At night they looked like the old-fashioned perforated tin lanterns, leaking light in a thousand places.   These were the luxurious homes provided for the high officials of the government of which so much has been said !

We paid for them an annual rental amounting to ten per cent of their cost, which had of course been excessively high on account of the necessity of packing everything used in them, except the lumber, up the Naguilian trail.

However, we were in no frame of mind to be critical. We had put in three years of killing hard work, labouring seven days in the week, and keeping hours such as to arouse a feeling little short of horror among old British and other foreign residents.   We were all completely exhausted, and Mr. Taft was ill.   For my part, I would gladly have paid almost any sum for a tent under the pine trees and the privilege of occupying it for a few weeks.

On the trip up Mr. Taft had ridden a magnificent saddle horse which had been given to him by General Chaffee. At the time he left, Manila had been burning hot.   When he was at last seated on the porch of the little house which

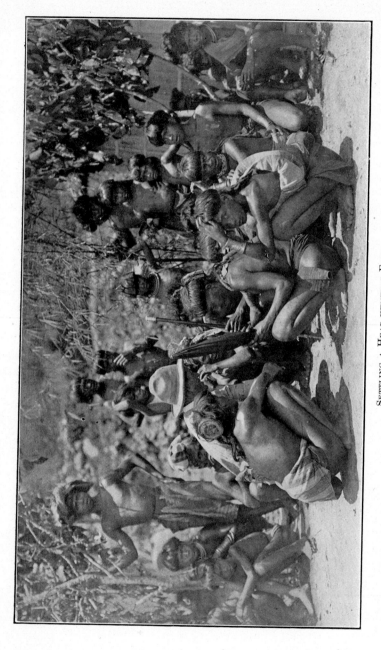

SETTLING A HEAD-HUNTING FEUD.

This picture shows Lieutenant-Governor Walter F. Hale, of Kalinga, persuading Kalinga head men of Mañgali and Lúbao to settle amicably a head-hunting feud of long standing.

was to be his home for weeks, with a cool breeze sighing through the needles of a spreading pine tree close at hand, his satisfaction knew no bounds. Already his magnificent constitution had begun to respond to the stimulation of the wonderful mountain air, and filled with enthusiasm he summoned a stenographer and dictated the following cablegram to the secretary of war : —

"April 15, 1903.

"SECWAR,

"WASHINGTON.

"Stood trip well, rode horseback 25 miles to 5000 feet altitude. Hope amœbic dysentery cured. Great province this, only 150 miles from Manila with air as bracing as Adirondacks or Murray Bay. Only pines and grass lands. Temperature this hottest month in the Philippines in my cottage porch at three in the afternoon 68. Fires are necessary night and morning.

"TAFT."

As quick as the wires could bring it, he received the following reply :

"WASHINGTON, D.C., April 16, 1903.

"TAFT,

"MANILA.

"Referring to telegram from your office of 15th inst., how is horse?

"ROOT."

When he read it his shouts of laughter, rolling over the hills of Baguio, must have been audible half a mile away !

Mr. Taft's sojourn in the hills put him again in fine condition and made it possible for him to return to Manila and resume the heavy burden of work which there awaited him. The other members of the commission also greatly benefited by their stay in the hills.

While there we heard disquieting rumours as to the practicability of completing the road. There was a difference of opinion between the engineer in charge and one of his immediate subordinates as to the route which should be followed. The consulting engineer of the commission was accordingly requested to make a survey to determine a practicable route for the unfinished portion of the road and estimate the cost of completing it. In due time he advised us that it was practicable to complete it, but that the cost would be at least $1,000,000. Warned by our experience with Meade, we wished additional expert advice, so summoned to Baguio Colonel L. W. V. Kennon, a man of great energy and executive ability, who had had large experience in engineering work in mountainous country, and requested him to go down the Bued River valley and report on the progress of the work, and the practicability of completing the road on the route which had been determined upon.

Being the youngest and most active member of the commission, I was detailed to accompany him. On this trip I became convinced that all of the engineers interested, except the consulting engineer, had grossly understated the difficulties which must be overcome before the road could be completed. Colonel Kennon decided that it was entirely feasible to build the road, but that the comparatively short stretch already completed from Baguio into the upper end of the cañon must be abandoned and a new line adopted. Furthermore, he gave us some very definite and extremely unpleasant information as to the probable cost of completing the work, his statements on this subject confirming those of the consulting engineer.

The commission was thus put face to face with the hard facts but did not flinch. On the contrary, it passed the following resolution on June 1, 1903 : —

"On Motion, RESOLVED, That it be declared the policy of the Commission to make the town of Baguio, in the Province of Benguet, the summer capital of the Archipelago and to construct suitable buildings, to secure suitable transportation, to secure proper water supply, and to make residence in Baguio possible for all of the officers and employees of the Insular Government for four months during the year, that in pursuance of this purpose the Secretary of the Interior, the Consulting Engineer to the Commission, the Chief of the Bureau of Architecture, and Major[1] L. W. V. Kennon, United States Army, whom it is the intention of the Commission to put in actual charge of the improvements in Benguet Province, including the construction of the Benguet Road, the erection of the buildings and the construction of a wagon road from Naguilian, be appointed a Committee to report plans and estimates to the Commission for the proposed improvements in the Province of Benguet and to submit same to the Commission for action and necessary appropriation, and

"BE IT FURTHER RESOLVED, That steps should be immediately taken looking to the increase of the capacity of the Sanitarium by at least twenty rooms, to the construction of seven more cottages on the grounds of the Sanitarium, to the construction of a Governor's residence on the site overlooking the big spring which is the source of the Bued River immediately south of the Sanitarium proper, to the construction of an Administration building sufficient for the Commission, the Commission's staff and the Executive Bureau, of at least twenty-five rooms, and to the making of a plan for a town site for the municipality of Baguio; but that the details of construction and improvements, with such variations from the indicated plan as may seem wise, shall be left to the committee appointed under the previous resolution."

In his annual report dated November 15, 1903, Governor Taft said : —

"In connection with the subject of health, reference should be made to the province of Benguet and to Baguio, the capital of that province. The secretary of commerce and police will refer to the work now being done in the construction of the Benguet road from Pozorrubio, through Twin Peaks, to Baguio. There have been serious engineering mistakes made in the road, and it is proving to be much more costly than was expected; but when completed its importance in the development of these islands can hardly be overestimated. One of the things essential to progress in the islands is the coming of more Americans and Europeans who shall make this their business home. If there can be brought within twelve hours' travel of Manila a place with a climate not unlike that of the Adirondacks, or of Wyoming in summer, it will add greatly

[1] He had the volunteer rank of colonel, but was a major in the regular army.

to the possibility of living in Manila for ten months of the year without risk.   It will take away the necessity for long vacations spent in America; will reduce the number who go invalided home, and will be a saving to the insular government of many thousands of dollars a year.   It will lengthen the period during which the American soldiers who are stationed here may remain without injury to their health and will thus reduce largely the expense of transportation of troops between the islands and the United States.   More than this, Filipinos of the wealthier class frequently visit Japan or China for the purpose of recuperating.   People of this class are much interested in the establishment of Baguio as a summer capital, and when the road is completed a town will spring up, made up of comfortable residences, of a fine, extensive army post, and sanitariums for the relief of persons suffering from diseases prevalent in the lowlands.   It is the hope of the government that the Roman Catholic Church will send American priests as it has sent American bishops to the islands, to assist in the moral elevation of the people.   The fear of the effect of the climate has kept many from coming.   The Roman Catholic Church authorities have announced their intention of erecting rest houses at Baguio for the purpose of the recuperation of their ministers and agents.   The Methodists and Episcopalians have already secured building lots in Baguio for this purpose.   It is the settled purpose of the Commission to see this improvement through, no matter what the cost, because eventually the expenditures must redound to the benefit of the government and people of the islands.   We have already stated, in the report on the public land act, that it is proposed, under that act, which allows the organizing of town sites, to sell the public land in suitable lots at auction so that every one interested shall have the opportunity to obtain a good lot upon which to build a suitable house." [1]

Mr. Taft would be delighted could he see to-day how completely his anticipations have been fulfilled.

Colonel Kennon was put in charge of construction work, and things began to move.   They kept moving until the road was finished.   From this time on we knew that the expense involved would be out of all proportion to the original estimate, but we were determined to push the

[1] Report of the Philippine Commission, Part 1, 1903, p. 58.

work through, having reached the decision that it was worth while to open up communication with Baguio at any cost within reason, because of its future certain value to the people of the islands as a health resort.

On April 1, 1904, I rode over the road in a vehicle nearly to Camp Four, and came the rest of the way to Baguio on horseback over a new trail which zigzagged up a mountain side near Camp Four and followed the crest of the range from there in. A little later the Commission came by the same route, and spent the hot season in the cool Benguet hills.

On January 29, 1905, Colonel Kennon drove into Baguio in the first wagon to arrive there over the Benguet Road, which was opened for regular service on March 27th of the same year. The cost of the road on November 1, 1905, had, as previously stated, been $1,966,847.05, and the cost of the heavy work in the cañon had been approximately $75,000 per mile, which is not excessive when compared with the cost of similar work in the United States, especially as this sum included maintenance of the portions constructed during previous years.

The fact that a certain amount of congressional relief funds was expended on the construction of this road has been made the subject of very unjust criticism. A large number of poor Filipinos, who were in dire straits, were thus given an opportunity for remunerative employment, and the distribution of a portion of the congressional relief fund in this way was in entire harmony with the fixed policy of the commission to avoid pauperizing the people by giving money or food outright to able-bodied persons, and to afford them relief by furnishing them opportunity to work for a good wage. A further reason why the expenditure of money from this fund on the Benguet Road was appropriate is found in the fact that the region opened up is destined to play a very important part in the cure of tuberculosis, which is the principal cause of death among the people of the lowlands, but is practically unknown among the Igorots of the hills.

During the earlier years after the road was open owners of bull carts in Pangasinán made large sums transporting freight over it.   This is not the case at the present time, as the growing volume of freight requiring to be moved led to the blocking of the road with bull carts and necessitated the installation of an automobile truck line so that it might be more expeditiously handled.

In December, 1904, the great landscape architect, Mr. D. H. Burnham, visited Baguio, and made a plan for its future development.   He was enthusiastic over its possibilities, and gave his services free of charge.   His plan is being closely adhered to, and although funds are not now available for going far toward carrying it out, we have at least avoided anything which would interfere with it.

The next important event in the history of Baguio was the first sale of residence and building lots, which took place on May 28, 1906, and was conducted in accordance with the provisions of the Public Land Act relative to town sites.

Although a howling typhoon was sweeping Benguet at the time, 91 residence lots and 15 business lots were disposed of at this first sale, and at a subsequent one held in Manila a few weeks later all the remaining lots then surveyed were sold.

The town site includes two hundred sixteen square miles, and new lots are surveyed as required.   All sums derived from the sale of lots are used for the improvement of the town site, and thus Baguio is made to help build itself.

In the spring of 1900 the Baguio Country Club was organized.   Because of the extraordinary false statements made concerning it by certain unscrupulous politicians, I give its history somewhat fully.   Its purpose was to afford a meeting place for the people of the town and to give them an opportunity for outdoor sports.   It purchased a hundred acres of land on which a low assessment had been placed in view of the semipublic purpose which it was to serve.

ENTERTAINING THE KALINGAS.

They are listening with great interest to the reproduction of a speech which one of their chiefs has just made into the receiving horn of a dictaphone.

At the outset the "club house" was a rude, grass-roofed shed made of pine slabs. Its doors and windows were mere openings which could not be closed. It was erected in about a week. Three holes of a golf course and a croquet ground had been prepared. These decidedly primitive club facilities nevertheless served to bring the people of Baguio together and give them an opportunity for a good time out of doors.

In February, 1907, a Country Club Corporation was organized with a capital stock of $5000, of which $3000 have thus far been subscribed. The shares cost $50. No single subscriber owns more than three, with the sole exception of Mr. Forbes, who took ten to help the club get started. Ownership of stock brings no emoluments, but, on the contrary, indirectly involves expense which the present owners have been willing to bear for the public good.

From these small beginnings the Baguio country club has grown into an important institution. As funds became available from the sale of stock, the payment of dues and the generous donations of a few members, an excellent nine-hole golf course was completed, and tennis courts and facilities for trap-shooting were installed. In March and April, 1908, a modest club house was built at a cost of some $5000. It has two small locker rooms, a large living room, a tiny office, a little bath, a kitchen, and nine single sleeping rooms. Three very small cottages, costing $375 each, were erected on the club grounds for the use of the members. Five larger cottages have since been constructed.

Any person of good character is eligible to membership. The entrance fee is $25, but officers of the army, navy and marine corps stationed at Baguio are admitted without the payment of this fee, and persons temporarily there may secure the privileges of the club by paying at the rate of $5 per month. The annual dues are $20. The families of members are entitled to the privileges of the club. Among its members are the highest officials of the insular government and teachers, clerks, stenographers and other employees drawing small salaries, as well as numerous permanent residents of Baguio.

It knows no race or creed, and Filipinos take advantage of its privileges quite as freely as do Americans. Representatives of every nationality in the islands may be found on its golf course on a pleasant afternoon. It is the common meeting place of Baguio, and hardly a day passes without the giving of some pleasant luncheon or dinner in its little living room or in the outdoor space covered by an overhanging roof at its eastern end. No more democratic institution ever existed.

Congressman Jones, in his attacks on the Philippine administration, is fond of stating that "there is a club for officials at Baguio." The statement is true, but reminds one of that other statement of a ship's first mate who came on board intoxicated just before the vessel sailed. The following morning, happening to look at the ship's log for the previous day, he saw the entry "The mate drunk to-day." It was his first offence, and he begged the captain to erase this record, but the captain said "It is true, is it not?" and insisted that it must stand.

A little later the captain was taken ill. Upon resumption of duty he found an entry in the log reading: "The captain sober to-day." When he furiously insisted that it be erased, the mate said "It is true, is it not?" Now, it is true that there is a club for government officers at Baguio, but in making this statement Mr. Jones and his ilk have neglected to say that there is also at Baguio a club for employees; a club for private citizens; a club for Americans; a club for Filipinos; a club for foreign consuls and other foreign residents of the islands; a club for business men; a club for clerks; and that all of these institutions are one and the same, namely, the Baguio Country Club, which is now strictly self-supporting and meets its obligations from the funds derived from the dues of its members. These dues are absurdly low in view of the privileges which it affords.

Although Mr. Forbes does not like to have it known, I cannot refrain from stating that the club has not always been self-supporting, and that he has repeatedly made up deficits from his private funds. The cost involved in getting the golf course into shape was out of all proportion to the resources of the organization. Sufficient funds were not available to pay for the club house and cottages when they were constructed, and had it not been for the generosity of Mr. Forbes the club would not exist to-day in anything like its present form.

The polo field at Baguio has been referred to as another evidence of extravagant governmental expenditure. It is true enough that it was in the first instance an expensive luxury, as an immense amount of earthwork had to be done in order to make a level piece of ground of sufficient size. The field is administered by the Country Club, and is open to the use of the public for any form of amusement which will not interfere with its use for polo. The detractors of the government have neglected to mention that the cost of its construction and maintenance have been met from the private funds of Mr. Forbes.

Returning now to the story of the growth of Baguio, the next step forward was the construction of an official residence for the governor-general, for which $15,000 were appropriated. Mr. Forbes had not the slightest personal interest in this appropriation. When it was made he had no knowledge of the fact that he was later to become governor-general, and his private Baguio residence was decidedly more comfortable and commodious than this official one. His subsequent occupancy of the latter building involved a real personal sacrifice.

In 1908 a modern hospital and the governor-general's residence were completed. No other government official is furnished a free house. All have to rent government cottages or stay at hotels, unless they choose to build for themselves. The policy of giving the governor-general an official residence in Baguio is in accord with that which gives him one at Manila.

In April, 1908, there was opened a "Teachers' Camp," to which came American school teachers from all over the islands. They were housed in a hundred and fifty tents, which were set up under the shade of the pine trees. Larger tents served as kitchen, dining room, storehouse and recitation rooms, while a structure of bamboo and nipa palm, erected at a total cost of $150, was utilized for general assembly purposes. Four talented lecturers were employed to instruct and entertain the teachers. At one time there were a hundred and ninety persons in the camp.

The credit for initiating this very important move is due chiefly to William F. Pack, at that time governor of the province of Benguet, who strongly advocated bringing the teachers to Baguio, and did everything in his power to make the first assembly the great success which it was.

It has now become a fixed institution, and has accomplished untold good. Americans who spend too many years in out-of-the-way municipalities of the Philippines without coming in contact with their kind are apt to lose their sense of perspective, and there is danger that they will grow careless, or even slovenly, in their habits. It is of the utmost benefit for school teachers to get together once a year, learn of each other's failures and successes, and profit by each other's experiences, forget their troubles while engaging in healthful athletic sports, listen to inspiring and instructive discourses, and above all else benefit by open-air life in a temperate region.

The Teachers' Camp is now a beautiful and attractive place. A fine system of walks and drives make every part of it readily accessible. It has an excellent athletic field. The teachers live in tents, but good permanent buildings have been provided in which are located the mess, a social hall, recitation rooms, etc., and several comfortable cottages have been constructed for the use of visiting lecturers and others. An outdoor amphitheatre which seats a thousand persons has been built at small expense by taking advantage of peculiarly favorable natural conditions. Filipino teachers share the pleasures and benefits of the camp with their American associates, and the "assembly" certainly does great good.

During the hot season of 1908 the Bureau of Lands transferred a number of its employees to Baguio, quartering them in tents. This was done in order to ascertain the practical effect of sending American and Filipino employees to this mountain resort. The conclusion was reached that the small additional expense involved was more than justified by the larger quantity and higher quality of the work performed as a result of the greatly improved physical condition of the workers. Every Filipino sent to Baguio gained in weight, with the single exception of a messenger who had to run his legs off! Other bureaus subsequently followed the example of the Bureau of Lands, with similar results.

During the 1909 season, the railroad having reached Camp One, five large Stanley steam automobiles were operated by the government in transporting passengers from this place to Baguio, and more than two thousand persons were thus moved over the road.

Meanwhile, the unexpectedly heavy expense involved in completing the road had been made the subject of severe criticism by the public press of Manila. Most of the critics were entirely honest, having no idea of the character of the country opened up, or of the importance of making it readily accessible.

Just at the time when the commission should have crowded its programme through to conclusion, it faltered. The only government construction work performed at the summer capital that year, in addition to what has been mentioned, was the erection of a small office building and of a barrack building for labourers, the enlarging of five government cottages, the addition of out-buildings, and the enlarging of a building which served as a combination sanatorium and hotel.

This policy of inaction was a mistaken one. It made the Benguet Road seem like the city avenue which ran into a street, the street into a lane, the lane into a cow path, the cow path into a squirrel track and the squirrel track up a tree, for while one could get to Baguio, there was very little there after one arrived. The accommodations at the sanatorium were strictly limited, and there was some apparent justification for the charge freely made that the Philippine Commission had voted to spend very large sums of money to open up a health resort from which only its members and its staff derived benefit.

The government had at the outset been obliged to construct its buildings on a piece of private land purchased from Mr. Otto Scheerer, as prior to the passage of the Public Land Act and its approval by the President and Congress, building on public land was impossible. Now, however, a town site had been surveyed, and plans for the future development of Baguio had been made by one of the world's most competent experts. The time had arrived for action. Mr. Forbes, then secretary of commerce and police, argued vigorously for the carrying out of the original plan of the commission by the construction of adequate public buildings. To help the development of the place, he purchased two adjacent building lots and on the tract of land so secured built a handsome and expensive home, where he subsequently entertained not only his personal friends, but guests of the government, as well as various persons who had no other claim on him than the fact that they were officers or employees of the government who were in need of a change of climate and could ill afford to seek it at their own expense. Among his house guests were General Aguinaldo, Speaker Osmeña and many other Filipinos. It was Mr. Forbes's idea, and mine as well, that members of

AN IFUGAO FAMILY.

The man is Gulned, the most influential of the Ifugao chiefs.

the commission ought to set the example by building at Baguio. I followed his example to the extent of buying a lot and constructing on it a simple and inexpensive house, thus obtaining the first and only home that I have ever owned.

Ultimately Mr. Forbes formulated a plan for the construction of a group of government buildings, a mess hall and a large number of small and inexpensive cottages for rental to government officers and employees so that the executive offices of the government might be transferred to Baguio during the heated term and it might become the true summer capital of the Philippines. This plan was adopted in substance, and it was decided to transfer the bureaus of the government to Baguio for the coming hot season, so far as practicable.

Funds were appropriated for the carrying out of Mr. Forbes's plan, but before the construction work had fairly begun there occurred, on October 17, 1909, a destructive typhoon. Eighteen inches of rain fell in nine hours, and twenty-six inches in twenty-four hours. The Bued River quickly rose fifty feet, carrying away trees and rocks which obstructed its course, and seriously injuring the road for miles. Four of the largest bridges were swept away and the work of constructing government buildings, which was just about to begin, was greatly retarded. It was not thought possible to transfer the bureaus of the government to Baguio for the coming hot season as planned. Indeed, there were not lacking those who insisted that no one would be able to get there. Mr. Haubé, the energetic and capable young engineer in charge, had the road open on the twentieth day of December, and the projected buildings ready for occupancy in February, a noteworthy and highly creditable achievement.

It was then thought that the storm which had done such serious damage to the road was of unprecedented violence, but there was worse to come. On July 14 and 15, 1911, a terrific typhoon swept across northern Luzón, bringing down one of the world's record rainfalls. Between noon of the 14th and noon of the 15th, forty-five and ninety-nine hundredths inches of rain fell at Baguio. A mountain forming a part of the wall of the Bued cañon split from the top and the detached portion toppled over into the river, damming it to a depth of about a hundred and fifty feet at a time when it was carrying an enormous volume of water. When this dam burst, an avalanche of earth and rock, swept onward by a huge wave, rushed down the cañon, leaving complete destruction in its wake. Every bridge in its course was carried away, and the road was left in such condition that it would have cost $300,000 to open it for traffic. Then Providence, having apparently done its worst, relented and sent another typhoon which washed away most of the débris left by the first one, uncovering the road-bed and making it possible to reopen communication for $50,000.

The cost of maintaining the Benguet Road has proved excessive. Mountains tower above it on both sides to a height of four to seven thousand feet and the drainage basin which finds its outlet down the narrow gorge through which the road runs is enormous. Even so, under ordinary climatic conditions its maintenance does not offer very exceptional difficulties, as much of it is blasted out of rock; but during extraordinarily heavy storms the danger of destruction by overwhelming floods is great.

While a century may pass before there is another storm like the one which brought down the terrific slide above described, there may be one at any time, and when the railroad has once reached Baguio, it is hardly probable that such extensive repairs as were necessary after the last destructive typhoon will ever again be made, especially as the horse trail built on a carriage road grade from Baguio to Naguilian in the lowlands has been widened little by little, until it is now safe for small automobiles. The maintenance of the bridges alone, on the Benguet Road, is a very formidable item, while there is only one short bridge on the Naguilian Road before the province of Union is reached. As it runs on or near the crests of ridges all the way, there are no extensive watersheds above it, and it is not liable to serious injury during the most violent storms. The total cost of the Benguet portion of this road to date[1] has been only $33,405. This stretch is seventeen and a half miles in length and does not include that portion of the road which lies within the city of Baguio. The total distance from the centre of Baguio to Bauang, the nearest railroad station on the coast, is thirty-four miles.

With the completion of the new government buildings and the transfer of the several bureaus to Baguio for the season of 1910 a real boom began. The old sanatorium building had long been leased to a private individual who used it for hotel purposes, adding to it from time to time. A second hotel had been built. The railroad had been extended to Camp One and a regular automobile service established for the convenience of the public between Camp One and Baguio. The Jesuits had constructed a great rest house and meteorological observatory on a commanding hill. The Dominicans had purchased a neighbouring hill top and prepared to erect thereon a very large reënforced concrete building to serve for college purposes and as a rest house for members of the order who required a change of climate.

Development began early at Camp John Hay, an extensive and beautiful military reservation set aside within the Baguio town site. Some progress had been made in this direction prior to the coming of Major-General Leonard Wood. That highly efficient and far-seeing officer gave a tremendous impetus to the work. He had been something of a sceptic on the subject of Baguio before visiting the place, but, like all other responsible persons who take the trouble to see it, promptly became an enthusiast when he had an opportunity to observe conditions for himself. Many army officers and their families who

[1] May 1, 1913.

could not obtain accommodations in the limited number of buildings on the reservation were glad to take tents for the season, and the Camp promptly began to serve useful ends. It has steadily grown and developed ever since, and is now a well-organized army post. Its remarkable progress has been due in large measure to the initiative and ingenuity of Captain M. R. Hilgard, who has been its commander since October, 1905. Great progress has been made in erecting buildings, but they are still far short of the needs of the service. At the present writing [1] there are many tents in use by officers and their families. These serve very well during the dry months, but with the oncoming of the heavy showers, which usher in the rainy season, become damp and uncomfortable and make it necessary for the occupants to return to the lowlands just at the time when Baguio is growing most attractive and the heat of Manila is becoming most oppressive.

The ground set aside in the military reservation is adequate for a brigade post, and such a post should be established as soon as the railroad reaches Baguio. The different commands in the islands could then be ordered there in succession, and officers and men given the benefits of one of the best climates in the world.

Baguio has continued steadily to develop, and the Benguet Road no longer ends by running up a tree. The government has not only erected a residence for the governor-general, but has established offices for the chief executive, the secretaries of departments, the Philippine Commission, the Executive Bureau, and the Bureaus of Agriculture, Civil Service, Education, Forestry, Health, Public Works and Constabulary. There are also a hospital, a series of tuberculosis cottages for the treatment of patients from the lowlands, cottages and dormitories for government officers and employees, a great mess hall where meals may be had at moderate cost, an automobile station, a garage, storehouses, a pumping plant, and labourers'

[1] April 15, 1913.

quarters. At the Teachers' Camp there are a separate mess hall, an assembly hall and a fine athletic field.

The city of Baguio has a city hall, a storehouse, a corral and market buildings. Lot owners who have built summer homes for themselves have brought up friends to show them what Baguio was like. Curiously it has never seemed possible to convey any adequate idea of its attractions and advantages by word of mouth. Again and again I have urged sceptics to come and see for themselves. When after the lapse of years they finally did so, they have invariably asked me why I had not told them about it before, forgetting that I had exhausted my vocabulary without being able to make them understand. Practically without exception, the persons who actually visit Baguio become "boosters."

It is fortunate in a way that the boom did not come quicker, for the hard truth is that up to date the rapidity of the growth of the summer capital has been determined absolutely by the local lumber supply. The original Filipino hand-sawyers were ultimately replaced by small portable mills, and these in turn by large modern mills to which logs are brought by skidding engines or overhead cables, yet it is true to-day, as it has always been true, that no sawmill has ever been able to furnish dry lumber, for the simple reason that the green output is purchased as fast as it can be sawed.

For a time the lumbermen took advantage of the necessities of the public, but when timber on the government concessions first granted them had been exhausted and they applied for new cutting areas, my turn came. I fixed maximum prices on lumber which they might not exceed without forfeiting their concessions. I also fixed a minimum annual cut which they were compelled to make, and imposed a regulation providing that at least half of the total cut should be offered for sale to the public.

There is no justification for the claim that Baguio is a rich man's city. The town site is very large and can be indefinitely extended.   Good lots may be had at extremely moderate prices, and the cost of houses is strictly a matter of individual means and taste.   A large section is given up to small dwellings for Filipinos.   The man who earns his living with a bull cart has no more difficulty in establishing a home there than does the Filipino millionnaire, and rich and poor are building in constantly increasing numbers.

While experience has taught me that I cannot convey by words alone any adequate conception of what Baguio is like, I must nevertheless here make the attempt.

Twenty-one miles of well surfaced roads wind among its pine-covered hills and afford beautiful glimpses of the luxuriant vegetation along its numerous small streams. There are building sites to suit all tastes, and each house owner is convinced that his particular location is better than that of any one else.   One spring supplies exceptionally pure water sufficient for the needs of at least ten thousand people, and an abundant additional supply can be obtained when needed.   The scenery is everywhere beautiful, and in many sections truly magnificent.

Gently rolling hills enclose valleys with sides sometimes steep and precipitous and sometimes gently sloping. The country is watered by numerous streams bordered by magnificent tree-ferns, and by trees, shrubs, and plants requiring a large amount of water, while the dry hillsides bear noble pines standing at wide intervals and often arranged as if grouped by a skilled landscape artist. During the rainy season they are covered with ferns and orchids, while exquisite white lilies, larger than Easter lilies, dot the hillsides.   The dense *cógon* of the Philippine lowlands is absent.   Bamboo grass or *runo* occurs sparingly in the immediate vicinity of streams and springs, but the hills are covered with a short grass seldom more than knee high, so that one may ride or walk over them in almost any direction with comfort.   A system of excellent horse trails affords communication with neighbouring provinces where one may see wonderful tropical vegetation, magnificent scenery, strange wild peoples, and the most remarkable terraced mountainsides in the world. These regions may be visited with safety and comfort, as public order is well-nigh perfect and rest houses have been provided at reasonable intervals on all important main trails.

The delightfully cool climate of Baguio makes active outdoor exercise enjoyable, and insures the speedy restoration to health and vigor of persons suffering ill effects from tropical heat, or recuperation from wasting diseases. Open fires are comfortable morning and evening throughout the year, and the pitch pine wood burns beautifully. Except during typhoons the rainy season weather is delightful. When one wakens in the morning the atmosphere and the landscape have been washed clean. The air is clear as crystal, and mountain peaks fifty or seventy-five miles away stand out with cameo-like sharpness. The needles of the pines fairly glisten and their delightful odor is constantly in one's nostrils. The whole country is green as a lawn. Roses, violets, azaleas, "jacks-in-the-pulpit," and several kinds of raspberries and huckleberries, all growing wild, make one feel as if back in America. One may visit the neighbouring Trinidad valley and see cabbages and coffee, bananas and Irish potatoes, flourishing on one piece of land. Strawberry plants imported from America bear continuously from December to May. Fresh vegetables of all sorts tickle palates which have grown weary of the canned goods of the lowlands.

Anywhere from twelve to three o'clock, the clouds begin to roll in and heavy showers fall, usually lasting until nine or ten at night. Then the stars come out. The next day is like its predecessor.

After the first rains, which usually come about the middle of April, there is as a rule a month of beautiful weather with very little precipitation. Then the rains begin to come steadily again, and keep it up until the end of the wet season, falling in the manner already described so that one can get one's outdoor exercise in the morning, while the afternoon showers are conducive to industry.

The following table shows the average maximum, minimum and mean temperatures for each month of the year, the figures covering the period January, 1902, to January, 1908 : —

MONTH	AVERAGE MAXIMUM	AVERAGE MINIMUM	MEAN
	° F.	° F.	° F.
January	75.1	50.2	63.3
February	75.4	45.8	61.6
March	77.5	49.4	64.1
April	78.2	51.9	65.7
May	77.7	54	66.2
June	77	56.8	66.2
July	75.9	55.9	65.4
August	76	54.9	65.1
September	75.2	56	65.2
October	76.4	53.8	65.1
November	76.4	49.8	64.1
December	76.1	50.3	64.1

All of the above figures are for temperatures at a height of six feet above the ground. Temperatures nearer the ground are decidedly lower. It has been found that in the Baguio plateau the lowest temperatures correspond to the deepest valleys. In such places white frost is not rare during the months of January, February, and March, while on the tops of hills the temperature is milder, frost being almost unknown. During typhoons conditions do not differ essentially from those experienced elsewhere in the islands, except that the rainfall is exceptionally heavy.

Major-General J. Franklin Bell, who has given special attention to mountain resorts the world over, vigorously asserts that Baguio has no equal on the globe. Certainly the climate is more nearly perfect than any other of which I have personal knowledge, and the delightful

Ifugao Dancers.

coolness and the bracing air afford heavenly relief to jangling nerves and exhausted bodies, worn out by overwork and by a too prolonged sojourn in tropical lowlands.

One of the very important things about the Baguio climate is its marvellous effect upon victims of tuberculosis.

Persons suffering from this disease in its earlier stages may confidently look forward to restored health if willing to live out of doors under the pine trees, and there have been a number of extraordinary recoveries among those in advanced stages.

A series of little cottages which can be thrown wide open have been operated for some time in connection with the government hospital, in order practically to demonstrate the effect of the climate on tuberculosis victims.

The results are conclusive, and whenever funds are available there should be established a settlement of such cottages on some one of the numerous good sites sufficiently removed from the town to avoid any possible danger of infecting healthy persons. There should also be a large mess hall from which good nourishing food can be served, and plenty of level ground on which tents can be erected during the dry season. Baguio's potential importance as a resort for victims of the great white plague justifies every cent of expenditure necessary to make it readily accessible.

The Sisters of the Assumption have erected a handsome building which serves as a rest house and a girls' school. The sisters known as the "Belgian Canonist Missionaries" are erecting a building which will afford them a place to come for recuperation when wearied by strenuous work in the lowlands, and will make it possible for them to open a school for Igorot girls, which they are planning to do.

Bishop Brent has established an excellent school for American boys, situated on a sunny hilltop. The instruction is very good, the food excellent, and a healthier, heartier-looking lot of youngsters than those who enjoy the privileges of this institution cannot be found anywhere. There is abundant opportunity for them to play basket-ball, tennis and golf. Some of them indulge in polo, playing on Filipino ponies.

Bishop Brent also has a mission school for Igorot girls, and plans to open a boarding school for American girls in the near future.

The Belgian missionary priests, locally known as the "Missionary Priests of the Church of San Patricio," have their headquarters at Baguio, where the chief of their order resides and where they come occasionally for rest and recuperation. Archbishop Harty has a modest home on one of the numerous hilltops.

The building of a school for constabulary officers, to which young men arriving from the United States are sent before entering upon active service, crowns another hill and commands a magnificent view of the surrounding country.

Several business concerns, such as the Compañia General de Tabacos de Filipinas, have erected rest houses for their officers and employees, while the number of attractive private homes increases as rapidly as the supply of building materials will permit. Filipino residents of Manila have recently invested more than a hundred thousand dollars in Baguio homes.

But this is not all. No description would be anything like complete without mention of a unique structure which is certain to become famous the world over. It has been built under the immediate supervision of Major-General Bell, who has given freely of his time and thought to make it the extraordinary success which it is. I refer to the wonderful amphitheatre which stands at the side of the official residence of the major-general commanding the Division of the Philippines. Advantage has been taken of the existence of a natural amphitheatre with remarkable acoustic properties. Man has added what Nature left undone, and the result is an imposing and beautiful auditorium capable of seating four thousand people, throughout which a whisper can be heard. It is utilized for religious services, concerts, lectures, theatrical performances and other public entertainments. No charge is exacted for its use, but if an admission fee is collected, a liberal percentage of the proceeds must go to some worthy charity. It has been terraced in stone by Igorot labourers; the trees originally standing in it have been protected, and tree ferns, shrubs and flowering plants have been added. The result beggars description, and photographs do it scant justice.

Igorots from Bontoc, and even Ifugaos, now visit Baguio with increasing frequency, attracted by a large market established especially for the benefit of the hill people, where they may sell their manufactured articles or agricultural products, and may purchase at moderate cost the commodities which they need. The Benguet Igorots do not raise rice enough for their own use. Formerly they had to make up the shortage by eating *camotes*, but they have now become so prosperous that they can afford to buy rice, which is carted in over the Benguet Road.

There are promising gold mines close at hand. Their development would have been impossible had not the construction of the Benguet Road made it feasible to bring in the necessary heavy machinery.

Some of the fruits, many of the flowers and practically all of the vegetables of the temperate zone can be advantageously produced in Benguet. They are being shipped to Manila in steadily increasing quantities.

One would gather from the criticisms of the enemies of the Philippine government that the Benguet Road was a pleasure boulevard. The government motor trucks transported over it during the last fiscal year 22,390 passengers and 7696.24 metric tons of freight.

Railroad corporations are inclined to be a bit soulless. The Manila Railway Company is extending its line to Baguio by means of a branch leaving the main line at Aringay. The building of this extension is now [1] fifty-

[1] May 1, 1913.

five per cent completed, and the company is bound under the terms of its agreement to finish the road by August, 1914.   In the event of its failure to do so, it must pay a monthly penalty amply sufficient in amount to cover the cost of maintaining the Benguet Road.   Baguio will continue to develop steadily until the railroad is opened and then will go ahead by leaps and bounds.   It is sure to prosper because it meets a very real and very imperative need.

In this connection the following extracts from a letter of August 7, 1913, from the director of medical services in India to the department surgeon of the Philippines are of interest : —

" In reply to your letter of June 31st I attach a statement showing the number and location of the hill stations in India with the approximate capacity of each, and their height above sea-level.

"With regard to your inquiry regarding the number of cases treated in these sanitaria we use these hill stations not only for the treatment of convalescents, but also for giving healthy men an opportunity of spending the Indian hot weather under the best climatic conditions procurable.   To this end, so far as is practicable, all units are sent to the hills for the first hot weather after their arrival in India, and they are thus able to settle down to their new conditions of life without being immediately exposed to the trying and enervating environment of a plains station in the summer months.   We also send as many soldiers as we can of the older residents from hot stations to summer in the hills.

*   *   *   *   *   *   *

"Practically all soldiers' wives and families are given an opportunity of a change from the more unhealthy stations to the hills during the hot weather.

*   *   *   *   *   *   *

"Our experience shows that the following cases are most benefited by a change to the hills : —

"1. All cases of malarial fever and malarial cachexia.

"2. Patients recovering from acute diseases.

"3. Convalescents after surgical operations.

"4. Cases of anaemia and debility.
"5. Cases of chronic venereal diseases.
"6. Neurasthenics."

Not only are all such cases greatly benefited at Baguio, but patients suffering from dysentery and chronic diarrhœa are also greatly benefited and often cured by a sufficiently long sojourn there. This is the experience of the civil government at its hospital and of the military authorities at the Camp John Hay hospital, according to General Bell.

Continuing the quotations from the letter of the director of medical services in India : —

"We have found that by the judicious use of hill stations for convalescents both the invaliding and death rate of the British troops in Indian have been enormously reduced and the efficiency of the Army has been increased with a considerable financial saving to the Government.

"It is advisable that all troops and families should be accommodated in huts, especially during the rainy season in the hills, but there is no doubt that they are benefited by the change even if they have to live in tents and are thereby exposed to considerable discomfort."

The importance attached by the British to hill stations is shown by the fact that there are no less than 29 in India, their height above sea-level varying from 2000 to 7936 feet. Of these eleven have no permanent accommodations and are used for men only.

I add the following extracts from a letter of Major P. M. Ashburn, Medical Corps, U.S.A., president of the army board for the study of tropical diseases : —

"A man can remain in the tropics indefinitely without being actually sick, if infectious diseases are avoided. This is fast leading to the fallacy that we can advantageously remain many years in these latitudes. The fact that while a man may never be sick, he yet may have his physical and mental vigour greatly impaired by prolonged exposure to heat is thus lost sight of. No man can do his best work, either physical or mental, if he is hot and uncomfortable. The same feeling of lassitude and indisposition to exertion is experienced at home during the hot summer, which after a few years here becomes chronic."

"It is a matter of official recognition that government employees need to get away from the heat of Manila each year, hence the removal to Baguio.

"It is likewise commonly recognized that many women and children become so run down and debilitated as to need to go to Japan, Baguio or the United States.

"It is often true that monotony and discomfort are the cause of nervous and mental breakdown, witness the often-mentioned insanity among farmers' wives and the nervous breakdowns attributable to pain and strain, even though it be, as in many cases of eyestrain, so slight as not to be recognized by the patient."

In short, it is the monotony of a tropical lowland climate which makes an occasional change so imperatively necessary. Shall residents of the Philippines be forced to seek that change, at great expense of time and money, in Japan, the United States or Europe, or shall we make and keep available for them a region which admirably answers the purpose, distant only half a day's travel from Manila?

I give extracts from a memorandum of Col. William H. Arthur, Department Surgeon of the Philippines, which are important in this connection: —

"3. Experience has shown that long residence in the Philippines has a marked effect on the mental and physical vigour of people not born and raised in the tropics. This is manifested in many ways, and men, women and children who are not actually ill, seem to lose their energy, become listless, irritable, and forgetful, and find the least exertion burdensome. This is much aggravated in the hot season, and very few individuals manage, without permanent mental and physical deterioration, to live through many hot seasons in the plains.

"4. There are in the Philippine Islands two places where relief from these conditions can be found: — (1) Camp John Hay, near Baguio, in the mountain province of Benguet, Island of Luzón; and (2) Camp Keithley, in the Lake Lanao District of the Island of Mindanao. Camp John Hay, in the province of Benguet, is in the mountains at an elevation of approximately 5000 feet and is 175 miles from Manila, most of which distance is covered by railroad. Within 18 months it is expected that the railroad all the way to Baguio will be completed.

An Ifugao Dancer.

"5. Experience has shown that a large number of cases of disease or injury, or patients convalescing from surgical operations, recover much more rapidly in the cool mountain climate of Baguio than in the depressing heat and humidity of the plains. Before the establishment of this mountain refuge from the heat of the plains, many cases of this class were transferred to the United States that are now brought back to health at Camp John Hay and Camp Keithley. The beneficial effect of the change in climate is particularly noticeable in people who have become run down after one or more hot seasons spent at the lower levels.

"6. The great value of a refuge in the mountains from the effect of prolonged heat is shown in enclosed reports, which indicate the classes of cases especially benefited, but there are a great many others not reported and not actually sick but whose vitality and resistance are more or less diminished and who find great benefit from an occasional sojourn in the mountains of Benguet or the highlands of Mindanao, especially during the hottest part of the year."

I have quoted thus at length from communications of a distinguished British medical officer, of a well-known and able special student of tropical diseases, and of the ranking United States army surgeon in the islands to show the consensus of opinion among experienced experts as to the necessity of hill stations in the tropics. I might give numerous additional similar opinions of equally competent men but will only add two more statements of Major Ashburn, the latter of which seems to me admirably to sum up the situation : —

So firm is my belief in the efficacy of the place that I have at considerable expense kept my two sons in school there, instead of keeping them at home in Manila at no expense for schooling, and so satisfactory has been the result in normal, vigorous growth and robust health for both boys, that I consider the money so spent about the best investment I have ever made.

* * * * * * *

I state all this to show the faith that is in me. To experience Baguio and to see the rapid improvement of visitors there is to be convinced that it is a delightful and beneficial climate. To appreciate the full degree of its delights it is only necessary to compare in one's own experience (not in weather reports) a hot season in Manila and one there.　To appreciate its benefits it is necessary to compare in one's own experience (not in statistics) the appearance of health of the people seen at the two times and places.　As recent work on beriberi has clearly shown the vast importance in diet of substances formerly not known to have any importance, so, I think, are the factors in climate not to be recorded by wind gauges, thermometers or other meteorological instruments, and factors in health and efficiency not recorded in books on physiology, bacteriology, pathology or health statistics."

Let no one think that the summer capital of the Philippines has been built solely for the benefit of Americans. The Filipinos need it almost as much as we do, and many of them profit by the change with extraordinary promptness.

It is really almost incredible that such a place should exist within eight hours' travel of Manila, and every possible victim of tuberculosis in the islands, which means every inhabitant of the lowlands, has a right to demand that it should be made, and kept, readily accessible.　Existing accommodations are nothing like adequate for the crowds which desire to take advantage of them during the season.　Hotels are filled to overflowing. There are always several different applicants for each government cottage.　Many persons who would be glad to spend the hot months in the Benguet mountains find it impossible to do so, because they cannot obtain accommodation, and at present many more are obliged to shorten their stay in order to give others a chance.

In the early days, when we were facing unforeseen difficulties and discouragements, I was for a time the one member of the Philippine Commission who was really enthusiastically in favour of carrying out the original plans for the summer capital.　It was then the fashion to charge me with responsibility for the policy of opening up communication with the place and for the mistakes made in the construction of the Benguet Road, although I had never had any control over the road work and had been one of five at first, and later one of nine, to vote for every appropriation found necessary in order to complete it.

It was the enthusiasm of Mr. Forbes which at a critical time finally saved the situation, and now that Baguio has arrived, and the wisdom of the policy so long pursued in the face of manifold discouragements has been demonstrated, my one fear is that he will get all the glory and that I shall be denied credit for the part which I actually did play in bringing about the determination to establish quick communication with one of the most wonderful mountain health resorts to be found in any tropical country, and in giving that determination effect. But I have had a more than abundant reward of another sort. My wife, my son and I myself, when seriously ill, have been restored to vigorous health by brief sojourns at this one of the world's great health resorts.

It has been very much the fashion for Filipino politicians to rail at Baguio, and now that the dangerous experiment of giving them control of both houses of the legislature is being made, they may refuse to appropriate the sums necessary to make possible the annual transfer of the insular government to that place. The result of such a bit of politics would be a marked increase in the present extraordinarily low death rate among government officers and employees, American and Filipino,[1] beginning in about two years, when the cumulative effect of long residence in the lowlands makes itself felt.

Meanwhile, Baguio can stand on its own feet, and if, as the politicians suggest, the government buildings there be sold at auction, purchasers for all dwelling houses should readily be found. Too many Filipinos have learned by happy experience the delights of this wonderful region, to let such an opportunity pass. Baguio has come to stay.

[1] This rate, for the fiscal year 1913, was 3.33 per thousand for Filipinos and 2.49 per thousand for Americans.

CHAPTER XVIII

The Coördination of Scientific Work

WHEN Americans landed at Manila, they found no government institutions for the training of physicians and surgeons and no hospital in any sense modern or indeed worthy of the name.

There did exist the equipment of what had been called a municipal laboratory, outfitted for a limited amount of chemical work only.

When the Philippine Commission arrived on the scene, it fell to my lot to draft the necessary legislation for placing scientific work on a firm foundation, and, later, as secretary of the interior, to exercise ultimate executive control over practically all such work carried on under the insular government.

The complete initial lack of adequate hospital facilities and of means for making chemical and bacteriological investigations had been promptly remedied by the establishment of army hospitals and an army laboratory. Although these could not be placed fully at the service of the public, they nevertheless bridged the gap for the time being, and in formulating laws and making plans for the future I was inclined to say, "Blessed be nothing," as we were not hampered by useless employees or archaic equipment, but were left free to make a clean start.

I had thoroughly learned one lesson at the University of Michigan while a member of its zoölogical staff. We had a zoölogical laboratory in which were conducted the zoölogical half of a course in general biology and numerous other courses in animal morphology, mammalian anatomy, comparative anatomy and embryology. There was also a botanical laboratory in which all of the botanical work

488

of the institution was carried on. This did not involve any overlapping, but there was overlapping of the work of the zoölogical laboratory and that of the medical department, which had an anatomical laboratory, a histological laboratory, a pathological laboratory and a so-called hygienic laboratory. The professor of anatomy thought that his students would understand human anatomy better if they knew something of comparative anatomy, and instead of sending them to us wished to start his own courses. The histologist dabbled in embryology and was soon duplicating our course in the embryology of the chick. He was constantly at war with the pathologist over the question of where histology left off and pathology began, and both of them were inclined to differ with the man in charge of the hygienic laboratory over similar questions of jurisdiction. Furthermore, we had a chemical laboratory split up into various more or less independent subdivisions, and a psychological laboratory. In these several institutions for scientific research there was much duplication of instruction and of books, apparatus and laboratory equipment. Great economies might have been effected by the establishment of a central purchasing agency, which could have obtained wholesale rates on supplies ordered in large quantity. Nothing of the sort existed. One laboratory chief would order from the corner drug store, while another bought in Germany.

There was danger that a similar condition of things might arise in the Philippines. The Bureau of Health would want its chemical and its biological laboratories; the Bureau of Agriculture would need to do chemical work covering a wide range of subjects, and botanical and entomological work as well. The Bureau of Forestry would of course require a large amount of botanical work, and would also need to have chemical work done on gums, resins and other forest products, to say nothing of investigating insects injurious to trees and more especially to timber after cutting. The latter class of destroyers do enormous damage in the Philippines. Much chemical work would be required by the Bureau of Customs, which as a matter of fact later insisted upon the necessity of a "microscopical laboratory" to provide facilities for the examination of fibres, etc. Obviously there would be a large amount of work for the general government in connection with investigation of the mineral resources of the country, and the testing of coals, cements and road materials.

Smallpox was decimating the population. There was need of the manufacture of great quantities of virus with which to combat it, and of other common and necessary serums and prophylactics as well.

Here then was a golden opportunity to start right. In imagination I saw a Bureau of Science for scientific research and for routine scientific work, a great General Hospital, and a modern and up-to-date College of Medicine and Surgery, standing side by side and working in full and harmonious relationship. The medical school would give to the youth of the land the best possible facilities for theoretical training in medicine and surgery, while access to the wards of the hospital would make possible for them a large amount of practical bedside work. Its operating amphitheatres would increase the opportunity for clinical instruction, as would a great free outpatient clinic, conducted primarily for the benefit of the poor. Professors in the college would hold positions on the hospital staff, not only in order to give to them and to their students every facility for clinical demonstration work, but to enable them constantly to "keep their hands in." Promising Filipino graduates would be given internships and other positions on the house staff of the hospital. Patients would be admitted to its free beds subject to the condition that they allow their cases to be studied by the faculty and students of the college. The necessary biological and chemical examinations for the hospital would be made in the laboratories of the Bureau of Science, which would at the same time afford every facility for the carrying on of scientific investigation by advanced students, by members of the faculty of the college and by members of the hospital staff. Members of the staff of the biological laboratory would have the use of the great volume of pathological material from the hospital, and with free access to its rooms and wards, would have an almost unparalleled opportunity for the study of tropical diseases, while some of the officers and employees of the Bureau of Science and of the Bureau of Health might be made members of the faculty of the college and their services utilized as instructors.

As we had neither laboratories, hospital nor college at the time, the realization of this somewhat comprehensive scheme seemed rather remote. It was commonly referred to as "Worcester's dream," and one of my friends in the army medical corps probably quite correctly voiced public sentiment when he said, "Poor Worcester has bats in his belfry." However, he laughs best who laughs last! After the lapse of a good many years my dream came true. The three great institutions which I hoped might sometime be established are to-day in existence, and are doing the work which I hoped that they might perform. Now let us consider how they came to be.

In the early days I drafted an act providing for the establishment of a Bureau of Government Laboratories which should perform all of the biological and chemical work of the government under the direction of one chief, and on July 1, 1901 the commission passed it.

I was more than fortunate in securing as the director of this bureau Dr. Paul C. Freer, then professor of general chemistry at the University of Michigan.

Dr. Freer obtained leave of absence for a year, in order to help us get started. This leave was twice extended for additional periods of one year each, and in the end he decided to sever his connection with the university and throw in his lot with the Philippine government.

He remained in charge of the Bureau of Government Laboratories and of its successor, the Bureau of Science, until his death on April 17, 1912.

Himself a chemist and investigator of note, he had a wide and catholic knowledge of science in general, and no better man could have been found for this important piece of constructive work. For nearly a year the two of us laboured over plans for the laboratory building and lists of the necessary books, instruments, apparatus, glassware, chemicals and other supplies. At the end of this time we submitted to the commission what I do not hesitate to say was the most complete estimate for a large project which ever came before it. Much forethought was necessary in order to time the orders for books, instruments and apparatus so that it would be possible to house them properly when they arrived, and the estimated expense was distributed over a period of two and one-half years.

Meanwhile work had begun in cramped temporary quarters in a hot little "shack," for it deserved no better name, back of the Civil Hospital. Here under almost impossible conditions there were performed a large volume of routine biological and chemical work, and a considerable amount of research, the results of which proved to be of far-reaching importance.

With the employment of the first chemists and bacteriologists there arose a class of questions which I determined to settle once for all. There is a regrettable tendency among some scientific men to try to build barbed-wire fences around particular fields of research in which they happen to be interested, and to shoo every one else away.

At the outset I gave all employees clearly to understand that such an unscientific and ungenerous spirit would not be tolerated in the Bureau of Government Laboratories. The field which opened before us was enormous. There was work enough and more than

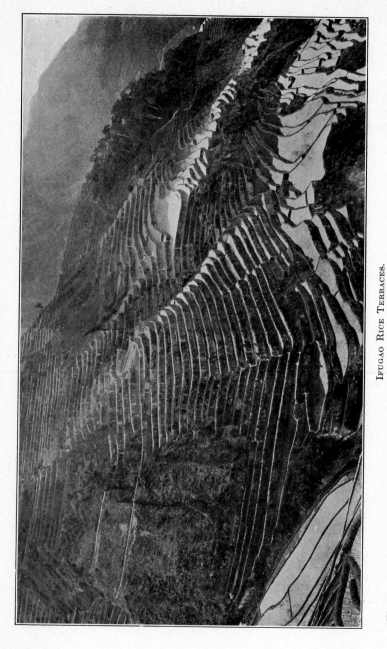

IFUGAO RICE TERRACES.

The wonderful irrigated rice terraces of the Ifugaos sometimes extend up steep mountain sides for thousands of feet. They afford an extraordinary example of successful primitive hydraulic engineering.

enough for all, and we should at the outset adopt a spirit of friendliness and helpfulness toward every scientific man who desired to lend a hand.

This rule of conduct has been steadfastly adhered to. Numerous well-known scientists have visited the Philippines and to each we have extended all possible assistance, furnishing laboratory quarters, instruments, apparatus and reagents, and, whenever practicable, material as well. Indeed, many of our scientific guests have been made employees of the bureau without pay, so that there might be no questioning of their right to use government equipment.

Two important results have followed this policy. One is that we have established the friendliest and most helpful relations with numerous research institutions. The other is that we have been able to assist in the performance of much valuable work which has borne important results, and which would perhaps have remained undone had it not been possible for us to aid those who undertook it.

In due course of time came our fine new building, with good facilities for performing all kinds of laboratory work. When it was equipped and occupied, we were able to say that the opportunities offered at Manila for investigating tropical diseases were probably unequalled elsewhere, and there was a deal of such investigation urgently needing to be made. Our equipment for chemical research was also very complete and the vast undeveloped natural resources of the islands presented a practically virgin field for such investigation.

At the outset absurd rumours spread as to the cost of buildings and equipment, and there was much popular outcry against the supposed wastefulness of the government. A simple statement of the facts served to kill these foolish tales, and people soon began to see that the creation of the Bureau of Government Laboratories was merely the application of common-sense to existing conditions and had resulted in greatly increased economy and efficiency.   Indeed, at the suggestion of a committee appointed to make a study of the government service and suggest measures for its betterment, the principle which I had adopted was carried still further.   Not only was all zoölogical and botanical work transferred to this bureau, but the Bureau of Ethnology and the Bureau of Mines were abolished as separate entities and were made divisions of it, and its title was changed to "The Bureau of Science."   Little by little the scope of the work has steadily widened.

The scientific books and periodicals of the government were scattered among half a dozen different bureaus and were not being well cared for.   I arranged to have them all temporarily transferred to the library of the Bureau of Science and catalogued there.   Those said to be really needed for frequent reference were then returned to the several bureaus but were kept under observation by the bureau of science librarian, who took particular pains to look after the binding of serial publications as rapidly as the volumes were completed.

The list of books requested by the several bureau chiefs for reference was suspiciously long.   I gave orders that each set of bureau bookshelves be provided with cards and a box into which to drop them, and each time a book was used a card was made out for it and placed in the box. After six months I quietly gathered up the cards and had them checked against the lists of books for which the several bureau chiefs had asked, and was then able to order a large proportion of them back to the library for the reason that they had not been used at all.

The result of this policy is that we have to-day a central scientific library in which are catalogued all the scientific books of the government.   Books needed by the several bureaus for frequent reference are placed where they can be used conveniently, and the card catalogue indicates where they are, so that they can readily be found.   In this way it has been possible to avoid much needless and expensive duplication.   The library now contains 26,652 bound volumes.

We were extremely fortunate in the men whose services we secured in the early days, and the volume of research work turned out was unexpectedly large.   The question of how best to arrange for the prompt publication of our results became urgent, and in the end we answered it by publishing the *Philippine Journal of Science,* now in its eighth year and with an assured and enviable position among the scientific journals of the world.

In the early days before we knew what we now know about the preservation of health in tropical countries there was a deal of sickness among government officers and employees.   While the army was more than liberal in helping us meet the conditions which arose, it was of course very necessary that we should establish our own hospital as soon as possible.

On October 12, 1901, the so-called "Civil Hospital" was opened in a large private dwelling, obtained, as we then fondly imagined, merely as a temporary expedient.   Together with two adjoining and even smaller buildings it continued to be our only place for the treatment of ordinary medical and surgical cases until September 1, 1910 ! I can here only very briefly outline the causes of this long delay.

At the outset the building was large enough to meet immediate needs.   At the time when it began to grow inadequate there was a plan on foot for a large private institution, in which the government was to secure accommodations for its patients, and a hospital building was actually erected, but interest in this project waned, the private backing which was believed to have been assured for it failed, and the whole scheme went by the board.   Then plans for a great general hospital were called for.   A very large amount of time was consumed in their preparation and when they were finished the expense involved

in carrying them out was found to be far beyond the
means of the government.   Ultimately I was charged
with the duty of securing other plans involving a more
moderate expenditure.   Again long delay necessarily
ensued.   When semi-final plans were submitted, the consulting architect insisted on a series of arches along the
sides of the several ward pavilions which were doubtless
most satisfying from an artistic point of view, but would
have shut off light and fresh air to an extent which I could
not tolerate.   A three months' deadlock was finally broken
by his acceding to my wishes, but in October, 1906, just
as the completed plans were finally ready to submit
to the commission, I was compelled by severe illness to
return to the United States.   There remained three American and three Filipino members of the commission.   One
of the former was Mr. W. Morgan Shuster, then secretary of public instruction.   Prior to the time when he
became a candidate for a secretaryship he had been
bitter in his criticism of the Filipinos.   Coincidently
with the development of this ambition he became
almost more pro-Filipino than some of the Filipino
politicians themselves.   For a time he seemed to control the Filipino vote on the commission and largely as a
result of his activities every important matter which I
left pending, including that of the establishment of the
great general hospital so vitally needed by the people of
the islands, was laid on the table.   I was informed that
Mr. Shuster had announced that we could have $125,000
for the hospital and no more !   We needed $400,000.

Beginning on the day after my return the following
April these several projects, including that for the Baguio
Hospital and that for the Philippine General Hospital.
were taken from the table and passed.

Construction work goes slowly in the tropics.   One
ward pavilion of the Philippine General Hospital was occupied on September 1, 1910.   Soon afterward the four
others came into use.

On June 10, 1907, a medical college was opened. It was called "The Philippine Medical School." Its creation at this time was made possible by the existence of the Bureaus of Science and Health. Its staff was at the outset recruited very largely from these two bureaus. The director of the Bureau of Science was made its dean and continued to hold this position until his death. To his unselfish efforts and to those of the director of health is due the well-organized modern college which we have to-day. In lieu of better quarters the first classes were held in an old Spanish government building which was altered and added to until it answered the purpose reasonably well.

The preparation of the act which provided for the establishment of this college was intrusted to me. I called for the assistance of a committee of technical experts and asked that they submit a draft for my consideration, which they did. It contained a provision to the effect that the college should be under the administrative control of the secretary of the interior. I struck out the words "secretary of the interior" and inserted in lieu thereof the words "secretary of public instruction" for two reasons. First, the school theoretically belongs under that official, in spite of its necessarily close relationship with the Bureau of Science and the Bureau of Health. Second, I wanted the support of the secretary of public instruction for the measure, as it involved considerable expenditure and I was not sure how the bill might fare in the commission. It happened that the incumbent of that position was very much inclined to take a liberal view of bills which extended his jurisdiction. Mr. Taft, when he visited the Philippines in 1909, reached the conclusion that I was guilty of an error of judgment in doing this, and a little later expressed the view that the Medical College ought to be under the control of the secretary of the interior, because of its intimate relationship with the bureaus above mentioned. I might perhaps even then have had this change made, but refrained from attempting to do so, believing that all would go well under the existing arrangement. So long as Dr. Freer lived this was the case.

He was a man of absolute honesty and sincerity of purpose, and was far-seeing enough fully to realize that the interests of the government, and of individuals as well, would best be served by carrying out the broad and liberal policy which was then in effect.

The next event of importance was the establishment of the University of the Philippines, which was provided for by an Act passed on June 18,1908.

The Philippine Medical School was in due time incorporated with the university as its College of Medicine and Surgery, passing under the executive control of the university board of regents.

At this time the plan of which I had dreamed so many years before was in full force and effect and was working admirably. Members of the Bureau of Science staff served on the college faculty and held appointments in the Philippine General Hospital as well, one of them being the chief of a division there. Members of the college faculty carried on research work at the Bureau of Science. The great working library installed in the building of the latter bureau served as the medical library. Members of the college faculty also rendered important service in the Philippine General Hospital, where two of them were chiefs of divisions, two held important positions on the house staff and numerous others served as interns. Officers of the Bureau of Health were appointed to the faculty of the college and carried on research work at the Bureau of Science. The staff of the latter bureau made the chemical and biological examinations needed in connection with the work of the hospital as well as those required by the Bureau of Health. The Bureau of Science manufactured the sera and prophylactics required by the Bureau of Health in its work. The two large operating amphitheatres in the Philippine General Hospital were planned with especial reference to the accommodation of students, who could pass along a gallery from one to the other. The work of the free clinic, attended daily by hundreds of Filipinos seeking relief, was largely turned over to the college faculty, and increased opportunities were thus given for medical students to study actual cases.

The arrangement was an ideal one. It excited the admiration of numerous visiting European and American experts, who were competent to judge of its merits, and its continued success was dependent only upon the honesty of purpose, loyalty and good faith of the several parties to it.

Then came the untimely death of Dr. Freer. A few months later an attempt was made by certain university officers to secure control of the professional work of the hospital for that institution, leaving the director of health and the secretary of the interior in charge of the nurses, servants, accounts and property, and burdened with the responsibility for the results of work involving life and death, but without voice in the choice of the men who were to perform it.

Those who were responsible for this effort evidently had not taken the trouble to read the law, and I had only to call attention to its provisions in order to end for the time this first effort to disturb the existing logical distribution of work between the two institutions.

Before I left Manila in October, 1913, a second attempt was being made to secure control of the professional work of the hospital for the university, but this time the plan was more far-reaching, in that it contemplated the transfer to the university of control of the Bureau of Science as well; and more logical, in that a bill accomplishing these ends had been drafted for consideration by the Filipinized legislature.

The original plan for the coördination of the scientific

work of the Philippine government was sound in principle
and will, I trust, eventually be carried out, whatever
may be done temporarily to upset it during a period of
disturbed political conditions. There is much consolation to be derived from contemplating the fact that pen-
dulums swing.